Table of Contents

Acknowledgements

I would like to express my appreciation to the staff at the Filmoteca Nacional in Madrid for the assistance that they gave me in my research. In particular, I would like to thank Dolores Devesa and her staff at the library of the Filmoteca for their many helpful suggestions, as well as technicians Juan Peña and Pepe Fernández Guardón. I am grateful to the many Spanish film producers who furnished me with stills and information for the illustrations for this study. I am deeply indebted to my friend Gerardo Pastor for his generosity and for all the assistance that he gave me in obtaining many of the stills. I would also like to express appreciation to my wife Isabel for her encouragement and support throughout this project.

Research for this study was made possible through a Travel to Collections Grant from the National Endowment for the Humanities and through a Faculty Development Grant from Western Maryland College.

Portions of this study have appeared in "Cinematographic Adaptations of Two Novels by Camilo José Cela," *Film/Literature Quarterly* 16.4 (1988); "From Page to Screen: Contemporary Spanish Cinema," *The Spanish Civil War in Literature*, ed. Janet Pérez and Wendell Aycock, Lubbock, TX: Texas Tech UP, 1990; and "Cela on Screen: *La colmena*," *Camilo José Cela: Homage to a Nobel Prize*, ed. Joaquín Roy, Coral Gables, FL: University of Miami UP, 1991. Reprinted with permission.

Introduction

Spanish film often reflects the passions of Spanish society, and especially its politics. The behavior of Spaniards with regard to many recent films manifests the conflux of passions both on and off screen. Upon viewing films such as Basilio Martín Patino's *Canciones para después de una guerra* (Songs for After a War),[1] José Luis Garci's *Volver a empezar* (To Begin Again), and Mario Camus's *Los santos inocentes* (The Holy Innocents), audiences in Spain reacted with hearty applause, either during or at the end of the projection. Taking this phenomenon one step further, a crowd of 500,000 enthusiastic aficionados turned out in Barcelona to provide vocal approval for the debut of *La Plaça del Diamant* (Diamond Square) as a film that represents a triumph of the Catalan language and culture. On the negative side, an attack by fascist guerrillas on director Manuel Gutiérrez Aragón provided the creative impulse for a film called *Camada negra* (Black Litter) whose debut would elicit theater bombings by these same groups. The political content of Carlos Saura's *La prima Angélica* (Cousin Angélica) caused such outrage on the right that fascist thugs attacked projection booths and bombed movie theaters. On the comic side, an accidental shooting of General Franco's daughter in the derrière during a hunting expedition provided director García Berlanga with the idea for a comedy filled with black humor that he entitled *La escopeta nacional* (National Shotgun). Thus, Spanish cinema, never divorced from Spanish history and politics, has found new avenues of expression and new perspectives on historical and political matters in recent years. Many of the changes in Spanish movies over the past two decades are due to radical transformations in Spanish society, and the relationship between the government, the

---

[1] I have attempted to maintain the English translations of film titles that have been used in previous studies (particularly Besas) for the sake of consistency. I will include quotes of dialogue from the films in Spanish followed by a translation, in order to give the flavor of the original scripts. All translations, unless otherwise noted, are those of the author.

Catholic church, and the film industry. There is no more state censorship of films, and no longer does the Catholic church have the control over Spanish society's morals that it once did, determining what films were appropriate for Spaniards to view.   Ana Mariscal humorously depicts the moral state of affairs regarding cinema during the 1940's and early 50's in her film adaptation of Miguel Delibes's novel, *El camino* (The Road, 1960), in which we see parish women try to cover the projector lens and stop the projection of a "risque" Latin American movie. Travellers to Spain during the 1950's and 60's such as James Michener saw warnings posted by priests on church doors about the dangerous nature of certain films: "This should be seen only by those ninety-four and above" (Michener 61).   Freed from prior constraints, the Spanish film industry now produces a wide variety of movies of excellent quality that achieve both critical and popular acclaim on the international scene.   On this side of the Atlantic, Spanish film festivals in New York and Washington have met with great success in recent years.   Festivals dedicated exclusively to Spanish cinema have been held in Miami and Buenos Aires, and Spanish films have also appeared in festivals in Chicago, Los Angeles, and Toronto.   The prizes won at these festivals together with those from Cannes and Berlin, as well as the 1983 Oscar for Best Foreign Film to José Luis Garci's *Volver a empezar* attest to the quality of current production in the cinema industry in Spain.

Spain has recently made a remarkable transition from dictatorship to democracy, distancing itself from the shadow of the Franco regime, which was the result of the Spanish civil war. This conflict (and its aftermath) is one of the fundamental recurring themes in contemporary Spanish cinema. Indeed, Spanish critic Emilio C. García Fernández in his recent study, *Historia ilustrada del cine español* goes so far as to categorize these films as a genre.[2]   Antonio García Rayo has commented that for a time it looked like the Civil War movie "could

---

[2]Madrid: Planeta, 1985, pp. 267-69. García Fernández includes in this genre the following films: Furtivos (Poachers); Canciones para después de una guerra (Songs For After a War);   Las largas vacaciones del 36 (The Long Vacation of '36); Retrato de familia (Family Portrait); La casa de las chivas (The Kids' House); La casa grande (The Big House); Gusanos de seda (Silk Worms); La ciudad quemada (The Burnt City); and Pascual Duarte. Other films that analyze the postwar period from the perspective of the present include: Camada negra (Black Litter); Jo, papá (Gosh, Dad); Caudillo; and Asignatura pendiente (Course Incomplete) (269).

well become and should become a genre like the western" (qtd. in Kovács 5). On the other hand, Antonio Gutti is of the opinion that films about the Spanish civil war "never became a genre" but is rather a type of "recurrent subgenre" (19). With regard to the many films concerning the past fifty years in Spain, i.e, the Civil War, the Franco regime and the transition to democracy, it is difficult to determine a category of "Spanish Civil War films." This is due in part to the nature of the conflict itself. The Nationalist uprising began on July 18, 1939, but it is impossible to separate the events during the Spanish Republic from this uprising; indeed, as eminent a historian as Hugh Thomas can even ask the rhetorical question in this regard, "When does the civil war begin?" (xv). Although victory was declared by Franco on April 1, 1939, for Spaniards, the conflicts did not terminate until many years later. Spanish intellectual Ignacio Sotelo has declared that "the war ended with the death of Franco" and that he pertains to "a generation that, with having consciously lived the war, was marked in an indelible way by the fratricidal conflict of our parents (11). In an interview in April of 1976, film director Carlos Saura stated, "the Spanish civil war has been and is still weighing down on us; it belongs to an immediate past that can hardly be separated from our present" (Camos 37). Film critic Haro Tecglen notes, "the civil war is a past that is in the present. All of Spanish reality is impregnated with the civil war" ("La huella" 12). Using these comments as criteria for the study of film narratives about the Spanish civil war would mean that November 20, 1975--the date of Franco's death--would mark the narrative end point for films of this category, but even this chronological limitation proves unsatisfactory. A film such as Fernando Fernán Gómez's *Mambrú se fue a la guerra* (Mambrú Went Off to War), which depicts how a "mole" (a Republican who lived "underground" during the Franco regime) goes public after the death of Franco, deserves to belong to this category as much as Alfonso Ungría's *El hombre oculto* (The Hidden Man), a film that portrays the life of a mole during the regime. Likewise, it is impossible to separate the events that took place during the Republic with those of July 18, 1936 and the following years.

Certainly the films that directly portray the bellicose conflict or the concurrent events in the rear-guard--films that narrate events from 1936 to 1939, such as Alfonso Ungría's *Soldados* (Soldiers), or Jaime Chávarri's *Las bicicletas son para el verano* (Bicycles are for

Summer)--are the easiest to place in the category of "Spanish Civil War films." However, in spite of the fact that the war officially ended on April 1, 1939, the fighting continued on in many rural areas. The "maquis" or anti-Franco guerrilla fighter is the theme of films such as Mario Camus's *Los días del pasado* (Bygone Days) and Manuel Gutiérrez Aragón's *El corazón del bosque* (The Heart of the Forest). Both the "maquis" and the hardships of city life during the post-war era are portrayed in Pedro Olea's *Pim, pam, pum...fuego* (Bang, Bang... You're Dead), and the misery of Madrid in the early 40's is reflected in Mario Camus's adaptation of the Camilo José Cela's novel, *La colmena* (The Hive). The psychological repercussions of the war carry on for many years after the termination of the conflict, and characters attempt to realize a cognitive reconstruction of this crucial period of their past or try to analyze the effects of the war on their lives. Films such as Carlos Saura's *La prima Angélica*, Jaime Camino's *España otra vez* (Spain Again), and Jaime de Armiñán's *Jo, papá* (Gosh, Dad) exemplify films whose protagonists delve into the past. In addition to the portrayal of a "mole" in Fernando Fernán Gómez's *Mambrú se fue a la guerra*, which brings the chronology of the narration to the period just after the death of Franco, other films, such as Manuel Gutiérrez Aragón's *Camada negra*, and Juan Antonio Bardem's *Siete días de enero* (Seven Days in January), which portray the ideological and social divisions in Spanish society through the narration of the actions of ultra-rightist groups, stretch the chronology even further into the period of the transition to democracy in Spain.

The limitations of this study would be best expressed with reference to M. M. Bakhtin's concept of "chronotrope" or "the intrinsic connectedness of temporal and spatial relationships that are artistically expressed in literature" (84)--or in this case, in film. We begin with films that portray the social turmoil that lead up to the civil war, continue with films that portray the actual conflict on the front line and the repercussions of the war on the civilian population in the rear guard, and analyze the cinematographic representation of various aspects of the aftermath of the war--the anti-Franco guerrilla movement, the misery and black market, the "moles," attempts to relive the past, the long-standing social divisions in Spanish society, and the documentary films that attempt to reconstruct the past. Thus, we wish to eschew a strict categorization of "Spanish Civil War films," and instead focus on films that manifest a somewhat broader phenomenon of Spanish culture known as *cainismo*, or a fraternal antagonism within Spanish society.

Spain is a heterogeneous culture, and Spaniards proudly point to the many groups throughout its history who have contributed to its culture: Iberians, Celts, Greeks, Carthagineans, Romans, Goths, Moors, Jews . . . . Under the new constitution, there are many autonomous regions which are often the contemporary manifestation of traditional regions with their own customs and sometimes even their own language (Cataluña, Galicia, Andalucía, etc.). Nevertheless, such famous historians as Ramón Menéndez Pidal and Américo Castro proposed the thesis of "two Spains," a concept later studied in depth by historian José María García Escudero. In a recent study, Vicente Cacho Viu points out that the concept of two nations is not exclusive to Spain, but he admits that "the image of two Spains seems to gain a certain amount of popularity as we approach the fiftieth anniversary of the Spanish civil war . . . [and] the two Spains are expressly or subliminally interpreted as the purely Spanish fruit of our cainism [although] after the 1930's, it is a different situation" (49). Although Manuel Tuñón de Lara favors the concept of "multiple Spains," in a recent study, he states that "each one of the 'two Spains' was a fraction that attempted an operation of hypostatization, that is to say, confusing a part, that which was constituted by its own interests and their ideologization, with the whole, the whole of Spanish society" (11).

The Spanish Civil War brought the *cainismo* theme to the forefront, and Spanish intellectuals who saw their nation once again divided by the rife of fratricidal conflict manifested the theme of *cainismo* in their writing. Two authors that especially manifest the *cainismo* theme are from the so-called "Generation of '98": Miguel de Unamuno and Antonio Machado. Indeed, the poet Machado, in his "La tierra de Alvargonzález" (Alvargonzález's Land) would say "Mucha sangre de Caín / tiene la gente labriega" (Laborers have a lot of Cain's blood, 111), and in his "Por tierras de España" (Through the lands of Spain), he refers to Spain as "un trozo de planeta / por donde cruza errante la sombra de Caín" (a slice of planet where Cain's errant shadow passes, 90). Some of Machado's verses referring to the Cain myth even find their way into Spanish film, as the professor in Jaime Camino's *Las largas vacaciones del '36* (The Long Vacation of '36) recites Machado's "Recuerdo infantil" (Childhood Memory):

Es la clase. En un cartel
se representa a Caín
fugitivo, y muerto Abel
junto a una mancha carmín.

(It's class. A poster shows fugitive Cain, and Abel dead next to a carmine stain.) Unamuno seemed almost obsessed with the theme of *cainismo*; perhaps the most famous manifestation of the theme in his works is the short novel *Abel Sánchez*. According to Unamuno, the very concept of civil war, "began with the fraternal assassination of Abel by his brother Cain" (*La ciudad* 13). Although the conflict from 1936 to 1939 represents the culmination of this tendency toward *cainismo* in Spanish culture, it has persisted throughout the postwar years, and is only now being put slowly to rest. This process of moving away from a concept of Spain based on fratricidal divisions is apparent in the influential pen of Juan Tomás de Salas, editor of the weekly news magazine *Cambio 16.* The concept of *cainismo* appears in a 1977 editorial regarding violent events in which he laments that "we were still going around with Cain's knife at our neck" ("Dónde estará" 7). As the transition to democracy became consolidated, the attitude toward *cainismo* began to change, and in September of 1983, referring to a survey conducted for his magazine, Salas comments, "If you observe that 73 percent of Spaniards today, according to the poll, have the opinion that 'the civil war was a shameful period of Spanish history that is better to forget,' you will understand why Cain's insanity in this land has given way to a militant civil pacifism that equally condemns both sides. That being the case, one would say that no one won the civil war: we all lost" ("Nunca jamás" 3).

This study analyzes the theme of *cainismo* in feature-length films directed by Spanish directors and which are Spanish productions (or co-productions with companies from other countries), and that have had their debut between 1965 and June of 1986. Prior to 1965, in the decades following the civil war, film production in Spain was in great measure a reflection of the difficult social and economic conditions that existed in the country.   The post-war period was a bleak time in Spanish culture. Spain's largest cities and centers of film production, Madrid and Barcelona, had been in the Republican camp during the war, and the victorious entrance of Franco's troops meant the arrival of hard times for many of the cities' inhabitants. In Barcelona, the use of Catalan was prohibited; in Madrid, money issued during the

Republic was declared null and void, thus leaving many families virtually destitute. Many feel, however, that one of the most important repercussions of the conflict was the truncation of the spectacular rebirth of Spanish culture that had occurred only years before. The assassination of the young poet Federico García Lorca symbolizes this phenomenon, and many artists and intellectuals who did not meet his fate emigrated from Spain at the end of the war. This fact, together with the imposition of a monolithic regime that recognized only one political party, one religion, and carried out strict censorship of the press and of the film industry, meant that the artistic development of cinema in Spain in the 1940's in Spain was stifled.[3]

In the 1950's, the situation slowly began to change, mainly due to the efforts of two film directors, Luis García Berlanga and Juan Antonio Bardem. The former's *Bienvenido, Mr. Marshall* (Welcome, Mr. Marshall) won an Honorable Mention at the 1953 Cannes film festival, and Bardem's 1954 film, *Muerte de un ciclista* (Death of a Cyclist), which shows the influence of Italian neo-realist directors such as Rossellini, won the International Critics Award in 1955. That year also saw an important conference on Spanish film sponsored by the University of Salamanca. The document that resulted from these "Cinematographic Conversations," as they were called, began by stating, "Current Spanish cinema is 1. Politically ineffective. 2. Socially false. 3. Intellectually abject. 4. Aesthetically null and void. 5. Industrially stunted" (Castro 439). Director Juan Antonio Bardem issued the battlecry, "Spanish cinema is dead. Long live Spanish cinema" (qtd. in Besas 41). A renewed interest in Spanish film as manifested by these "Conversations" led to the founding of magazines dedicated to this topic, such as *Film ideal* (begun in 1956). García Berlanga and Bardem continued to direct important films, such as *Calabuch* (Calabuch, 1956) and *Los jueves, milagro* (A Miracle Every Thursday, 1957) by the former, and *Calle mayor* (Main Street, 1956) by the latter.

In 1962, under the direction of Manuel Fraga Iribarne, Minister of Information, there was a certain liberalizing movement in Spanish culture. This was at a time when Spain was undergoing fundamental social transformations, with Opus dei technocrats in government posts

---

[3]See Antonio Castro, El cine español en el banquillo.

and an influx of foreign tourists who brought not only foreign currency but foreign mores, as well. With the naming of José María García Escudero as Under-Secretary of Cinema, there were important changes in that industry. In February of 1963, the Norms of Film Censorship were published, and they represented a liberalization of the artistic climate because from that moment directors at least had written guidelines within which they could work. In the following year, legislation created the "special interest" category for films, which entitled movies that qualified to receive larger state subsidies and set distribution quotas for foreign and domestic films. In 1963, García Berlanga directed *El verdugo* (The Executioner), a compelling film about capital punishment and the individual's role in modern society, which represented Spain at the Venetian film festival and caused a scandal because of the reaction of the Spanish ambassador, Sánchez Bella, who called the film "one of the greatest libels ever perpetrated against Spain" (qtd. in Besas, 79). In addition to García Berlanga and Bardem, several young directors began to be active in Spain in the 1960's. Many of them were products of the "Escuela Oficial de Cinematografía" (EOC), and they received government subsidies for their productions. Thus, under the protection of García Escudero, the movement known as the "New Spanish Cinema" was born.[4] The two main innovations of the movement were, according to José Angel Rodero, a spirit of "renovation with regards to all that earlier Spanish cinema meant" and an aesthetics "capable of shaping a real vision of our society with its problems, its people, its circumstances" (7). By the middle of the decade, the directors such as Carlos Saura (*Los golfos* [The Troublemakers], *La caza* [The Hunt]), Basilio Martín Patino (*Nueve cartas a Berta* [Nine Letters to Berta]), Mario Camus (*Con el viento solano* [With the Easterly Wind]), Manuel Summers (*El juego de la oca* [Goosey Game]) were having an important impact on Spanish cinema.

Of course, during the first decades of the Franco regime, films dealing with the civil war narrated the official view of the conflict. What can be termed a "political" cinema did exist, but according to

---

[4]Critics Carlos and David Pérez Marinero contend that the government intervention actually stifled the aesthetic development of Spanish film, and that this movement was simply a propagandistic operation for the outside world. See their Cine español 25.

Diego Galán, it consisted of films with historical, religious, and folkloric themes, and it offered support for the regime instead of a critical vision of the times.[5] The year 1965 marks an important change in Spanish cinema with reference to the topic of our discussion, since it is the year in which both Saura's *La caza* and Martín Patino's *Nueve cartas a Berta* have their debut. Critics--both at the moment of its debut and with the perspective provided by the passing of time--view the former as a film that opened important new directions for Spanish cinema. A *Fotogramas* review of *La caza* after it opened commented on its aesthetic breakthrough, saying that it represents "a new cinema, definitely separated from the old trunk of Spanish cinema that was still rooted in theater, and more precisely, in melodrama or burlesque" ("*La caza*" 11). Emilio C. García Fernández, in his *Historia ilustrada* notes the thematic rupture of the film with regards to earlier Spanish cinema: "it had a number of themes that appeared for the first time in Spanish cinema: it took a look back at characters that had created and lived a historical situation" (254). Likewise, *Nueve cartas a Berta* has stood the test of time, impressing both contemporary and later critics. José Monleón wrote in 1966 that it was "one of the most important films that Spanish cinema has presented us" (61). Enough critics agreed with Monleón to award the film the "Concha de Plata" at the San Sebastián film festival as well as the Premio de la Federación Nacional de Cine-Clubs. In his 1986 study on Spanish film, Emmanuel Larraz calls it one of the most important Spanish films of the 1960's both for its formal qualities (voice "off," inserts, frozen images, and the division of the film into nine chapters) but also for the "accuracy with which Basilio Martín Patino has interpreted the problems of his generation--its anguish, its desire to break through the rigid limits of the institutions installed after the civil war" (174-75). Due to the importance of these two films, we have chosen 1965 as the year with which we begin our analysis of contemporary Spanish cinema.

---

[5]See his "El cine 'político' español" in Enrique Brasó, ed., Siete trabajos 87-107.

Chapter 1

Social Turmoil

The early decades of the twentieth century in Spain were a time of social turmoil. The defeat of Spain in 1898 in the Spanish-American war, industrialization and concurrent rise of the labor movement with the socialist UGT (Unión General de Trabajadores or General Union of Workers) and the communist CNT (Confederación Nacional del Trabajo or National Confederation of Labor) which led to clashes between workers and police, war in Africa in an attempt to maintain the semblances of empire, the dictatorship of Primo de Rivera, and the declaration of the Republic in April of 1931 were all socially tumultuous events in the years preceding the civil war.[6] Although several Spanish films from the past decade deal with the tumultuous events of these early decades of the twentieth century in Spain, we shall limit our analysis of the pre-Civil War period to movies whose narrative framework includes 1936, the year that the Civil War began.[7] Films which meet this criterion include two from 1977--Ricardo Franco's *Pascual Duarte* (Pascual Duarte) and Fernando Fernán Gómez's *Mi hija Hildegart* (My Daughter Hildegart)--as well as Jaime Camino's 1986 film, *Dragon rápide* (Fast Dragon).

The Ricardo Franco film is, of course, a cinematographic version of the famous post-war novel by Camilo José Cela, *La familia de*

---

[6]The period of the Republic is crucial for understanding the outbreak of the civil war. Important studies of the republic include Juan J. Linz's The Breakdown of Democratic Regimes: Europe, Gabriel Jackson's The Spanish Republic and the Civil War, 1931-1939, Stanley Payne's The Spanish Revolution, the first volume of Ricardo de la Cierva's Historia de la Guerra civil española, and Paul Preston's The Coming of the Spanish Civil War, 1931-1936 and Revolution and War in Spain 1931-1939.

[7]Antoni Ribas's 1976 Catalan film, La ciutat cremada (The Burned City), chronicles the events of the so-called "Tragic Week" of 1909 in Barcelona. This was the first film of the post-Civil War era in Catalan, and it received a very enthusiastic reception in Catalonia. Ribas's 1985 work, Victoria (Victory), was released as three separate films, and also deals with the pre-Civil War years.

Pascual Duarte (The Family of Pascual Duarte). The film won several important awards, including the Best Actor award at the Cannes Film Festival in 1976 to José Luis Gómez for his portrayal of Pascual. *Pascual Duarte* portrays the life of its protagonist, a poor peasant living in Extremadura in the years prior to the civil war, as he is caught up in webs of violence both of his own making and of society. The chronology of the film narrative begins in 1937 with Pascual arrested for homicide, and then a series of flashbacks alternate the narrative between the past--one of Pascual as a youth, with the rest as a young man in the 1930's--and the present of his incarceration, and finally, execution. The first flashback commences with a young Pascual reading from the Bible to a priest: "Allí viviréis dichosos y sueltos y llamó Abrahán a los suyos . . ." (You will live happy and free there, and Abraham called his family members). The choice of this text is significant: the script to the film indicates that this text shows "the concept of the promised land and of homeland . . . and the element of violence, even family violence" (Martínez Lázaro 35). Critic Hernández Les points out that "the Biblical reference to the sacrifice of Abraham serves as a foreshadowing of a possible interpretation of the character. Pascual sacrifices, but he is also sacrificed" (*"Pascual Duarte"* 30). Indeed, the concept of land also becomes one of the fundamental themes of the film because of the socio-political element with which director Franco imbues his cinematographic text. This begins in the sequence in which Pascual's father, Esteban, reads from the newspaper, "Fusilados los de Reus," (Reus Criminals Executed by Firing Squad) followed by a close-up of the headline, "Fusilamiento de Ferrer" (Ferrer Executed by Firing Squad), both of which refer to the social turmoil of the events of the "Tragic Week" of 1909 in Barcelona and its aftermath. The following scene, in which Pascual and his father visit the rich landlord's farm and Esteban diagnoses a sick pig as having "el mal rojo" (the red sickness) is certainly not fortuitous, and must be read metaphorically. The metaphorical reading of this scene, which is derived in part from its syntagmatic relationship with other scenes in the text, has to do with the associative relationship between the landlord and this particular animal, as well as the multiple signifieds of "rojo," which here takes on possible socio-political

connotations[8].   A later scene which occurs at the landlord's home
further emphasizes the socio-political element. When Pascual writes to
his sister Rosario, who has abandoned the family and gone to Trujillo
with her lover, "el Estirao," Pascual's mother mentions to him that he
should thank her for the money which the sister sent by way of "el
Estirao" (who is also her pimp). A close-up of Pascual's letter, with
the words, "Otra vez a ver si este año algunos van a quedarse sin
trabajo" (Let's see if some men are going to be left without work again
his year), triggers the transition to the scene at the landlord's home,
where two men are fighting outside of the house. Don Jesús, the
landlord, appears at the window, to tell the laborers that there is no
work for them, and that they should go away. The reverse low and
high-angle shots visually underscore the social hierarchy of Spanish
society, and the fistfight of the two laborers metonymically represents
the strife among Spanish workers as a whole. Two other brief scenes
show the landlord's influence and importance in the community: after
don Jesús deposits his ballot in the transparent urn during the election
scene, a low angle shot captures him pronouncing that all should vote,
since it is their obligation. In the next scene, Pascual's wedding to
Lola, don Jesús arrives on horseback, dismounts for a quick drink of
wine to everyone's applause, but he refuses to sit with the other
guests. He gives Pascual some money, with the wish "Espero que
todo os vaya bien," (I hope that everything will go well for you), and
then leaves. Both scenes connote his power, wealth, and a certain
condescending attitude toward the lower class, of which Pascual is
certainly a member.   Again, the juxtaposition of scenes is not
fortuitous, and the next one finds Pascual at night listening to a radio
broadcast of the declaration of the Republic: "Viva España y viva la
República" (Long Live Spain and Long Live the Republic).
    The animosity between Pascual and "el Estirao" builds in a bar
scene during which there is a type of singing contest. The first song,
sung by an old man and directed metaphorically to the protagonist,
further underscores the characterization of Pascual as victim:

---

[8]Monterde believes that "Franco's film unequivocally calls for a metaphorical
reading" because of its style and its temporal placement during the Second Republic (13).
Hernández Les holds a similar opinion, stating, "Pascual Duarte's character is erected
as a symbol of a certain type of conduct, of a disillusioned attitude, and lastly, of a
nausea that occurs in the historical malaise of our time" (29).

Civil crimes in a militarized context: Franco's <u>Pascual Duarte</u>, starring José Luis Gómez. Courtesy Elías Querejeta, P.C.

> Ningún hombre debe ser
> a garrote sentenciado
> por meterse en un cercado
> a desprender un clavel.

(No man should be sentenced to be garroted for getting into a fenced in garden to cut free a carnation). "El Estirao's" song contains a negative allusion to Pascual's shotgun marriage to Lola (Hay algunos que se casan / por cumplir una obligación [Some men get married to fulfill an obligation]), which causes Pascualito to attack "el Estirao," and although he is restrained by others, it serves as a foreshadowing of the violent murder of "el Estirao" which Franco considers a "substitute homicide," since Pascual kills his brother-in-law instead of his sister (Balagué 14), thus underscoring the *cainismo* theme. The matricide, preceded by a lengthy shot of Pascual shining his shotgun, which is the murder weapon, and the homicide of don Jesús, the landowner, complete the cycle of violence. The use of the shotgun as the murder weapon (a radical change from the original novel) seems to implicitly link Pascual to the concept of armed struggle and the fratricidal conflict which was to follow.

Of course, the literary text is so tremendously violent that it caused critics to coin the term *tremendismo* to refer to the text. The visual images of the film make the cinematographic text even more so. Spanish critic Manolo Marinero praises how the film visually captures this style with its splendid photography and how Ricardo Franco obtained an ideal atmosphere for the coarseness and barbarity of the story" ("*Pascual Duarte*" 47), and Juan Carlos Rentero describes the film as having a "a latent, ferocious, savage, tremendous, incredible, but magnificently exposed violence, with an exasperating and destructive coldness" ("*Pascual Duarte*" 38). Part of the audience's reaction to the violence in the film is the result of a deliberate aesthetic distancing on the part of the director.[9] Of course, the graphic images heighten the sense of violence in the film, but there is a deliberate lack of linkage or cause and effect with regards to some of the violent scenes, and Hernández Les reports that the resulting lack of a moral sanction or humanizing vision is precisely what caused the most repugnance among Spanish audiences (29). Thus, for example, in the novel, violence appears in the context of cause and effect: Pascual kills his mule after the animal threw Lola. In the film, however, there is a mere juxtaposition of scenes: after his mother calls Pascual away from the bar scene, we witness Lola in bed, unconscious, as Pascual looks on, horrified, and in the next scene (exterior, day), Pascual knifes his mule to death, a scene which caused an acute reaction in cinemas throughout Spain. Most of the violent scenes take on a metaphorical meaning, however. Angel A. Pérez Gómez considers that none of the violence in the film is gratuitous, since Pascual's decisions to kill "el Estirao," his mother, and don Jesús "obey an unconscious desire to end the injustice of which he has been a victim. And by shooting at them, he is rebelling against a broader model: against the complete underdevelopment in which he is forced to live" (220). In his interview with C. Balagué, Ricardo Franco states that the violence "became the only viable language for a class that was stripped of any

---

[9] Luis Quesada refers to "an aseptic coldness that distances the story from the audience" (450). Santoro notes that Pascual Duarte has a "minimalist aesthetic", constituted by a spare mise-en-scène (including a "minimum of props, a minimum of actors and a minimum of movement and speech produced by these actors") which helps to distantiate the viewer in the Brechtian mode (84-88). For Gabriel Blanco, this distancing, which is achieved in part by the sound track, is a defect in the film (42). The music for the film, composed by Luis del Amo, consists mainly of an ominous five-note phrase which is repeated throughout the film, and especially at key moments, such as immediately preceding or following the murder of his dog, his mule, "el Estirao," etc.

A harsh landscape takes its toll: Franco's <u>Pascual Duarte</u>, starring José Luis Gómez, Diana Pérez de Guzmán, Paca Ojea, and José Hinojosa. Courtesy Elías Querejeta, P.C.

identity. Pascual only assumes his own life when he exercises this violence; he has no other means for communicating his frustration" (14). The historical circumstances of the Spanish peasant during the 1930's constitute a harsh reality that foments frustration and social turmoil: daily wages for agricultural laborers of less than one peseta per day; clashes with civil guards in many small towns such as Casas Viejas (1933) result in massacres, and Haro Tecglen points out that in *Pascual Duarte*, "the schematic and almost silent biography of the protagonist and those who surround him is precisely an almost mathematical demonstration of the social pressures on Spanish country dwellers during the years that lead to the civil war" (28). Carmen de Elejabeitia and Ignacio F. de Castro note that this social pressure was to the inequitable distribution of wealth--particularly land--and that this leads to a metonymical reading of the film: "in a parallel way, Pascual Duarte's life leads to the garrote and his final desperate shout, and the history of the country leads to the civil war and its dark night. In the story and in history, the cause that unchains the tragedy is money and landholding" (13).

Although the homicide of "el Estirao" results in Pascual's incarceration, the amnesty declared by the Republic allows Pascual to regain his freedom. An important deep shot from inside a train car shows Pascual returning home, and outside, written on a wall, are clear graffiti of a political nature: "CNT," (Confederación Nacional del Trabajo or National Confederation of Labor, the anarchist union) and more importantly, "Tierra y libertad" (Land and Freedom), which at once underscores the political emphasis with which Ricardo Franco has imbued the film, and also manifests the principal source of conflict. The final homicides of the film cause Pascual to return to prison, this time to face the execution by garrote. Hernández Les contemplates the effect on Spanish audiences of the final gripping still shot of the film, "a terrible frozen shot that inexorably provokes reflection in the spectator . . . [which in turn provokes] a scream for our conscience as Spaniards" (30). *Pascual Duarte* is a superb film on many counts, a film which combines superb aesthetic qualities with an important sense of social theme.

Mi hija Hildegart (My Daughter Hildegart), the 1977 film directed by Fernando Fernán Gómez, stars Amparo Soler Leal as Aurora Rodríguez Caballeira, and Carmen Roldán as her daughter, Hildegart. The movie is based on a novel by Eduardo de Guzmán entitled, *Aurora de sangre* (Bloody Aurora), which is in turn based on a series of historical events: a notorious homicide and resulting trial which occurred in 1934. Although the majority of the narrative is concerned with the turbulent years preceding the Civil War, the actual chronological limits of the film are expanded through the use of flashbacks. Indeed, the main portion of the narrative is in itself a flashback, since the story is narrated in the present by Aurora's lawyer for the case, Eduardo, who, now an old man, is telling the story at a bar. Fernán Gómez uses Aurora's trial as the vehicle for the narrative, and events prior to the main narrative include Aurora as a child with a doll; the night of Hildegart's conception, when Aurora mechanically performs the sexual act with a man in order to be able to have a child; Hildegart as a young girl; and the declaration of the Republic. Director Fernán Gómez handles these flashbacks in a rather primitive fashion, using tinted frames to signify a chronological change in the narrative: red for Eduardo's narrative in the bar, and brown for the flashbacks to the earlier events.

Pistol shots heard "off" return the narrative from the initial bar scene to the past as Aurora leaves her apartment building to inform her lawyer that she has killed Hildegart. The flashbacks thus function to explain how this woman came to commit such a heinous crime. The return to Aurora's childhood constitute the earliest events of the narrative: as a young girl, she clutches a doll and asks her father, "Papá, cuando sea mayor, tendré una muñeca de verdad y nadie me la va a quitar?" (Daddy, when I am older, will I have a real doll that no one will take away from me?). Of course, her daughter Hildegart later becomes the doll, and Aurora cannot stand to see her/it reach maturity and become independent. Indeed, Hildegart was a mere object to be manipulated from the moment of her conception, as Aurora explains to the jury during her trial: Hildegart "debía consagrarse a la liberación de la mujer" (she had to consecrate herself to women's liberation). This liberation, in Aurora's mind, was both sexual and political. It is clear that Aurora views sexual relations with great disdain. After the scene in which she confesses that her daughter was certainly not the fruit of a passionate encounter, since the presence of the male procreator did not represent gratification, but was simply a mere biological necessity, Aurora tries to organize women in prison against the "exploitation of the body" and in favor of the prohibition of prostitution. Another example of Aurora's attitude toward sexual exploitation occurs in a later scene when Hildegart is in her late teens: Aurora accompanies her daughter and a friend, Antonio Villena, to a fair and they witness a midway game in which boys throw balls at a target in order to make women fall out of their beds. Aurora becomes furious, calling the game "barbarous" and "filthy." (Footage of this scene also appears during the opening credits, further reinforcing the sexual theme). The themes of possessiveness and sexual inhibition culminate in the scene in which Hildegart is about to leave on a date with her friend Antonio: the mother takes her into the bathroom and writes "Aurora" on the girl's stomach, chest, and back, telling her that if the signatures are erased when she returns, she is "lost." Aurora's exclamation during the trial, "Hildegart solo era mía. Aquel hombre no tenía ningún derecho sobre ella" (Hildegart was mine alone. That man had no right to her), further underscores the possessiveness theme. As Hildegart tearfully leaves, she strikes the keyboard of the piano, and the discord of the notes symbolizes the irreconcilable discord that has arisen between herself and her mother. Of course, such divisions did not always exist between mother and daughter. Aurora tells the jury that Hildegart was a precocious child; she wrote her first article in the *Socialista* at the age of fourteen, and her first book appeared two years later. Hildegart's request that her mother sign a copy of the book symbolized their unity at that time.

As vice president of the Young Socialists, the daughter echoed her mother's ideological convictions, stating in speeches that matrimony represented sexual enslavement, and that solving women's problems solved social problems in the interest of humanity. Hildegart came under attack for her views, and both mother and daughter become disenchanted with the party to the point that Hildegart turned in her membership card. Aurora justified this act, commenting, "quien se ha alejado del socialismo es el partido" (the party itself has grown away from socialism). This loyalty theme is also fundamental to the relationship between mother and daughter. Just before the day of the murder, Hildegart tells her mother that she is leaving to go to Mallorca alone. When Aurora threatens to call the police, we see a close-up of Hildegart telling her that she (Hildegart) has sacrificed herself and done everything for her mother. Aurora's reply is, "¿Estás segura? No será al revés?" (Are you sure? Isn't the opposite true?).

The day of the crime, Aurora tries to justify her attempt to maintain her dream and prevent Hildegart from leaving her. Aurora waits at night for Hildegart to return home, and as she loads a pistol, the camera pans the wall with its testimonials to Hildegart's achievements and their former unity: diplomas, photos of mother and daughter together. Aurora sees a book written by her daughter entitled *Sexo y amor* (Sex and Love), and she reads (with Hildegart's voice "off") the section on "Caín y Abel": "Abel nació para aceptar el orden constituido; Caín, para destruirlo y cambiarlo por otro más justo. Caín es el símbolo del progreso, el primer anarquista que se presenta en la leyenda hebraica. Cuando tropecemos con un Abel en nuestro camino, que en nombre de arcaicos principios se burla de nuestros esfuerzos, la única conducta acertada, legítima, justa, es la que siguió Caín" (Abel was born to accept the established order; Cain, to destroy it and change it for a more just one. Cain is the symbol of progress, the first anarchist in Hebrew legend. When we bump into an Abel on our path, who in the name of arcane principles makes fun of our efforts, the only correct, legitimate, just conduct, is that which Cain followed). This political interpretation of the myth provides a unique twist to the theme of *cainismo* in Spanish film, and in this narrative provides Aurora with a justification for her crime. As she tells the jury, however, "No es fácil a una madre quitar la vida a su hija" (It's not easy for a mother to take away her daughter's life), and Aurora's sobs wake her sleeping daughter for a final confrontation as the mother holds a pistol to the daughter's temple. Aurora tells her daughter that she only wants to save her--from herself and from her own weakness, and she again accuses Hildegart of a lack of loyalty: "No serás la primera en traicionar el proletariado" (You won't be the first one to betray the proletariat). The flowers that fall from Aurora's hands to the floor of the courtroom symbolize the end of her internal conflict, and the death of Hildegart as narrative weaves back from the trial to the final moments of the daughter's life. Hildegart, at only nineteen and still very much under the influence of her mother, tells her to kill her, and Aurora's ironic shouts, "No estoy loca" (I'm not crazy), accompany the homicide.

The abolition of capital punishment during the Republic meant that Aurora's sentence consisted of incarceration. In July of 1936, however, prison doors were opened (a truck marked "CNT" appears in the street to the tune of "A las barricadas" [To the barricades]), and women prisoners, including Aurora Rodríguez Caballeira, were set free. The film ends as it begins, with a caption regarding the historical events: "Pero desapareció para siempre. Se ignora si está viva todavía o si ha muerto. No se ha vuelto a saber de ella" (But she disappeared forever. We do not know if she is still alive or if she is dead. No one knows anything about her). Nevertheless, recent investigations have discovered that Aurora Rodríguez died in 1955 at the insane asylum of Ciempozuelos in the province of Madrid (Fajardo 130). *Mi hija Hildegart* suffers from an over-ambitious story, with overly crude markers to denote transformations in the narrative. The scene in which we see Hildegart's bare breasts as Aurora paints her name over her daughter's torso corresponds to the *destape* phenomenon,[10] whereby after the death of Franco, Spain seemed to suddenly discover sexual freedom. There is a sad irony in the film, however, in that this rather gratuitous display, which seems geared toward better box-office receipts, goes completely against Hildegart's beliefs regarding sexual exploitation.

Jaime Camino's 1986 film, *Dragon rápide* (Fast Dragon) takes its name from the airplane that General Franco used to fly from the Canary Islands to Tetuan in order to then lead the revolt of the Army of Africa against the Republican government on July 18, 1936. Camino used historian Ian Gibson as a consultant on this film in which actor Juan Diego plays the *caudillo* (leader), Franco. This role was a

---

[10]Destape means "uncovering," and in the period following the death of Franco, depiction of nudity on screen and in magazines proliferated.

The first fictional representation of Franco: Camino's <u>Dragon rápide</u>, starring Juan
Diego. Courtesy Tibidabo Films, S.A.

difficult one, especially since it was the first time that Franco had been
portrayed by an actor on screen since his death. The film narrative
occurs between July 4 and July 19, 1936, and it traces the machinations
of Spanish rightists to rent the airplane in England, the role of both
General Franco and General Mola in the plot, and the investigations of
liberal Madrid newspaper reporters during those tense summer days.
A problem with the film is that it has an excess of spatial references:
we are momentarily in Madrid, Biarritz, Barcelona, London, Santa
Cruz de Tenerife, Morocco, Navarra, etc. Although Camino captions
each scene with its location, you almost get lost in the constant jumping
around. Seemingly superfluous moments in the narrative also dilute the
structure of the film: the scenes in which we see Pau Casals directing
an orchestra in Barcelona add nothing to the plot, unless Camino feels
that the rendition of "The Ode to Joy" in response to the news of the
Nationalist uprising is supposed to symbolize a transcendence of the
negative political and military events about to unfold.

Camino tries to portray a complete and objective portrait of Franco,
showing both the military leader and the man. There are numerous
details regarding his personal life: his request for a simple egg omelet
for supper shows his parsimonious character; his self-doubts appear as
he tells his wife Carmen that he once met a Russian taxi driver in Paris

Intimate moments with the caudillo: Camino's Dragon rápide, starring Juan Diego and Victoria Peña. Courtesy Tibidabo Films, S.A.

who had been a general, and as he wonders if he should shave his moustache (Camino accomplishes this in purely visual terms: a close-up of Franco in a mirror shows him put his finger over his upper lip). On July 18, he is even "indisposed" due to his nerves. Nevertheless, his wife provides constant support, ranging from advice on his clothing to the affirmation that he is the only one with enough prestige to save the fatherland. As military leader, Franco plans the details of the plot on a blackboard, and convinces his fellow officers that betraying their country means not saving it. As a counterweight to the rightist activities, a pair of newspapermen ironically speak of "los eternos salvadores de España que no han hecho otra cosa que depreciarla" (the eternal saviors of Spain that have done nothing other than to scorn her), ending their conversation with the rhetorical question, "¿Cuándo nos dejarán en paz?" (When will they leave us in peace?).

The film shows the intimate story of these events; there is no attempt to portray masses of people on the screen. Indeed, exterior scenes were shot with either small groups or else the crowds are heard "off." Although the movie is slow at times, it helps provide a valuable historical perspective on the crucial days leading up to the outbreak of the Civil War.

Chapter 2

The Front Line

Of the large number of films produced since 1965 which deal with the Spanish Civil War, relatively few actually portray the confrontation of troops on the front line as a fundamental element of the narration. Nevertheless, there is a large variety of basic aesthetic elements such as point of view, tone, and the use of time in the narratives of the conflict on the front line. These films include Pedro Lazaga's *Posición avanzada* (Advanced Position, 1965), Isidoro Martínez Ferry's *Cruzada en la mar* (Crusade at Sea, 1968), José Antonio de la Loma's *Golpe de mano* (Surprise Attack, 1969), Luis Lucía's *La orilla* (The River-Bank, 1970), Rafael Gil's *A la legión le gustan las mujeres* (The Legion Likes Women, 1975), Alfonso Ungría's *Soldados* (Soldiers, 1978), Luis García Berlanga's *La vaquilla* (The Little Cow, 1985), and Ricardo Palacios's *¡Biba la banda!* (Long Live da Band!, 1987).

Pedro Lazaga is a director who had already earned a reputation for previous films dealing with the Spanish Civil War, such as *La patrulla* (The Patrol, 1954), *El frente infinito* (The Infinite Front, 1956), and the famous 1959 production, *La fiel infantería* (Faithful Infantry). His 1965 film, *Posición avanzada* (Advanced Position), was shot in black and white, presumably in order to portray the stark realism of wartime events. The film narrates, through the use of a single flashback, a front line situation from the point of view of a nationalist soldier. The film opens with a long shot of a dam and some fields, and then with a wide angle shot that shows Juan, a farmer, working on a tractor. Both the dam and the tractor symbolize economic prosperity and peace in the Franco regime during the 1960s, in contrast with the soldier's helmet that Juan's son finds and brings to him to identify. Juan recognizes the over-sized helmet with a bullet hole in it as that of a companion, and a close-up of the helmet triggers the flash-back to the war and a spot on the front line known as "Frying Pan Villa." Second Lieutenant Laso is in charge of a unit of nationalist troops that maintain a position along a river that divides them from the Republican forces. The expression that sums up this front line situation is "sin novedad" ("no news"). The lack of bellicose action is reinforced when the nationalist sergeant Ayuso announces a truce so that soldiers from both sides can go fishing. The truce manifests an element which is important to this and several other films that deal with the conflict: humor. When the sergeant yells across the river to inquire if the Republican captain, Trueba, is there, the latter's response is, "No, estoy en San Sebastián veraneando" (No, I'm in San Sebastian on summer vacation). Likewise, when asked about the commander's orders not to fraternize with the enemy, Trueba's response is, "Le he mandado a hacer puñetas" (I told him to fuck off). Both retorts exemplify the humorous element of the film.

The truce also manifests a motif which is common to many civil war films: the common good-will and affection among troops from the opposing sides. As they return to their positions, Ayuso comments that Trueba "es un tío muy majuco" (he's a really swell guy). The aura of goodwill comes to an abrupt end, however, when the nationalist soldier Leandro gives the signal for a new truce, and is killed by a Republican bullet. We discover that the change in attitude on the part of the enemy troops is due to the fact that the opposing Spaniards have been replaced by members of the International Brigades, referred to as "hijos de perra" (sons of bitches) by the Nationalist soldiers. Their arrival also signals a change in the immediate rear guard, and this prompts the Nationalist soldier Juan Ruiz (the farmer of the opening sequence) to leave his position under the cover of night in order to visit his wife and child in a village just behind enemy lines. The rhythmic montage of the next sequences provides the only note of suspense of the entire film, since Ruiz must negotiate his way among the enemy troops, while the Lieutenant, who discovers that Ruiz is missing, will only wait until dawn to report that the latter has deserted. Ruiz, wounded during his return, becomes a hero, however, since he has discovered that the enemy troops plan to attack that morning. The final sequence is the enemy attack filmed with reverse angle shots so as to underscore the dichotomy of attackers and defenders as well as to heighten the suspense; the final hand-to-hand combat results in the death of virtually every soldier in the field. A long shot of the helmet completes the flashback and returns us to the picnic lunch with the farmer and his family, in which Juan tells his son, "Es mejor soñar esas cosas que vivirlas" (It's better to dream these things than to live them).

It is not surprising that conservative critic Fernández Cuenca extols

A Nationalist perspective of the conflict: Lazaga's <u>Posición avanzada</u>, with Manuel Zarzo and Antonio Ferrandis. Courtesy Filmoteca Nacional.

Posición avanzada as an exceptional film, and he implies that the fighting portrayed in the film is merely the result of the intervention of the International Brigades, since they "do not understand, nor do they have to understand the reasons for enemies getting along with each other" (1: 597). Both this critical view and the portrayal in the film seem to constitute a very simplistic and sophistic representation of a complex historical reality. In particular, it represents a tendency on the part of certain film directors (and critics) who were sympathetic to the Nationalist cause, and whose earlier films portrayed the "official" version of the war, to portray the International Brigades in an unfavorable light. From a narrative point of view, however, the presence of the foreign troops provided a turning point in which the director was able to take a monotonous story line to a rapid and action-filled conclusion. The international soldiers fighting for the Republican cause are portrayed linguistically as being German, a motif which appears in more than one film, and which is not without a touch of irony, since the more important German intervention occurred on the side of the Nationalists. Can it be that directors such as Lazaga wish to draw our attention away from this fact?

Isidoro Martínez Ferry's 1968 film, *Cruzada en la mar* (Crusade at

Sea) is another film which represents a pro-Nationalist point of view. The director is quite straight-forward in acknowledging this fact, as he opens the film with a narrator who quotes from Admiral Carrero Blanco's book *La marina española* (The Spanish Navy) extolling the nationalist naval forces' valor and military success, and states, "Esta película intenta modestamente paliar este olvido y al mismo tiempo rendir homenaje a nuestra marina de guerra" (This film modestly attempts to palliate this oversight and at the same time pay homage to our navy).[11]

As in the previous film, the narration begins with a flashback which is completed at the end of the narration. Here, the first sequence opens with an old sailor, Captain Enrique Mendoza, visiting the abandoned skeleton of his former ship, the cruiser Almirante Cervera, just before it is about to be dismantled. The zoom-in to the ship's bell is the trigger for the temporal leap backwards to the summer of 1936, when Mendoza was twenty years of age, and his voice "off" announces "Fue el barco de mi juventud" (It was the ship of my youth). The director signals this flashback with a red tint that lowers the aesthetic quality of the film considerably. The narration combines two biographical strands: Enrique's action in the war and his amorous adventures with his girlfriend, Mary. The outbreak of war on July 18 brings a separation of the couple, since Mary is destined to a military headquarters in Gijón with her father (who is an officer), and Enrique is assigned to sea duty. For the latter, Martínez Ferry uses both historical footage and reconstructions.

One surprising use of historical footage is that showing José Antonio Primo de Rivera, founder of the right-wing Falange party who was executed in a Republican prison. He speaks of the triple division which menaces Spain--the local separatist movements, political parties, and class struggles. Martínez Ferry justifies the inclusion of this propagandistic footage by previously characterizing the protagonist as being politically ingenuous: "Yo no entendía bien lo que pasaba. . . los jefes no hablaban de política, hablaban de España, y por España habrían de sumarse al movimiento nacional" (I did not understand very well what was going on . . . the officers didn't talk about politics, they talked about Spain, and they would have to join the Nationalist

---

[11] For an account of the war at sea during this conflict, see Willard C. Frank, Jr., "Naval Operations in the Spanish Civil War, 1936-1939."

movement for Spain).

After a skirmish to control the arsenal at El Ferrol and a duel between opposing officers to control the cruiser Almirante Cervera, which Fernández Cuenca (1: 562) claims to be historically authentic, Enrique finds himself at sea. While lying in a hammock, his memories of Mary lead to another flashback, this time in black and white, of a visit by Mary and her father to the ship, and the return to the narration by means of red-tinted frames seems extremely primitive. Martínez Ferry uses rhythmic montage in this film to present concurrent narrations: Mary in the Simancas headquarters which is under heavy attack by Republican troops, and Enrique on board the Almirante Cervera which is steaming to her rescue. The desperate attempt of the Nationalist patrol to sneak out of the headquarters and silence the enemy howitzers is unsuccessful, and the final scene of this sequence shows Mary sitting next to the radio operator who is signalling the ship that the headquarters has been taken by the enemy, while a Republican soldier enters the room and fires two shots at them. Although the viewer is left with the impression that Mary has been killed, much later in the film, Enrique receives a letter from her, and we discover that she was miraculously saved. One can only question the verisimilitude of the narrative at this point.

The director dedicates much of the intervening narration to the action of small ships in the Nationalist forces called *bous*, Franco's crossing the strait of Gibraltar from Africa to Spain, and the action of the cruiser in the Mediterranean against various Republican ships. A significant bit of filler is the sequence of the visit to the Pantheon of Illustrious Mariners. In addition to the name of Magellan, the name of Don Cosme Damián de Churruca appears prominently as the camera lingers over his tomb. This sailor was killed at the battle of Trafalgar in 1803, but his importance to contemporary Spaniards lies in the 1941 landmark film entitled *Raza* (Race), directed by José Luis Sáenz de Heredia, with a script by none other than General Franco under the pseudonym of Jaime de Andrade. This film has as its protagonists members of the Churruca family from the time of the Spanish American War to the Spanish Civil War, and it contains a dose of pseudo-autobiographical elements of the *caudillo*.[12] The importance

---

[12]See Román Gubern, <u>Raza, el ensueño de Franco</u>.

which Martínez Ferry gives to Churruca here can only be seen as an attempt to indirectly eulogize General Franco. This is reinforced by later inclusion of historical footage of Franco at a naval review in 1939. The film is overly melodramatic, and is plagued by too many long shots of ships at sea which serve to give the film enough footage to be considered a feature-length film, but which do not contribute to the progression of the narration or to the creation of atmosphere. The overall poor quality of the film is evident from the opening shots of the old captain, whose face when seen in a close-up shot is so caked with makeup that he seems to have escaped from some horror film set.

José Antonio de la Loma's 1969 movie, *Golpe de mano* (Surprise Attack), is a film about personal vengeance and duty. The action occurs in 1938 along the Ebro front. The nationalist soldier, Second Lieutenant Andrés Novales, is from the town of Monteharo, located just behind the enemy lines, and after saving Captain Andújar's life in a skirmish, the former explains his ardent desire to liberate the nearby territory: "A mi padre los rojos lo mataron los primeros días de la guerra. Le estuvieron torturando toda una noche. . . . Al amanecer le cortaron sus partes y machacaron la cabeza a culetazos" (The reds killed my father during the first days of the war. They were torturing him all night . . . . At dawn they cut off his organs and they pounded his head to pieces with their rifle butts). The captain's angry reaction, "¡Basta! Monte guardia y vuelva" (That's enough! Mount guard and return!), defines his character at this early juncture as one in which duty is of foremost importance. The arrival of a civilian (Marcelino Solorzano) who has escaped from Monteharo suddenly changes the situation, since the Nationalists discover that the Republicans are planning to destroy a strategic bridge. Novales's personal motives again surface when he asks Solorzano about "el Pernas," the laborer who killed his father. The lieutenant's plan to divide into two squads to attack machine-gun nests and the bridge allows for the use of rhythmic montage, which creates a sense of suspense in the film. The narrative structure in the following sequences is really cuadripartite, since it involves the advance of Novales's squad and that of the squad led by Sergeant Requena (nicknamed "Casquete"), as well as the anxious waiting of Captain Andújar (heightened by a call received too late from headquarters which prohibited any squads from leaving), and the actions in the Republican camp. The scene in this fourth group shows a Republican captain with a conspicuous CNT armband, which identifies him as an anarchist, in the house of "el Pernas" as the latter refuses to evacuate the town. The suspense culminates in the moment in which "Casquete" finds the dynamite cables at the base of the bridge just as the Republican captain (Paco, "el Fulminante") is about to detonate the explosion. After this initially unsuccessful attempt, Fernández Cuenca (2: 577) points out that de la Loma subtly manifests the undercurrent of dissension and rivalry between anarchists and communists in a meeting between Paco and the famous communist leader known as "el Campesino." The latter tells the captain, "Eres anarquista pero te conozco bien y sé de lo que eres capaz" (You're an anarchist, but I know you well, and I know what you are capable of).

In contrast to the Republicans' ineptitude, Novales's Nationalist soldiers are successful in knocking out the machine-gun nests, and he is able to reach a house in town. He identifies it as being his family's, and a close-up shot of his face triggers a flash-back to the night in which "el Pernas" and his mob burst through the door to capture his father as Novales escaped through the back of the house. The return to the present also occurs with a close-up of the lieutenant, and "el Pernas" discovers that Novales has returned. Although the laborer's son identifies the Nationalist soldier as "Andrés, el hijo del amo," (Andrés, the son of the boss), the father retorts, "Ya no hay amos" (There aren't any bosses any more), and the theme of the class struggle which was implicit in the conflict is reinforced in his declaration, "Me cargué al viejo Novales porque era un cacique y no tenía derecho de seguir explotando a la gente" (I got rid of the old Novales because he was a boss and he didn't have any right to keep on exploiting people). De la Loma shot the sequence of the confrontation between "el Pernas" and Novales with a combination of reverse high and low angle shots in order to maximize the sense of conflict between the two (Pernas, with a shotgun, is in a second-story window; Novales takes cover on the ground outside of the building). The lieutenant again manifests his personal motivations in this confrontation as he yells, "He venido a matarte, ¿me oyes? Te voy a matar como un perro." (I've come to kill you. Do you hear me? I'm going to kill you like a dog). After a cut to the scene which depicts the fighting at the bridge, we return to see Novales's plans thwarted by the daughter of "el Pernas," who drops a bucket on Andrés's head and knocks him unconscious, symbolized by the shot going out of focus. Captain Andújar explains to Novales, who is now in bed, that "el Pernas" and his son surrendered and are incarcerated, to which the lieutenant

Personal vengeance over honor: De la Loma's Golpe de mano, with Simón Andreu. Courtesy Filmoteca Nacional.

replies, "En la cárcel, no; tienen que morir" (No jail for them--they've got to die). This desire for vengeance almost becomes reality when we see Novales (in a low angle shot representing the point of view of the incarcerated laborer) burst into the jail cell with a submachine-gun and assassinate "el Pernas" and his son; however, the fact that the shot is both out of focus and tinted red signals that it is just a dream. The murder again almost becomes reality in a variant of this scene in which Novales does indeed enter the cell with his weapon. However, the haughty and condescending attitude of "el Pernas," who calls the lieutenant "un señorito de mierda" (a fucking master) as he turns his back to him, causes Novales to throw his submachine-gun aside and attempt to strangle the prisoner. The captain, who symbolizes duty and honor, intervenes, and the next scene comprises the final confrontation between the two characters and the values that they represent. Captain Mendoza angrily blames the lieutenant for the deaths of his comrades at the bridge: "Los dejaste morir sin ayudarles porque tu venganza no podía esperar. . . . Eres el tipo más repugnante que me he echado a la cara. No eres digno de vestir ese uniforme y menos aun de llevar esa estrella" (You let them die without helping them because your vengeance couldn't wait. . . . You are the most repugnant fellow that I ever laid eyes on. You aren't worthy of wearing that uniform, much less that star). The close-up of Mendoza's hand ripping the insignia from Novales's chest visually reinforces the moral tone that de la Loma gives the film. He further reinforces this tone in the final shot as the camera zooms in from the long shot of the captain and his soldiers crossing the bridge to the crucifix in the river that had been worn by the slain Nationalist Sergeant "Casquete," a visual juxtaposition that underscores the Nationalist belief that their fight was a crusade.

The first half of the film is interspersed with jokes similar to those found in *Posición avanzada*. For example, as the Nationalist squad leaves on its mission, a soldier comments, "Nos vamos de ronda" (We're going serenading); later, when they have to ford a river, another says, "No podemos seguir; me he olvidado el traje de baño" (We can't go on; I forgot my bathing suit). This trend toward humor should be kept in mind when we consider the 1985 García Berlanga production, *La vaquilla*. Although de la Loma is able to create suspense through rhythmic montage, it suffers somewhat in the final confrontation at the bridge between "Casquete" and "el Fulminante." The latter, in his attempt to drive the Nationalists away, throws a grenade at an enemy soldier standing guard, and with the medium shot of "Casquete" standing in the water at the base of the bridge, a severed arm that is too obviously from a mannequin falls and almost hits him on the head. In reaction, the sergeant shoots and kills "el Fulminante" with nary a drop of blood in sight.

In spite of the director's claims that he eschewed subjectivity (Fernández Cuenca 2: 574), the narrative point of view is clearly that of the nationalist soldiers, and De la Loma visually underscores the righteousness of the nationalist cause. Nevertheless, the film does contain a moral message which is quite clear: duty and honor as a soldier must come before any personal objectives, especially base vengeance.

La orilla (The River-Bank), a film directed by Luis Lucía which had its debut in 1971, also contains a significant moral element derived from the conflict of the protagonists' ideals. Lucía begins the film with a narrator in a voice "off" who makes the following dedication: "Esta película está dedicada a los que desde un bando u otro, desde una u otra orilla, lucharon con nobleza y generosidad por una España mejor, la que día a día va fructificando en nuestra paz" (This film is dedicated to those from either faction, from either side, who fought with nobility and generosity for a better Spain, which day by day is yielding fruit in our peace).   Thus, from the very beginning, it is evident that reconciliation is a fundamental theme of the film.

Juan Castro, the male protagonist, is a Republican soldier who is known as "el Teniente Melenas" due to the length of his hair. He is clearly identified in the initial scene as an anarchist by the CNT insignia which he wears on the chest of his uniform. His commanders give him the mission to destroy four enemy Junkers for which he must cross a river and pass by a convent to get to Nationalist territory. Thus, we can base an initial reading of the title of the film on the geographical feature which divides the two armies. Lucía underscores the proximity of the convent to the front line through the use of sound effects "off" heard from the perspective of both groups, soldiers and religious: Juan hears the convent bells from his headquarters, and the first shot of the nuns praying contains the sounds of gunfire. Because two Republican soldiers cross over to the Nationalist side and betray Juan, he is the only survivor of his squad; badly wounded, he must seek shelter. The remark made by the Nationalist captain regarding the fallen Republican soldiers, "Han caído como unos valientes" (They fell valiantly), represents what Fernández Cuenca (2: 608) calls the "integrating spirit" of the film. This continues in the reactions of the nuns when Juan tries to gain entrance at the convent: although Sister Francisca calls the anarchist soldier "un rojo" (a red) and "un enviado del diablo," (sent by the devil), the Mother Superior replies, "Es un ser humano" (He is a human being). The latter saves Juan's life by extracting the bullets, with the help of a blood transfusion from the novitiate Sister Leticia. The image of the soldier and the novitiate united through this life-giving process (see photograph) is a portent of how their relationship is to develop.

The Mother Superior represents the "integrating spirit" throughout the film, and her comments made to the priest in the confessional constitute a second, metaphorical reading of the title of the movie which is hinted at in the dedication: "Si cada español se hubiera ganado el afecto de uno de la otra orilla, no andaríamos ahora a tiro limpio, Don Senén. Unos con su egoísmo y otros . . . con su resentimiento nos han traído tanta tristeza, tanta sangre" (If each and every Spaniard had won the affection of one on the other side,[13] we

---

[13]Note that <u>orilla</u> refers physically to the river-bank and metaphorically to the other side of ideological division that racked Spain.

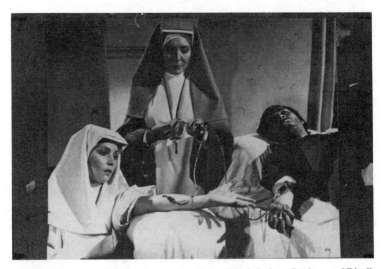

Impossible love: Lucía's La orilla, with Juan Castro, María Dolores Pradera, and Dianik Zurakowska. Courtesy Filmoteca Nacional.

wouldn't be shooting at each other now, Father Senén. Some have an ego, and others . . . with their resentment have brought us so much sadness, so much blood).

Juan is initially unable to understand the sacrifice that the nuns make on his behalf, and conflict between their respective value systems is symbolized by a clash in song: while the nuns intone chants in praise of the Virgin Mary, Juan, from his bed, tries to drown them out with renditions of "A las barricadas" (To the Barricades) and "En el frente de Jarama" (At the Jarama Front), popular songs from the Republican camp. A change in attitude accompanies his recuperation, however, and the montage sequence of close-ups of Juan watching Sister Leticia pray marks a new element in the narration: love. The image of Leticia with loose hair (without her veil) symbolizes the awareness in Juan of her beauty and sexual attractiveness. Nevertheless, the conflict of ideals remains. When Leticia later asks Juan, "¿Es posible que no creas en nada?" (Is it possible that you don't believe in anything?), he responds, "Creo en algunas cosas: en la muerte, en la revolución y los que padecen injusticia y sufren hambre" (I believe in some things: in death, in the revolution, and in those who suffer injustice and hunger). Although Juan adds that he is also beginning to believe in love, Leticia says, "Pues Dios es amor" (God is love) and the close-up image of their almost--but not completely--joined hands forebodes the impossibility of the consummation of their relationship. When Juan abandons the convent to return to his comrades, he leaves her a note which manifests the two levels of meaning in the title: "Me voy a la otra orilla, a mi sitio. Mientras viva me acordaré de ti" (I'm going to the other side of the river, to my place. As long as I live, I will remember you). Leticia runs after him, and following a final departure scene, Juan enters the river, only to be cut down by gunfire. Leticia, pursuing him, is also killed; the two bodies float away, and the camera shifts upward for a shot of the night sky, as if to symbolize an almost mystic union of the two in their deaths.

The "integrating spirit" that Fernández Cuenca relates to the theme of reconciliation between soldiers from the opposing sides, occurs only, it seems, on Nationalist terms. When the Nationalist Captain Losada finally discovers Juan in the convent, he decides to not take him prisoner so that the anarchist can protect the convent against his Republican comrades. Conversation between the two results in their self-evaluation as "dos españoles típicos" (two typical Spaniards) and a "par de fanfarrones" (a couple of braggers). This theme is carried to the extreme that Juan makes the improbable statement about the founder of the fascist Falange party: "No me caía mal a mí ese José Antonio. Lástima que no estuviera en nuestro bando" (That José Antonio didn't seem bad to me. Too bad he wasn't on our side). On the other hand, Lucía includes the theme of rancor between different factions of the Republican cause. When Losada informs Juan that the Nationalists have almost won the war, the anarchist comments about his comrades, "Son una banda de ineptos. Todo por hacer caso a los comunistas" (They are a bunch of incompetents. All because they paid attention to the communists). In a second encounter Juan and Losada agree to attempt to establish a truce so that no more lives are lost now that the war is almost over, and the captain admits, "Usted y yo podríamos llegar a ser muy buenos amigos" (You and I could become very good friends). This points to the theme of a better future, a theme which also appears in conversations between Juan and Rami, a young boy who visits the convent as assistant to the priest. The wounded soldier declares to the boy, "A lo mejor tú tendrás suerte y cuando ya seas hombre puedes vivir tranquilo. Yo creo que tanta sangre tiene que servir para algo" (Maybe you'll be lucky and when you're a man you can live peacefully. I believe that all this blood has to be for something). Rami, of course, represents ingenuous youth, who does not comprehend any justifications for the war among brothers. His conversation with Juan manifests the theme of the inexplicableness and nonsensicalness of a fratricidal conflict. After he explains that his two brothers fight on different sides, he comments, "A mí me parece que esta guerra está mal organizada. Los hermanos debían estar juntos" (It seems to me that this war isn't run right. Brothers should be together).

An important feature of the first half of the movie is the element of humor which is similar to that of other films of this category. Most of the examples occur in exchanges between Juan and the Mother Superior, such as when she hands him a new shirt with the emblem of the Nationalist troops, and says, "Lo siento, se nos han terminado los de la CNT" (I'm sorry, but we've run out of CNT emblems), or when Juan confesses that he is afraid of dying and in a low-angle shot the camera focuses on a statue of an angel which hangs precariously above the head of his bed. However, melodrama prevails, and the two protagonists, Juan and Leticia, meet untimely but romantic deaths.

León Klimovsky is a director of Argentine birth whose films on the Spanish Civil War include *La paz empieza nunca* (Peace Never Begins, 1960), and *La casa de las chivas* (The Bitches' House, 1971). The latter film makes the claim to have been based on historical occurrences, as a narrator states during the opening black and white sequence that "la casa ha existido y aún existe" (the house existed and still exists). Although the work does not feature as its main narrative element the confrontation of the two warring factions, the action does take place at the front, mainly in a house of two young women, Petra (Charo Soliano) and Trini (María Kosti), which has been occupied by Republican soldiers. As the film shifts from the "historical" to the "narrative," and changes from black and white to color, the narrator, in a continued voice-over, proclaims that house contained only the most primordial elements of human existence--life, death, hate, and sex--to which one would have to add religion. Indeed, this film is unique because it manifests a Nationalist point of view from within a narrative that is composed of Republican characters. This is possible because of the religious beliefs of Juan (Simón Andreu), the Republican soldier who stands out from his comrades who are also quartered at this civilian house. Indeed, the central conflict of the film is not between two armies or two ideologies, but between sex and religion.

From the beginning of the film, the moral standing of Petra and Trini is brought into question. The women in town insult the older sister (Petra), and insinuate that she obtains her food in exchange for sex. Klimovsky immediately establishes the inner virtue of this character, however, as we see her defend her honor and fight with the woman who has insulted her, as well as leave the army truck that has picked her up on her way home when the soldier/driver attempts to proposition her. Petra, then, represents the primordial tension that exists in the film between sin and redemption. Petra is the object of sexually-charged jokes on the part of the soldiers, and indeed, she appears in bed on different occasions with Villalba and Guzmán. Nevertheless, she shelters and defends her younger sister from the soldiers, an action for which Juan praises Petra. Trini seems bent on losing her innocence, however, and as the soldiers arrive at their home, she undoes her braids, a symbolic gesture which manifests the passage from girl to woman, and which manifests her sensuality. Trini's sexual impulses are directed toward Juan; when she finds him alone under a tree, she appears as a temptress, but to no avail. Later, Trini enters his bedroom and kisses his bare torso, waking him with the imploration, "Tómame" (Take me). His continued scorning of her causes Trini to plot revenge, and she rips her petticoat and shouts for help, accusing Juan of attempting to rape her. Petra chastises Trini with a comment that both refers to her mother's bad reputation, and provides the title to the movie: "Sí . . . es hija de la chiva" (Yes . . . she is the bitch's daughter).

Juan's continued rejection of Trini contrasts sharply with the behavior of the other Republican soldiers, who seem to be always looking for sex. Juan shows other character traits which also set him apart: in his initial scene, he shares his food with his comrades; he philosophizes in a pseudo-religious vein--"Ningún ser humano puede decir lo que vale otro. Eso no corresponde a los hombres" (No human being can say what another one is worth. That is not man's job); Trini accuses him of preaching "sermons" to her; and after a bombing attack he stops to attend to a dead soldier (as he explains to Petra, "También hay que ocuparse de los muertos, ¿no crees?" [We also have to take care of the dead, don't you think?]). We slowly realize that Juan, in spite of being among the ranks of the Republicans, is a very religious man who would like to become a priest. He awakens certain religious sentiments in Petra, and dialogues with her about religion. After showing her a photograph of a romanesque icon, Petra expresses her

incipient religious feelings: "Debe ser hermoso creer en algo grande
. . . en Dios" (It must be beautiful to believe in something big . . . in
God).   Petra's inner conflict comes to the surface after her sexual
encounter with a young Republican soldier called "el Nene" (the baby)
whose virginity was the cause of jokes by his older comrades.   After
the young soldier dies during a bombing, and Juan becomes angry with
Petra when he discovers their sin, she offers a justification which
continues her religious development in the film: "Quizá esa inocencia,
esa timidez era lo que buscaba en él" (Maybe it was that innocence,
that timidity that I was looking for in him).   As the camera zooms in
to a close-up of her face, she beseeches Juan, "Dame la paz, la
necesito" (Give me peace, I need it).   Petra implores him for a cross
as she climbs aboard an army truck to be evacuated, and as the truck
pulls out, Juan, in a close-up, makes the sign of the cross, saying,
"Que Dios te bendiga, mujer. Que Dios nos bendiga a todos" (May
God bless you, woman. May God bless us all).   Although Oms points
out that this is the first Republican sign of the cross on the *franquista*
screen since 1939 (*La guerre* 218), it is Republican in uniform, not in
spirit.   The melodramatic tone of the film climaxes in the final
sequence, as Trini, who had gone to live with Mariano, returns,
pregnant, and in a final fit of desperation drives a truck across a mined
bridge to her death. The final scene of the narrative shows Juan in a
high angle shot, praying on his knees and asking God's pardon for
everyone. The film then returns to black and white--the historical--as
the voice-over proclaims that this is a true story, we see an old
women--Petra--go to the door of her house.

Although the narration does not occur on the front line of battle,
the occasional bombings and the resulting evacuation of the house merit
the film's inclusion in this category. However, it shares some themes
with films which portray life in the rear guard: the interaction between
civilians and soldiers, and the attempt by civilians to retain some
normality in their existence, a theme poignantly displayed in the scene
in which Petra's father tends to his garden even though his house will
soon belong to no-man's-land. It is also one of the few films which
deals with the topic of deserters, and Klimovsky ties this theme into the
theme of religion. The Republican soldier Alonso complains about
"this damned war" and is later shot and killed while trying to escape.
His comrades flippantly remark, "A lo mejor era un cura camuflado"
(Maybe he was a camouflaged priest) to which Petra retorts, "Pues no

se ha portado como un cura, te lo digo yo" (He hasn't behaved like a priest, let me tell you). The first remark connotes a condescending attitude toward the clergy, and the second, with its sexual innuendos, manifests a type of humor which is typical of the Nationalist films of this period, and which underscores the main conflict of the film. The protagonist, Juan, contrasts sharply with his fellow soldiers, and through his example, changes the lives of the young women. However, Juan's character would have seemed more appropriate on the other side, fighting for the Nationalist cause. Nevertheless, *La casa de las chivas* represents a further attempt at reconciliation on the part of Klimovsky, a theme which at least superficially is evident in many of the "Nationalist" films in the late '60's and early '70's.

Rafael Gil is a director who began work in the 1940's and who is well known for films about the Spanish Civil War, such as *Murió hace quince años* (He Died Fifteen Years Ago, 1954). His 1975 film, *A la legión le gustan las mujeres* (The Legion Likes Women), is a comedy in which the point of view is from the Nationalist side. The opening scenes (during the credits) show various groups of soldiers--first Romans, then Christian knights and seventeenth-century musketeers-- who capture groups of women; although Gil fails here to provide any transcendence to the movie, he does set the tone for what is to follow. As the title suggests, the sexual motif is the basis of much of the humor.

The story involves a group of Nationalist soldiers who make an unauthorized foray into enemy territory in order to save the girlfriend (Pili) of their commanding officer, Second Lieutenant Josele. Their adventures include sight-gags such as the "talking" bear named "Stalin" whose voice-over makes satirical comments to his bear-like master, "el Peman," and the pickpocket's loot from a Republican movie theater which includes four wallets and one garter. The principal gags of a sexual nature occur during the banquet and orgy between the Nationalist soldiers and Republican women, such as Aurora, Jacqueline (the wife of Mr. DuPont), and Natacha (the Russian translator). These include sight gags such as the disappearance of a jar of bicarbonate followed by that of aphrodisiac, as well as those based on sound effects (Jacqueline's repeated giddy laughter "off" which signals her sexual pleasure). At times, the sexual motif is combined with a religious motif, such as in an early comment by the prudish Doña Irene: "Después de la victoria, una cuaresma de mil años" (After the victory,

a one-thousand year Lent).   Religion also appears in the sequence
filmed in a hospital in Republican-controlled territory.   In another sight
gag, we see a portrait of Lenin that the Nationalists in enemy territory
quickly flip over when the contingent of their soldiers arrive to reveal
a portrait of the Virgin Mary. The derogatory epithet which an old
woman   uses   toward   her   captors--"perros   judíos"   (Jewish
dogs)--underscores the Nationalist attitude that their fight was indeed
a crusade.

As in other films made by directors who had previously portrayed
the official version of civil war during the Franco regime, the most
derogatory attitude concerns the International Brigades.   Their
commanding officer appears to be a greedy individual ready to ravage
Spain of her treasures: when he spies a Goya painting in his
headquarters, he commands, "que me lo embalen" (have them rap it up
for me).   When the Nationalist soldiers manage to cross into enemy
territory by commandeering a Republican hospital truck, the soldier
who drives has an absurd conversation in macaronic English with
British guards.   Their comment as the truck pulls out is "Fucking
Spaniards," which manifests a very condescending attitude on their part
and shows them in very derogatory light.   Indeed, the very name of the
leader of the International Brigades, "Commander Merdy," represents
a play on words which can only be meant to continue this derogatory
vein.   In addition, the Republican women appear as lascivious and
traitorous (they assist the Nationalist soldiers in their mission), as
opposed to the chaste, faithful, and courageous Pili.

Unlike the International Brigades, the Spanish Republican soldiers
generally appear in a positive light. Comments exchanged between the
closely positioned trenches again reveal the religious motif as a source
of humor: when the Republicans insult the Nationalists as "Hijos de
cura" (Sons of priests), the reply of the latter is, "Hombre, alguno
habrá por aquí, pero decirlo de todos . . ." (Maybe there is one over
here, but to say it about everyone . . .).   However, they decide to call
a truce and exchange items (cigars and wine for cigarette papers and
newspapers), and their subsequent appraisal of each other--"majos"
(swell) and "cachondos" (ribald)--reflects the superficial reconciliation
motif which appears in other films.

The Nationalist squad prepares a "sorpresa (surprise) 'Made in
Spain'"--a   mock   bullfight   which   exhibits   gross   caricature--to
successfully accomplish their mission.   They even return with the
captured Commander Merdy, who, in the final shot of the film, is

greeted by the Nationalist soldiers with a Bronx cheer. Although *A la legión le gustan las mujeres* is not a quality film, it is significant that it manifests many motifs which are common to other Nationalist oriented films of the period: the reconciliation motif, the portrayal of the International Brigades in negative light, etc. It is also significant to note that this is a film which deals with the Civil War in a comic tone a full decade before García Berlanga's smash hit, *La vaquilla* (The Little Cow).

Soldados (Soldiers), the 1978 film by Alfonso Ungría, contrasts with *A la legión le gustan las mujeres* in both point of view and tone. This is the first movie of this category, films which portray the conflict at the front, to adopt the point of view of the Republican side of the conflict. There is also a contrast with the farcical tone of the previous film; indeed, Ungría has referred to *Soldados* as simply a melodrama which manifests the "impossible search for goodness" (qtd. in *Cine español* 281). The film portrays the lives of Republican soldiers Agustín and Tellines, and two women in their lives, Remedios and Tula, both during and before the war. *Soldados* is based on the novel by Max Aub, *Las buenas intenciones* (Good Intentions), but Ungría has significantly changed the narrative structure. Abandoning linearity, he has woven a complex narrative through the use of the flash-back technique. This important transformation in the narrative structure serves to focus our attention on the discourse itself, which Ungría, as Juan Hernández Les points out, elegantly carries out in this film ("*Soldados*" 25).

The first protagonist, Agustín Amparo, (played by Ovidi Montllor), is a Republican soldier who enters a small town with his comrades, only to be ambushed by local Nationalists. The point of view is immediately established in the film in this opening sequence, since the low angle shots of the second-story windows from where the shooting which is killing many of the Republican soldiers originates immediately places the spectator at Agustín's side, in danger. After his escape from the ambush, a close-up of his eyes triggers the first flash-back of the film. In a luxurious setting, a woman named Remedios informs us that her child was sired by Agustín Amparo, but we discover that the culprit was the lecherous Agustín père. In order to not endanger his ailing mother's health, the young Agustín offers to marry Remedios, and subsequent flash-backs develop the contrast between the moral character of the father and the son: while the father continues to attempt to seduce Remedios, the younger Agustín maintains a chaste relationship with her, treating her with kindness and tenderness. Remedios testifies to her husband's essential goodness in her good-bye note in which she says that he is a "most decent person." However, this love triangle constitutes an untenable situation for Agustín, and he suffers deep emotional problems because of it. One evening Remedios finds her husband crying on the floor near the entrance to their home, a scene artfully photographed by José Luis Alcaine with the camera at floor level to better capture Agustín's inner agony. After suffering from sexual impotence with a prostitute, Agustín, manifests his subconscious anguish and hostility toward Remedios in a dream sequence in which he crucifies her. The discovery of the note announcing her departure is an existential limit point for Agustín, and in the next scene, as his tuxedo-dressed father returns home from an evening escapade, Agustín kills him with one shot to the head. Another male protagonist who has a violent past is Tellines, who after being rejected by gangster boss Don Rodolfo in his request for a job, decides to shoot up the night-club where the boss does business. Tellines must later escape from Don Rodolfo's men who seek vengeance, and during the war, he is a comrade in arms with Agustín.

Unlike these two characters, a third Republican soldier, Javier, brings an ideological dimension to the film. He is a communist who meets and has an affair with Pilar, a somewhat older woman who runs a bookstore. Like Agustín, Javier is basically a decent person: after his first night with Pilar, he leaves her a note which says, "No soy un chulo" (I'm not a bastard). However, he is caught up in the historical circumstances, and after political discussions with some anarchists, he decides to leave for the front. This decision devastates Pilar, who, in a fit of rage, kills her daughter, and ends up in an insane asylum. Javier's failure on a personal level mirrors that on the ideological level. Arriving for active duty with an armload of books results in a sharp rebuke on the part of his captain--"No aguantamos propaganda de ninguna clase" (We won't stand for propaganda of any type)--which the officer combines with the threat of a firing squad. On the front line, amidst a pouring rain with persistent gunfire "off," Javier admits that the concept of revolution makes no sense there.

Like Remedios, who, after leaving Agustín, goes to a brothel to seek employment, the other female protagonist, Tula, also becomes a prostitute. Director Ungría interweaves the narrative strands of these characters' lives as they meet on the front line and try to escape the

The perspective of the vanquished: Ungría's <u>Soldados</u>, with Ovidi Montllor and Francisco Algora. Courtesy Filmoteca Nacional.

Nationalist troops. As they attempt to cross a river, Tula desperately attempts to return to the water's edge to retrieve her missing treasure, but her friends restrain her. A close-up of her laughing face triggers the flash-back that provides us with information about her past. As a young girl, her parents inform her that she will marry "master Vicente," but the relationship proves to be unsatisfactory. One night the pregnant Tula discovers her husband in bed with a prostitute, and she rushes out of her husband's house into a storm. After the resulting miscarriage, Tula abandons "el señorito Vicente" with the declaration, "Me marcho, pero no voy a morirme de hambre" (I'm leaving, but I'm not going to die of hunger). The following scenes artfully show how she kept her word: a brothel setting with close-ups bordered by dissolves of feminine hands which contain money or which place a pearl necklace into a jewelry box. This narrative information, taken in syntagmatic relationship with Tula's laughter at the river's edge, gives that wartime scene an acute sense of the absurd.

After the dissolve following the brothel scene, we observe the three protagonists sleeping in an open field, an image which symbolizes their passive acceptance of their fate--their defeat. In their struggle to survive, however, Agustín kills a threatening soldier whom he later identifies as a fellow Republican. His reaction to this incident is both erbal and non-verbal: not only does he exclaim, "Estamos todos locos" (We're all crazy), but he abandons his   rifle, a gesture which culminates the symbolism of his despair and of the absurd. His verbal response echoes Tula's comment from her first encounter with Agustín which also manifests the absurdity of their situations. When Agustín fails to understand something that she says, Tula responds, "Eso es lo que pasa, que nadie entiende nada" (That is what is happening, nobody understands anything). When the three friends reach Alicante, port of departure for the Republican soldiers who are fleeing the onslaught of the Nationalist troops, Agustín decides that he will return to Madrid. Tula's recommendation of a brothel for shelter in the capital leads him to a chance reuniting with Remedios and the consummation of their relationship. The length of this scene--with a change in camera angle in a tracking shot from the foot to the side of the bed--is justified by its importance in the narration. It marks a contrast with both his earlier unhappiness and his impotency, and it forebodes (recalling the French concept of "la petite morte") his subsequent death. After the Nationalist soldiers burst into the brothel and capture him, they take him on a "stroll" and assassinate him. The penultimate shot of the film, a close-up of the dead Agustín's head with the camera at ground level, parallels the earlier crying scene. The form of assassination of the prisoner also culminates the wanton violence portrayed throughout the film, such as the initial assassination of the village mayor and the killing of the civilian driver when the Republican soldiers commandeer an automobile.

The characters all move from pre-war situations of frustration and failure to end-of-war situations of defeat and death. The despair and frustration portrayed in the film are also the result of the social and artistic climate in which Ungría worked, however. He has stated that this tremendous frustration was the result of having lost not just any war, but the Spanish civil war (Rentero, "Entrevista" 45). *Soldados* is an excellent film on many counts. Superb acting by Ovidi Montllor, brilliant photography by José Luis Alcaine, and excellent direction by Alfonso Ungría add to its significance as the first film portraying action at the front which adopts the point of view of the Republican camp.

The 1984 film, *Memorias del General Escobar* (Memoirs of General Escobar), which portrays the war-time activities of an actual Republican general, received notoriety because of the legal proceedings following allegations of plagiarism against the film's director, José Luis

Madrid. The year before the film had its debut, José Luis Olaizola had won the Planeta literary prize for his novel, *La guerra del General Escobar* (General Escobar's War), and there were plans for director Antonio Mercero to make the film version of the novel. Before Mercero was able to do this, however, director Madrid used a script by the Catalan scriptwriter Pero Massip and was able to take advantage of the popularity of the novel on the same topic. Massip expressed his intentions regarding the script in an interview in which he stated, "I want to remember [the war] and avoid another situation like that one, and in my contribution to the film, I also want to take advantage of the opportunity to pay homage to all the soldiers of Catalonia" (Vidal 33).

The opening scene shows General Escobar (Antonio Ferrandis) writing his memoirs in a Nationalist prison cell, with a voice-over of the protagonist which narrates the action. This is the basic narrative ploy of the film, used four times during the movie, and on each occasion, there is a flashback to the historical and personal events which constitute the story. The film narrates the events of the three years corresponding to the Civil War, since the first element of the story is the rebellion of the Nationalists in 1936 at a time during which Escobar is a Colonel in the Civil Guard. Like many other films that deal with the war, *Las memorias del General Escobar* manifests the essence of *cainismo* in this fratricidal conflict: Escobar's son José, who is a Falangist, is wounded in the street violence and must flee to Italy; the other son, Antonio, is stationed with the Republican army in Madrid. In a telephone conversation with the latter, the Colonel expresses his sentiments regarding his role in the conflict: he will maintain his fidelity to the government, and uphold his oaths of loyalty. This conversation manifests, then, what scriptwriter Massip believes is the essence of the film: the victory of duty over conscience (Comelles 28). Director Madrid visually shows this loyalty in his recreation of the historical moment in which Escobar leads his Civil Guards into the plaza before the governmental palace with Prime Minister Tarradellas on the balcony: high and low reverse-angle shots capture the sense of unity between the government leaders on the one hand and Escobar and his men on the other. Escobar's military salute and exclamation, "A sus órdenes, mi Presidente" (At your orders, my President), constitutes his pledge of loyalty, and is greeted with shouts in Catalan of "Long Live" the Republic, Catalonia, and the Civil Guard. His sense of duty remains firm until the very end of the conflict. With impending defeat, other Republican soldiers urge him to flee to Valencia in order to go into exile, but he replies, "Mi puesto esta aquí y aquí me encontraré" (My post is here, and here is where I'll be). During his trial before a Nationalist military tribunal, he wears the uniform of the Civil Guard and rests his defense on the notion of loyalty and obedience: "¿Qué podía hacer un modesto Guardia Civil sino cumplir sus juramentos u obedecer a sus superiores?" (What could a modest Civil Guard do except follow his oaths or obey his superior officers?). This motif leads to some weak points in the script however, such as when a Nationalist prison guard orders him to clean the latrines. Although other incarcerated Republican soldiers think that it is a disgrace that their leader has received such an ignominious task, Escobar points out, "Las órdenes se cumplen, no se interpretan" (Orders are carried out, they aren't interpreted), to which the soldier replies, "Este hombre tiene un par de cojones" (What a pair of balls this guy has). A colleague of General Goded notes that in addition to his profound sense of loyalty, Escobar had profound religious convictions and was an authentic man of honor. Director Madrid treats this aspect of the protagonist in the second flashback, as the General writes in his Memoirs that "los incontrolables sembraban terror y muerte" (the uncontrollables were spreading terror and death) in the streets of Barcelona. He tells Prime Minister Tarradellas of his repugnance at the burning of convents, and he saves a priest who is about to be assassinated by a group of men who have gotten out of a car that has the conspicuous anarchist label, "FAI/CNT," and who claim that the priest is an enemy of the people. Indeed, his strong religious convictions are manifested throughout the film. He suffers two serious wounds during the conflict, and after recovering from the second, he makes a pilgrimage to Lourdes to give thanks for his recovery. He also quotes the Bible on several occasions, and uses phrases like "Que sea lo que Dios quiera" (Whatever God wishes) and "Hágase la voluntad de Dios" (May God's will be done) in reference to his impending capture by Nationalist forces and later execution. Finally, his visual signal to his firing squad to carry out their orders is the raising of a crucifix in his right hand. The religious aspect of the film also contains an implicit criticism of Nationalist ideology and their view of the war as a crusade when Escobar inquires of President Azaña, "Usted cree que Dios puede estar al lado de alguien en una guerra?" (Do you believe that God can be on anyone's side in a war?).

The transformation of the Civil Guard into the Republican National

Guard, and Escobar's transferral to Madrid is accompanied by the use of documentary film shown in brown tint, and other uses of this technique in the movie occur to show the Nationalist attack on Madrid, the funeral of Durruti, and refugees at the end of war. His arrival in the capital allows the narrative to introduce the figure of an ingenue to bring into question the very nature of the conflict. In this case, it is his grandchild who asks, "Abuelo, ¿para qué sirven las guerras?" (Grandpa, what are wars good for?), to which the General replies, "Yo creo que para nada--sólo para que mueran muchos hombres" (I believe that they aren't good for anything--they only cause many men to die). Nevertheless, after the tragedy of losing his son José in the fighting, it is the General himself who questions the conflict's *raison d'être* when in October of 1938, he asks the other Republican generals the rhetorical question, "¿Para qué nos ha servido esta guerra?" (What has this war been good for?), to which the only response can be "Que nos sirva de ejemplo para que no se vuelva a repetir" (May it serve as an example so that it does not happen again). At the end of the conflict when he is in prison, he does not receive a pardon, and is sentenced to die. The voice-over of a letter that he writes exclaims, "Si mi vida y la de todos que han caído sirve para que esto no se vuelva a repetir, nuestra sangre no habrá sido estéril" (If my life and the lives of all those who have fallen mean that this will not happen again, our blood will not have been sterile). After his death, the final voice-over continues along the same vein as the camera hovers over the document of his Memoirs in his cell: "Un millón de muertos. Una guerra entre hermanos. ¡Qué horror!" (One million dead. A war between brothers. What horror!), and the final close up shows the last words of the document--the rhetorical "Dios mío. ¿Por qué?" (My God. Why?), which again show his incomprehension.

The theme of reconciliation seen in other Civil War films also appears in *Memorias del General Escobar*. When the protagonist receives word that both José Antonio and Durruti have died, he exclaims, "Los dos eran valientes" (They were both brave). Later, in another overly-melodramatic scene involving a Christmas Eve truce, Escobar comments that all of the soldiers speak "the same language" as a low-angle shot shows the silhouettes of enemy troops as they join together to sing a carol.

The film suffers from several defects, and perhaps some of the defects can be attributed to the speed in which director Madrid worked on this project. This is certainly not Antonio Ferrandis's best performance, as he renders Escobar's character too melancholy and lachrymose (as when he erroneously discovers that his son José may be among the Nationalist troops who are attacking his position) or shows a lack of dramatic intensity (as when his visit to the front line in the Casa del Campo in Madrid appears to be a stroll down the Paseo de la Castellana). One can only wonder how Mercero would have dealt with essentially the same narrative material.

Luis García Berlanga is one of Spain's most important directors, and his long career includes such important films as *Esa pareja feliz* (That Happy Couple, 1951), *Bienvenido, Mr. Marshall* (Welcome, Mr. Marshall), the film which won an Honorable Mention at the 1953 Cannes Film Festival, *El verdugo* (The Executioner, 1964), and the so-called Leguinache trilogy, which consists of *La escopeta nacional* (National Shotgun, 1978), *Patrimonio nacional* (National Patrimony, 1981), and *Nacional III* (National III, 1983). In May of 1986, García Berlanga achieved recognition for his long and illustrious career in cinema when he became the first film director to receive the coveted "Premio Príncipe de Asturias de las Artes" (Prince of Asturias Prize for the Arts). At the end of 1986, when the Spanish Film Academy (Academia de las Artes y las Ciencias Cinematográficas de España) was founded, García Berlanga was awarded the title of Honorary President. His 1985 production, *La vaquilla* (The Little Cow), is based on a script that Berlanga had prepared as early as 1956 but which had been rejected by the censors of the Franco regime on numerous occasions. At the time of its filming, it was the most expensive Spanish movie ever made, with a budget of 270 million pesetas, but it also turned out to be one of the biggest box-office hits in the history of Spanish film, earning almost 500 million pesetas in the first eight months of its showing. The film's success among Spanish movie critics was likewise notable, and Joan Salvany calls the film "one of the most brilliant allegations of the uselessness of war in the history of cinema" ("*La vaquilla*" 43). The action takes place on the front line in Aragon (the movie was filmed in the town of Sos del Rey Católico), but we must speak of confrontation rather than fighting, since not a single shot is fired in this "war" movie.

In the initial sequence, a voice emanating from a loud speaker in Nationalist-held territory invites the Republican troops to join them in a feast in honor of the patron saint of their town, Perales. The

Animal symbolism: García Berlanga's <u>La vaquilla</u>. Courtesy Sogepaq, S.A.

announcement, which includes the menu and the mention of an "encierro" or driving of cattle into the penfold is meant to demoralize the Republican troops.   Sergeant Castro (Alfredo Landa) devises a plan to ruin the Nationalists' festivities and at the same time raise the morale of his own troops: steal the bull and return with the meat. However, his lieutenant (José Sacristán) decides to take charge, and recruits three other soldiers for the mission. Their incredible foray into enemy territory is the story that the movie tells.

Critics refer to the film as a comedy, but often categorize it as an example of the *esperpento*, the genre invented by Ramón del Valle-Inclán.[14]   The *esperpento* represents a systematic distortion of characters and indeed reality that Valle-Inclán created in his dramas and novels.   In *Luces de Bohemia* (1920), the protagonist Max Estrella

---

[14]Manuel Hidalgo refers to the film as "a Spanish comedy, between the farce [sainete] and the esperpento" ("La vaquilla" 36) and José Luis Guarner regards it as an example of "the choral esperpento" ("La vaquilla" 34). Regarding the aesthetics of the esperpento, see Anthony Zaraheas's <u>Visión del esperpento: teoría y práctica en los esperpentos de ValleInclán</u>, Rodolfo Cardona's <u>Visión del esperpento</u>, and María Eugenia March's <u>Forma e idea del esperpento</u>.

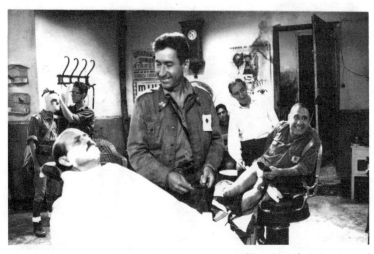

A comic vision of the conflict: García Berlanga's <u>La vaquilla</u>, with Alfredo Landa, José Sacristán, and Agustín González. Courtesy Sogepaq, S.A.

proclaims, "Classical heroes reflected in concave mirrors give us *Esperpento*" and "Spain is a grotesque deformation of European civilization" (106). For Valle-Inclán, in order to portray the reality of Spain, one must use the grotesque, the absurd, and the ridiculous.

García Berlanga utilizes many techniques to achieve a comic tone in the film. Notable in the linguistic element of the film is the repeated use of billingsgate by the soldiers, such as Mariano's exclamation when he discovers upon returning to his home that his almond grove has been ruined-- "¡Me cago en la madre que los parió!" (Motherfuckers!)--or the Lieutenant's complaint after stepping on a thistle--"¡Que tengo el pie jodido, coño!" (My foot is fucked up, dammit!). The linguistic component of humor is also fundamental in the scene in which the Republican Lieutenant, formerly a barber, has to shave the Nationalist commander. Disguised in a Nationalist uniform, he must nervously invent a new identity ("Donato, uh, López, uh, Pérez") and hurriedly invent follow-ups on slips of the tongue.   The rhythm and timing that García Berlanga maintains throughout the film contribute to many comic situations. Just as the squad has their victim cornered and are about ready to kill the animal, the cattle drive begins, and in their attempt to run ahead of it, Sergeant

Scatological humor: García Berlanga's <u>La vaquilla</u>. Courtesy Filmoteca Nacional.

Castro is horned in the buttocks. In a scene in a stable involving Mariano, Guadalupe, and the Nationalist Lieutenant Alfredo Carrasco, the latter grabs for his rival just as the Republican soldier slips away, and the Lieutenant is left holding a bridle. The director uses another sight gag when the five disguised Republican soldiers hear a moo "off" and exit through an archway left in pursuit of their prey. They immediately return, pursued by a Nationalist band of trumpeters; when they exit right, they again return followed by a wagon loaded with food. This type of humor causes Manuel Hidalgo to state that the script for this film is "an indefatigable machine of verbal comicality, wild situations and excessive characters that the director paroxystically agitates and shakes, with his characteristic inclination toward chaos, a chaos that Berlanga organizes in the interior of sequences of very long duration" ("*La vaquilla*" 36).

A strong sense of irony pervades the entire film. The animal which the Republican soldiers pursue turns out to be not a bull, but the little cow announced in the title of the film. They discover a group of whores who have come to town from Zaragoza just for this religious festivity. After a zealous Nationalist chaplain yanks them from the brothel, they must participate in the religious procession. This artfully

filmed scene begins with a low-angle shot of the Christ figure which is
being carried on the shoulders of the devout; the camera then pans
down to show the infiltrated Republican Lieutenant as one of the
statue-bearers. Likewise, Sergeant Castro carries the Virgin figure.
The scene is accompanied on the sound-track by what can only be
described as equally ironic music. A priest gives the "Republican
sacristan" money with the admonition, "Por nuestra cruzada" (For our
crusade). The Nationalist commander then orders them to carry the
Marquis, who is confined to a wheel chair, to the top of the church
bell-tower so that he can get a better view of his vast land holdings.
García Berlanga enriches the obvious symbolism of the wheel-chair by
the fact that these Republican soldiers must support him and carry
him. The director is also not above using scatological humor for a
laugh. In their initial encounter with the cow, Sergeant Castro has to
push "el Limeño," a former bullfighter who was hand-picked for the
job, by the seat of the pants toward the animal. In a knee shot, Castro
smells his hand and exclaims, "Pero si se ha cagado" (He shit his
pants). Later, during the "bullfight," the Republican band takes
refuge under a wagon filled with female spectators. The sudden
"rain" without a cloud in the sky is explained as being a "town
custom" by which the women thus chastise any men who would cower
under the wagon during the bullfight.

The machismo of the soldiers is constantly undermined. Not only
does "el Limeño" soil his uniform during the confrontation with the
cow (an accident which the soldier comically tries to justify with the
excuse of having eaten green plums), but the entire assembly of
Nationalist troops runs wild in fear and confusion when the Republican
infiltrators set off some fireworks during the   "encierro" as a
diversionary tactic. Later, during a dance in the plaza, the Lieutenant
leads Sergeant Castro as his partner in a "paso doble." The Republican
tailor who made the counterfeit uniforms for the squad is a blatant
homosexual, and he later distracts the Nationalist guards in their
nearby trench with a sexually suggestive monologue.

Since the cow escaped during the diversionary fireworks, "el
Limeño" and his rival Nationalist matador, "el Cartujano," must
follow it at dusk into no-man's-land between the two enemy lines. The
incongruous image of the former dressed in a matador's suit of lights
with an army helmet on his head captures the absurdity of the entire
affair. As "el Limeño" grabs it by the horns, the animal succumbs,
and the rivals embrace. This symbolic gesture is the culmination of

the reconciliation motif which appears earlier in the film when the Republican squadron is bathing in a stream, and a group of Nationalist soldiers arrive and hold a congenial conversation with the infiltrators. When the Nationalists depart, the camera zooms in to Sergeant Castro, who comments, "Aquí en pelota, ni enemigos ni nada. . . y además nos invitan a desayunar" (Here we are in our birthday suits and we're not enemies at all . . . and they even invite us to breakfast). The nudity of the soldiers in this scene symbolizes man in his essential, primal state, unencumbered by cultural or ideological trappings. Later, the idea of equality with regard to the basic necessities of man appears during the scene at the brothel. After quoting Aristotle (undoubtedly via the Archpriest of Hita's fourteenth-century Spanish masterpiece, *The Book of Good Love*) on man's need for sexual coupling, the Republican "sacristán" comments, "Que si comunismo, pero si fascismo, pero a la hora de meterla en caliente, todos de acuerdo" (So what fascism, what communism? When the time comes to stick it in, we all agree). Manuel Hidalgo comments that *La vaquilla* manifests García Berlanga's conception of the individual as "the only possible author of human behavior" and that the film is "not a version of the Spanish civil war in accord with the ideas that came into play at that time, but a vision of man in his reduced stature of an antihero who tries to save himself from the conflagration, and, if possible, come out on top in the most everyday matters" ("*La vaquilla*" 36).

Egoism, as opposed to ideological considerations, is indeed the prime motivation in the film. The Republican soldier Mariano, in an initial exchange of tobacco and cigarette paper between opposing troops, offers to exchange places with his Nationalist counterpart simply because their girlfriends and families are in opposite zones. Sergeant Castro slaps him in slapstick fashion and adds the reprimand, "¿Te has creído que la guerra es una broma?" (Did you think that war was a joke?). Other comments between the sergeants about soldiers who do not have "patriotismo ni espíritu militar" (patriotism nor military spirit) and the rhetorical question, "¿Cómo vamos a hacer una guerra con tipos así?" (How are we going to fight a war with guys like these?) further underscore this motif. Later, Guadalupe chides Mariano that everything is his fault because he voted for the leftists, and the girl's mother adds, "Todo por las condenadas ideas" (All because of his damned ideas). This scene also includes another important motif which appears in other films: the mole. Roque,

Guadalupe's father and a Republican, has been in hiding in the house since 1936. The Marquis, who superficially provides much support for the Nationalists, also proves to be a mere egotist in two comments that he makes: when the Nationalist commander inquires in which front his son is serving, the Marquis replies, "Biarritz"; after the sumptuous banquet, the aristocrat chides his steward: "¿Por qué entregaste cincuenta ovejas al ejército?" (Why did you hand over fifty sheep to the army?). As Octavi Martí states, the main concept behind *La vaquilla* is that no one defended any ideals, but only acted out of obligation, fear, or to satisfy their own interests ("Un encierro" 27).

Although critics like Octavi Martí (27) and J. M. López i Llaví (27) take exception to the very comic tone which García Berlanga employs in *La vaquilla*, García Berlanga clearly enjoys the artistic freedom--now that censors no longer impede him!--to choose whatever tone he wishes to do a film about the Spanish Civil War, and the director has clearly declared that his intent in this film was to demythify the war (Tirado 3). Indeed, as the Republican commander ironically says to the assembled squadron at the end of the film, "Esto no es una guerra, es una verbena" (This isn't a war, it's a festival). The final scene of the movie shows the dead cow in the middle of no-man's-land the next day. After a zoom in, the camera, in a high angle shot does a complete 360 degree pan of the countryside; with guitar and Spanish singing "off," a second zoom in shows buzzards amidst the "banderillas," eating the cow. The symbolism is quite evident, for as Thierry Maliniak points out, the little cow was simply Spain (*Cine español* 1: 312). No other visual image better captures the sentiment expressed by Juan Tomás de Salas regarding recent public opinion polls: the real loser in the Spanish civil war was, indeed, Spain.

In 1987, actor Ricardo Palacios had his debut as a director with the film *¡Biba la banda!* (Long Live da Band). This attempt at comedy falls way short of its mark. Although Carlos Heredero states that the film most closely related to this one would be *La vaquilla*, by Luis G. Berlanga" ("*Biba*" 67), a more appropriate analogy would be with an earlier comedy in which Palacios himself had a major role: *A la legión le gustan las mujeres*. The basic narrative structure and the political viewpoint of both films is the same: the plots revolve around an incursion behind enemy lines with the purpose of saving a soldier's amorous relationship, and both films have a Nationalist point of view.

Indeed, *¡Biba la banda!* is the first Spanish film in twelve years to have Nationalists as its protagonists.

The soldiers of the film are not combatants, however, but musicians in a Nationalist band, whose music is to reflect the "spiritual values of the west." When Agustín receives a letter from his girlfriend Verónica in which she tells him that the bank is going to take her family's land away because they cannot make the payments on it, Agustín goes to her rescue, helping to harvest the wheat. The band is rehearsing for a concert for the *caudillo*, and since Agustín is an important member of the band, the sergeant (Alfredo Landa) sends a contingency of soldiers to bring Agustín back immediately. All this is possible because of the fortuitous breaking of the glasses of the Comandante (Antonio Ferrandis), who is unable to distinguish who is present for rehearsals. The absence of so many soldiers puts a strain on the band, however, and they must resort to subterfuge in order to convince the Comandante that rehearsals are running smoothly: a record of marching music makes the band leader think that they play better without him, until his new glasses allow him to discover the shocking truth. The twenty-four hour deadline before the concert adds the element of suspense to the film, which Palacios attempts to heighten through rhythmic montage, alternating the harvesting scenes and later obstacles for the soldiers' timely return (sheep blocking the road, etc.) with the Comandante's pending appearance before the *caudillo*.

The incursion into enemy territory becomes complicated as red guerrillas, led by Verónica's brother Manolo, descend upon the Nationalist troops. As Verónica and her mother defend the good-willed soldiers who fight for Franco, we see a theme that appears in several other films with Nationalist protagonists: apparent brotherhood and harmony ("Esto no es una guerra civil, ni esto no es nada" [This isn't a civil war or anything]). When the tension between the two groups who are working together to finish the harvest later erupts, Emilia (mother of Verónica and Manolo) imposes order on the "children." Slapstick elements abound (the priest falling into an irrigation ditch, etc.), but the comedy of the film never takes off. After a triumphant concert, the final image of the film, the "bird" that the delinquent soldiers give to Lt. Urquiza, represents an exact parallel to the Bronx cheer at the end of *A la legión le gustan las mujeres*. Although it is important to note that *¡Biba la banda!* continues the category of pro-nationalist comedy movies well into the period of democratization, it is of even lesser quality than its predecessors.

¡Ay, *Carmela!*, by Carlos Saura, virtually swept the national cinematographic awards for 1990. It won Goyas for Best Film, Best Director, Best Adapted Script, Best Actor (Andrés Pajares), Best Actress (Carmen Maura), and Best Supporting Actor (Gabino Diego). In addition, Andrés Pajares won the Best Actor award at the Montreal Film Festival. Although a caption establishes the spatial and temporal location of the action as the Aragonese front in 1938, the film does not narrate fighting, but rather, the adventures of the troupe of "Carmela y Paulino, varietés a lo fino" (Carmela and Paulino's excellent variety show) who entertain the Republican soldiers. The opening sequence of the film, a panned long shot of buildings in ruins, is accompanied by the famous civil war song "Viva la quince brigada" (Long Live the Fifteenth Brigade), which has "¡Ay, Carmela!" as its refrain. This music, together with the pan of walls covered with graffiti (CNT, FAI) and Republican propaganda posters, immediately establishes the political point of view of the film. The degree of destruction seen in the initial images, and the sorry state of the posters--ripped, torn, and nearly falling off the wall--manifest not only the doomed condition of the Republican cause, but also serve as a foreshadowing of fate of the protagonists, Carmela (Carmen Maura) and Paulino (Andrés Pajares), and their mute companion, Gustavete (Gabino Diego). The sound of German planes "off" that interrupts their show is an image that constitutes the underlying threat that finally materializes in the climax of the film. Saura uses color symbolism similar to that in his *Prima Angélica* when he shoots the fog through which the troupe travels toward Valencia with a blue filter: when we hear men singing in the distance, we know that they must be Nationalist troops. The low-angle shot of the Nationalist officers both on horseback and as they drag Gustavete to the truck establishes the physical domination of Nationalists over these representatives of the Republic. Paulino mistakenly--or ingenuously--greets the officers with a Republican salute: left hand raised with a clenched fist, and the words, "Salud camarada. Trabajador del teatro en turno y homenaje al glorioso ejército republicano" (Hail, comrade. A theater worker on duty and in homage to the glorious Republican Army). The officer hits Paulino's hand with his pistol, and retorts, "¿No sabéis saludar como buenos españoles?" (Don't you know how to greet us like good Spaniards?) underscores the dichotomy between "good" and "bad" Spaniards based merely on political considerations. Paulino's immediate switch--the raised right hand in a fascist salute, with the words, "Arriba España" (Up with Spain) is essentially a visual gag, and exemplifies the humorous vein that runs throughout the film. Paulino's ingenuousness continues when they are sent to a school used as a prison, and he tries to allay the fears of a woman political prisoner saying, "Los que somos inocentes, no tenemos nada que temer" (We who are innocent have nothing to fear). When fascist soldiers enter the room and choose men that they will take out, Paulino's ingenuousness turns to mere callousness when he exclaims, "No pasa nada" (Nothing is going to happen). Carmela, on the other hand, intuits their fate: "Que los van a matar, Paulino" (They are going to kill them, Paulino). The high angle shot of the firing squad belies the Lieutenant's earlier comment, "En la zona franquista, se hace justicia" (In the zone controlled by Franco, justice is done).

When interrogated about the presence of a Republican flag in their truck, Carmela invents an answer that allows them to escape the fate of the assassinated Republicans: she exposes her left breast so that the Italian Lieutenant would think that their flag number in the show that they performed for the Republicans was "una cosa de cachondeo" (a joke). Lieutenant Ripamonte, the Italian artistic director for the fascist troops, coerces the actors into performing for the Nationalist soldiers. However, Carmela's criticism of the fascists and her adherence to her ideals contrasts with Paulino's capitulation. Even while in the Republican camp, Paulino's billingsgate during their meager supper-- "Me cago en la puta guerra de la madre que la parió" (This fucking war)--indicates a certain egotism based on his displeasure at the hardships that the war has personally caused him. His use of the possessive pronoun in statements to the Nationalist officers--"No salimos de la España nacional, ésta ya es nuestra casa" (We're not leaving Nationalist Spain, this is already our home), and that it would be an honor to perform for "vuestros, bueno, nuestros soldados" (your, well, our soldiers)--connotes a willingness to collaborate with the Nationalists in order to save his own skin. He also repeats on more than one occasion the motto of the Italian fascist: "Creer, obedecer, y combatir" (Believe, obey, and fight). However, his cynicism toward both sides of the conflict appears in a statement that he makes when he memorizes the verses that Lieutenant Ripamonte has given him for the performance before the fascist troops: when he reads of the "glorioso alzamiento que ha devuelto a España el orgullo de su destino imperial" (the glorious uprising that returned the pride of its imperial destiny to Spain), he comments, "Anda, que también estos . . ." (Boy, these guys also . . .). On the other hand, Carmela's Republicanism and criticism of fascism builds in a slow crescendo throughout the film. She befriends Polish members of the International Brigades who are imprisoned in the schoolhouse, and protests against the flag number (a routine that ridicules the Republican flag and cause) that Lieutenant Ripamonte has included in their program. The fascist theatrical director plans to dedicate the number to the Polish prisoners, since they are barbarians from the north, without culture or spirituality. To Carmela, the number is not only "una marranada y una ordinariez" (a vile deed and a piece of vulgarity), but to perform it the night before sending them to the firing squad is a "putada" (dirty trick). As Carmela becomes more upset while putting on her makeup (the camera functions as the mirror), Paulino's cynicism again surfaces: "No te pongas así; son cosas de la guerra" (Don't get like that; that's the way war is). On stage, the point of view shot through the hole in the curtain that shows the Polish prisoners in the balcony of the theater elicits the same dichotomy between the entertainers: although Carmela protests and refuses to do the flag number, Paulino retorts, "Nosotros somos artistas y hacemos lo que nos mandan" (We are artists and we do what they tell us to do), and reminds her of the fate of the other prisoners. Nevertheless, Carmela's defiance grows throughout the performance, as she refers to the lack of freedom of the prisoners of war, makes fun of the Nationalist audience with so many medals and so many commanders, and dedicates her song and dance number to the Polish soldiers in the balcony. The close-up of the two entertainers backstage just before Carmela is about to perform "Suspiros de España" underscores the dichotomy between the two, and is a visual symbol of Carmela's displeasure with the whole performance and of the turmoil that is about to engulf the leading lady: while Paulino, in the background is in focus, Carmela in the foreground, is out of focus.

The flag number contrasts with the finale of their original show for the Republican troops. In that performance, the Republican flag was a backdrop to the three of them: Paulino dressed as a Republican soldier, Carmela represented justice, and Gustavete was the lion, representing Spanish parliament and democracy. In the parody written by the fascist theatrical director, Paulino represents a gay physician, Carmela, who represents the Republic, wears the flag as a tunic and acts as a sick patient; Gustavete, dressed in a fur cap and red shirt with

A fascist satire of the Republic: Saura's ¡Ay, Carmela!, with Andrés Pajares, Carmen Maura, and Gabino Diego. Courtesy Iberoamericana Films.

a hammer and sickle drawn on the chest, represents Carmela's (the Republic's) husband, the Soviet Union. The mere sight of the Republican flag elicits outrage on the part of the fascist audience, as they shout "whore," "disgusting," and "get out." The flickering, strobe-like light of the projector as well as the distortion of the image of the entertainers in the close up shots of them creates an atmosphere that Antonio Castro relates to expressionism ("¡Ay, Carmela!" 29) and serves to underscore the growing tension in the scene and foreshadows the final eruption between Republicans and fascists in the theater. The rapid rhythm of the end of this sequence is derived from the montage of shots showing parallel actions in the three locations within the theater: on stage, in the fascist audience, and among the Polish prisoners of war in the balcony. Shouting in all three locales creates a cacophony and disorder.

This sequence manifests numerous parallelisms in the narrative structure of the film: both the performance for the Republicans and the performance for the Nationalists contain songs and dances--"Caminito de Jerez," "Suspiros de España" (Little Road to Jerez, Sighs of Spain)--as well as poems--Antonio Machado's "A Líster" (To [General] Lister) and Federico de Urrutia's "En el cerro de los Angeles" (On the

hill of Los Angeles). In the tumultuous finale, Carmela bares her
breast a second time, an indication that for her the performance truly
is "una cosa de cachondeo" (a joke), and therefore, constitutes one of
her insults to the fascists. And Paulino's farts that entertained the
Republican troops are transformed into a protest against the
Nationalists, as the low angle shot that shows him facing his rear end
toward the camera is a point of view shot of the Nationalist soldiers.
Carmela further insults the Nationalists--"Cabrones" (Bastards)--and
she sings from "La quince brigada," "Acabar con el fascismo, Ay,
Carmela, Ay, Carmela" (End with fascism, Ay, Carmela, Ay,
Carmela), a song that is in counterpoint to the Nationalist soldiers'
rendition of the fascist hymn, "Cara al sol" (Facing the Sun). The
climax of the scene occurs when a Nationalist soldier takes out a pistol,
shouts, "Cierra la boca" (Shut up), and shoots Carmela in the forehead.
The slow motion fall of the dead actress provides a dramatic contrast
with the rapid rhythm of the montage sequence. The cut to a long shot
pan of the countryside and cemetery where Paulino and Gustavete place
flowers and a marker[15] on her grave, and the final long shot
accompanied by the music of "La quince brigada" parallels the opening
of the film and thus constitutes a framing of the narrative.

The humor in the film creates a certain ambiguity of tone, since it
contrasts with the dramatic events of the prisoners of war, firing
squads, and murder of Carmela. There are times in the middle of the
film in which the pace seems to slow and some of the jokes fall flat
(especially during the dressing room scene). However, much of the
humor has political undertones, as in the transformation of the above-
mentioned scatological element. Lieutenant Ripamonte voices approval
when Paulino recites Antonio Machado's "El crimen fue en Granada"
(The Crime Was in Granada), a poem in memorial to the assassination
of Federico García Lorca, and the resulting irony constitutes the first
in a series of satiric barbs against the Italian fascists. When Lieutenant
Ripamonte gives the actors "freedom" in exchange for the promise that
their hands are free of blood (and for their collaboration in the
entertainment of the Nationalist troops), Gustavete, who communicates
by writing on a slate board, writes "Viva Mulosini." The visual gag

---

[15]Gustavete supposedly lost his voice due to a traumatic war experience, and the
shock of Carmela's murder has caused him to recover it; he places his chalk board as a
marker on her grave.

A tragicomic tone: Saura's ¡Ay, Carmela!, with Gabino Diego and Andrés Pajares. Courtesy Iberoamericana Films.

of the misspelling is accentuated since Gustavete always hyphenates words on his small slate, and the division "Mulo-sini" emphasizes the play on words (*mulo* means mule). A humorous, satirical effect is inherent in the repetition of the "i" when Paulino and Carmela mention their honor to perform for a son of Italy, the cradle of art that also gave us "'Miguel Angel, Dante, Petrarca, Puccini, Rossini, Boccherini, Mussolini.' 'Que sí, mi Teniente'" (Why of course, Lieutenant). The incongruence of Mussolini's inclusion in this list of artists represents further satire of the fascist leader. When Paulino quotes a Latin proverb, the Italian soldier who apologizes for not understanding Spanish is made to be a fool, and when high-stepping Italian troops in feathered helmets perform for the troops, General Franco exclaims to a fellow officer, "Estos no tienen arreglo" (There is no hope for these guys), to which the Spanish officer retorts, "Una banda de maricones" (A bunch of queers). Thus, the satire of the Italian soldiers even comes from their fellow fascists. The humorous tone, then, is not superficial, but complements the horror and outrage at the fascist atrocities, and contributes to make the film's garnering of both national and international awards well deserved.

Chapter 3

The Rear Guard

While the soldiers from both sides waged war from 1936 to 1939, civilians in the population centers away from the front felt the effects of the conflict. The most notable effect of the war on civilians occurred when the fighting reached near their homes. In Madrid, apart from the initial conflict at the Montaña barracks in July of 1936, fierce fighting occurred on the very edge of the city during the battle of Madrid in November of 1936, and to this day, visitors to the Parque del Oeste near the University of Madrid can see bullet holes on statues and old machine-gun nests. In addition, the Spanish civil war was the first conflict in which systematic bombing of civilian populations took place; the famous bombing of the Basque town of Guernica on April 26, 1937 by German Heinkels perhaps took 1,000 lives (Thomas 625). This act caused international indignation and served as an inspiration to Pablo Picasso in painting his masterpiece named after the town. Bombing of Madrid began as early as August 27, 1936. Shortages of food, the need to evacuate portions of the civilian population, and even psychological effects of the war on the civilian population are also themes that recur in films dealing with the rear guard.[16]   There is a wide variety of films within this category: García Serrano's *Los ojos perdidos* (The Lost Eyes, 1966), Lazaga's *El otro árbol de Guernica* (Guernica's Other Tree, 1969), Giménez Rico's *Retrato de familia* (Family Portrait, 1975), Camino's *Las largas vacaciones del '36* (The Long Vacation of '36, 1976), Velasco's *Uno de un millón de muertos* (One of a Million Dead, 1976), Rodríguez's *Gusanos de seda* (Silk Worms, 1976), Martín's *Tengamos la guerra en paz* (Let's Make War Peacefully, 1976), Betriu's *La Plaza del Diamante* (Diamond Square, 1982) and *Réquiem por un campesino español* (Requiem for a Spanish

---

[16]For a study of life in the rear guard for citizens in Nationalist territory, see Rafael Abella, La vida cotidiana durante la Guerra Civil: La España nacional.

Peasant, 1985), Chávarri's *Las bicicletas son para el verano* (Bicycles Are for Summer, 1984), and Benito Rabal's *El hermano bastardo de Dios* (God's Bastard Brother, 1986).

Rafael García Serrano is the author of the novel *La fiel infantería* (Loyal Infantry), which was adapted to the screen by Pedro Lazaga in 1959, and he both wrote and directed the 1966 film, *Los ojos perdidos* (Lost Eyes). The hero of this film is a second lieutenant, Luis Valle. The main stylistic element of the narrative is the flashback: at the beginning of the film, a soldier gives Margarita Sanz a letter that contains Luis's insignia, a metonymical device to symbolize Luis's death. The chronology of the rest of the film is straightforward, narrating the brief hours that Luis and Margarita have after they meet and fall in love in San Sebastián before the lieutenant has to report to the front. García Serrano underscores the theme of religion in the film from the moment the protagonist appears on screen. In his first scene, Luis enters a church to pray for courage, for his comrades, for chastity, less of a desire to drink, a just victory and peace for all--an almost incredible wish-list, even for the Nationalist hero that the director wishes to portray. His prayer, intercut with views of the crucifix in church, manifests a combination of religion and the theme of reconciliation between the two sides as he prays "por todos los milicianos en la guerra bajo cualquier bandera y a los de las Brigadas Internacionales. Esos tipos también son tus hijos y mis hermanos" (for all the soldiers in the war under any flag and for the International Brigades. Those guys are also your sons and my brothers). Nevertheless, these "conciliatory" words seem to mask a condescending tone, especially toward the International Brigades ("esos tipos") which is a common element in many films by pro-nationalist directors. The heroic aspect of the protagonist is echoed in his statement to Margarita: "Yo lucho para que todo lo que suceda mañana sea más bello de lo que sucede hoy" (I fight so that everything that happens tomorrow will be more beautiful than what is happening today). The religion theme later reappears in the comment, "Tú ya sabes que los muertos en campaña van derechos al cielo" (You already must know that those who die during the campaign go right to heaven), a comment which underscores the crusade ideal of the Nationalist side. A more important attempt in the dialogue to put forth the theme of reconciliation between the two sides of the fratricidal conflict occurs in Luis's words in the barbershop: "Mi padre está tan a gusto en el otro lado como yo en éste. Y con la misma lealtad. El cree que estoy equivocado; creo que el equivocado es él. Esto se llama guerra civil" (My father is as happy on the other side as I am on this one. And with the same loyalty. He thinks that I'm wrong, and I think that he is. This is what they call a civil war). This speech represents the theme of *cainismo* in an almost literal sense--the division and fighting within the family, but here with a sense of respect for each other.

All of the action of the film takes place in San Sebastián; repeated long shots of the city and the beach give the film a "touristy" look at times. The film also includes icons of Nationalist leaders--there is a clearly displayed photograph of the young General Franco in a bar, and one of José Antonio in a jewelry store. We only see the war through documentary "No-Do" footage when Luis and Margarita go to the movies. Otherwise, the director seems to take a two-fold approach to the fighting itself. On the one hand, there is an attempt at humor, with references to it as "un jaleo" (an uproar) and "las cataratas del Niágara" (Niagara falls) or the joke in the dialogue that accompanies the shot through the window of a convoy of trucks carrying soldiers to the front: "'Van al fregado.' '¿Tú crees?' 'A menos que se trate de una excursión de fin de semana'" ("They're going to where the action is." "Do you think so?" "Unless it might be a weekend excursion"). On the other hand, the fighting is portrayed as so horrendous that the civilian population cannot comprehend it. When the Nationalist soldier Pablo gives a short story that he has written to a newspaper man, the latter complains that it is a cruel story, and that "la guerra que pinta es feroz" (the war that you portray is ferocious). Nevertheless, the war is never seen, as the film limits its portrayal of a day in the life of the rear guard. Although the title and the opening scene in which Margarita receives the announcement of the death of the soldier portend the theme of the loss, García Serrano does not delve into its consequences, as we see in films such as *La Plaza del Diamante*.

In 1969, Pedro Lazaga filmed *El otro árbol de Guernica* (Guernica's Other Tree), with a script written by Pedro Masó and Florentino Soria based on a novel of the same name by Luis de Castresana. It is a movie which deals with the problem of child refugees from the Basque country. During the credits, Lazaga includes documentary footage of war scenes, the only real bellicose action of the entire film. The narration centers on two young children, Santi and Begoña Celaya Fernández, whose parents decide to send them to

Belgium from their native Bilbao for safety's sake. The recurring motif that the war will end soon appears on more than one occasion in this film; first, during the emotional departure of the children from their parents, and at a point in the narration one year later when the children receive a letter from their parents in Spain. Sound effects of sirens and bombs "off" sometimes accompany the voice-over of the mother reading the letters, belying the hopes of the civilians.

As in other films, children here perform the function of the ingenue who asks the difficult question of the adults, "¿Por qué hacen los hombres la guerra?" (Why do men wage war?). The occasion here is a beach scene after a boat delivers the children to Belgium, and one of them discovers a helmet from World War I in the sand. Santi poses the question to Don Segundo, the man who is escorting the children to their temporary new homes. His response, "Las guerras vienen muchas veces sin saber por qué" (Wars often come without knowing why), glosses over the reason for the conflict and constitutes an overly-facile answer. Although one could justify it in the context of the narrative--young children cannot indeed always understand the complexities of the adult world--it seems to follow a pattern whereby certain Nationalist directors such as Lazaga dismiss the reasons for the war. As we shall examine in Chapter 9, some documentary films, both by Nationalist directors such as Mariano Azores (*Morir en Madrid* [To Die in Madrid]) as well as those on the other side, such as Diego de Santillán (*¿Por qué perdimos la guerra?* [Why Did We Lose the War?]) do examine the pre-war period in great detail, but generally with a lack of objectivity.

The majority of the narrative deals with the children's relationship with their new environment. Although Begoña is content with her new family, Santi has difficulty accepting the kindness and hospitality of his hosts, the Defout family. When they give him a new bicycle and sign the card from "mamá" and "papá," Santi's negative outburst and crossing out those words of kindness causes an equally immature reaction in Madame Defout, and the young Spaniard must move to a boarding school. His life there also has its trials and tribulations, mainly due to the fact that Santi has confrontations with school personnel, Belgians that are portrayed with almost xenophobic zeal. When a small Spanish boy named Eusebio suffers from enuresis because of his psychological suffering, Madame Jacob calls him a "cochino español" (Spanish pig) to which Santi retorts, "Usted es una

cochina belga" (You are a Belgian pig) in his defense. Madame
Jacob's mean character surfaces again when Montse, Santi's little
Catalan friend, has an altercation with a Belgian girl over a sweater.
When Madame Jacob unjustly takes the sweater from Montse, Santi
seeks refuge and solidarity with the other Spanish children under the
giant tree in the school courtyard which reminds them of the famous
tree of their homeland that provides the title of the movie.[17] Santi then
leads a successful protest to regain the sweater and their rights. Even
the Belgian children do not escape the xenophobic view of the director.
The only one that is accepted by Santi and the other Spanish children
is André, who, in order to gain the full confidence of the group, must
become "Hispanified" through the name change of Andrés. The worst
confrontation between Belgians and Spaniards, however, occurs in
Santi's history class when the Belgian professor lectures about how
Spaniards killed Indians in the new world and makes the condescending
remarks, "los españoles han sido, son y serán salvajes" (Spaniards have
been, are, and will be savages) and "¿qué esperas de un pueblo cuya
fiesta nacional son los toros?" (What do you expect from a country
whose national pastime is bullfighting?).   Although Santi has an
immediate reaction--calling the professor a liar and a coward--he later
decides to escape the boarding school, not without leaving the
proclamation "Viva España" written on the blackboard.   This
provides the opportunity for some brief "touristy" shots of Brussels,
but luck would have it that the very next morning, Santi sees that the
headlines of the newspaper *Le matin* proclaim the end of the war in
Spain. At this juncture, Lazaga includes the only other documentary
footage in the film, that of Nationalist troops triumphantly marching
into Madrid. The children return by boat to Spain, and the last scene
contains a long shot of the port of Bilbao and the children sing in their
joyous return to their homeland. No mention is made, of course, of
the difficult times that lay ahead for these children of Basque and
Catalan Republicans, and an epigraph that dedicates the film to all
Spaniards attempts to strike a conciliatory note. Although director
Lazaga has stated that it was a love movie, not a war movie (Castro
243), Gubern points out the Nationalistic bias of the film, as it equates
"Spanish" with Francoism and makes the countries that gave asylum to

---

[17]The tree is a symbol of Basque nationalism, since Spanish kings had to travel to
Guernica in order to swear that they would uphold the traditional Basque rights (fueros).

Republican children seem like places of sequestration (*1936* 150). *El otro árbol de Guernica* has problems with the script, but director Lazaga was able to obtain solid performances from the child actors which help bolster the quality of the film.

   Retrato de familia (Family Portrait), a film from 1975 directed by Antonio Giménez Rico and starring Antonio Ferrandis, Amparo Soler Leal, Mónica Randall, and Miguel Bosé, is an adaptation of Delibes's 1953 novel entitled, *Mi idolatrado hijo Sisí* (My Idolized Son Sisí). The change in title is a significant indication of the director's intention to portray a bourgeois family which is caught up in turbulent events in Spain in the 1930's.   This family consists of Cecilio Rubes, a prosperous merchant of bathroom fixtures, his wife Adela, and one son, named Ceci after the father.   The opening shot of a newspaper with headlines about the elections of February, 1936, and the following sequence of political speeches and gangs of right-wing thugs who break up meetings, place immediate emphasis on the political element. Cecilio is an egotistical and vacuous character whose sole   motivation is that of self-interest, and in this context, he chooses to not become involved.   He praises neutrality, and tells Adela, "La política no es todo en esta vida; donde hay una buena copa . . ." (Politics isn't everything in this life; as long as you can have a good drink . . .), and he later exclaims, "Lo mejor es no comprometerse con nada ni con nadie" (The best thing to do is not get involved with anything or anybody). The inexorable march of events begins to engulf Rubes, however, and Martin-Márquez notes that a shot in which Rubes sits on the right hand side of the frame and a newspaper occupies the left-hand portion of the frame "is a traditional two-shot, containing the two principal characters of the film: Rubes and politics" (116). However, Rubes's egotism persists, and even when events begin to strike close to home and his store windows are broken, he only views the event in terms of his own benefit: he tells his assistant to augment the damage report, since everything is completely insured. His wife, in contrast, attempts to become involved in political events, and wishes that her son Ceci would follow suit.   She works for the CEDA (Confederación Española de Derechas Autónomas [Spanish Confederation of Rightist Autonomous Parties]), giving speeches to women in which she praises the values of the right: "Dios, patria, familia, orden y trabajo" (God, fatherland, family, order, and work). Although she is worried about the Falangist activities of her son, she tells her husband, "Por lo menos

War envelopes a bourgeois family: Giménez Rico's <u>Retrato de familia</u>, starring Antonio Ferrandis and Amparo Soler Leal.   Courtesy Filmoteca Nacional.

tiene ideales, cree en algo" (At least he has ideals, he believes in something).   After the war breaks out, she tells Cecilio that her son will have to enlist.   When he finally does so, she tells Ceci, "Cumple con tu deber" (Fulfill your obligation).   Cecilio, however, is against his son's involvement, out of fear for his safety.   The father unsuccessfully speaks with General López, who is a friend, in an attempt to obtain a safe, rear-guard post for his son.   In a burst of emotions which both manifests his fears and foreshadows the tragic events to come, he exclaims to Adela, "Esta guerra, esta guerra, esta guerra--me cago yo en la guerra.   Cualquier día se nos agarran al chico y lo llevan a morir como un perro" (This war, this war, this war--war sucks.   One of these days, they're going to grab our boy and take him away to die like a dog).   The emphasis on the historical period from 1936 to 1938 is evident in the chronology of the narrative, as Giménez Rico radically departs from the mainly linear depiction of events that Delibes utilizes in the novel, whose opening line places the action in 1917.   Since the film narrative begins in 1936, all prior events are subordinated to that historical present through the use of the flashback technique.   Indeed, the film makes use of seven major flashbacks, going back to the moment of Ceci's conception, and including the boy's rebellious youth, signs of social unrest, and Ceci's death in the war.

The first flashback occurs when Ceci first appears on screen, coming from his falangist activities. He looks at his father, and after a closeup of Cecilio's face, we are taken back to the moment of Ceci's birth, with Adela's screams and entreaties to her husband, "Júrame que no tendremos más hijos" (Swear to me that we won't have any more children). The second flashback is signalled by a zoom-in to a pearl earring warn by a woman called Lina, who is Cecilio's lover. The chronological point of the narrative is when Ceci is a baby; the father explains to Lina that he has made a promise to God that in return for curing his sick son, he shall refrain from his sexual promiscuity. The next flashback begins with a shot of a victrola, an object that symbolically represents Lina (connoting the sensuous dance of forbidden lovers). Lina feels that she deserves to be the mother of Cecilio's child, and she has a great desire to at least see the boy. This is followed by a sequence in a park in which Lina casually encounters the Rubes family, and she views the baby in a carriage. The fourth flashback occurs when Ceci, who as a young man of twenty has met Lina and has taken her on as a lover; we jump from a shot of Ceci in bed with Lina to the time when Ceci was thirteen and, rebelling against his mother ("Vete a la mierda, idiota" [Fuck off, idiot]) leaves the house to go on his first adventure with girls. During a ride in his car at night, Cecilio witnesses several signs of civil unrest--a bonfire, gunshots, a graffito "Death to . . .". The latter triggers a jump to a scene which shows the death of Cecilio's mother, another moment of rebellion for the thirteen year old Ceci: when his distraught father slaps him, the boy retorts, "No te acerques, idiota. Y no se te ocurra volver a tocarme" (Don't you come close to me, idiot. And don't ever try to touch me again). As a twenty-year old, Ceci seems to have a real romantic interest in Elisita, a neighbor girl. As she plays the piano for him, the camera zooms in to a close-up of Ceci, and the piano is now that of a prostitute in a brothel as the thirteen-year old Ceci looks on and accepts a cigarette from a friend. This sequence, with a prostitute who leads the young boy to her room and initiates him to sex, placing his hands on her bare breasts, created a scandal in Spain and was the object of most of the negative criticism about the film. The final flashback occurs after the death of Ceci, whose truck was bombed by an enemy plane. Martin-Márquez comments that Giménez Rico deliberately uses the setting of a party at their neighbors' home to disclose of Ceci's death: Cecilio and Adela sing the Nationalist hymn with great emotion and Rubes embraces war-veteran Luis, "nuestro héroe" (our hero); "by embracing Luis, the representative of fascism, Cecilio embraces fascism" and the juxtaposition of the party scene with the scene of Cecil's truck exploding implies an ironic punishment of Rubes for having chosen Nationalism (122). Rubes goes to the front to collect the remains, and during the return trip by car, his mind (manifested in his voice "off") wanders back to the earliest point of the film story, the moment of his son's conception. The memory of the words, "¿Sabes lo que he pensado esta tarde? Que quiero tener un hijo" (You know what I thought about this afternoon? That I want to have a son), precedes his pulling back a curtain and the shot of a naked Adela, twenty years ago.

The death of his son has a profound effect on the bourgeois merchant. He becomes a recluse, and later irrationally demands that Adela give him another child. Time and again, we observe that he cannot comprehend his tragedy: when he collects his son's remains, he asks the general amid tears, "¿Por qué me has engañado?" (Why have you deceived me?) and "¿Qué has hecho de mi hijo?" (What have you done with my son?). At home, he comments to Adela about the war, "Vosotros armáis la guerra para que paguemos los que no tenemos nada que ver con ella" (You start up a war just so we who don't have anything to do with it end up paying). Finally, when he goes to see Lina, his lover, who seeks consolation over Ceci's death in drink, we see his strongest statement set against a background of sirens, bombs, and blinking lights, elements that in an even stronger sense than as Miriam Rice (18) has pointed out regarding the original narrative, bring the odious war right into Rubes's bedroom: "Cabrones, hijos de puta. ¿Qué habéis hecho de él? Tú, ella, ella entre todos lo habéis matado" (Bastards, sons of bitches. What have you done with him? You, her, above all her, you have killed him). His combination of rage, depression, and lack of understanding lead to his final act: suicide, throwing himself from the window of Lina's apartment. Ironically, Cecilio and Ceci live on in Lina, who announces to the father in his final visit that she is pregnant by his son. Giménez Rico artfully captures this last tragic moment with a frozen shot of the drunken Lina as the final shot of the film.

Fernando Méndez-Leite observes that *Retrato de familia* is the "first film of the post-Franco era that directly deals with the theme of the Spanish civil war" (16), and Gubern comments that the film demythifies the so-called "crusade" of the victorious side (*1936* 168-

69). *Retrato de familia* is an excellent depiction of the war's effect on one segment of the rear guard, and portrait of an egotist whose destruction brings to mind Trotsky's maxim that "You may not be interested in war, but war is interested in you."

A film from 1976 which had considerable critical and commercial success is Jaime Camino's *Las largas vacaciones del '36* (The Long Vacation of '36), which featured an all-star cast including Conchita Velasco, José Sacristán, Francisco Rabal, Angela Molina, Amalia Gade, Ismael Merlo, Vicente Parra, Charo Soriano, and José Vivó. This film is of capital importance in the development of the Spanish cinematographic treatment of the civil war; as Caparrós Lera comments, the novelty here consists of the fact that "those who have always been the 'bad guys' are now the 'good guys,' or vice versa" (*El cine político* 71-2).[18]

The action is set in Camino's native Catalonia, near Barcelona. Catalan music--the melody to "La princesa está maleva" (The Princess Is Ill)--accompanies the opening shots, and there is an announcement for a *sardana* concert on July 19, 1936. The temporal setting thus begins with the outbreak of the Nationalist rebellion, and temporal progression is marked throughout the movie by captions ("Spring, 1938," etc.). The title of the film is most appropriate, for as author Carlos Barral points out, "for almost all of the boys my age, the war had been a long and strange vacation" (13). The narrative centers on a middle-class Catalan family that was on vacation when the war broke out, and indeed, at first they treat the disruption in their lives as if it were an extended vacation, with outdoor gatherings and cookouts during which they manifest a cavalier attitude toward the war: "Mientras podamos hacer paellas como ésta. . ." (As long as we can make paellas like this one . . .). The common motif that the war will end very soon appears in their conversations. Although some talk with indifference toward the conflict, and are only concerned about their own personal welfare ("¿Qué pitos toco yo en esta guerra, eh?" [What the hell do I have to do with this war?]), others speak of going to the

---

[18]José Enrique Monterde comments that with this film, producer José Frade makes a decisive step in the recuperation of Spanish history and popular memory (11). Other Spanish critics (those of the "Equipo 'Cartelera Turia'") note that Las largas vacaciones del 36 points the way to a new chronicle of the civil war on the post-Franco Spanish screen (Torres: Cine 237).

front to fulfill their duty. Although the family supports the Republican side, as did the family of Jaime Camino, we see the political division within the family in the characters of Uncle Alberto and his wife who hide their automobile in the family garage and praise "el glorioso levantamiento" (the glorious uprising). They say that the Spain of the Cid and Pelayo has said "enough" to communists and socialists, and augur that the army will drive the "masons" into the sea. This friction within the family manifests itself primarily in verbal confrontations between Alberto and young Quique. When the former calls the boy a "rojillo" (little red) the lad threatens to denounce him to the authorities. Later, Quique surprises Alberto and says "Manos arriba, fascista" (Hands up, fascist) with a pistol in his hand, to which his uncle replies, "Republicano de mierda" (Fucking Republican).

Indeed, the children in the film seem affected by the war as much if not more than the adults. Although at first their activities are those of any normal vacation--riding bicycles, skipping rope--the violence that surrounds them intrudes into their world when they discover a man with a bullet hole in his head in a cemetery. The children begin to play at being soldiers (even at being firing squads!) and Mercedes comments, "No hay forma de que los niños acaben con esos juegos" (There is no way to get the children to stop playing those games). Of course, their schooling is also affected by the war, and the parents hire a teacher to set up a classroom. Here, the question of "good guys" and "bad guys" explicitly arises for the edification of both the young students and the audience: when a boy asks Mr. Rivas, the teacher, if he is a red, he answers affirmatively. The student then responds that according to his father, "reds" are bad; the teacher calmly replies, "Ni robo, ni asesino; sólo enseño" (I don't rob or kill, I only teach). To further prove the point, Mr. Rivas incorporates as part of his lesson the poem "Recuerdo infantil" by Antonio Machado, another "red":

> Es la clase. En un cartel
> se representa a Caín
> fugitivo, y muerto Abel
> junto a una mancha carmín.

(It's class. A poster shows fugitive Cain, and dead Abel next to a carmine stain.) A shot of the map of Spain on the wall which divides the country into Republican and Nationalist-held territories further underscores the theme of *cainismo* that appears in the poem.

As the war progresses, and the Republican army becomes more

Mimicking adults: Camino's <u>Las largas vacaciones del '36</u>.   Courtesy Filmoteca Nacional.

desperate, young Quique receives conscription papers and must serve in what is facetiously called "The Pacifier Brigade." The boy's love letters to Alicia augur an unhappy ending ("Puede ser la última carta" [This could be my last letter]) while showing great courage ("Yo no tengo miedo" [I'm not afraid]). The latter sentence is heard in a voice-over after a soldier visits his house and says that he was a friend of Quique. A close-up of the boy's watch metonymically conveys the news of his death. The war, then, never appears on screen, but is always a menacing specter. The only actual shooting occurs at the very beginning (July 19, 1936) when Republican militia capture some rebels in a church. Otherwise, the occasional airplane overhead, cannon fire heard "off," and comments of people coming from Barcelona ("Ha sido una carnicería" [It was a slaughter]) keep the war just below the surface.

Camino provides a crescendo for the hunger theme throughout the film. The middle class families begin with marvelous *paellas*, and the receipt of a package which contains truffles and Bordeaux wine maintains a sense of well-being. The latter scene, however, is juxtaposed with another meal in which there are only two loaves of bread; Quique wants to exchange a tomato and a potato for a sardine, and they talk of killing horses. By the winter of 1938, hunger really begins to set in, and Mr. Rivas, the teacher, has to admit to his pupils, "No me da vergüenza preguntaros si tenéis algo que comer" (I'm not ashamed to ask you if you have something to eat). Finally, Jorge finds a solution to the family's needs, but they must use Alberto's hidden car to go to a farmer who sells black market food in exchange for gold, a sequence which ends with the men fighting among themselves over the food.

As the end draws near and Republican troops in retreat pass through the streets, there is at once a feeling of despair and uncertainty. The zoom-in to closeup of the grandfather crying (filmed with beautiful chiaroscuro lighting) at news of the Republican defeat at the Ebro, together with his later remark, "¡Dios Mío! ¿Qué será de nosotros?" (My God! What will become of us?) capture the emotions of almost all of the family. There is also a sense that there will be a return to prior social mores. At the beginning of the film, some boys defend the fact that they are smoking cigarettes by saying, "Ahora sin curas, no hay pecado" (Now without any priests, there is no sin). Children playing in the cemetery proclaim that there are no longer ghosts. And the family maid--who provides Quique with his first sexual encounter--refers to herself as "Comrade Encarna" and proclaims, "No soy más una oprimida y se acabó" (I'm no longer oppressed, and that's it). At the end of the film, however, after Alicia greets a priest, we hear that "Hasta ya vuelve a haber pecado" (Even sin has already come back). Of course, Uncle Alberto and his wife are ecstatic about the turn of events, and his final comment, "Tengo ganas de poner el coche en marcha" (I feel like starting the car), indicates that their white automobile now symbolizes the victory of their side, and their future material well-being and domination. This is in contrast with the scene that precedes it in which a Republican soldier gives what he calls a gift from Negrín to the children--a Republican five-peseta coin that is now totally worthless. The final shot is a long shot of Moorish cavalry troops from Franco's army advancing toward the camera with what Jorge Abbondanza calls a "marvelous hammering force" (11). Indeed, this scene caused problems with Spanish censors, and for a time, there were two versions of the film, one with this final shot excised, and another in which it was included. In spite of its problems with Spanish censors, Román Gubern comments that *Las largas vacaciones del '36* broke many taboos in Spanish cinema's treatment of the civil war, including images of the Republican flag and of Catalan president Campanys, and that audiences often applauded after viewing the film (*1936* 173).

Tengamos la guerra en paz (Let's Make War Peacefully) is a film from 1976 directed by Eugenio Martín which takes its title by giving a comic twist to a common Spanish expression ("Tengamos la fiesta en paz" [Let's not make a fuss]). This sets the tone for the film, which is a light sex comedy set in a small town during the war. Documentary footage of the war during the credits and the famous quote by Larra, "Aquí yace media España, murió la otra media" (Half of Spain lies here, the other half died), set the stage for the action to occur during the fratricidal conflict of the 1930's. The narrative begins with two burials which show the divisions in the town: during one, relatives and friends of the deceased soldier sing the International with clenched fists raised; during the other, there is a conspicuous cross on the tomb. In the next sequence, Daniel, a Nationalist prisoner, escapes while his clothes are being washed, and enters the town naked in the dead of night. He finds an unlocked window and takes refuge, but the next morning he discovers (!) that he has slept in bed with Catalina, the beautiful daughter of Pascual, the anarchist mayor of the town. When the mayor attempts to interrogate his prisoner in order to ascertain his political leanings, Daniel responds, "Depende con quien me encuentre" (It depends on whom I'm with), an answer that shows that the film is to be devoid of any ideological content. Although Pascual considers sending Daniel before a firing squad, the women of the town defend him, since the only other "young" man left in town is fifty-five years old: "Al único joven que hay no se lo van a cargar" (They're not going to do away with the only young guy that there is). In an attempt to escape from his predicament, Daniel falls into the hands of Carmelo, the Nationalist mayor of the town and father of the beautiful Lourdes. Although Pascual's wife is certain that Daniel is a Republican in a scene in which he is unable to respond to her queries about how certain saints met their ends, Serafín, the priest, announces to him that he will serve the noble and just cause of having children. Thus, a wedding with Lourdes is planned. Daniel falls back into the hands of Pascual, however, and the wedding turns out to be with Catalina. This includes more attempts at comedy, such as the transformation from a reluctant groom to one who repeatedly leaves the wedding bed--a sequence shot with image reversals--in order to refortify himself with both water and *anís* during the prolonged sexual consummation. The arrival of Nationalist troops causes changes of the flag and of street names, and also of Daniel's fate, as he now must marry Lourdes in a church ceremony. His choice is to join a Nationalist patrol, or to accept a "Chinchón" (*anís* liqueur) at the local bar in order to accept the idea of the wedding. His answer, "Bueno, si es Chinchón seco, seco" (Okay, if it's a really dry Chinchón), is typical of the humor seen throughout the film. A subsequent encounter with a jealous Catalina causes Daniel to end up in jail, where the jailor's daughter takes off her blouse and tries to seduce him. Her statement, "Dos tetas tiran más que dos carretas" (Two tits pull more than two carts), actually sums up the film, where the *destape* of the two wives is sometimes played out to the maximum with slow pans of their naked bodies, thus pulling the weight of the film for Spanish audiences unaccustomed to seeing much flesh on screen. After what is absolutely the most contrived battle scene of all movies dealing with the Spanish Civil War, in which Nationalist and Republican soldiers enter the main square of town and kill each other off to the very last man, the town is left with Daniel to carry on the "noble cause." The final scene shows the protagonist sitting between his two conspicuously pregnant wives, who discuss who gets to have him when, as the camera cranes up for the last shot. Not even the epilogue with words by Claudio Sánchez Albornoz that call for a reconciliation of the two Spains can save this film from oblivion. Indeed, Daniel's statement to Catalina, "Es que estamos en la guerra, y tenemos que tragar con todo" (Since we're at war, we have to put up with everything), easily applies to this movie.

Another film that attempts "a recuperation of the past through a nostalgic and pro-Franco cinema" (Monterde, "Crónicas" 12) is *Uno de un millón de muertos* (One of a Million Dead), directed by Andrés Velasco, a film from 1977 that manifests a hostile view to amorality and anti-religious sentiments on the left and false religious views on the right. The crux of the narrative is a love story which is set against the turbulent actions of the war. The opening scenes depict a church in flames, and then Republican soldiers in a truck marked FAI and who sing "A las barricadas" (To the Barricades) burn a convent. Rosa, a novitiate, escapes--ironically--to a brothel, where Doña Paca, a kind-hearted madame, takes her in and protects her by telling everyone that Rosa is her niece. Some lamentable humor from the light sex-comedy genre occurs in this sequence, when one client (played by the obese

Ricardo Palacios; cf. his role as Pemán in *A la legión le gustan las mujeres*) exclaims to a prostitute that "A las mujeres hay que aprovecharlas como a los cochinos, de cabeza a rabo" (You have to take advantage of women from head to toe, just like pigs). This cheap attempt to obtain a laugh from the audience is not totally out of context with the rest of the film, however, since it must be taken in conjunction with other comments which portray the Republican troops as morally depraved. Thus, one prostitute states that they have more clients than ever because of the war, and as a group of soldiers enters the plaza singing the popular civil war song, "Si me quieres escribir" (If you want to write to me), another prostitute exclaims, "vienen como becerros" (they are coming in like heifers). Although the madame tries to protect Rosa, saying that she is her niece, an officer spies Rosa and exclaims, "No hay sobrina que valga para un héroe de la Revolución" (A hero of the Revolution should get any woman he wants). Paca intercedes, however, and Rosa leaves the brothel to board a train where she meets Angel, a Republican doctor. From the moment that he offers her his blanket so that she can keep warm, we know what the outcome of their relationship will be. A Nationalist air attack on the train leaves many dead and wounded, and provides the opportunity for the protagonists to express their sentiments against the war: Rosa exclaims, "Dios mío, qué horrible es todo esto" (My God, how horrible this all is), while Angel later states, "Maldita guerra. Esto es una carnicería absurda" (Damned war. This is an absurd slaughter) and proposes that they escape to France. Their arrival in Madrid has no justification within the narrative except to include some documentary footage that would help justify a *franquista* point of view which shows the "Puerta de Alcalá" with huge portraits of Marx and Lenin as well as a banner that proclaims, "¡Rusia! Nuestra admiración y nuestra gratitud" (Russia! Our admiration and our gratitude).

Angel and Rosa successfully cross the Pyrenees, and they live at the home of a Dr. Verdonier. At this juncture, the narrative divides between the idyllic existence that Rosa and Angel lead on the farm in France, and the certain religious phenomena in Spain. A priest preaches that the war is the "decisiva batalla por la salvación de la fe en Cristo" (the decisive battle for the salvation of faith in Christ) and with high and low angle shots showing the priest and Rosa's parents in the congregation, the priest exclaims that everyone hopes for the reconquest of justice, and peace that will come with the Nationalist

Casualties of war: Velasco's <u>Uno de un millón de muertos</u>, starring Sara Lezana and Antonio Mayans. Courtesy Filmoteca Nacional.

victory. A later radio broadcast includes such Nationalist propaganda as "El pueblo Español prefiere morir de pie que vivir de rodillas" (The Spanish people prefer to die on their feet than live on their knees). Such statements would be more likely to occur in a film from 1957 or even 1967, but seem totally out of place in this film from 1977, two years after the death of Franco.

Velasco relates the religious theme with the lovers through a cult to Rosa that has developed in her home town, since she was presumed martyred in the convent-burning episode. The narrative cuts back and forth between the growing love affair between Angel and Rosa in France, and the development of this false cult back in Spain, in which devout believers proclaim miracles before a board of priests, religious processions with the image of "Santa Rosa" parade through the streets, and the bedroom of her home has been converted into a sanctuary. Just after Rosa and Angel finally consummate their relationship, a young Republican refugee breaks their idyllic existence when he arrives at the farm in southern France and asks for food. The war has ended, and director Velasco includes more documentary footage in a very propagandistic way as he attempts to depict the generosity of the Nationalist troops as they distribute food to the citizens of Madrid. The lovers decide to return to their native Spain, but as they cross the

French border in the opposite direction of the hordes of Republican refugees, they are greeted with epithets such as "fascistas de mierda" (fucking fascists). As they cross a gully, a Republican soldier shoots and kills Angel. As the camera zooms into the horrified Rosa, her interrogative, "¿Por qué? ¿Por qué?" (Why? Why?) underscores the futility of this death, one of the million to which the title alludes.[19] Her return home causes a problematic situation, since if the townsfolk discovered that she has come back, it would destroy their faith. In addition, the fact that Rosa admits to being pregnant converts her into a "zorra" (bitch) in the eyes of her father and brothers. Her father, Leoncio, says that her place is in heaven, and the final shot, a frozen image in brown of the back of his legs as he ascends the staircase, portends Rosa's death at the hands of her own father. Although *Uno de un millón de muertos* ostensibly attacks bellicosity and hypocrisy, it is a poor quality film with serious defects, mainly in the script.

Gusanos de seda (Silk Worms) is a film from 1977 directed by Francisco Rodríguez and starring some of the luminaries of contemporary Spanish film, including Esperanza Roy, Antonio Ferrandis, Rafaela Aparicio, and Agustín González. The narrative takes place in the 1930's, just prior to and during the Civil War. These historical events of this period serve as background to a sordid tale of greed, manipulation, and exploitation in which a domineering mother (Rafaela Aparicio) marries her middle-aged, spineless son Alberto (Antonio Ferrandis) to Rosalía (Esperanza Roy), a retarded woman who is the sole heir to a sizeable fortune. Greed motivates both Alberto's mother and Rosalía's father Ernesto (Alfredo Mayo), and they both see the birth of a grandchild as a means of accomplishing their goal--in Ernesto's case, so his estate will not go to the government in taxes, and Alberto's mother makes allusions to a large amount of money that awaits her and her son if they provide the desired grandchild to their rich benefactor. Rosalía's relatives worry about her, saying that she should be in a hospital, since she cannot speak and can only walk in a very halting manner. Her physical helplessness makes her an object of exploitation on the part of her new husband and mother-in-law, and it

---

[19]The allusion to a million deaths during the Spanish civil war has become a cliché. Although it is extremely difficult to obtain precise numbers, the most current studies show this number to be considerably less than one million. See Ramón Salas Larrazábal, Pérdidas de guerra, and Los datos exactos de la Guerra Civil.

is mainly the latter who shows her disdain toward the bride. On the wedding night, the mother-in-law undresses Rosalía, calls her son, "Albertito," and then comments about the bride, "Todavía es virgen, y a su edad . . ." (She's still a virgin, at her age . . .). The use of the diminutive in her son's name on this occasion indicates how the domineering mother treats her grown son as a little boy, a tendency which grows throughout the narrative. Thus, when the mother-in-law decides to punish Rosalía by locking her up, her pusillanimous son can only respond with the incredulous question, "¿Toda la noche?" (All night long?).

Rosalía attempts to escape on two different occasions. Her first attempt, during which she is able to leave the building where their flat is located and cross the plaza, incorporates the theme of social conflict, since gunfire in the plaza causes her mother-in-law to look out the window and discover both Rosalía's flight and the body of a dead man. Earlier radio broadcasts with political news of the "Popular Front" and the "UGT" set the tone of social turmoil, and the mother warned Alberto that his marriage has placed him in another social position in which they now have a lot to lose. Her second attempt to escape is more pathetic, as she is unable to open the front door to her building and can only sit and moan. On this second occasion, it is Alberto who discovers her when he awakens from a dream sequence in which his mother cajoles him, "Ponerla encinta es la primera cosa que tienes que hacer en tu vida solito . . . solito . . ." (Getting her pregnant is the first thing that you have to do in your life all alone . . . all alone . . .). His subconscious recognizes his own incapacity and manifests it in this reference to the lack of his virility. Indeed, the film hints that Alberto never consummates his relationship with Rosalía; on their wedding night, the bedding sequence terminates with Alberto, still dressed in undershorts, embracing Rosalía in bed, and the morning after, he is not very forthcoming when his meddling mother inquires, "Bueno, ¿qué? ¿No me vas a contar nada?" (Well how did it go? Aren't you going to tell me anything?), responding only, "Pues bien, todo bien" (Fine, everything went fine). Her suspicions mount, and when Rosalía does not become pregnant, she cajoles Alberto, "Espabílate" (Get with it).

When the social conflict begins to heat up, the family must abandon Madrid, and they go to live in Don Ernesto's country home. There, Rosalía attempts to escape again, this time through suicide, as she throws herself into the swimming pool. Her rescue and later treatment by Dr. Lemos includes a somewhat enigmatic comment regarding her past: "¿Pero qué es lo que estabas haciendo en la piscina, eh? Como cuando eras pequeña, ¿verdad? Pero eso no puede volver, hija, ni siquiera para ti" (What were you doing in the swimming pool? Just like when you were little, right? But that cannot return, child, not even for you). [20] The other character that knows Rosalía from her past is the mayor of the country town (played by Agustín González), who is surprised to learn that she has married. When they have no more food and Alberto desperately seeks employment from him, he suggests that Alberto go to the front line. The domineering mother again intervenes, retorting that the mayor should go himself, whereupon the mayor threatens to lock her up until she rots, since he says that "Yo tengo aquí mi propia guerra" (I've got my own war right here).

The mother's desperation drives her to even greater depths of moral depravity, and she blackmails her maid's husband into sleeping with Rosalía in attempt to finally impregnate her. Her son's response-- bowing his head in shame--as well as the shouts and crying of Rosalía during the comparatively long love-making scene (with a close-up of Rosalía crying, and shifts in camera position and angles) indicates that this is a scene of both physical and psychological defloration of Rosalía. There is a crescendo in Rosalía's physical suffering as her mother-in-law even denies her food, hoping that she will die now that word has come that Don Ernesto has been taken prisoner and lost everything. The moral depravity reaches its nadir, however, when the mayor, who has amorous intentions toward Rosalía, rescues her from her captors, sends Alberto to jail, and maintains his mother as a sort of "madame" who arranges Rosalía's dress, paints her lips, and advises her to "make him happy" in preparation for the visits of the new lover.

The silk moths that give the film its title appear on three different occasions during the narrative. First, during a visit of Don Ernesto to his daughter's new home, he receives the news that "Rosalía está estupendamente" (Rosalía is doing great). Following a close-up of a box with silkworms on some leaves, there is a loud noise "off" of things falling down. Alberto opens the bedroom door as his mother exclaims, "¿Pero qué hace esta loca?" (What is this crazy woman doing?), to see Rosalía's bed stained with urine. The sound effect and

---

[20]The inability to recapture the past (even for the child-like Rosalía) is a major theme of films that deal with cainismo; see Chapter 7, "Returning to the Past."

visual image contradict the earlier statement about Rosalía's condition, and place the image of the silk worms in a negative context. On the second occasion, the close-up of the box containing the silkworms occurs after the mayor of the country town where they have taken refuge exclaims his surprise at Rosalía's marriage. The silkworms apparently did not survive the trip to the country, and Alberto cries out, "Mis gusanos. Los han matado" (My silkworms. They've killed them), a statement which continues their negative imagery. On the third occasion near the end of the film Alberto examines them with his magnifying glass to discover that all that remains are mere shells. The metaphor here is based on the concept of exploitation. Just as Alberto would exploit his silkworms but is unsuccessful in doing so, his attempt to exploit Rosalía is also in vain. Hernández Les states that this film represents "a reflection on the exploitation of human beings" ("*Gusanos*" 17). Although superficially it is a film that focuses more on the individual than the socio-historical, the characters can be seen allegorically, as Francisco Rodríguez paints a very negative, black portrait of the Spanish bourgeois who exploit a defenseless cripple.

La Plaza del Diamante (Diamond Square), a 1982 film directed by Francesc Betriu, is the first movie in the history of Spanish cinema made with an express agreement between a film-maker and Spanish Television. The film, based on the novel of the same name written by Mercé Rodoreda, was released in both Catalan (*La Plaça del Diamant*) and Castilian, and had both a standard film version of one hour fifty-five minutes, as well as a television version with four one-hour episodes. The debut of the film was seen as an important manifestation of Catalan culture, and 500,000 people crowded the streets of Barcelona in celebration of the event.   Perhaps the most important stylistic technique of the film is the constant voice-over of the female protagonist, nicknamed Colometa.   Betriu chose this technique to correspond to the use of interior monologue by the protagonist in the novel, and it allows us to achieve a more profound glimpse into the character of this resilient woman. Silvia Munt's poignant portrayal of Colometa is certainly one of the strongest points of the film, and it launched the young Catalan actress into stardom.

Colometa meets her future husband, Quimet (Lluís Homar) at a dance at the Barcelona locale of the title, but their blissful relationship is marred when she later pursues their young son Toni under a bed, only to discover a package which contains a blue shirt, symbol of

A happy marriage destroyed by war . . .

Quimet's involvement in the Republican militia. Although her husband tries to assuage her fears, her voice-over declares, "Lo que debía ser muy corto se alargaba" (What should have been brief kept getting longer). This remark is preceded by a close-up of doves, accompanied by a siren "off," and followed by a chest shot of Colometa dressed in black, and a long shot of search lights piercing the night, accompanied in turn by gunfire.   These elements all presage the negative consequences of the war and their social situation.   Quimet goes to the front in Aragón to fight the Nationalist troops, and in Barcelona, civilians take refuge in the Metro while bombs explode and the electricity is interrupted.   When Colometa encounters an old girl-friend, Julieta, the protagonist becomes aware of the fact that her friend is not the same, that war changes people.   The change is manifested physically in both her husband, who now appears with a beard dressed as a soldier, and in her friend Mico who cries when he takes leave of her to go to the front; Colometa's voice-over declares, "Era la primera vez que veía llorar a un hombre hecho y derecho" (It was the first time that I saw a real man cry).

The movie contains many common motifs to films that portray the rear guard.   Civilians in the rear guard often hope for an end to the conflict and plan for the future.   In a close-up before she kisses her

. . . and a widow who survives: Betriu's <u>La Plaza del Diamante</u>, with Silvia Munt, Lluis Homar, and Joaquim Cardona. Courtesy Fígaro Films, S.A.

husband, Colometa speaks of her plans for after the war, thinking that the conflict will soon terminate: "Cuando todo esto se acabe, me meteré en casa como la carcoma se mete en la madera y nadie me volverá a sacar" (When this is over, I am going to get into my home like a woodborer gets into wood, and nobody will take me out again). Quimet's death prompts the inquisitive comment about the nature of the conflict on the part of the ingenue; in this case it is their daughter who asks her brother, "¿Qué es la guerra, Toni?" (What is war, Toni?), to which he responds, "Donde unos se matan a otros a tiros" (It's where some people shoot others to death). The Nationalist victory brings many changes with it, manifested in the image of the change of street signs, as a hammer smashes the Catalan and Republican sign, "Plaça de la Revolució" (Revolution Square) and the Castilian and Nationalist sign, "Plaza de la Unificación" (Unification Square), takes its place. Changes take place in people, as well, both during and after the conflict. When Quimet goes off to fight, Colometa's employer rejects her, saying, "Nos hemos enterado de que su marido está metido en ese lío, y con personas así no queremos tener tratos" (We found out that your husband is mixed up in this affair, and we don't want to have anything to do with people like you). Rejection also comes at the end of the war, when Colometa seeks employment and is met with the harsh response, "¿Que quiere trabajo? Pues que se suba aquí" (You want work? Well climb aboard), as the man makes an obscene gesture toward her, or by the comment, "Preferimos tener la casa sucia que tener que tratar con . . . cierta gente" (We would rather have a dirty house than have to deal with . . . certain people). The following sequence includes a tracking shot of lines of people in the street waiting for food, a voice-over by Colometa ("Todos están muertos, muertos . . . y muertos los que han quedado vivos, muertos como si los hubiesen matado" [They are all dead, dead . . . and the living have become dead, just as dead as if someone had killed them), a shot of a man painting stencils of Franco on building walls, and a long shot of parishioners dressed in black leaving a church, which all create the impression of the terrible social conditions in post-war Catalonia. Her personal tragedy of the loss of her husband is on the one hand ameliorated by her second marriage to Antonio (Joaquim Cardona), the shop-keeper whose war-time wound has made him impotent, and on the other hand exacerbated by the fear that Quimet might not really be dead and might reappear. This fear gives rise to a dream sequence that terminates in Antonio comforting his emotionally distressed wife, a scene which symbolizes the support that he provides Colometa to help her survive. Indeed, Colometa does survive--she survives the hunger, the pain, the rejections and the fears. In her most important speech of the film, Colometa, on her balcony at night, looks directly at the camera in a medium shot and speaks about her ability to survive in beautiful metaphors: "Cuando alguna vez había oído que las personas estaban de corcho, no sabía lo que querían decir. Por fin lo entendí. Porque yo era de corcho, tuve que hacerme de corcho con el corazón de nieve. Porque si hubiese sido como antes, de carne que cuando te pellizcan te duele, no hubiera podido pasar por un puente tan alto, tan estrecho y tan largo" (When I once heard that people were made out of cork, I didn't understand what they meant. At last I understood. Because I was made of cork, I had to become cork with a heart of snow. Because if I had been like before, of flesh that when they pinch you it hurts, I wouldn't have been able to go over a bridge that was so high, so narrow, and so long). Francisco Marinero praises this scene as the "best and most daring moment of the film," since it consists of a language that is clearly literary, a shot that interrupts the fiction ("*La Plaza*" 34). Colometa represents the lives of many Spaniards--

particularly in Catalonia--who survived the difficult years after the war.[21]

Betriu imbues the film narrative with a poetic quality through the use of three recurring images. Over the span of many years, Colometa sees a toy bear in a store window, symbol of the happiness which is always out of reach for the protagonist. On two occasions, during her courtship with Quimet and again near the end of the film in her old age, there is a close-up of Colometa's finger tracing the image of a scale on the wall, an image linked to the balance of happiness and sadness in her life. Finally, images of doves take on importance throughout the film. Stills of doves begin and end the film, and there are numerous instances in which these birds enter into the narrative. In an early scene, Colometa picks up a wounded dove, an act that symbolizes her tenderness and care that will maintain her in difficult times. Letting some doves out of their cage provides a lesson for the children on freedom, and a later close-up of a dying dove serves as a foreshadowing of the death of her husband. The final shot of the film, however, which shows a dove in flight, is an image of hope and happiness, since Colometa has indeed survived, has found consolation and company in her husband Antonio, and has seen her children grow and marry.

Weighing against these poetic elements of the narration is the apparent lack of resources--in spite of the contract with Spanish television--in the filming of exterior sequences. The high-angle shot of the demonstration marking the inauguration of the Republic shows a pitifully small group of extras, and the entrance of Nationalist troops into Barcelona is marked by a miserly single truckload of soldiers. Greater attention to detail and authenticity in these important historical scenes would certainly have improved the overall quality of the film.

Spanish critic Jenaro Talens calls the 1984 hit, *Las bicicletas son para el verano* (Bicycles Are Only For Summer), a film directed by Jaime Chávarri that was based on the drama by Fernando Fernán Gómez, "one of the most important testimonies about the civil war" (Cristina Gil vii). However, the film does not narrate the military aspects of the confrontation, but rather, the daily lives of a family that lived in Madrid during the war.

---

[21]Marcel Oms indicates that Colometa, together with her wounded husband, mark the sacrifice of a whole generation to assure that life will go on (Cine español 241).

The film has something of a circular construction--or perhaps the image of a spiral is more appropriate, since the opening and closing scenes feature Luisito (Gabino Diego) and take place in the same physical location, a lot on the outskirts of Madrid, but the condition of Luisito has changed: the young boy who merely imagines the war at the beginning of the film has become a victim of it at the end. Indeed, the still images of Luisito which imitate Robert Capa's famous photograph of a Republican soldier being hit by enemy fire serve as a foreshadowing of his victimization, for although Luisito is not physically wounded, he nonetheless will suffer the consequences of not being on the victorious side of the conflict. His family, with parents, Luis (Agustín González) and Dolores (Amparo Soler Leal), and older sister Manolita (Victoria Abril) is an example of the middle class of the capital; Luis works at a warehouse. Luisito's plans for the summer of 1936 suddenly change when his "F" in Physics prevents him from receiving the bicycle that his parents had promised, and the rising of social tensions and outbreak of the war prevent him from going to Murcia to visit his cousin. Up until this disruption, the youth had manifested a certain naiveté about the social conditions. His father's dire warning, "No sé adónde va a llegar la situación. Esto acabará afectando a todos" (I don't know where this situation is going to lead us. This is going to end up affecting us all), is met with an ingenuous response of "Pues aquí estamos contentos" (Well we're just fine here) by Luisito. His father also suffers from the same shortsightedness, however, as we see the common motif that the conflict will not last a long time: even after the family receives the news of the Nationalist rebellion on the radio, Luis tells his son, "En cuanto acabe, compraremos la bici y tienes todo el verano adelante" (When this is over, we'll buy the bike, and you'll have the whole rest of the summer to ride it)--a sentiment later echoed by the phrase "Esto sólo va a durar quince días" (This is only going to last a couple of weeks). Radio broadcasts inform the family of the progress of events--the move of the government to Valencia, the official attitude of non-intervention of certain European countries--and they provide an important historical dimension to the film.

The war comes closer to the family as we see images of sandbags in the street, a military parade of Republicans with clenched fists and banners that proclaim, "No pasarán" (They shall not enter), and a rock that comes through their window, accompanied by the shout of "Quita esa luz" (Turn out that light) which is followed by the sound of an

The war's effect on civilians: Chavarri's <u>Las bicicletas son para el verano</u>, with Amparo Soler Leal, Gabino Diego, and Victoria Abril. Courtesy Sogepaq, S.A.

explosion and the image of flames caused by the bomb which has fallen near their home. Luis's attitude about the duration of the conflict now changes, as he cries out in frustration, "A ver cuándo cojones quiera Dios que acabe todo esto" (I wonder when the hell this is going to end). Sounds of machine-gun fire, sirens, and shouts often keep the combat just below the surface. A later bomb attack sends the family and their neighbors to the basement of their building, where many pray to a statue of the Virgin. The film thus shows elements of daily life which break down trite stereotypes: not all of the inhabitants in Republican Madrid during the war were atheist reds.

Another major impact that the war has on the family is their lack of food. In a very poignant scene, Luis confronts the family with the situation, and each member confesses taking a spoonful or two from the pot when they pass through the kitchen--Luisito, to quell his hunger, Manolita, because her milk has dried up and she can no longer feed her baby, etc. At the end of the confessions, Dolores's imploration, "Que llegue la paz" (May peace come), leads to something of a verbal confrontation based on the What if. . . hypothesis between husband and wife that manifests a contrast in political leanings within the family. Luis complains about both communist and fascist atrocities, and when he says, "Y si las potencias democráticas hubieran ayudado hace dos

Daily life in the rear guard: Chávarri's <u>Las bicicletas son para el verano</u>. Courtesy Sogepaq, S.A.

años, esto estaría ya liquidado" (If the democratic powers had helped two years ago, this would already be over), his wife retorts, "Y si los revolucionarios no hubieran hecho tantas barbaridades al principio" (And if the revolutionaries hadn't committed so many barbarities at the beginning). Luis's response, "Sí, coño, pero ¿quién tenía razón?" (Yes, dammit, but who was in the right?), shows an essential element of his character. Luis, like Cecilio in *Retrato de familia*, is a non-partisan in this fratricidal conflict, but is caught up in the flood of historical events; he is a victim who is critical of the fanaticism and excesses on both sides of the confrontation, and represents, in the words of Carlos Boyero, the defense of life against barbarism (*Las bicicletas* 17). Luis's rationality appears not only in a political context, but in terms of everyday family problems as well: when he discovers that Manolita wants to become an actress, his defense of his daughter's wishes shows his tolerance and good will in a difficult situation. The goodness of his character is also manifest in the anguish that he suffers when economic hardship forces him to send their maid (who has provided Luisito with his sexual initiation) to her village. Of course, the socio-political changes of the time give rise to a change in mores. In a dialogue reminiscent of *Las largas vacaciones del '36*,

Antonia declares, "Se acabó el pecado" (There is no more sin), and in a humorous touch, Doña Marcela decides to obtain a divorce after forty-eight years of marriage because of incompatibility.

Little by little, the war impresses its negative impact on the family: Manolita confesses to her mother not only that she is pregnant and single, but that the child's father, a Republican captain, has been killed. Although Dolores's initial reaction is to exclaim, "Esta guerra, esta maldita guerra" (This war, this damned war), her daughter's predicament causes her to change her way of thinking and to become more tolerant as well. The tragic shattering of their lives inexorably grows as Julio, the awkward neighbor boy who marries Manolita, is killed; Luis loses his job; and Luisito cannot register at school because of his political background. After the war ends, violent confrontations between civilians and Nationalist soldiers in the streets create a climate of fear, and Luis is apprehensive that he himself will be arrested. In the final sequence, which takes place in the field where the action began, Luis shares a cigarette with his son. This act serves as a symbol, along with the change in the boy's name (the diminutive now disappears) that his son is now a young man who must shoulder the burden that lays before him. In one of the most famous lines from all of the contemporary Spanish films which deal with the Civil War, in a close-up shot, Luis tells his son, "Es que no ha llegado la paz, Luis, ha llegado la victoria" (It's not peace that has arrived, Luis, victory has arrived). The young man must now help provide for the family, and his father has obtained a job for him as a delivery boy. He will finally get his bicycle, but it will not be to ride with a young girl, as he had hoped. Thus, as Juan Bufill points out, the material object of the title takes on an important symbolism, becoming an undesirable symbol of defeat and bitterness (35).

Las bicicletas son para el verano is an important contribution to the historical memory of Spain, since, as Miguel Bayón points out, the principal endeavor of the film is to reconstruct those landscapes, those rooms, filling them with the passions and the sorrows of the people who lived through the war (El Madrid 93).[22] It stands out as the best film about the rear guard of the Spanish civil war in contemporary Spanish cinema.

---

[22]L. G. Egido praises designer Parrondo's magnificent work in recreating the historical atmosphere of the 1930's on the set of this film.

Réquiem por un campesino español (Requiem for a Spanish Peasant) is a film from 1985 directed by Francesc Betriu, and based on the novel of the same name by Ramón Sender. Regarding the debut of the film in Zaragoza, the capital city of the province where the action (and filming) took place, B. Rovira (Estreno 26) noted that members of the audience were moved because their memories of the conflict are still very much alive, thus giving testimony to the emotive power of cinema that deals with the theme of *cainismo*. The cinematographic story has the same structure as does the novel: the present time-frame consists of the mass that Mosén Millán (Antonio Ferrandis), the village priest, says for the soul of Paco; prior events are subordinated to this moment in flashbacks, with close-ups of the priest signalling a return to the present. The earliest point of the narrative is the baptism of Paco by Mosén Millán; thus, the relationship between the peasant and the priest is inexorably linked from the beginning of the former's existence. This relationship grows during Paco's youth, since he serves as an altar boy for the priest, a period that manifests the fundamental characteristics that will mark Paco's future. As an eight-year old altar boy, he invokes the priest's ire when his wooden pistol falls from his pants to the floor during mass. The pistol itself serves as a symbol of the violent end that will meet Paco, and his defense of the incident before the priest, placing himself in the position of scapegoat, is actually a subconscious attempt to defer guilt: "Si lo tengo yo, no lo tienen otros chavales peores que yo (If I have it, then other kids who are worse than I won't have it). During his confirmation ceremony, he tells the bishop that he wants to be a laborer like his father, and have three mules. This comment reflects his desire to improve his lot in life, a desire which will later inexorably cause him to clash with authorities. He later accompanies Mosén Millán to a cave to give extreme unction to a parishioner. Close-up shots of Paco indicate his incredulity, and when he questions the priest about the man's poverty, Mosén Millán acknowledges the young boy's virtues, which will later form the basis of his social consciousness: "Tienes buen corazón. Tu compasión es virtuosa y caritativa" (You have a good heart. Your compassion is virtuous and charitable). This episode also manifests an important feature of Mosén Milán's character. His comment to Paco that "Cuando Dios permite la miseria y el dolor sus razones tendrá" (When God permits misery and pain, he must have his reason) shows an air of resignation that will be crucial to the outcome of Paco's fate.

Paco's transition to manhood occurs in a scene in which he swims in a pond across from where a group of women who are washing clothes comment, amid much laughter, that he is now "todo un hombre" (really a man). As Paco (Antonio Banderas) begins to work in the fields, he comes to realize the extent to which the landowners exploit the peasants. An evening in the village square provides him with the opportunity to question his mentor about such abuses, but the priest brushes his complaints aside as "alegatos peregrinos" (strange allegations) and says that he should worry more about himself and the scandal that he caused by bathing naked in front of the washer women. This scene constitutes an indictment against the role of the church in pre-war Spain. More concerned with sexuality than social injustice, Mosén Millán contributes to the social turmoil that follows.

Paco's wedding occurs just as social tensions in the town and in the country begin to mount, and the narrative of the film interweaves the two. The shoemaker--representative of the popular social conscience-- warns, "el rey se tambalea y si cae muchas cosas se van a caer con él" (the king is shaky, and if he falls, a lot of things are going to fall with him). The local and national political situations intersect when Paco becomes involved in the elections of April, 1931, much to the chagrin of landowners. The laborer tells Mosén Millán that these are new times, and that the renters plan to stop rent payments to the landowners. After a long shot of the town, a shot of Paco on his white horse symbolically contrasts with the entrance into the town square of two automobiles from which a band of youths dressed in black military uniforms emerges. These outsiders are fascists who begin to terrorize the town with beatings and murders. In one of the most poignant scenes in the film, they gather the townsfolk into the square and force them at pistol point to sing the fascist hymn, "Cara al sol" (Facing the Sun). Paco eludes the fascist manhunt and comes to town at night-- again on his white steed--to inquire of his mentor about his family. This will cause his downfall, however, since the priest collaborates with the fascists and betrays Paco's whereabouts. The closeup shots of Mosén Millán crying--both as the authorities interrogate him, and when Paco is about to be executed--show how actor Antonio Ferrandis attempted to imbue his role with an emotional depth worthy of the Sender character. The same moral justification for suffering that the priest showed in the early scene at the cave of the dying parishioner resurfaces when Paco asks him why he must die: the priest ignores both the injustice of the fascist executions and his own complicity, only responding, "A veces Dios permite morir a un inocente" (Sometimes God permits an innocent man to die), a comment that imbues Paco with Christ symbolism. The priest not only ignores the righteousness of the laborers' protests, but overtly sides with the landowners from early on. Only the priest's guilty conscience causes him to not accept payment for the requiem by the landlord's administrator (Fernando Fernán Gómez) When word comes that the king has fled, the administrator visits Mosén Millán to warn of bad times, and suggests, "Deberíamos permanecer unidos" (We should stick together), Betriu visually captures the collusion of the church and the oligarchy in the last scene of the film, when Mosén Millán enters the church to say the mass for Paco: although there are no townspeople, the landlord's administrator is conspicuously present. However, the intrusion moments before of Paco's white horse, poetic symbol of the peasant's goodness, freedom, and strength, into the church, shows that Paco's spiritual presence lives on in the town. The intrusion is seen as a sacrilege, just as Paco's struggle for justice was viewed as a violation of a God-given social order. The presence of the riderless horse in the church serves as a foreshadowing of the ending--the capture and assassination of Paco--as well as a haunting reminder to the priest of the tragic error that he has committed, since this scene immediately follows that in which the priest confesses Paco's hiding place to the fascists.

Betriu and photographer Raúl Artigot make excellent use of dark lighting throughout the film to presage the denouement, and in general the photography is excellent. Although *Requiem por un campesino español* may not have entirely captured the tragic dimensions of novelistic narrative, it does portray the repression and terror experienced by a small town in the rear guard.

Benito Rabal made his directing debut with the 1986 film, *El hermano bastardo de Dios* (God's Bastard Brother). Rabal divides the narrative into five segments: 1939, the months before the war, at the beginning of the conflict, at the end of the war, and we finally return to the opening scene and continue the action in 1939. The dedicatory epigraph of the film, "A todos aquellos que eran niños o no lo pudieron ser por proscripción gubernativa" (To all those who were children or who were not allowed to be so because of governmental proscription), indicates from the very beginning that the point of departure of this movie is a common one: the war seen from the perspective of a child. Although the protagonist, Pepe Luis, is indeed a child, the perspective here is really that of the adult who remembers his childhood in the provincial city of Cuenca during the war, since the voice-over that conveys his thoughts is that of a grown man who has sought answers to philosophical questions and reflects upon the meaning of life. The early sequences--the discussion about the execution of Don Jacinto, the school teacher; the children killing the cat; or the close-up of a photograph of his grandparents--elicit the comment by this voice of his conscience (voice "off"): "Yo tenía pocos años, pero sabía lo que era la muerte" (I was young, but I knew what death was). Nevertheless, the reason for death's existence is a question that he pursues all his life.

Although there is no actual fighting in the film, death and suffering inevitably surface from the background. The child protagonist functions as the ingenue who does not understand the reasons for the outbreak of the conflict ("Nadie le aclara nada para un niño en semejantes circunstancias" [No one clears up anything for a child in circumstances like these]) and whose questions lay bare the inherent absurdity of war (Pepe Luis: "¿Qué hacen en el frente de batalla?" [What do they do at the battle front?] Trini: "Matarse" [Kill each other]) or the additional problems of a civil war ("No sabía distinguir rojos y nacionales" [I couldn't tell reds from nationalists]). Pepe Luis witnesses the suffering among the adults as Trini, who writes letters dictated by Alejandra to her son at the front ("Hay que ser valientes y acabar con los fascistas" [You have to be brave and put an end to these fascists]) must now comfort her friend over her boy's death. Pepe Luis's uncle Julio returns from the front with a bad wound, and he must have his leg amputated. The family visit to the hospital where Pepe Luis sees the suffering of his uncle and other patients causes the boy to reflect on God's goodness and conclude with a thought that serves as the film's title: "Sólo el hermano bastardo de Dios podría permitir tales cosas" (Only God's bastard brother could permit such things to happen).

This film handles the religious theme in a unique way. In a scene in the local grocery before the war breaks out, Ramona predicts, "Aquí va a pasar algo muy gordo" (Something really big is going to happen here), and she states, "La culpa es del clero y de la oligarquía" (The clergy and the oligarchy are to blame). She has special criticism for priests, speaking of "mucha sobrinita" (lots of nieces) with reference to the hypocrisy regarding their sexual behavior. The family of Pepe Luis, however, is Catholic. When they take down and put away a painting of the Virgin, the young Pepe Luis talks about religion with

Trini, who explains, "Este gobierno que tenemos aquí prohibe que la gente crea en Dios" (This government that we've got prohibits people from believing in God). Although this statement is not accurate regarding the legal situation regarding religion under the Republic, it may reflect an individual Catholic's perspective of the *de facto* situation during the war.[23] When the youngster plays with some companions in the stable, they discover hidden religious statues. A slow-motion shot of the statues flying through the air to their destruction is a portent of later harassment that Pepe Luis's family will suffer. Near the end of the war, soldiers break down their door in search of a projector that they claim the family uses to communicate with the enemy. When Rosendo, the grandfather, protests that it is only a toy, a soldier hits him.

After the war, with the Nationalists now in power, Pepe Luis becomes an altar boy. One of the weakest parts of the film are scenes imagined by Pepe Luis at mass: a cathedral in the sky accompanied by the voices of children singing. Director Rabal includes two other such scenes: when Pepe Luis is knocked unconscious by falling rocks in a cave and imagines Pilarina putting roses on his casket, and when he serves as an altar boy at a funeral and imagines that the dead man awakens and greets everyone. Death is the key image in Pepe Luis's subconscious, and death seems to fill the entire atmosphere of the post-war period as well. The voice-over states, "Ya no se mataba en el frente; ahora se mata en los juzgados o poco juzgados" (There wasn't any more killing at the front; now they killed at the courts of justice or injustice), a humorous but barbed criticism of injustices committed after the war by the Nationalists. In this regard, we return to the execution of the school teacher, Don Jacinto. At the beginning of the narrative, we discover that his sin consisted of being "liberal, ateo, de todo y de nada" (liberal, atheist, everything and nothing). The lesson that he teaches his class near the end of the war concerning the lack of

---

[23]According to Article 3 of the constitution that was approved in 1931, "The Spanish State has no official religion." Article 25 allowed for freedom of religion, but allowed it to be practiced only inside churches. Other restrictions on religion, such as dissolution of the Jesuits, nationalization of church properties, proscription of education by religious orders and congregations, and legalization of divorce, certainly represented dramatic changes that might result in the hyperbole of Trini's statement. In addition, fanatics' attacks on buildings of a religious nature created a climate of extremism on either side. See Thomas 49 ff.; also Montero Moreno; Narbona; Aguirre.

generosity of the Christians after the conquest of the Muslim kingdom of Granada in 1492 is a foreshadowing of the lack of generosity and clemency of the Franco regime. When civilians beat the prisoner on the way to his execution, he falls as if he were Christ on his way to Golgotha. The fact that unlike the others, Pepe Luis does not take pleasure in the poor man's suffering points out one of the strengths of the film: its lack of a dogmatic, single-sided perspective. Making the protagonist the child of a Catholic family that fights for the cause of the Republic puts him in a somewhat ambiguous position. Although Pepe Luis never finds answers to many of the questions that he asks, *El hermano bastardo de Dios* poignantly records the memories of those questions of a child in the rear guard of the fratricidal conflict.

Chapter 4

The *Maquis*

The term *guerrilla* ("little war") originated in Spain during the Napoleonic invasion when small groups of armed Spaniards harassed the French troops. There were certainly guerrilla activities during the Spanish Civil War, and when the conflict officially ended in April of 1939, some Republican soldiers took to the mountains to continue the fight. These men became known as *maquis*, after the French term. They are the subject of numerous historical studies[24], and the theme appears in films prior to 1965 such as Pedro Lazaga's *Torrepartida* (1956) and León Klimovsky's *La paz empieza nunca* (1960). In March of 1986, the *maquis* was still very much in the news. In San Fiz de Asma, at the tomb of José Castro Veiga, Galicians paid homage to this last of the anti-Franco guerrillas, who was killed by the Guardia Civil on March 10, 1965. On March 3, 1986, three former *maquis*, Marcelino Fernández, Mario Morán, and César Ríos, told their story on "Vivir cada día" (Living Each Day) a program produced and aired on Spanish television.

In films made after 1965, this figure appears as both a primary and a secondary figure. He is most important in Mario Camus's *Días del pasado* (Bygone Days, 1977) and Manuel Gutiérrez Aragón's *El corazón del bosque* (The Heart of the Forest, 1978), two powerful and fascinating movies about the *maquis* in Asturias, as well as in Julio Sánchez Valdés's *Luna de lobos* (Wolves' Moon, 1987); a film that centers around guerrilla activity during the war is Manolo Matji's *La guerra de los locos* (The Madmen's War, 1987); the *maquis* appears in a secondary role in Pedro Olea's *Pim, pam, pum, fuego* (Bang, Bang

---

[24]See Víctor Alba's Historia de la resistencia antifranquista (1939-1955); Tomás Cossías's La lucha contra el maquis en España; Daniel Arasa's Años 40: Los maquis y el PCE; and Alberto E. Fernández's La España de los maquis.

You're Dead) (1975), *Kargus* (Kargus), directed by Miñón and Trujillo
(1981), Vicente Aranda's *Si te dicen que caí* (If They Tell You That I
Fell, 1989), and Víctor Erice's *El espíritu de la colmena* (The Spirit
of the Beehive, 1973), which is one of the best Spanish films ever
made.
      Mario Camus is a director who studied at the I.I.E.C. (Instituto de
Investigaciones y Experiencias Cinematográficas), precursor of the
Escuela Oficial de Cinematografía, and who collaborated on some of
Carlos Saura's early films. He often transposes literary works of art
into film, such as Ignacio Aldecoa's novel *Con el viento solano* (With
the Easterly Wind, 1965), Camilo José Cela's *La colmena* (The Hive,
1982), and Miguel Delibes' *Los santos inocentes* (The Holy Innocents,
1984). His film about the *maquis*, *Los días del pasado* (Bygone Days,
1977), won both popular and critical acclaim. Fernando Méndez Leite
comments that it is "without doubt, one of the best films of the past ten
years" ("El cine español" 19) and Marcel Oms refers to it as an
"essential work for understanding Spanish life" (qtd. in *Cine español*
1: 100). The movie's success among the general public was due at
least in part to the casting (and excellent performances) of two popular
performers to play the title roles: Antonio Gades is the *maquis*
Antonio, and Marisol (the professional name of Pepa Flores) plays
Juana, the school teacher who is in love with him. The film begins
with the epigraph: "Las arenas del mar, las gotas de la lluvia y los
días del pasado . . . quién podrá contarlos?" (The sands of the sea, the
raindrops, the bygone days . . . Who will be able to count them?).
According to Camus, this quote represents the motto of an entire
generation in which what predominates is "the anguish of the process
of recovery. The recovery of those 'bygone days' diverges in two
ways: the general, overall history of those who lost the war and would
not accept it, and the individual history of a few for whom love is the
inspiration for daily silent rebelliousness" (Frugone 123).   Indeed,
these very elements--love, rebellion, and the inability to accept
defeat--are the motifs that dominate the movie. Filmed in Asturias with
superb photography by Hans Burmann, the movie takes on the magical
qualities of the lush green mountainous scenery of the region. The

frequent long shots capture the importance of the elements of nature--the forest, the river, the mist, the rain--or of elements of country life in the 1940's--a farmer walking with a cow, the one-room school building, the arrival of the school inspector on bicycle, or a panoramic shot of the town itself. Director Camus also uses close-ups to underscore salient elements of this atmosphere: a shot of wooden shoes with a pan up to capture Juana's face under her umbrella is important because of the implicit contrast with her past. Juana is from Málaga, with a markedly distinct climate, and she often is depicted as an outsider who does not fit in: a series of fade-outs separate scenes in her bedroom upon her arrival that show her shivering in bed, putting on a sweater, or putting on woolen stockings as she attempts to face the rigors of the northern climate; in her nocturnal meeting with Antonio in her bedroom, a close-up of her face also shows her to be cold, and she complains, "No me acostumbro" (I can't get used to it). The sound track also contributes important elements in establishing the physical and psychological atmosphere: the frequent bird calls (especially those of the owls) lend an air of mystery and suspense (the *maquis*, constantly pursued by the Civil Guards, can come to town only at night). The musical theme that repeats throughout the film as a motif for the *maquis* (when Juana sees wanted posters of the guerrillas, when a *maquis* scans the countryside with his binoculars, etc.) is a guitar rendition of "Ay, Manuela," the popular Republican war song. The love scenes, however, are accompanied by accordion music, so that even the musical score reinforces the dichotomy and underlying conflict between Antonio's desire to continue fighting and to give up the armed struggle for his girlfriend.

In the opening sequence, while Juana travels on a train north, the voice-over of Antonio provides us with both his motivations and a temporal framework for the action. The latter appears in his comment that seven years have passed like an instant, thus placing the temporal setting in the mid 1940's. His initial complaint, "Nos amenazaban con llevarnos a España y así trabajamos sin parar . . ." (They would threaten to take us to Spain, so we worked without stopping . . .), connotes the misery of French concentration camps where Republican refugees were held. However, he manifests a sense of optimism in his renewed struggle: "Ganamos la guerra, Juana; cayó París, cayó Berlín, y ahora que los soldados dejan las armas, volveremos a empezar" (We won the war, Juana; Paris fell, Berlin fell, and now that soldiers are laying down their arms, we will begin again).   Their armed resistance to the Franco regime consists of guerrilla actions such as the blowing up of an electrical tower or the ambush of a patrol of civil guards. Nevertheless, the admission "Nos llaman los huidos" (They call us renegades), and Captain Lucio's rhetorical question and answer, "A qué hemos venido? No lo sé" (What have we come to? I don't know), connote a fatalistic acceptance of their eventual defeat.

The schoolhouse where Juana teaches symbolizes both the poverty and the cultural repression of the era. The children explain to the new instructor that there was no one there before her; fundamental material objects such as chalk and firewood for the woodstove are also missing. Although Juana lectures the students about "cántabros y astures" --ancient tribes who defended their mountain lands against foreign intruders, the school inspector chides her, "basta enseñar algo sobre los Reyes Católicos" (it's enough to teach something about the Catholic Kings), referring to Fernando of Aragon and Isabel of Castile, who were idolized by the Franco regime for qualities that it sought to emulate, such as centralization of government and unification of religion. (Indeed, the shot of the inspector clearly shows his Falange emblem, and the Falange took its symbol of the yoke and arrows from this icon associated with Fernando and Isabel).   Nevertheless, the schoolhouse also provides Juana with a means of contacting her fugitive boyfriend.   Angel, a student whose father was killed by the Civil Guard, knows both the mountain and the *maquis*, and he informs Juana of their nocturnal visits to town. She seeks Antonio in an abandoned winter stable, justifying her visit to that isolated location with a school field trip. The empty building provides no reward for her quest: her inquiry of the youth who is sweeping in the darkness of the interior, "Alguien estuvo aquí la noche pasada, ¿verdad?" (Somebody was here last night, right?), receives an answer that is less than unequivocal: "No lo sé" (I don't know). This episode thus symbolizes the ingenuous search for an elusive reality that she is not able to pin down, and which ultimately turns out to be empty. The sudden entrance of armed men dressed with berets and blankets adds both to the suspense and to the ambiguousness of the episode. The initial visual impact suggests that they are *maquis*; however, they turn out to be Civil Guards who order her and the children back to town.

When Juana finally encounters Antonio, their reunion is less than ideal,   reflecting a certain mutual misapprehension.   The *maquis* exclaims, "Estás loca, ¿pero qué haces aquí?" (You are crazy. What are you doing here?), to which she responds, "Dios mío, qué flaco estás" (My God, how thin you are). The physical change in Antonio reflects other deeper changes as well. Although he touches her face with his hand and they finally embrace in a close-up shot after they walk to the bridge, his silence elicits her query, "¿Por qué no hablas?" (Why don't you speak?). She diffuses her inner suffering and incomprehension of his motivations with the generalization, "Nadie entiende por qué faltas" (No one understands why you are missing), but his elusive response symbolizes what will ultimately be the unbreachable void between them. This void is even more noticeable in their final encounter. Juana travels by bus to meet Antonio in a house by the sea. Although she pleads, "¿Por qué no nos vamos, Antonio? A Francia, a vivir" (Why don't we leave, Antonio? Go to France to live?), his response, "Estoy cansado, Juana" (I'm tired, Juana), is more elusive than ever, and he falls asleep as a train whistle sounds in the distance. Again the sound track acquires importance through the connotation here of beckoning of escape for Juana, a distant call unheeded by Antonio. The beautiful chiaroscuro photography that Hans Burmann uses in a close-up shot of Juana in this scene, as she caresses the hair of her sleeping boyfriend, underscores this culminating moment in her inner struggle as she is torn between her love for Antonio and her desire for a happy, normal existence. (Juana herself has become like the pursued; she was questioned at the police station and later furtively left the road so that a passing car would not notice her.) When he awakens, she has made her decision: "No tengo fuerza, no puedo más. Voy a mi casa con mi gente" (I don't have any strength, I can't go on. I'm going home to be with my folks). Juana does indeed abandon Antonio, and the last scene shows a panoramic view of Málaga and then a close-up of a pensive Juana in a short-sleeved dress (symbol of the change in climate and contrast with the earlier scenes with warm clothing in Asturias), sitting in her classroom as the children recite their lesson "off." The scene then cuts to a close-up of a tree branch and a tracking shot through the forest, with four important sounds "off": gunshots, the barking of dogs, the panting of a running man, and the guitar rendition of "Ay, Manuela." Like an ancient Spanish ballad whose narrative is truncated at a moment of suspense, *Los días del pasado* has an ending that is both poetic and powerful in its understatement and inevitability.

Director Camus imbued *Los días del pasado* through what J. L.
Martínez Montalbán calls a brilliant use of ellipsis and metaphor (182),
and García Fernández points out the important utilization of symbolism
in the film stating, "Camus recreates the tragedy by means of symbols:
the landscape, the house, the school, the children, the inspector, the
cold, the forest" (309). *Los días del pasado* provides an excellent
portrayal of the *maquis*, and is one of the many superb films that
director Mario Camus has given the contemporary Spanish screen.

Manuel Gutiérrez Aragón is a director who began as a script
writer, working in that capacity on films such as Betriú's *Corazón
solitario* (Lonely Heart, 1972), Borau's *Furtivos* (Poachers, 1975),
Camino's *Las largas vacaciones del '36* (The Long Vacation of '36,
1976), and García Sánchez's *Las truchas* (The Trouts, 1977). His
career as a director began in 1973 with *Habla mudita* (Speak, Little
Mute), and continued in 1976 and 1977 with *Camada negra* (Black
Litter) and *Sonámbulos* (Somnambulists). His 1979 production, *El
corazón del bosque* (The Heart of the Forest), is a film concerned with
the theme of the *maquis*.[25] Like many other contemporary Spanish
films, it too is based on--at least in spirit--a literary work of art. In
this case, however, it is not a Spanish novel, but an English one:
Joseph Conrad's *Heart of Darkness*.[26] In addition, the influence of
actual Spanish history on the film is fundamental. The director, who
is from Northern Spain, knew of the case of a guerrilla fighter named
Juanín who continued fighting until the 1960's and who had
degenerated into a bandit in order to survive (see Torres 102).

As in the case of *Los días del pasado*, *El corazón del bosque* (The
Heart of the Forest) was shot in the mountains of Asturias, this time
with the superb photography of Teo Escamilla, which won him the
Luis Buñuel Prize for best film photography of the year. Again,

---

[25]The director denies that this film is about the maquis, saying that it is about
"getting near pursued beings, with their fatalism, the irremediable destiny" (qtd. in
Antolín, 40).

[26]Several Spanish critics point out this relationship. Miguel Juan Payan and José
Luis López in their monograph entitled, <u>Manuel Gutiérrez Aragón</u> state that they agree
with Matías Antolín that <u>El corazón del bosque</u> is <u>Heart of Darkness</u> "made into pure
cinema" (71). However, the director only concedes that the movie is LIKE <u>Heart of
Darkness,</u> and that indeed, the title is derived from the novel, but that it is not a film
adaptation of Conrad's work (Torres, <u>Conversaciones</u> 103).

nature--the mountains and forests, rain and mist, corn fields and cows--becomes a protagonist in the film. Gutiérrez Aragón accomplishes this not only through the long shots that capture the beauty of the countryside, but also with a supporting sound track. Mirito Torreiro calls the sound track, with its bird songs, sound of the rain and of the wind in the corn fields, "an entire code of gestures, an entire manual of expressions that do not have anything to do with our own expressive forms, and that constitute one of the most interesting elements of the film" (55-6). The intensity of the images on screen results in what Francisco Marinero calls "an overwhelming film where you can feel the rain and the cold" ("*El corazón*" 47). The film opens with an epigraph that confirms the historical background of the movie: "Esta historia está basada en diversos sucesos y personas que existieron en los mismos montes y bosques en que la película ha sido filmada" (This story is based on diverse events and people who existed in the same mountains and forests in which the movie has been filmed).[27] After a medium shot of guerrilla fighters shooting their machine-guns and the explosion of an electrical facility, another written text on screen both introduces the temporal setting and the protagonist and explains the preceding action: "1 de septiembre de 1942. Hace cuatro años que terminó la guerra civil española. Andarín y su grupo de "escondidos" mantienen una resistencia esperanzada en las montañas del Norte" (September 1, 1942. The Spanish civil war ended four years ago. El Andarín and his group of hidden men keep up a hopeful resistance in the mountains of the North). The following night scene of an open-air dance is crucial to the development of the film. The cross-cutting between Andarín dancing with old women and medium shots of a little girl, together with a superb use of visual metonymy--close-ups of Andarín's feet while dancing and when walking back to the forest--serve to carry out the process of mythification of the *maquis* in the eyes of the youngster. A fade-out gives way to a third caption that explains not only a temporal jump, but also introduces the Cain figure to the film: "1 de septiembre de 1952, diez años más tarde. El grupo del Andarín aún sobrevive en las montañas. La organización a la que pertenece el Andarín ha decidido poner fin a la resistencia armada. Se envían sin resultado un enlace

---

[27]In Spanish, <u>historia</u> means both "history" and "story", and this double meaning of the term underscores this confirmation.

tras otro. Juan P., oriundo del lugar, es el último" (September 1, 1952, ten years later. Andarín's group still survives in the mountains. The organization that Andarín belongs to has decided to put an end to armed resistance. They send one liaison after another without success. Juan P., a native of that place, is the last one). The name of this character connotes a certain Kafkaesque touch; the information provided about him--that he is originally from this place--is fundamental. It implies that he, too, must know the forest well, and that his return will lead to both a search for Andarín, as well as for his own past. Indeed, Jorge de Cominges states that the film is a reflection on "fidelity and betrayal, man and his double, memory and reality" ("El hombre" 29). Gutiérrez Aragón symbolically introduces the theme of the self and the double during the credits. The red letters on a black background--which in itself connotes blood, darkness, and death--are accompanied in the upper right-hand corner by a pair of rhomboids. The introduction of Juan P. into the film during another dance scene (the annual village feast that Andarín always attends) begins the parallelism between the two brother figures, a parallelism that slowly begins to dissolve into oneness as the film progresses.

The little girl who idolized Andarín is Amparo, Juan's sister, who is to marry Suso, a shoemaker who plays the saxophone for the dance. The sister provides Juan with initial information on the location of Andarín: in a scene reminiscent of *Los días del pasado*, she informs him that he must go up the mountain to the winter stable. On the way, however, he has an encounter with the Civil Guards, and in another superb use of visual metonymy, Andarín saves the man who seeks him out: in the darkness of night amidst the bushes, we see only a hand reach out and drag Juan to safety. The identity of the hand is later confirmed through periphrasis. When Juan awakens in the hut, a man informs him only that "Lo ha traído aquí él" (He brought him here). This mysterious allusion later becomes clear, however, when Juan asks a little girl, "Dónde está el Andarín?" (Where is Andarín?), and she replies, "Shhh . . . se dice 'él'" (Shhh . . . you say 'him.'" Her intervention parallels that of the young Amparo in the mythification of the *maquis*. The process is heightened here as the little girl recognizes but ignores (in her contradictory statements) the sad reality of her hero: "Es guapísimo. Lo que pasa es que ahora tiene unas bubas en la cara y hay que llevarle medicinas" (He's really handsome. The trouble is that now he has some pustules on his face,

Ideals betrayed: Gutiérrez Aragón's <u>El corazón del bosque</u>, with Luis Politti. Courtesy Luis Megino, P.C.

and we have to take medicine to him). However, she provides Juan with clues to the whereabouts of Andarín through a folk song that she sings.[28]

---

[28]Gutiérrez Aragón states that "the film is like a riddle in which the 'ritornello' of the little girl gives clues (Torres 106). A similar interpretation is offered by Ramón Freixas when he states that <u>El corazón del bosque</u> is "a difficult film with an open structure that needs collaboration on the part of the audience" ("Manuel Gutiérrez

The animal similes that a former *maquis* uses in a conversation
with Juan to describe Andarín connote the demythified reality of the
guerrilla fighter: "Es como un bicho.   Habría que matarle. . . .
Consigue que él baje; si no, va a morir como un perro" (He's like a
bug. He would have to be killed. . . .   Make him come down; if you
don't, he'll die like a dog). His other comment, "No está con nosotros
desde hace mucho" (He hasn't been with us for a long time) comprises
part of the faithfulness motif; here, it is faithfulness to a cause.
Andarín's later rhetorical question, "¿Hay alguien que no sea traidor?"
(Is there anyone who is not a traitor?) reveals the other perspective:
only HE has remained faithful to the cause, to the fight begun so many
years before.   Juan's conversations in the forest with the former
maquis also provide the opportunity for Juan to come to grips with his
past. A bird call elicits Juan's unsuccessful attempt to identify it and
to name it (at first he can only recall its name in French).
Conversation about Juan's youth is accompanied by flashback images
of a cow and of Juan as a child dressed in a blue bobby.   This
sequence in particular can lead to a metaphorical interpretation of the
film; Mirito Torreiro recognizes that this film is about "the Odyssey
of a man to find another, but also the desire of the emissary to recover
his memory of objects, people, animals. Thus, the character's search
of his own past is also Manolo Gutiérrez's search for the collective past
of his country" (55-56).

The final phase of Juan's search manifests the transformation of the
seeker. In order to survive in the forest, he becomes capable of even
taking food from a cadaver. Although Andarín saves Juan (who has
been wounded by the Civil Guards) again, the latter shoots the *maquis*
on the mountain top, and the guerrilla fighter's last words, "Me cago
en dos" (Fucking Gosh; literally "I shit on two") constitute a
euphemistic oath against God as well as a curse against his double,
Juan, who has caused his death. The mist that envelopes Andarín's
body shows again how nature is a principal protagonist in the film.
The image of Juan scratching his chest and legs parallels early behavior
by his dead companion, and the final scene   completes the
transformation of Cain into Abel: when Juan, recuperating in bed,
tells his sister that he wants to leave, her husband retorts, "Ya no
puede ser" (It's too late). The sound "off" of a truck arriving and

Aragón" 52).

footsteps on the stairs can only mean one thing, and Juan shrieks the same curse emitted earlier by Andarín. The transformation is complete. The final shots of the film consist of a slow pan of the corn field followed by a long shot of the mountain,[29] which completes the poetic atmosphere that Gutiérrez Aragón has created in this haunting film.[30] *El corazón del bosque* is indeed one of the most important Spanish films that manifests the *cainismo* theme.

In 1987, Julio Sánchez Valdés directed yet another film about the *maquis*, *Luna de lobos* (Wolves' Moon), based on the novel of the same name by J. Llamazares. The movie stars Antonio Resines in a dramatic rather than his normal comic role, together with Santiago Ramos, Alvaro de Luna, and Kiti Manver. The narrative takes place over a nine-year period, from 1937 until 1946, and traces the gradual attrition and disappearance of a group of guerrilla fighters in the mountains of León and Asturias. The opening line of the film, "Bueno, parece que esto se acaba" (Well, it looks like it's all over), is a prelude to the inexorable elimination of these *maquis*. Indeed, in the opening scene, as six men sit around a campfire, shots ring out, and two of the group are killed. Throughout the rest of the film, the remaining *maquis*--Angel, Gildo, Ramiro, and Juanín--struggle to survive as the Civil Guard hunts them down one by one.

As in previous films about the *maquis*, contact with villagers who

---

[29]This final shot is followed by this epilogue which really adds nothing to the movie: "Suso y Amparo tuvieron varios hijos.

Al cabo del tiempo, Juan P. volvió a casa y se quedó a vivir allí.

Suso se marchó y ha puesto una zapatería en Llanes. Juan y Amparo viven de vender leche de sus vacas.

Los tres se ven una vez al año el día de la romería."
(Suso and Amparo had various children. After a while, Juan P. returned home and he stayed there to live. Suso left and has set up a shoe store in Llanes. Juan and Amparo make a living by selling milk from their cows. The three of them see each other once a year on the saint's day excursion).

[30]Regarding the poetic qualities of the film, critics focus on the imagery that Gutiérrez Aragón utilizes. Matías Antolín ("Revolucionarios" 38) states that it is "a film of atmosphere, whispered in images that are extraordinarily suggestive" and García Fernández states that "the grammar of the image is enough to narrate what is not narrated, to say what words do not express" (Historia ilustrada 332). Jesús Ruiz adds that El corazón del bosque is "an eminently poetic film. Poetry that dominates over the anecdote and which is the result of the atmosphere" of the film (33).

The <u>maquis</u> continues the battle: Sánchez Valdés's <u>Luna de lobos</u>, starring Antonio Resines. Courtesy Anola Films, S.A.

support their cause seems essential to their survival. Quite often, however, townspeople, such as the miller, want to have nothing to do with them, since it puts their own lives in danger. This is particularly the case of the priest, Don Manuel, whom the *maquis* kidnap (but later release) because he refused to aid Angel's brother. The guerrillas often attempt to contact family members, who provide them with food or boots, and one of the most important villagers to provide shelter and support for the *maquis* is María. Although the relationship is not as developed as that of Antonio and Juana in *Los días del pasado*, María's love for Ramiro helps him survive. Nevertheless, as in the earlier film, María finds her situation to be almost unbearable. Instead of leaving Asturias as does Juana, María compromises herself: when Angel receives a stomach wound from another ambush, Ramiro seeks María's help only to find her in bed with Sergeant Argüello, the Civil Guard who is hunting the *maquis*. When María later meets again with Ramiro, she explains, "Yo también estaba acorralada, Ramiro. Yo también sabía lo que es el miedo y la soledad" (I was also surrounded, Ramiro. I, too, knew what fear and loneliness are).

The first exchange between María and Ramiro clarifies the title of the film. When she exclaims, "Hueles a monte, Ramiro. Hueles como los lobos" (You smell like the woods, Ramiro. You smell like the wolves), he replies, "¿Y qué soy, María? ¿Qué soy ya más que un lobo?" (And what am I, María? What more am I than a wolf?). Sergeant Argüello also adds to the metaphor as he explains his strategy for capturing the guerrillas: "A un lobo no se le sigue, hay que esperarlo" (You don't follow a wolf, you wait for it). There are frequent night scenes with a full moon, and Ramiro comments, "La luna es el sol de los muertos" (The moon is the sun of the dead). Although this adds to the inexorable fate of these "wolves," a close-up of a wanted poster for Ramiro Luna Robles reveals that the title of the film refers not only to the metaphor and the visual imagery, but also to a play on words with one of the protagonist's surnames.

At the beginning of the film narrative, the *maquis* show a certain generosity and altruism: although they must steal to survive, they pay farmers for their losses, and even decline to take a sheep that is pregnant. In the next temporal segment, corresponding to 1940, they have become more criminal, robbing a bus of passengers, and killing a man in a store who calls them "hijos de puta" (sons of bitches) and reaches for a gun. In an attempt to acquire money with which to bribe their way across the border, they resort to kidnapping Don José, a mine owner. The Civil Guard attempts to ambush the *maquis*, and the slow-motion shots that Sánchez Valdés uses for both this scene and the previously mentioned shooting seem superfluous. After the death of Angel and the Civil Guard begin to close in on Ramiro, finding his cave and nearly discovering him hidden in a stable, his only recourse is to flee. Transformed by a shave, haircut, and suit, Ramiro is able to board the train, and a long shot of the train's departure ends the film.

At the beginning of the film, the narrator states of the guerrilla fighters: "Dejaron los mejores años de sus vidas y una estela imborrable y legendaria en la memoria popular" (They left the best years of their lives, and an indelible and legendary imprint on popular memory). They are never treated as heroes in this film, however. When Ramiro sneaks into the village to visit his father's deathbed, the women there reject his presence. Don José sums up the opinion of the townspeople regarding the *maquis*, saying, "Para unos sois unos simples ladrones y asesinos, y para otros, aunque no lo digan, unos pobres desgraciados que lo único que hacéis es tratar de salvar la vida"

A doomed struggle: Sánchez Valdés's <u>Luna de lobos</u>,   starring Antonio Resines.
Courtesy Anola Films, S.A.

(For some folks, you are simply thieves and assassins, and for others, although they might not come out and say it, you are a bunch of poor devils who are only trying to save your skins). When Ramiro decides to leave, his own self-exile is a recognition that he is an outcast among his own people in his own land: "Esta tierra no tiene perdón; esta tierra es maldita para mí" (This land has no pardon; this land is accursed for me). The exceptional photography by Juan Molina Temboury, with numerous long shots of the beautiful countryside of León and Asturias, and the thematic counterpoint in the music by Luis Mendo and Bernardo Fuster (the drum motif of the Civil Guard contrasts with the accordion motif of the *maquis*) add to the quality of the *Luna de lobos*.

La guerra de los locos (*The War of the Madmen*, 1987) is Manolo Matji's first film as director, and it represents a very auspicious beginning. Insanity has been linked to war in films such as Philippe de Broca's *Le Roi de Coeur* (King of Hearts, 1966), and Matji provides a new twist on this theme in what is one of the finest films on the Spanish Civil War in recent years. The opening caption places the action: "Agosto 1936. La historia que aquí se cuenta sucedió al

Fascist atrocities: Matji's <u>La guerra de los locos</u>, with Juan Luis Galiardo and Alicia Sánchez. Courtesy Manuel Matji and Xaloc, P.C.

comienzo de la Guerra Civil española" (August 1936. The story that is told here occurred at the beginning of the Spanish civil war). The film is indeed loosely based on a historical incident: patients escaped from an insane asylum in Toledo as General Yagüe's troops advanced from the south. The encounter between the "locos" and a group of republican guerrilla fighters led by "el Rubio de la Nava" (the Blond guy from Nava) constitutes the nexus of the film narrative.

In the opening scene of the film, a Nationalist physician, Don Salvador (Juan Luis Galiardo) inquires about "el Rubio" among the refugees fleeing the advancing troops. When Don Salvador and a group of fascist thugs arrive at night in Navagrande, the hometown of "el Rubio," they perpetrate the violence that was a scourge to the civilians in the rear guard: after changing flags at the town hall (a visual image symbolizing the radical change in people's fortunes), they assemble the townsfolk in the plaza at gun point, and the physician personally kills the wife of "el Rubio" in cold blood, ironically fulfilling his earlier admonition to the refugees: "Nadie puede escaparse de la guerra" (No one can escape the war). Rufino (Pedro Díez del Corral) witnesses the atrocity and rejoins the group of guerrilla fighters lead by "el Rubio." In a parallel action, when the

A quixotic battle: Matji's <u>La guerra de los locos</u>, with Alvaro de Luna, Patxi Catalá, Pedro del Corral, and Acmero Mañas. Courtesy Manuel Matji and Xaloc, P.C.

director of the sanitorium leaves, the internees rebel against the nuns that run the facility in his absence. One patient, Angel (José Manuel Cervino), assumes the identity of the director, dressing in a white lab coat. He soon discovers that the authority and power that he coveted carry heavy responsibilities: he is unable to control the unruly patients as they bang their metal plates against the dining room table, and he must resort to using tranquilizers in their food. When the Nationalist soldiers arrive, they requisition the hospital's truck, but Angel, repeating his rebellion against authority, steals the requisitioned truck and escapes with internees Roque (Luis Marín), Serafín (Emilio Laín), and Andrés (Pep Munne). They are only able to travel as far as the gasoline holds out, however. When "el Rubio" (Alvaro de Luna) and his men come upon them, they become suspicious when they see four full cans of gas in the back of the truck, but they welcome the "locos" into their group, since the stolen truck also contains a large supply of arms and ammunition, one of the many ironies of the film narrative. Rufino sees them as victims of society, and welcomes them into the guerrilla group proclaiming, "Para ganar, todos tenemos que arrimar" (In order to win, we all have got to lend a hand). Nevertheless, the attempt to incorporate the "locos" into the guerrilla group proves more difficult than imagined. During rifle training, Serafín accidentally shoots his rifle and grazes the head of one of the *maquis*; when the moment of actual combat arrives, the "locos" quickly retreat and huddle together in fear.

The level of violence escalates when at the end of the battle, the treatment by "el Rubio" of the captured Nationalists echoes the earlier fascist violence: the guerrilla leader summarily kills the local Nationalist leader after a mere reference to a "people's tribunal." In the next guerrilla attack, Angel becomes completely deranged when he learns that Don Salvador, the fascist doctor, has escaped to his hometown of Andones; Angel attributes this to deceit on the part of "el Rubio," and he shoots the guerrilla leader in the leg. The internees follow his lead and turn on their comrades, killing and wounding them. Earlier high-angle point of view shots showing the bald head of "el Rubio" which were intercut with reaction shots of Angel now become clear: Angel now has the opportunity to assume yet another personality of authority and power, and he shaves the center of his head to match the balding Rubio. He thus becomes the anarchist guerrilla leader, imitating his mannerisms and linguistically affirming his new identity: "No soy Angel, soy el Rubio" (I'm not Angel, I'm the Blond). The role playing is superficial, however; Angel does not imitate the idealistic, almost quixotic Rubio who succeeded in founding an agrarian cooperative against all odds; rather he is the guerrilla fighter who takes the violence to its extreme, killing and wounding civilians in his quest for the evil doctor. Just as in the asylum when Angel could not stand the shouting of the internees, the shouting of civilians in the church triggers his command, "Haz que se callen" (Make them shut up) which leads to their massacre by the other "locos" who wield a machine-gun. Matji uses rhythmic montage to represent the parallel actions of the two Rubios in their respective journeys to Andones, where the fascist doctor lives. Angel/Rubio drives the hospital truck now identified with the revolutionary label "UHP" ("Unión de Hermanos Proletarios" or Union of Proletarian Brothers), stopping to figure out a map, while the wounded Rubio is ironically taken in a horse-drawn cart by a country woman to Andones for medical attention precisely by the physician who wants to kill him. When Angel/Rubio arrives in Andones, his revolutionary slogan, "Ya no hay amos" (There are no longer any bosses), subsumes his character into that of the real Rubio. His capture and pending execution by the Nationalists causes the Spanish sense of

Who is insane? Matji's La guerra de los locos, with Emilio Laín, Pep Munné, Luis Marín, José Manuel Cervino, and Joan Potau. Courtesy Manuel Matji and Xaloc, P.C.

personal honor to prevail in the real Rubio, since he must clear his reputation of the atrocities committed by Angel in his name: his only recourse is to surrender to the fascists.

Matji subtly accomplishes a further fusion of the two characters in these final sequences of the film. When Don Salvador announces, "Vamos a fusilarte, Rubio" (We are going to shoot you, Rubio), he is standing next to the wounded Rubio, but he looks off screen toward Angel. When he says that they will return Angel to the insane asylum, a close-up reaction shot of Angel shows his negative reaction to the idea. His lips move as we hear the words "Hijo de puta" (Son of a bitch), but Don Salvador addresses his retort, "No vas a arreglar nada con los insultos" (You won't fix anything with your insults) not to Angel but to "el Rubio," as if the two characters spoke with one voice. After Don Salvador observes the execution of "el Rubio" from the balcony as we hear the firing squad "off," Angel commits his final rebellion against authority as he grabs the guerrilla leader's knife and stabs the evil physician. The fusion of the characters of the leader of the *maquis* and the leader of the internees occurs on another level as well. The guerrilla leader's nickname refers to both a physical characteristic and a place name, but the reference to his hometown of Navagrande is shortened to "la Nava." (*Nava* means "valley" in Spanish, and several towns in Spain use this word in their names). This abbreviation, together with the use of the definite article, creates a phonetic association with the words *la navaja* (the knife or razor) which Matji visually underscores. The first sequence in which "el Rubio" appears in the film begins with a close-up shot of his hands cutting a piece of cheese with his knife. The guerrilla leader later shaves himself in the mirror of the truck and significantly hands the razor to Angel so that he can also shave and feel like a new man. When Angel literally does become a new man, the final step in his transformation into "el Rubio" is accomplished by the razor blade that shaves the top of his head so that he too can be bald. When "el Rubio" turns himself in to the Nationalists in order to save his honor, Matji again uses a close-up as we see the guerrilla leader's hand place his knife on the Major's desk. When Angel/Rubio uses this same knife to kill Don Salvador, the physician's last word is "Rubio," as if this final act of vengeance totally fused the two characters. The final image of the film is a close-up still of the knife; instead of "el Rubio de la Nava," he might be called "el Rubio de la navaja" (the Blond guy with the knife).

Matji weaves the theme of insanity throughout the film narrative. Rufino suggests that the "locos" join the *maquis*, but his comrades think that he has lost his senses. Nevertheless, "el Rubio" decides to have the *maquis* masquerade as "locos" in order to travel through enemy lines with impunity. When Serafín accidentally wounds a *maquis*, "el Rubio" shouts "Are you crazy?" at him. The guerrilla leader's decision to turn himself in causes the insanity theme to resurface, as both the woman who shelters him and Don Salvador react saying, "Estás loco" (You're crazy). "El Rubio" sees his own death as a sacrifice for a cause that will eventually triumph, as he tells Don Salvador, "Si yo muero, no significa nada. Hay miles, millones de hombres como yo en el mundo. ¿Podrás matarnos a todos? Ellos llevan la vida; son la vida" (If I die, it doesn't mean anything. There are thousands, millions of men like me in the world. Will you be able to kill all of us? They carry life inside them; they are life). Matji shoots this declaration by "el Rubio" in a close-up two shot, with "el Rubio" leaning on his elbow and looking up at Don Salvador, who is inclined over him. For his enemy, however, the very cause that "el

Rubio" fights for is a manifestation of insanity: "Nunca estuvistes en tus cabales. Mira que pretender poner el mundo patas arriba" (You never had all your marbles. Imagine, trying to turn the world upside down). Before this response, Don Salvador pulls away from "el Rubio," and we see him in a low-angle shot. Although he continues to look straight down at the wounded *maquis*, when he pronounces the word "estuvistes", his eyes look up as if he were including Angel as well. ("Estuvistes" may be more than a subconscious slip of the tongue, since it represents almost a blend between the gramatically correct singular form, "estuviste," and the plural form "estuvisteis"). Who, then, in the film are the true "locos"? Perhaps the greatest irony of all occurs when the Nationalist captain arrives at the asylum and proclaims, "Lo único que temo en el mundo es la locura" (The only thing in the world that I'm afraid of is insanity).

La guerra de los locos is one of the best films about the civil war: it weaves a tight narrative with a rich layering of themes, and it transcends the propagandistic element that is so easy to include in cinema dealing with this subject. Indeed, Matji seems aware of the dangers of this phenomenon as we see the reaction of the woman who shelters "el Rubio" to his decision to turn himself in: "Si ganan ellos, dirán lo que quieran, contarán la guerra a su modo; y si al contrario, ¿qué te importa?" (If they win, they'll say what ever they want to say, they'll tell their version of the war; if the opposite happens, what does it matter to you?). Although the Franco regime did tell its official version of the conflict for many years, perhaps the contrary would have been true of a Republican victory. Although the director believes that "underneath any war there is nothing but a struggle for power" (Heredero, "La guerra" 46), the fact Matji started working on the script in 1974 but was unable to produce the film until 1987 meant that the script dealt much more with the theme of obsession with power. Questions of power, insanity, identity, and the Spanish Civil War make this a gripping film that will surely stand out for years to come.

The films that deal with the theme of the *maquis* in a secondary fashion are *Kargus* (Kargus), *Pim, pam, pum, fuego* (Bang, Bang, You're Dead), *Si te dicen que caí* (If They Tell You That I Fell), and *El espíritu de la colmena* (The Spirit of the Beehive). The first of these productions, *Kargus*, is a film from 1981 by two young directors, Juan Miñón and Miguel Angel Trujillo. The movie consists of a series of sketches that are bound together by the fact that they all represent short stories written by a character named Juan who hopes to present them to a rich, mysterious patron named J. R. H. Kargus, who is soon to arrive in Madrid (according to Juan's friend Eva). The first of these sketches deals with the theme of the *maquis*, but in a very tentative and unsatisfactory fashion. This narrative segment of the movie begins at a rural train station with a steam-engine locomotive ready to pull out. Two *maquis* furtively kill a Nationalist guard in order to get on board, and they are able to escape. Later, while walking through a forest, a woman armed with a pistol surprises them, threatening to kill them. Ironically, she confesses that she needs their help, and says, "Quiero pasar al otro lado" (I want to cross over), meaning to go to France. Contradictory to her statement of needing help, the woman serves as guide when the three continue their journey. When they reach a small boat and they set out to sea, a patrol boat discovers them and begins to attack. The directors intercut shots of the patrol boat shooting at the *maquis* together with the amorphous forms of a Gestalt test in order to bring this narrative segment to a close: Juan, on a couch in a psychiatrist's office, sees dead bodies in the Gestalt form. In itself, this sketch is not well developed enough to present a clear theme. However, in conjunction with the other sketches, which bring us chronologically up to the death of the "caudillo," it offers a clear political message regarding the struggle against a repressive regime, or at least the attempt to cope with one's limitations within the context of political, cultural, and sexual repression.

Pim, pam, pum, fuego (Bang, Bang, You're Dead) is a film from 1975 directed by Pedro Olea and starring Concha Velasco as Paca, a show-girl who has great difficulty finding employment, José María Flotats as Luis, the *maquis* who befriends Paca, and Fernando Fernán Gómez as Julio, the black marketeer who loves the show-girl. The love triangle of these characters is set against the poverty and squalor of post-war Madrid. Paca first meets Luis on a train travelling to the capital, and she hides him in the lavatory from inspectors who are checking the documentation of all passengers. Once they arrive in the capital, the *maquis*'s lack of documentation prohibits him from obtaining lodging at a boarding house, so he follows Paca home. Once again she saves him by allowing him to stay at her apartment with her father, a Republican who is bed-ridden due to a wound suffered in a bombing attack in 1938. Luis has abandoned the *maquis* because he realized that it was a futile fight; as he explains to Paca, "Nos estaban cazando como conejos" (They were hunting us down like rabbits). His only hope now is to escape to France, so he must wait in Madrid until friends can obtain false documents for him. During his wait, he and Paca fall in love, but the suspense builds as the police find and destroy the printing press that his friends had used to print documents, and as the powerful and possessive Julio discovers a tell-tale sign (a smoldering cigarette butt) that signals the presence of a clandestine rival. The sudden arrival of documents and a train ticket for Luis seem too good to be true, and indeed they are. We discover through the close-up of a headline of an article in the *ABC* newspaper, "Captura y muerte de un *maquis*" (Capture and death of a *maquis*), that Julio had arranged things to eliminate Luis. Julio's final sentence in the film, "Conmigo no se juega, y tú has jugado" (You don't play arouind with me, and you did) precedes his cold-blooded homicide of the show-girl. Clearly, the *maquis* theme is merely a tangential aspect of *Pim, pam pum, fuego*. Indeed, the *maquis* as such (in the role of guerrilla fighter) is not even developed at all. Instead, the focus is on the urban environment of post-war Spain, and the political aspect of the film is channelled through the inter- personal relationships (the triangle) of the three main characters. The film was released shortly before Franco's death, a fact that undoubtedly had an impact on the amount of socio-political criticism in the film.[31]

Si te dicen que caí, directed by Vicente Aranda (1989) is the cinematographic version of the novel by Juan Marsé. The *maquis* in this film are urban guerrillas who do not suffer the privations of their rural counterparts. They eat sumptuous paellas at home or enjoy cognac and cigars at a bar. A close-up of the wife of a *maquis* cutting a melon in half, followed by the wife and her husband smelling how good it is, indicates the companionship and plenty that these guerrilla fighters enjoy.

Ideological questions among the m*aquis* almost give rise to squabbling, but they are set aside to get to the heart of the matter. Palau (Lluís Homar) says, "No me canso de repetirlo. Nuestra primera obligación es vaciarles el bolsillo" (I don't get tired of repeating it. Our first obligation is to empty their pockets). Indeed

---

[31]The other aspect of social criticism in the film falls under the category of the misery of post-war Spain (see Chapter 5).

he doesn't tire of it, since in a later scene in a bar, he tells the other *maquis*, "Si quieres acabar con los fachas, quítales la cartera" (If you want to get rid of the fascists, take their wallet away from them), and in a final sequence in the present (the movie theater in the background when Luis and Palau meet is showing Martin Scorsese's *Last Temptation of Christ*, from 1989), the elderly Palau exclaims, "Mientras los ricos tengan dinero, yo me dedicaré a quitárselo" (As long as the rich have money, I will dedicate myself to taking it away from them). Although during the first meeting of the *maquis*, one of them responds, "Que no somos atracadores, tú" (We're not robbers), it appears that they truly are little more than that. Aside from a brief shot showing a bomb blowing the doors off of a bank, and a *maquis* throwing propaganda pamphlets from the rooftop of a building, the main activity of the *maquis* is to rob fascists in brothels. Their bursting into rooms to interrupt the activities of the fascists with their whore contributes to the portrayal of moral decadence of the period. When one of the clients turns out to be merely a plumber, the *maquis* give him money back so that no one will say that they abandon workers, but it seems to be a weak attempt at solidarity.

The wanton violence of the members of the losing side of the civil war appears in two scenes. In a flashback to the beginning of the war, Republican soldiers drag a fifty year old man to the front of an automobile in which Marcos (Antonio Banderas) and Aurora Nin (Victoria Abril) are seated. Although the man begs on his knees for Aurora to tell them that they have the wrong person, that they must be after his son, Conrado, one of the soldiers shoots him in the back of his head with his pistol. When Aurora shouts in horror that he was not Conrado, the soldier glibly replies, "Tan hijo de puta será éste como el otro" (He's probably as much of a son of a bitch as the other guy). Just as the lack of rational and legal justification makes this a crime, the later killing of the prostitute Menchu by the *maquis* is also a crime without solid justification, and Palau even backs out for that reason. It is especially ironic that the kidnapping and killing of Menchu because she is the lover of a rich black marketeer contradicts earlier convictions regarding prostitutes as expressed in street banners of the Republic which proclaim "Libertario de la prostitución" (Defender of the freedom of prostitution). Unlike other Spanish films that deal with the subject, *Si te dicen que caí* demythifies the *maquis*, and portrays him as one of the many negative elements of post-war Spain.

El espíritu de la colmena (The Spirit of the Beehive), a film from 1973 by Víctor Erice, is perhaps the best movie in the history of Spanish cinema. The film is the winner of various awards, including the Golden Shell (first place) at the 1973 San Sebastián Film Festival, and awards in Chicago and London. Although it was not a huge box-office success in Spain, surveys of Spanish film critics consistently rank it as number one because of its aesthetic qualities. The film stars Fernando Fernán Gómez as Fernando, Teresa Gimpera as his wife Teresa, and two child actresses who portray their children: Isabel Tellería as Isabel, and Ana Torrent, who gives a majestic performance in her acting debut as Ana. The epigraph of the film, "Erase una vez" (Once upon a time) followed by the caption, "Un lugar de la meseta castellana hacia 1940" (A place on the Castilian plateau around 1940) manifests the basic interplay between myth and history, fiction and reality in the film: although the caption provides spatial and temporal referents that suggest historical reality (north-central Spain immediately following the end of the Civil War), the linguistic mode of the epigraph is that of the fairy tale. This interplay continues as the town crier announces the arrival of a new film, James Whale's *Frankenstein*, and a master of ceremonies warns people not to take it very seriously. Ana, however, is too young either to heed such advice or to comprehend the film; that night in bed, she inquires of her older sister, "Por qué el monstruo mata a la niña y por qué luego le matan a él?" (Why does the monster kill the little girl, and why do they then kill him?). Although Isabel first responds by saying "Porque en el cine todo es mentira" (Because everything is a lie in the movies)--Erice adds a touch of irony to the fiction/reality dichotomy--she then tells Ana that the monster is really a spirit who lives in an abandoned house outside of town, and that you can communicate with him by closing your eyes and calling out, "Soy Ana, soy Ana" (I am Ana, I am Ana).

Ana's father is a bee-keeper and an intellectual who leads an irregular and solitary existence. Amidst his large library, he spends nights writing a book about bees. Fernando's voice "off" narrates his work in a tone that emphasizes the enigmatic element of the hive. Indeed, Erice has stated that the very title of the film attempts to capture the enigmatic aspects of life, since the title is "a term invented by Maurice Maeterlinck in his book *The Life of Bees* in order to describe this all-powerful, enigmatic, and paradoxical spirit that bees always obey, and that man's ratiocination has never been able to understand" and for that reason it synthesizes "the great mystery of nature . . . that you attempt to explain by means of myth--something that attempts to transcend the mystery of things" (Rubio "Victor Erice" 3-4).

Fernando's intellectual and political background is manifest in a photograph of a young Fernando together with Miguel de Unamuno, the famous rector of the University of Salamanca. (Unamuno, although both a paradoxical and a controversial figure, is generally viewed as a supporter of the Republic.) The intellectual affinity with this great figure is also manifest in the origami that Fernando practices, and for which Unamuno was famous. The political inclination of the family is also manifest in a letter that Teresa writes, also in her voice "off": "Las noticias que recibimos de fuera son tan pocas y tan confusas . . . . Aunque me doy cuenta de que ya nada puede hacer volver aquellas horas felices que pasamos juntos, pido a Dios que me conceda la alegría de volver a encontrarte. Se lo he pedido siempre, desde que nos separamos, incluso en medio de la guerra. Y se lo sigo pidiendo ahora, en este rincón donde Fernando, las niñas y yo tratamos de sobrevivir" (We receive little news from outside, and it is very confusing . . . . Although I realize that nothing can make those happy hours that we spent together return, I pray to God that he concede me the joy of finding you again. I have always asked it of Him, ever since we were separated, even in the middle of the war. And I keep on asking Him now, in this remote corner where Fernando, the girls, and I are trying to survive). A close-up of an envelope of a second letter that she writes shows the destination to be in care of the Red Cross in Nice; the addressee, then, is an exiled Republican, and the isolation, lack of communication, and lost happiness to which she refers can only mean that the family pertains to the vanquished side. The piano music that Teresa plays, the "Zorongo gitano" by the martyred Republican poet García Lorca, reaffirms this identity. The scene in which she plays the piano includes a montage of photographs of herself and her husband as young adults, and Ana reads the inscription to Fernando on one of Teresa's photographs. The discordant notes of the untuned piano underscore the break between the happiness of their pre-war existence and the lack of harmony--on both a personal and a political level--of their present life.

The film draws a parallel between the father and the Frankenstein

A child's innocence calls into the night: Erice's <u>El espíritu de la colmena</u>, starring Ana Torrent. Courtesy Elías Querejeta, P.C.

figure on various occasions. Riley points out that the first association between the two is based on a montage between the master of ceremonies announcing the Frankenstein film and the close-up of Fernando, "grotesque in his beekeeper's garb" (492). Later, when the girls are in bed, Isabel instructs Ana to call the monster and the footsteps that we hear lead us momentarily to believe that her wish is coming true, but a cut to Fernando pacing back and forth--his "nocturnal comings and goings" are the basis of complaints by Milagros (Laly Soldevila), the maid--formulates another association between the father and the monster. As Fernando sits down in the living room to read the paper, we hear the sound track of the *Frankenstein* movie coming through the window, and a character tells Dr. Frankenstein to sit down. In a dream sequence during Ana's escape, the Frankenstein monster that appears to Ana physically resembles Fernando, thus underscoring the relationship in the girl's subconscious mind. Inasmuch as we identify the Frankenstein monster with a paradigm (the Prometheus myth in which he provides access to the knowledge and power reserved to God),[32] the father also reflects this paradigm when he gives the girls a lesson on poison mushrooms in the forest. Nevertheless, there is another figure who competes with Fernando in this regard. One day, a wounded *maquis* jumps from the train that is passing through town, and he takes refuge in the abandoned house outside of town. Ana, seeking the spirit of Frankenstein there, encounters the fugitive. Just as Mary in the Whale classic offers flowers to the monster, Ana offers him an apple, which Hernández Esteve (227) identifies as an emblematic element that symbolizes "the assimilation of exterior reality and evoked reality," that is to say, the fusion of Ana's fantasy world with the historical reality. After a fade out, Ana brings him more food and some of her father's clothing. The *maquis* finds Fernando's pocket watch in one of the pockets, and entertains Ana with a sleight of hand trick, making it disappear. In a further gesture of friendship, Ana ties his shoe. Erice narrates the fate of the *maquis* by means of what Angel Camiña terms a perfect example of ellipsis in the film: "in a brief shot, you see and you hear shots in the night, and in the next shot, now in the daytime, you see the sign "Everything For the Fatherland" [the official slogan of the Civil Guard]. No other explanation is needed; everything has already been said regarding what happened to the fugitive" (121). A Civil Guard leads Fernando to identify the body and reclaim his belongings. The pocket watch that the captain of the Civil Guards winds is an important metaphorical object shared by both men, and Fernando's recovery of his watch symbolizes a shift in his political stance. Emmanuel Larraz notes that Fernando's beautiful house and very cordial relations with the Civil Guard "place him clearly on the side of the victors" (226). The silent breakfast during which Fernando opens his pocket watch and looks at Ana marks an important moment in the subtle competition between the two "Frankensteins" for Ana's affection. Her later return to the abandoned house in search of her "friend" and her subsequent fleeing from Fernando, as well as her final attempts to communicate with the spirit, all represent a rejection of her father, who if once represented freedom and intellect, now represents intolerance and hollowness.   Another parallelism in the film correlates the *maquis* with the Frankenstein monster, but in the positive sense of representing

---

[32]See Hernández Esteve, "Teoría" 215. See also Gérard Lenne, Le cinéma fantastique et ses mythologies.

the intangibles that both the "mad" scientist and the ingenuous child seek.   This parallelism   has to do with the spatial location of the *maquis*'s cadaver: the movie theater where the Frankenstein film was shown. Camiña notes that this creates a metaphorical relationship with "that other monster, created by men in the post-war era, who is abstract and evil, who is the enemy of the fatherland, who is at times a red, at times a Jew, or other times a Mason" (75). In *El espíritu de la colmena*, the *maquis* appears only briefly, but like all of the other elements of the film, is imbued with rich connotative values that contribute to the quality of this superb cinematographic work.

Chapter 5

Misery and Oppression

The post-war years were difficult in most parts of Spain. In addition to the continuation of the armed conflict on the part of the maquis, the civilian population suffered food shortages; indeed, these years were known as the "years of hunger."[33] Certain sectors of the population, however, felt the deprivation much less than others. In spite of the fact that during the first year in which sanctions were applied (beginning in September of 1940) nearly 5,000 black marketeers were imprisoned and even capital punishment was applied in the most severe cases, the *estraperlo*, as it was known, continued to flourish to the point that about one-third of the country's grain production ended up on the black market.[34] The 1940's was also a period of oppression for those who lost the conflict, as Franco imposed his political and religious views on all of Spanish society. Recent films that portray the material dichotomy in Spanish post-war society--the misery and the lucrative underground of the black market, as well as the oppressive political and religious climate of the period include: Erice's *El espíritu de la colmena* (The Spirit of the Beehive, 1973), Olea's *Pim, pam, pum, fuego* (Bang, Bang, You're Dead, 1975), Martín's *No quiero perder la honra* (I Don't Want to Lose My Reputation, 1975), Gutiérrez Aragón's *Demonios en el jardín* (Demons in the Garden, 1982), Camus's *La colmena* (The Hive, 1982), García Sánchez's *La corte del faraón* (The Pharaoh's Court, 1985), Trueba's *El año de las luces* (The Year of Lights, 1986), and Aranda's *Si te dicen que caí* (If They Tell You That I Fell, 1989).

---

[33] For details on this period, see Vizcaino Casas, Fernando. <u>La España de la posguerra</u> and Rafael Abella, <u>Por el Imperio hacia Dios: Crónica de una posguerra (1939-1955)</u>.

[34] The term <u>estraperlo</u> originated with a scandal involving individuals named Strauss and Perlo during the Republican government of Lerroux; it came to refer to blackmarketeering, especially in food. For more information about the black market, see Sueiro and Díaz Nosty, 21-40.

In addition to manifesting the *maquis* theme, Víctor Erice's *El espíritu de la colmena* captures the atmosphere of misery during the early 1940's in a small town in Castile: the opening sequence shows a marker with the town's name, Hoyuelos, together with the yoke and arrow symbol of the Falange, the political party that dominated postwar Spain. Erice initially intended to do a film about the Frankenstein monster, and this element provides an important narrative level on top of the merely historical. The director has stated that rather than presenting a story about the postwar, he has tried to capture the cadence and moral climate of the period (Rubio "Victor Erice" 3). However, although the mythical plane of the film ultimately transcends narrow temporal boundaries, the narrative is deeply rooted in a concrete chronological time frame. Indeed, the temporal rhythm of the film is one of its chief aesthetic elements; Angel Camiña points out that the slow rhythm, and length of shots "coincides with 'children's time,' the 'time of a small country town,' and the 'time of the post-war period' in which nothing seemed to happen" (122). The film has what critic Enrique Aberich calls "a powerful ability to describe the oppressive, sickly, and perennially painful atmosphere" of the post-war period (25). A key scene in which this atmosphere is manifest is the class in which the teacher tries to inculcate the children with certain values. For a biology lesson, the teacher uses a mannequin, "Don José," to teach the children body parts. To the repeated questions of the teacher, "¿Qué le falta?" (What is he missing?), the children respond with "the heart," "the lungs," "the stomach," until Ana, with help from a whisper from her older sister Isabel, has to supply the mannequin with eyes. For Vicente Hernández Esteve, besides the importance of sight, this sequence shows how elements of the exterior world--"order, repression, and isolation," are imposed on the infantile world, together with "a new model of conduct, the learning of Knowledge," which is coupled with Authority and Well-being, a model that Isabel accepts, but Ana does not (223). Camiña also points out that visually, it is obvious that "poor Don José" is also missing his sexual organs, and as such, is a "reflection of the absolute taboo"

regarding sexual education in that period (121).[35]   The classroom
scene also includes recitation of verses by the Galician poet Rosalía de
Castro, and Hopewell points out that the translation of her poetry from
Galician to Castilian is another example of cultural repression (207).
This work by Rosalía de Castro, Poem XIII from *Follas novas* (*New
Leaves*), underscores many of the themes in the film: the desire for the
unknown and the ineffable ("Only thirst, a thirst / for something that
is killing me"), the oppressive atmosphere ("Air, I need air!"), and a
pessimistic attitude toward a world wrought with danger ("I'm going
to fall where / whoever falls can never get up").   The portrait of
Franco on the classroom wall, and the drawing of the Virgin on the
blackboard underscore the political and religious aspects of
underpinnings of the educational system and Spanish society as a whole
in the 1940's.

The oppressive climate of the period appears most overtly in the
theme of isolation. Indeed, for Emmanuel Larraz, this film shows
"how a totalitarian system imposes isolation among human beings"
(226). Jaime Genover points out that the characters are isolated "as if
they were in each one of the cubicle of the beehive that the title alludes
to," and he notes that this implies a metaphorical reading regarding the
post-war period (25). Indeed, the hexagonal-shaped window panes in
the house provide a visual metonymy for the house-beehive concept,
and Higgenbotham notes that "color also contributes to the hive
metaphor," because Luis Cuadrado shot the interior scenes through a
yellow filter (117). Molina Foix indicates the importance of lighting
in the film, saying that "the light that gives character to *El espíritu de
la colmena* is a filtered, "censored" light that dominates the entire film
and acts as a leit-motiv" ("La guerra" 114).   The bee-keeper's
description of the atmosphere of the hive also underscores the concepts
of futility and nihilism: "the diverse and incessant activity of the
multitude, the cruel and useless effort, the coming and going with
fervent ardor . . . the very repose of death . . . (Erice and Fernández
Santos 58, 60). Fernando's task of writing seems to reflect the very
activity that he is describing: his assiduous observations, feverish
writing, and nocturnal pacing while laboring on a composition which

---

[35] For details on this phenomenon, see L. Alonso Tejada, La represión sexual en
la España de Franco.   See also C. Martín Gaite, Usos amorosos de la postguerra
española.

seems useless.

The dynamics between Fernando and his wife also constitute part of the negative atmosphere in the film. Their relationship--or lack of relationship--is most evident in the absence of communication between the two characters. After a night's work on his book, Fernando goes to bed. As Teresa lies awake, we see the shadow of Fernando projected on the wall behind the bed as he undresses, connotating a lack of substance in the husband, and further relating him to the monster, since Isabel had told Ana that he was a spirit with no body. When he lies beside Teresa, there is no sign of affection between man and wife: although she is awake, they do not exchange words. Instead, she looks toward the window, and we hear the whistle of a train in the distance. In an earlier sequence, Teresa had ridden her bicycle to the train station to deliver her letter to her exiled friend or lover. For Teresa, the train symbolizes a link with and a longing for the happiness provided by the other. The sound effect of the train whistle takes on a primary importance in the film in the closing scene: Ana, on the balcony with her eyes closed, summons the spirit, and we hear the train whistle, which symbolizes a beckoning from the outside world where perhaps a better life is possible.[36] This world is connected to the mysterious world of the spirit, and is not without danger. When the children listen to the train tracks for the oncoming train, Ana is mesmerized with this element of mystery and does not pull back from danger until the last second. Of course, we also directly associate the maquis with the train, since he arrived in town after jumping from a box-car.

The parents attempt--in vain, it seems--to have contact with this outside world. Fernando tries to listen to a ham radio, which is a constant symbol in Spanish films that portray this period of the attempt to overcome censorship and repression. Teresa writes to a mysterious man named Job, admitting that the little news that they receive from the outside is confused. The voice-over of Teresa as she sits at her desk writing the letter offers a grim view of the times based on recurring motifs of death, destruction, and solitude:

> Salvo las paredes, apenas queda nada de la casa que tú
> conociste. . . . Cuando miro mi alrededor y descubro tantas

---

[36]Molina Foix cites this scene as an example of the "potentiation of the desired" in which the border between fiction and reality becomes blurred ("La guerra" 117).

ausencias, tantas cosas destruídas y al mismo tiempo tanta
tristeza, algo me dice que quizá con ella se fue nuestra
capacidad de sentir la vida.

(Except for the walls, there is hardly anything left of the house that you
knew. . . . When I look around me and I discover so many absences,
so many things that have been destroyed, and at the same time, so
much sadness, something tells me that perhaps with all that our
capacity for feeling life has left us). After her second attempt to write
a letter, she throws it into the fire in frustration, and a close-up of the
envelope being devoured by flames shows that it was destined to Nice
in care of the Red Cross, thus connoting that the man is a Republican
exile. Although the fact that Teresa burns the letter symbolizes that she
has given up hope, that the mysterious man to whom she writes is
ostensibly dead, this death provides new hope for her relationship with
Fernando, since only now do we see her gesture of tenderness toward
him which attempts to break through the wall that had separated them:
she goes to Fernando who is asleep at his desk, removes his glasses,
and covers him with a blanket.

The entire atmosphere of the film is imbued with death: Ana
cannot comprehend the death of little Mary at the hands of the
Frankenstein monster; Ana's search for the monster/spirit manifests a
life/death dichotomy; Isabel tries to strangle their pet cat, and she later
feigns death and frightens her younger sister. Fernando gives a lesson
on poisonous mushrooms to his daughters; and there is the death of the
maquis, the wounded man to whom only the innocent Ana would offer
shelter and solace. E. C. Forster points out that their game of jumping
over the bonfire--with the freeze-frame of Isabel in mid-air surrounded
by flames--also links them to the idea of spirits, since there is a
conceptual link (despite the wintry scenery) with the bonfires of Saint
John's day in Spain (494). Furthermore, religion seems linked with
death in several montage sequences. Aside from the bedside miniature
of the Virgin that is shown preceding the girls' discussions of the
monster, a painting of St. Jerome that includes a prominent skull
appears in three montage sequences: after Ana paints her lips with
blood, after Isabel tries to strangle their cat, and as the camera cranes
back and up from a close-up of the painting, we hear Isabel's scream
"off," which is the beginning of the sequence in which the older sister
pretends that she is dead in order to frighten Ana.

El espíritu de la colmena was beautifully photographed by Luis

Cuadrado, and Hopewell notes that the lighting was consciously modelled on Dutch paintings by Vermeer and Rembrandt (208). In addition to many scenes shot in chiaroscuro, Erice often uses long fade-outs as a means of ellipsis which adds to the sense of mystery in the film. In addition, the film's musical score by Luis de Pablo contributes to what Genover calls "the totally musical structure of the film" (25). All in all, this haunting movie represents an important turning point in the development of Spanish film, opening new avenues of cinematographic expression to later directors. Even after the important resurgence in Spanish film during the past fifteen years, it remains one of the best in the history of Spanish cinema, and was voted best film on more than one occasion.

Post-war Madrid is the setting for Pedro Olea's 1975 film, *Pim, pam, pum, fuego* (Bang, Bang, You're Dead). The misery of the period first becomes manifest in references to food. When Paca initially meets Luis, the maquis, on the train, she is impressed that he is eating white bread which he brought with him from the countryside; although those living on farms may have had enough to eat, food was often lacking in the large cities, and this shortage is manifest in the scene in which women in Paca's apartment house in Madrid fight over chick-peas and ration booklets. A later market scene includes the news that five individuals were apprehended for selling horse meat, and women complain about the quality of the lentils that are for sale. Food also is an important element in the confrontation between the powerful and the powerless and the shady world of blackmarketeering, which is represented by Julio (Fernando Fernán Gómez). Although Paca is initially able to find employment as a teacher in a dance academy, and then as a cabaret dancer and singer, Julio is able to manipulate her when he bribes the cabaret owner to fire Paca. The bribe takes the form of coffee, sugar, and butter, thus symbolizing the incredible importance of food in post-war society--it was even more valuable than money. Julio then sets her up as a dancer in the more prestigious Martín Theater. Other symbols of Julio's power--his Mercedes automobile, the new apartment that he buys for Paca--signify not only his corruption and wealth, but his dominance over the show-girl: he transports her in the car, and he sexually violates her in the apartment. Also, Julio's cynicism and scheming appear throughout the film. In an early dialogue in his car, Paca accuses him of being involved in "dirty business," to which he replies, "¿Es que hay alguno limpio hoy en día?" (Is there anything clean these days?). When Julio shows her the new apartment, his complete dominance over her becomes clear as he confesses that he had her fired from the cabaret job, and he says, "Paca, si es necesario sabes que puedo hacer que te echen también de ese gallinero donde vives ahora" (Paca, if need be, you know that I can also make them throw you out of that chicken pen where you're living now). Paca realizes that she is powerless, but does not capitulate without protest. As she lifts her skirt and lies on the floor, she spits at Julio and disdainfully exclaims, "Anda cerdo, toma" (Go ahead, pig). Julio's cynicism, prevails, however, as he says, "¿Te das cuenta? Eres tú quien me está pidiendo" (You see? It's you that's asking me). The zoom-in of Paca moaning and covering her mouth visually represents her despair and lack of power. Her greatest humiliation at the hands of Julio, however, occurs at the end of the film. The black-marketeer takes her to a tavern, and after ordering chicken, he makes the sexually-charged statement, "No me gusta el muslo" (I don't like the thigh), and he gives the chicken to a low-life character at the next table. Although Paca protests, he physically threatens her, and she must endure his humiliation. Her final abasement occurs in his Mercedes: Julio drives to a deserted spot in the country in order to give Paca the newspaper which tells of the capture and death of her lover, Luis. Paca's realization of Julio's falsity and scheming is of no avail, since she is utterly powerless. Her sobbing as he pulls out his pistol and kills her parallels the rape scene in the apartment. The game alluded to in the title, *Pim, pam, pum, fuego*, ends with her fatal shooting.

In addition to the portrayal of the corruption and ruthlessness of the blackmarketeer, the film portrays other elements of repression of the post-war period. The wounded Republican grandfather listens to Radio London with earphones in his bed in order to obtain uncensored news. A theater censor later chides Paca about her cowgirl review costume, calling it "provocative" and "filthy." This film, which was released the year of Franco's death, represents a transitional phase in Spanish cinematic history regarding treatment of the post-war period. José Enrique Monterde points out that in the wake of films that allude to the past based in the present, *El amor del capitán Brando* (Captain Brando's Love) and *Jo, papá* (Gosh, Dad), *Pim, pam, pum, fuego* constitutes the "first reconstruction of the past" (11). As such, it was considered a politically charged film at the time of its release; when reviewing the 1975 edition of the San Sebastián Film Festival, Santiago de Benito called *Pim, pam, pum, fuego* "one of the most political films that Spanish cinema has made" (20).

Another film from 1975 that also attempts to capture the atmosphere of misery of the 1940's is Eugenio Martín's *No quiero perder la honra* (I Don't Want to Lose My Reputation). The film stars two important actors, José Sacristán as Miguel and Angela Molina as Isabel, and they are supported by other noted actors such as Laly Soldevila and Rafaela Aparicio. Martín sets the atmosphere of the period by using documentary footage during the credits, a technique which is common to many of the films in this study. Another key element to capturing this atmosphere is the sound track, which contains many popular songs of the 1940's: "Carita de Angel," "Rasca-yu," "Tico-Tico," and "La gallina papanatas," to name just a few. Although the narrative begins with soldiers fighting in battle, it is merely a reenactment of the Civil War, and director Martín does nothing to further develop the film-within-a-film theme, except to add a caption ("Madrid, en los difíciles años 40, cuando había que ganarse el pan en los oficios más insólitos" [Madrid, during the difficult '40's, when you had to earn your daily bread in the most unusual jobs) that turns out to be ironic, since the visual image that follows is a line of actors waiting to receive their salary. The "unusual job" of the protagonist, Miguel, is not acting however; he is a pimp who cannot make a living because of the incompetent prostitutes working for him, who not only do not charge soldiers who have tricked them into thinking that they are going off to fight the "reds," but, in a comic twist, the girls even give money to their soldier-clients. On the advice of Eugenio, Miguel decides to get an innocent country girl to liven up his business. Miguel is able to trick the orphaned Isabel into thinking that he is her cousin, and he brings her to Madrid. Her effect on business is the opposite of what he had intended, however, since, as the title of the film implies, the girl does not want to lose her honor. Miguel's disingenuous comment is "Ay, cómo está España. ¿Y para eso hemos hecho una guerra?" (What is Spain coming to? And we waged a war for this?). He then finds her employment in a cabaret review, but he falls in love with the girl. After legal difficulties (Miguel spends a few days in jail and has his head shaved for running a brothel), they decide not to see each other any more. Miguel now dedicates himself to black-market activities with Eugenio, but finally decides to seek out Isabel in her small town in order to live happily ever after.

The film suffers from cheap humor: many of the jokes are terrible, and the slapstick visual elements (José Sacristán falling into a fountain, etc.) are overdone. In addition, the musical element of the film often seems incredibly out of place, as the songs do not seem to correspond at all to the narrative that they are supposedly complementing. The talent of the cast was totally wasted on this film.

Demonios en el jardín (Demons in the Garden), the 1982 film directed by Manuel Gutiérrez Aragón, portrays a family in a small town in northern Spain during the post-war period. The director has noted in his conversations with Augusto M. Torres that there is a strong autobiographical element in the film, with elements such as the sick child and the store run by the grandmother ("In a way, I'm talking about my family, and that boy is me", 153). Nevertheless, the film in many ways is a portrait of an entire generation, since, as the director noted, after the film's projection at the film festival in San Sebastián, many people from the audience admitted to him that they saw their own lives in the film, because they were children during the 1940's (Torreiro 46). Gutiérrez Aragón organized a brilliant cast for the film: Encarna Pasó as Gloria, the dominating grandmother who runs the family store called "El jardín"; Eusebio Lázaro and Imanol Arias as Oscar and Juan, her feuding sons; Angela Molina as Angela, Juan's lover; Ana Belén as Ana, Oscar's wife; and the child actor Alvaro Sánchez-Prieto as Juanito. The film won critical acclaim (the International Critics' Grand Prize at the 1982 San Sebastián Film Festival; five awards, including Best Picture, by the New York Film Critics Association; and the Donatello René Clair Prize to the Best European Film of 1983) and was a success at the box office, being the sixth largest grossing Spanish film of the year.[37]

The opening scenes provide the spatial and temporal setting for the narrative: the green countryside and the roadside sign "Torre del Valle" with its accompanying Falangist symbol of the yoke and arrows, together with the graffito "Vivan los quintos del '42" transport us to northern Spain in the years following the civil war. The *cainismo* theme surfaces early in the film as Oscar confronts his

---

[37]In Spain, critical acclaim was not unanimous; several critics feel that the film is "irregular": both Diego Galán ("Retrato" 41) and Enrique Alberich ("Demonios" 57) consider that the film is marred by contradictory aesthetic tendencies.

brother Juan about selling a bull. Oscar, who wants to be rid of the animal, says, "A ese toro le voy a hacer chuletas" (I'm going to make chops out of that bull), in response to which, Juan, who favors keeping the animal, grabs Oscar's nose. This gesture constitutes an element of aesthetic incongruity in the film as we see a number of dramatic situations take unjustified comic turns. The wedding between Oscar and Ana proceeds, and the bull, which has broken loose, enters the church, causing a great commotion. The bull is a symbol of virility which the early narrative clearly associates with Juan; the symbolic gesture of it entering the church and disrupting his brother's wedding foreshadows later narrative information that Juan has had an affair with the bride. The confrontation between the brothers continues as Oscar discovers black-market goods in the family warehouse, and takes out a pistol in order to kill the bull. Juan shouts at his brother, "Eres un judío de mierda" (You are a fucking Jew), and after he defies his brother, pushing him and throwing black-market olive oil at him, Oscar pulls the trigger. The pistol does not fire, however, and Oscar exclaims, "Joder, casi te mato. ¿Me perdonas?" (Shit, I almost killed you. Will you forgive me?), to which Juan responds, "Sí, que te perdono, coño," (Fuck yes, I forgive you), and they walk out of the warehouse with their arms around each other. The billingsgate contained in their speech functions in a manner similar to the gesture mentioned above; although it elicits an easy laugh in the audience, there is something incongruous about the inclusion of a comic element at this moment, and the brothers' reconciliation seems overly facile.

Juan decides to try his fortune in Madrid, confident that he will obtain employment, since, as he boasts, "Yo soy falangista" (I am a Falangist). He abandons Angela, the family servant, who is pregnant with his child. Juan's mother, Gloria, then forces Angela to abandon the house, and the latter leaves to live in a hut on the mountain; Angela thus suffers what Paul Ilie has termed "inner exile" (2). During the years of Juan's absence, he is mythified in the eyes of the townsfolk: one man says that there is a photograph of Juan in the paper, and that he will be a cabinet minister; another confesses to Juanito that he is a friend of his father, or at least he was, until Juan became so important. When Juanito receives a cigarette lighter with the Falangist emblem of the yoke and arrows which belonged to his father, it metonymically underscores Juan's importance, especially when Ana tells the boy that his father was valiant. Juanito returns to live with his grandmother because of poor health, and after a trip to the physician, the boy's worsened condition is linked to the further mythification of the father figure, since Juan, who now has so much influence, is able to obtain scarce medication for the boy. A man who was with Juan in Madrid says that he is in Franco's body guard. Even Oscar tells Juanito that Juan has a position of great importance, and they say that he is going to appear in the "NO-DO," the official newsreel shown at Spanish movie houses during the Franco regime. Ana accompanies Juanito to the movies, and when the black and white documentary showing Franco appears on the screen, she tells her nephew, "está al fondo a la derecha" (he's at the back on the right), thus confirming by means of this official organ of the truth the importance of his father. The projectionist even cuts out a piece of film--visual proof--which shows Juan so that the boy can take it home.

Juanito's illness is ironically a source of power for the child, since it allows him to manipulate the family, who must follow the doctor's orders that he should be well cared for and never become upset. When Gloria brings Juanito an omelet, three grown men hovering over the boy are unable to make him eat, and they ironically consume the food themselves. In the following scene, Juanito's panting and shortness of breath cause his grandmother to capitulate to his whim that his mother feed him, in spite of the fact that Gloria believes that the boy is only faking his illness. This contrasts with a later scene, however, when Juanito's panting is not feigned. Franco comes to town to inaugurate a reservoir that has been built, and this gives Juanito the opportunity to meet his father. The family goes to meet with the dignitaries, and in a scene reminiscent of when the Americans pass by in García Berlanga's *Bienvenido, Mr. Marshall*, the entourage of guards on motorcycles and dignitaries in automobiles drives past, leaving the spectators literally in the dust. When the uniformed Juan meets his son, he says, "¿Sabes lo que llevo aquí? La comida del caudillo" (You know what I'm carrying here? The Leader's meal). The revelation that his father is a mere waiter is a shock to the young boy, and he tries to escape. When Angela finally catches him, Juanito is panting hard, and his mother reprimands him, saying, "No te hagas el tonto" (Quit fooling around). Now, however, his illness is genuine. This sequence manifests a key theme in the film: the demythification of the father figure. As Payan and López note, "it is precisely the father theme that introduces the possible political aspects of the film" (87). Director Gutiérrez Aragón points out in his conversations with

Hypocrisy: Gutiérrez Aragón's <u>Demonios en el jardín</u>, with A. Molina, A. Belén, E. Pasó, I. Arias, and A. Sánchez-Prieto. Photo Jordi Socias. Courtesy Luis Megino P.C.

Augusto M. Torres that Franco was a fundamental father figure (also mythified by means of the NO-DO) who is demythified in the film (159). The shattering of the father myth within this political context causes an existential dilemma for Juanito. Since his mother Angela, the internal exile, is referred to with the condescending term "rojita" (little red), which places her in the opposite political camp from Juan and the rest of the family, the boy can only query at this juncture, "Si papá es de Franco y tú eres rojita, ¿qué soy yo?" (If Dad is on Franco's side, and you are a little red, what am I?).

The *cainismo* continues as Oscar confesses to his wife concerning Juan, "Siempre le he odiado. . . por eso quise matarle y lo que es peor aún, lo quiero matar" (I have always hated him . . . that is why I wanted to kill him, and even worse, I still want to kill him). Of course the *cainismo* in this film is not based on political differences, but on deep-seated fraternal rivalry and jealousy. The latter is justified, since Ana--in spite of the fact that she refers to Juan as "a demon"-- continues her affair with him, and even furtively robs from the family safe to support him. Juanito's witnessing of an amorous encounter between his father and Ana triggers both a physical crisis, connotated by his panting, and a symbolic dream sequence: after a close-up of a bull's eye, the animal bellows and pursues Juanito through the street. Although Gloria blames Angela for the robbery, Oscar finds his brother in the barn and confronts him with the crime: "Con que eres tú quien nos ha robado" (So it's you who robbed us). This scene parallels that of their earlier confrontation: Juan again taunts Oscar, pushing him, even after giving him a pistol. Gloria interrupts the dispute, shouting, "Caínes, caínes, sois caínes" (Cains, Cains, you are Cains), while beating them with a wooden stick--a scene that constitutes the most explicit example of *cainismo* in contemporary Spanish film. Nevertheless, Gutiérrez Aragón uses the same formula as in the prior scene--quick reconciliation in which inclusion of billingsgate introduces an incongruous comic element: when Juan beseeches pardon from his brother and hugs him, Oscar replies, "Que te perdono, coño" (Shit, I forgive you). Although Juan is reincorporated into the family, he is incorrigible, and his amorous advances toward Ana ("Yo te prefiero a ti. Tú eres la única, la primera" [I prefer you. You are the only one, the first one]) during the festivities of Saint John's Day parallel the narrative sequence at the opening of the film. Although Ana confesses her love for him, she shoots Juan in the shoulder with a pistol. The festivities are to be commemorated with a family portrait, and with the photographer waiting, the wounded Juan throws his suit jacket over his shoulders and joins the others. The film ends with a still shot representing the photo, in black and white, of the family posed together. Gutiérrez Aragón notes that this technique of incorporating a still photo at the end of the film indicates that there will be no change in the hypocritical behavior that the characters have shown, that everything will remain the same (Torreiro 49).

The economic and political elements are intertwined in this film as they are in many others.   Angela's second exile, based on false allegations of thievery, falls into the pattern of irony used throughout the film, since it is the accusers who are the real thieves.   Here the fascists control the black market, and the images of bounty appear when Oscar shows the contents of the family store to his nephew when Juanito first comes down from the mountain to live with his grandmother: the camera lingers over the objects as Oscar shows them one by one to the boy-- sausages, chocolate, lentils, chick-peas.   This surely contrasts with the boy's meager prior existence in the hut, since his uncle shows them to him as if the boy had never seen such objects before.   Significantly, this scene also precedes that of women standing in line to purchase food at the store.   They are the have-nots, who are on the other side of the fence both economically and politically. Gloria passes judgment on them and instructs her grandson to beware. Although she initially warns, "Hay que tener cuidado con todas" (You've got to be careful with all of them), the grandmother is particularly wary of a woman   married to a man whom she describes as "very bad" because he had threatened to take the store away from the family; in other words, "reds" who must be watched over--or exiled--in order to avoid problems.   Gloria's façade of righteousness with her grandson only makes her hypocrisy all the more salient. Although the film has some incongruities in the script, it contains some excellent performances that made it very successful at the box office, and is an important film in the portrayal of *cainismo* on the Spanish screen.

In 1982, Mario Camus directed a cinematographic version of *La colmena* (The Hive), the famous novel by Camilo José Cela.   The action of the movie centers around the café "La Delicia" in 1943, and amidst the *tertulias* (social gatherings) of the intellectuals who frequent the establishment, it portrays the squalor and misery of the period.   The film was a smashing success with Spanish audiences, and it was the top-grossing national film during the year that it was released.   It also met with   critical acclaim both at home and abroad, winning the prestigious Golden Bear Award at the 1983 Berlin Film Festival. Hans Burmann provided splendid photography for the film, and the musical score by Antón García Abril is a   sometimes haunting, sometimes ironic complement to the narrative.[38] Camus and José Luis Dibildos were the screen writers, tackling the formidable task of reducing the novel's almost 300 characters to around some twenty-three principal roles. Camus filled the cast with stars of the Spanish screen, and even included a cameo appearance by the novelist, ironically cast as an "inventor of words." The long list of famous actors includes José Sacristán, Francisco Rabal, Francisco Algora, Agustín González, Imanol Arias, Victoria Abril, Concha Velasco, Ana Belén, and many others. José Sacristán as the impoverished *ultraísta* poet Martín Marco has what can be considered the lead role in a film which is, as Jesús Ruiz comments, "a movie with a choral structure in which each and every one of the characters is a protagonist of that 'slice of life' from the 1940's" (43; cf. Frugone 129). Sacristán comments that "*La colmena* is above all, a work that recuperates the history of Spain . . . . My character [Martín Marco] represents the resignation of those who had no choice but to accept defeat" (Pérez Ornia, "Retorno" 4). In order to capture the atmosphere of the period, Camus went to great lengths to recreate a café of the 1940's, attending to such details as magazines from the period, ration coupons, match boxes and cigarette packages made after drawings of the originals, and three-hundred bottles, half of which were authentic, behind the bar (Pérez Ornia, "El café" 4). The same is true for the scenes at characters' homes, which feature portraits from the 1940's of Franco and of the pope. Camus even included exterior footage of streetcars from the 1940's as well as an old newsreel during a scene in a movie theater in order to complement the interior scenes of the café and boarding houses.

The clients who frequent the café for their *tertulia* are so impoverished that they often sit there without ordering anything at all, much to the chagrin of Doña Rosa, owner of the café, who constantly chides the waiters. Miss Elvira asks for cigarettes with the promise that she will pay tomorrow. Led by Ricardo, the intellectuals occasionally dupe the aspiring academician Don Ibraín into reciting his boring acceptance speech into the academy, in return for which the elderly gentleman gregariously orders coffee for everyone at the table.

---

[38]Critic Pedro Crespo calls the score a "perfect counterpoint to the dramatic action" ("La colmena" 69) and Angeles Masó says that García Abril's compositions "punctuate the action perfectly" ("La colmena" 35). Francisco Marinero praises Hans Burmann's photography, which achieves chiaroscuro effects ("La colmena" 42).

Post-war misery in Doña Rosa's cafe: Camus's <u>La colmena</u>, with José Sacristán, Francisco Rabal, and Francisco Algora. Courtesy Filmoteca Nacional.

Other times they suffer the humiliation of being thrown out of the café, as when Martín orders thinking that a friend who never shows up would pay. Doses of Doña Rosa's ire include the epithets "bestia" (idiot) and "rojo" (red), when a waiter trips and falls, thus reflecting the subconscious political division of the moment. These divisions also appear in a confrontation between Leonardo and Don Mario de la Vega, and in the relationship between Martín and his brother-in-law, and in a conversation between two women, Visi and Filo. Leonardo is a man who conducts shady, and sometimes unusual business deals: he sells a pen to Don Mario, a man of means who smokes cigars worth an entire "duro" (five pesetas). Although Leonardo claims that the pen is an authentic Parker brought in by diplomatic pouch, Don Mario returns in a rage another day, saying that the pen leaked and ruined his suit. He claims that Leonardo cheated him and he threatens to denounce him to the police. Leonardo, however, is not a man to be threatened: he shows his medal from the war, which gives him a certain amount of moral authority. The scene ends with accusations of "estraperlista" (blackmarketeer) on the part of Don Mario, with a mention of olive oil that complements the thematics of *Demonios en el jardín*, which depicted the same social problem of the period.

When Martín visits his sister, their discussion includes a comment about Roberto, Martín's brother-in-law, and his country ("su país"), with the use of the possessive adjective connoting a distinction between the Spain of Martín and that of Roberto. This distinction is later underscored in a conversation between the two in which we see that they are men of different ideas and that the latter considers the poet a loafer. Roberto's Spain is clearly connoted in a scene at night when he and his wife listen to the radio with its martial music and cries of "Viva Franco" and "Arriba España" (Up with Spain) as the camera seeks out a photograph on the desk of Roberto in a soldier's uniform. The scene is charged with irony, however, because after the triumphant cries, the lights go out, and we see that electrical shortages are a common occurrence with Roberto's comment, "Sí que estamos buenos otra vez" (We're in fine shape again). Martín's Spain is that of the soup-lines and police interrogations as he tries desperately to survive. When the police stop him in the street late at night and ask for his documentation, he does not have it, and he nervously explains that he collaborates with the "Prensa del Movimiento" (the official press) and has written an article about Queen Isabel, to which the officer responds by allowing him to go. We later discover that he has earned one-hundred pesetas for an article that he wrote on Carlos V, monk and soldier. Although this is not stuff that an "ultraísta" poet is normally made of, his ideological capitulation to the political system allows him to survive. When Visi goes to Filo's house, it is to ask for a favor, since her husband is a veteran. She asks for intercession in the case of her husband, Roque, who needs a purification record ("expediente de depuración"). We know of Roque's "questionable" background, since we have learned that he listens to the BBC at 6:00. The reverse angle shots used in the conversation between the two women underscore the division of the have's and the have-not's (a division which is based on political considerations). As we see close-ups of Visi, she attempts to justify her request, saying that they even voted for Azaña in 1936. The belief in the efficacy of obtaining political favors through personal connections even extends to Suárez, the homosexual who tells his friend Pepe that he will soon have employment in the government-run union.

Everyone, it seems, must circumvent traditional morality in order to survive. Martín sleeps at a brothel in an empty bed when business there is slow. Leonardo, who complains of the stones and the insects in his lentils at his boarding house and who eagerly brings a hammer to help Ventura open his package of cheeses and other foods that arrives from the countryside, furtively steals an egg in the kitchen by piercing the shell with his medal and sucking out the contents. In order to obtain money for her phthisical boy-friend, Victorita finally overcomes her initial scruples (in her first encounter, she refuses to show more than her breasts) and prostitutes herself to the wealthy Don Mario. Likewise, Martín's old girlfriend, Nati, now wears pearls, has painted fingernails, and pays for their restaurant bill, which all connote her success at the expense of dignity. Sometimes, the deceptions are unmasked and we see a touch of humor as the characters' peccadillos are revealed. Ricardo, an intellectual at the café, unmasks Doña Rosa when he discovers that the marble table tops are really inverted tomb-stones, and the entire establishment becomes an uproar as everyone inverts their table. In order to have sexual relations, Ventura convinces his girl- friend Julita to visit him at a "safe" boarding house and give the password "Napoleón Bonaparte." She timidly enters the building but mistakenly calls at the wrong door, and they bluntly inform her, "La casa de citas es en el piso de arriba" (The whore house is upstairs). This sequence also ends with a humorous note as the shirt which Ventura wrapped around the light bulb which hangs from the ceiling so as to create a more romantic atmosphere bursts into flames and falls upon the couple. Not all, however, could tolerate the atmosphere of the period. One of the final sequences features the news that Doña Margot, mother of the homosexual Suárez, committed suicide. The police, who think that there may have been foul play involved, pick up Martín, as well as Suárez and Pepe, for questioning. After their release, the camera, in a tracking shot, seeks out the revolving door of the café (an image which suggests a circularity in which the existential situation of the characters cannot improve) as the narrator, in a voice-over, quotes from the novel that metaphorically refers to the city as a beehive, thus imbuing the cinematographic text with the flavor of the literary original.   Diego Galán praises the historical recreation of the   atmosphere of post-war Spain in *La colmena*, saying that Mario Camus reproduced, "with sensitivity and a certain amount of sorrow, the sordidness of that [post-war] atmosphere" ("Sensible" 41). *La colmena* presents a vivid portrait of post-war misery and the divided society in Spain in the 1940's.

In 1985, José Luis García Sánchez directed a musical entitled *La corte del faraón* (The Pharaoh's Court), based on the *zarzuela* (comic opera) by Perrín y Palacio (with music by V. Lleó) of the same name. García Sánchez set the performance of the operetta in the early 1940's, with the censorship of the period the main theme of the film. The opening scene shows the police throwing the performers out of the theater, and they then go to the police barracks. The rest of the film narrative alternates between the present of the police inquisition and a series of flashbacks concerning how the zarzuela came to be performed. The priest (Agustín González) complains about the performance to the chief of police (José Luis López Vázquez): the costumes are so scanty and the singing and dancing so lascivious, that even he had a "tremendous erection." The censorship that García Sánchez ridicules is a result of the Nationalist victory in the civil war, as the priest makes quite clear: "Que no se gana una guerra, que no se hace una cruzada para este resultado" (You don't win a war, you don't have a crusade for this). Images of José Antonio and Franco look down over the chief of police, who bumbles through the investigation, accepting bribes and listening to actors' confessions to the priest. A bribe comes in the form of a succulent paella offered by Roque (Fernando Fernán Gómez), the father of one of the performers. Roque is able to win the good graces of the police chief not only through his expenditures, but because he was a Nationalist soldier who fought at Brunete, a bit of information that results in a fascist salute by the commissioner.

García Sánchez artfully interweaves the fiction of the performance with the reality of the performers' lives. The zarzuela tells the Biblical story of chaste Joseph, Putifar, and the Virgin of Thebes. The role of the Virgin is performed by Mari Pili (Ana Belén), an actress who is engaged to Basilio, but falls in love with a seminarian chosen to play José (Antonio Banderas), and who attempts to resist her charms both on and off stage. Ana Belén's singing is a highlight of the movie, especially in the famous song, "Son las mujeres de Babilonia" (The Women of Babylonia). Her performance undoubtedly helped make the film a big box-office success (the sound-track also sold very well).

The sexual component of the film is not limited to the lascivious performance on stage: in addition to the kinky sex of Roque's wife and homosexual tendencies of his son, sex is also used to ridicule the censor/priest. The latter absurdly concludes the zarzuela is making fun of Franco, since Putifar represents the *caudillo*, and the desire to crown him means that their leader is a cuckold (based on a play on words with the verb *coronar*).

Censorship and oppression: García Sánchez's <u>La corte del faraón</u>, starring Ana Belén.
Photo by Felipe López. Courtesy Luis Sanz and Lince Films, S.A.

The film touches on other themes of the period such as the black
market (performers pry open coffins to discover smuggled food) and
political repression (when José states that someone in his boarding
house was listening to the radio with earphones, the commissioner
interrogates him about the perpetrator's identity). The final scene of
the film finds the police chief stating that he will use the "ley de vagos
y maleantes" (vagrant law) and will discover the clandestine press of
the subversives affiliated with Masonry, Judaism, Communism . . . *La
corte del faraón* is an excellent satire of the repressive atmosphere of
the 1940's.

Fernando Trueba's *El año de las luces* (The Year of Lights, 1986)
is a film which captures the atmosphere of the post-war period in the
setting of a sanatorium for children who are suffering from tuberculosis
a year after the end of the conflict. The center is only for young
children, but since the teenage Manolo (Jorge Sanz) is an "hijo de
caído" (the son of a fallen soldier) he is admitted with his younger
brother because he was a victim of malnutrition during the war. His
suffering occurred in Madrid when it was under siege, and this detail
endows the character with certain ambivalence: although he benefits
from the Nationalist victory by being admitted to the sanatorium, his

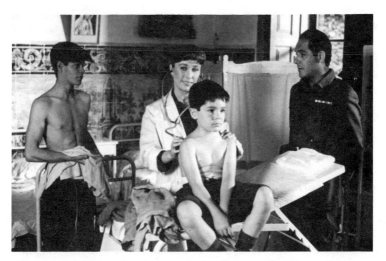

Medical treatment for veterans' children: Trueba's <u>El año de las luces</u>, with J. Sanz, V. Forqué, L. Martín and S. Ramos. Courtesy Compañía Iberoamericana Films, S.A.

residence in the Republican capital connotes a lack of conformity with the new regime's values. For a teenager, this logically relates to moral and sexual conduct. From the opening scene in the film in which close-ups show Manolo staring at a young girl at a kiosk, the theme of Manolo's sexual awakening predominates. This awakening is set against the background of oppression in which moral and political elements are constantly intertwined. A conciliatory note appears at the beginning of the film, however: on the bus that Manolo takes to the sanatorium, someone mentions that more people should be executed, and a priest responds that the war is now over, and that everyone should forget their prior animosity toward the other side.

At times, Trueba converts the viewer into a voyeur as we, along with Manolo, watch as the soldier on the bus masturbates a woman with his foot, or as Manolo observes the nurses undress behind the translucent glass window at night. Manolo's onanism is the basis for many humorous episodes in the film, such as when the girls look through the microscope at the sample of "milk" that he has supplied, or when during confession he shows the novice priest his calendar filled with the record of his ejaculations, causing the latter to faint. His sexual awakening culminates in his relationship with María Jesús. The fact that her father turns out to be the priest represents a subtle anticlerical criticism that recalls the scurrilous definition that some Spaniards give to this member of the clergy--"a man whom everyone calls 'father' except his children, who call him 'uncle.'" The priest is also the object of mockery in the scene in which he shoots at pigeons ("daughters of Satan") that are flying in his church. The main character that represents moral oppression, however, is Doña Tránsito (Chus Lampreave). When she leads the children in prayer, her litany of fascists ("pray for José Antonio, the fallen, the Führer, the Duce, the Emperor of Japan") humorously mixes the religious and the political. When Manolo's younger brother suffers from enuresis in class[39], Manolo defends him; for his "rebelliousness," Tránsito wants to hand the older brother over to the Civil Guards. This is not such an idle threat, since an earlier scene in which Civil Guards check the passengers on the bus for their documentation, and then take some away underscores this element of repression. Tránsito also prohibits close dancing, since it is a sin. As a counterbalance to this repressive figure, Emilio represents the opposite: he is a free-thinker who saves French books from an "inquisitorial" burning and whose paradoxical (and humorous) religious sentiments bring to mind those of Luis Buñuel. When Manolo asks Emilio if Hell exists, he answers that he is an agnostic, but if it does, "Que Dios nos coja confesados" (May God take us after having confessed). Buñuel's famous religious self-definition was "Soy ateo, gracias a Dios" (I am an atheist, thanks be to God).

The film suffers a bit in the final sequences, especially in the scene in which the priest and the others separate Manolo and his young lover. Nevertheless, the film is a solid addition to Fernando Trueba's works, and it admirably portrays the atmosphere of post-war Spain. Indeed, as Angel A. Pérez Gómez notes, its splendid evocation of the post-war atmosphere makes *El año de las luces* "one of the best Spanish films that refer to that period" (*"El año"* 107). There was personal incentive for Trueba to accurately evoke the Spain of the early 1940's in this movie, since the film narrative is based on actual events that occurred to his father-in-law.

Si te dicen que caí (1989), directed by Vicente Aranda, is the cinematographic version of the novel by Juan Marsé in which the

---

[39]This is a common motif in films that deal with war orphans, ranging from <u>El otro árbol de Guernica</u> to Louis Malle's <u>Au revoir les enfants</u>.

Sexual awakening in the post-war: Trueba'a <u>El año de las luces</u>, starring Maribel Verdú and Jorge Sanz. Courtesy Compañía Iberoamericana Films, S.A.

novelist from Barcelona has admitted that he "wanted to reflect in the hardest, most sordid, and most sinister way possible what had been my childhood in those years" of the postwar (Amell, 110). The film takes its title from a verse of the Falangist hymn, and therefore ironically subverts the sociopolitical discourse of the regime as it offers multiple images of the misery and oppression of post-war Barcelona.

Two sequences at the "Roxy" movie theater manifest the everyday oppression of the regime. The first sequence begins with an excellent example of visual synecdoche: a long shot of two *maquis* entering the movies is disrupted by the torso of a policeman crossing directly in front of the camera, and he stops so that only his right side (arm bent at the elbow with his hand on his hip above his pistol) appears in the foreground on the left side of the frame. This ominously foreshadows the violence of the next scene--the interior of the movie house, when the policeman asks the *maquis* for their identification--and the maquis gun him down. In a second movie house scene, Java (Jorge Sanz) sits next to the prostitute Ramona (Victoria Abril), and she charges him two pesetas for a feel. When the lights come on and the Nationalist hymn is played, with an image of the *caudillo* on the screen, their chatter results in a fascist shouting "Silence" and slapping

Java several times. Both scenes contain a montage of film from the
1940's, first from the official NODO newsreels that show images of
the Führer and announce General Franco's imminent meeting with
Hitler, and later, scenes from the film *Sin novedad en el alcazar* (No
News From the Alcazar), a film that glorifies the Nationalists troops'
resistance during the siege of the alcazar in Toledo and therefore
contributes to the regime's official discourse regarding the civil war.

The film hints at misery and repression on many levels. Origami
birds and an empty plate with a spoon are the telltale signs of the mole
theme, but in this case Java's brother Marcos (Antonio Banderas) is
hiding from both the fascists and the communists. Java's threat to
denounce a girl to the authorities for past crimes if she does not assist
him in his search for Aurora Nin serves as a foreshadowing of his
denouncement of his own brother to the authorities, which we can
surmise from a conversation on a park bench between Java and the
one-eyed fascist. When a woman opens the door to a bar in order to
raffle a chicken, the mere sight of the one-eyed fascist causes her to
retreat in fear.   The *maquis* refer to beatings of civilians by blue-
shirted fascists, and the shooting of prisoners of war, and when one of
the children suggests that they sell firearms that they have found to
the *maquis*, another retorts that they would be put in front of a firing
squad for doing so. The reappearance of Luis Lage, who has been
released from jail, represents a note of joy and happiness, as well as
the opportunity to undermine Nationalist propaganda, when Luis tells
his son to note that his hands are not stained with blood. Joy turns to
shame, however, when Luis later confronts his wife who prostituted
herself in his absence. She tearfully defends herself, saying that she
wanted to put some meat on their children's table, and did nothing
wrong.

The sexual degradation is most significant in character of Java,
the young rag collector. Conrado Galán (Javier Gurruchaga), a
Nationalist lieutenant who was wounded in the war and is now
confined to a wheelchair, pays prostitutes to perform as he
voyeuristically observes them from behind a curtain, showing his
displeasure or impatience by pounding his walking stick on the floor.
Java announces to Ramona (Victoria Abril) that the show must last one
hour, and the montage of the sexual activities and extreme closeups of
Conrado's eye as the sex becomes ever more degrading and brutal--
Java sodomizing her, beating her, and finally urinating on her--makes

for an extremely harsh sequence. This is even more the case because of director   Vicente Aranda's desire to cast his favorite actress, Victoria Abril, in this role, in spite of the fact that she was six month's pregnant at the time. Author   Juan Marsé comments that this resulted in scenes that were brutal in and of themselves being even more brutal, and that the film version was overly sadistic (Abad 101). The close-ups of Conrado's voyeuristic gaze are accompanied by chilling violin chords that bring the shower scene from Hitchcock's *Psycho* to mind, and become Conrado's motif on the soundtrack, together with an eerie, ominous squeaking of his wheelchair. Sex and violence are also linked in two later sequences in which Java and the other boys interrogate Juanita and Fueguiña about Aurora Nin. In the second of these, the children are in a costume shop and are playacting. Java's role is that of Conrado: he order the actors to be silent and to continue and strokes a hammer, analogous to Conrado's walking stick. (The close-up wide-angle shot of Java produces an expressionist distortion that recalls the early sequence preceding the initial sexual scene between Java and Ramona in which Java enters an elevator   as Conrado in his wheelchair enters the lobby: shots of both Java and Conrado through the old elevator glass create a distorting effect that foreshadows their moral warping as male prostitute and voyeur). Dressed in a cardinal's costume, when Java raises his hands, the cape is transformed into curtains, and an extreme close-up of Java peering between them, accompanied by the chilling violin chords associated with Conrado, complete the transformation of victim into victimizer. Fueguiña is tied to a crucifix, and when Java approaches her to interrogate her, the shot of him from the back in which he draws his cape over his head further transforms him into a vampire figure, and he draws blood as he kisses her through the knife blade that cuts her lip.   Combining sex and religious imagery occurs at other moments as well and serves as part of the overall social criticism of the film: in the early sex scene, Ramona at one point also wears a cardinal's cape and cap; when Conrado directs a school play, Lucifer (Java) at first attacks, then seduces Saint Michael, who is played by a girl, as the paralyzed lieutenant voyeuristically observes in close-up as he strokes his phallic walking stick; and on two occasions, prostitutes are said to be friends of the bishop.

The only characters in the film that escape the devastatingly negative portrayal of post-war Spanish society are the young boys who constitute Sarnita's gang of friends. The boys survive these difficult times partly by escaping into the fantasy world of their "aventis" or tales invented by Sarnita.

Chapter 6

The Mole

After the victory of the Nationalist troops in 1939, the Republicans who stayed in Spain often faced persecution and difficult times. Stanley Payne indicates that the Nationalist victory resulted in "the greatest single wave of political arrests in the country's history" and at the close of 1939, there were 270,719 prisoners (222). In order to escape arrest, some went into hiding, and their underground existence led them to become known as "moles"; their struggle has been documented in Jesús Torbado's study, *La historia del miedo* (translated into English as *The Forgotten Men*). Two very different films deal with "moles": Alfonso Ungría's *El hombre oculto* (The Hidden Man, 1970), and Fernando Fernán Gómez's *Mambrú se fue a la guerra* (Mambrú Went Off to War, 1986).

Ungría's work is a difficult film that critics refer to as "hermetic," and "cryptic" (Cebollada 42; Rentero, "Entrevista" 45). Filmed in black and white, this medium serves to better capture the bleak reality of years of underground existence. The opening images of the film provide keys to this existence: the close-ups of a clock with seconds ticking and the hand on different numerals which are not in sequence (8, 12, 10, etc.) symbolize the slowness of the passing of time under these circumstances, and the passage of large segments of time, as well as the seeming sameness of different times. The second image of a man lying on a bed, but upside down, connotes the inverted, nonsensical aspect of this existence. The claustrophobic life of the mole is accentuated by a frequent use of close-ups, of the protagonist (shaving, etc.) or of objects related to him (the tools with which he makes rosary beads, or the beads themselves). As Miguel Rubio points out, some of his acts acquire the status of ritual, such as the close-up of him cutting his toe nails and carefully depositing them in a jar with the others that he has collected ("*El hombre*" 23). Other activities, however, relate to the desire to maintain contact with the outside world and a hope for a better future: he listens to radio broadcasts with

earphones (an image of repression used in many films which deal with
the post-war era), and he labors over French lessons which he also
receives on the radio.   The radio also serves to underscore the
absurdity of his existence, indeed of all existence, as we hear a male
announcer state, "El universo es un caos . . . un abismo sin sentido"
(The universe is a chaos . . . an abyss without meaning).   The
inexorable march of time brings new technological devices, however,
and one day, when alone, he encounters a television set. His reaction
to this device--fleeing in fear from the image that he beholds when he
turns on the set--may seem exaggerated, but it corresponds to the
atmosphere which Ungría attempts to create in the film. The director
states that the film has "a theme of uneasiness, fear, the terror of little
things, the oppression of daily life, which was of main concern. Even
though the plot wasn't clear, the atmosphere was, and that was the
main concern of the film: to create an atmosphere" (Rentero
"Entrevista" 45).

The relationship between the "mole" and the other members of the
household is somewhat unclear. He reads the newspaper to a blind
girl, presumably his daughter, and yet there are sequences in which
Ungría strongly suggests through ellipsis a sexual relationship between
the two. In the second sequence, in particular, after she takes off her
dress, he comments,   "Está mal hacer estas cosas. No debes
comportarte así" (It's not right to do these things. You shouldn't
behave like that), before the fade out.   This use of ellipsis parallels
that in another sequence in which the "mole" spies on his other
daughter who has returned home with a boyfriend. As the two youths
disappear into the basement of the home, we hear giggles "off" before
the fade out. In spite of his efforts to keep tabs on the members of his
own household, he seems incapable of doing so. His wife confides to
him, "Santos se ha enterado que soy tu mujer" (Santos has found out
that I am your wife), and he reacts "¿Pero cómo ha podido?" (But how
could he?), and worries about what his situation will be now.   His
"situation" is   never   clearly   expressed: the   protagonist's
"imprisonment" is never justified in intra-textual terms. Indeed, there
are only oblique references to the war.   The first of these occurs
during a dinner conversation at the beginning of the film in which he
recalls to his family "those stupid explorations" while dressed as a
captain. Instead of a bellicose setting for his nocturnal observations,
however, he describes an oneiric urban setting in which he is unable to
cross an avenue.   Later, a man with no voice who plays cards in the

living room (and relies upon a young girl to interpret his guttural
sounds) is referred to as "comandante." Near the end of the film,
when Santos asks the "comandante," "¿Le importaría contar otra vez
aquello?" (Would you mind retelling that?), the wife objects, saying,
"No es verdad lo que dice" (What he says isn't true) and "Las cosas
hay que vivirlas de cerca.   Son cosas antiguas" (You've got to
experience things up close. That's ancient history). Her statement that
the girl is twenty-three years old constitutes an important temporal
marker.   After the blind girl shouts, "Fire," we hear the sound of
planes and bombs "off," before the screen fades to white. We can
only surmise that this is a flashback to her youth when she was blinded
in an air raid. Consequently, this would place the temporal framework
of the narration in the late 1950s or early 1960s. Finally, the "mole"
is able to leave his subterranean existence behind; he is able to go out
to the outside world. We see from the dirt that he wipes from his lips
that he has kissed the earth that he has not been able to walk on for so
many years. In the final shot, however, he stops to fix a string on his
sock, a sign that he is still a prisoner of an existence in which the
minute acquires primordial importance.   Freedom is not easily
exercised.

Whereas existence in the "mole's" house seems lifeless, as
symbolized by the rooms in which the furniture is covered with sheets
and not used, life "outside," symbolized by the parade with soldiers
and floats which they view on television, is a superficially happy
existence in a state controlled by the military apparatus.   There is
significant religious symbolism in the film as well. The story about the
animal that is half cat and half lamb (and wants to be a dog) is a
metaphor with both religious, and as Alfonso Sánchez points out,
Kafkian undertones (25). The protagonist, in particular, is identified
with Christ. This occurs both at the beginning of the film, when he
puts a Christ-figure on the crucifix of a rosary that he is making and
he injures his finger, as well as at the end of the film when his wife
nails a spike into his foot, a surrealistic sequence which parallels the
sequence immediately before the crucifix scene in which a cigarette
burns a hole in his pants' leg and then falls "into" his thigh. Although
these surrealistic scenes seem to manifest an obvious debt to Buñuel,
Sánchez states that their aesthetic lineage runs much deeper than that:
"Ungría applies a deformed figurative aesthetic in which he ties into the
whole Spanish tradition that includes Cervantes, Goya, Valle-Inclán,
and Buñuel" (25). Ungría himself has stated, "I make my deformed

aesthetics for the here and now, a gallery of concave and convex mirrors" (Cebollada, "El hombre" 42), a statement which certainly recalls Valle-Inclán's definition of the *esperpento*. The director feels, however, so that his deformed (and deforming) aesthetic does not apply simply to an individual, but to a society. When Juan Carlos Rentero asked in an interview if the film dealt openly with those individuals who took refuge after the war, Ungría's response was, "No, no. The film was about the gray and oppressed daily existence of a whole society. What most impressed me when I read the stories about these people, who appeared in public after being holed up in a garret for twenty years, is that when they told about the lives that they had led during all that time, I realized that was the same type of life that my next-door neighbor led. . . . So the film was about that: that there was a dreadful situation, one of a hidden nation . . . that lived within the borders of fear, oppression, and that didn't protest, didn't shout" (40). Thus, his main aesthetic goal was to search for an answer to the question that is analogous to that posed by Lewis Carroll about how one would see the light of a candle when it is out: "How, in a hidden society, would hidden men see the story of another hidden man? (Cebollada "El hombre" 42). Because of its hermetic nature, *El hombre oculto* did not receive popular acclaim. Nevertheless, Ungría's aesthetic exploration of this theme puts him squarely in the tradition of other difficult but ingenious Spanish artists, and is deserving of praise.

The second film concerning the "mole" provides a very different vision of this phenomenon. Fernando Fernán Gómez's 1986 movie, *Mambrú se fue a la guerra* (Mambrú Went Off to War), is a much more "commercial" production, and was even subsidized by the Ministry of Culture. With a script by Pedro Beltrán, music by Carmelo Bernaola, and excellent photography by José Luis Alcaine, the film stars Fernán Gómez as Emiliano (the "mole"), María Asquerino as Florentina, his wife, Emma Cohen as Encarna, their daughter, Agustín González as Hilario, her husband, and Jorge Sanz and Nuria Gallardo as the grandchildren, Manolín and Juanita.

The point of departure of the two films is completely different. There are no surreal elements in *Mambrú se fue a la guerra*; rather, there are many comic moments--an element not present in the earlier film about "moles"--even though the humor in Fernán Gómez's film is often very bitter. Whereas the narrative of *El hombre oculto* focuses on the underground existence of the "mole," with only the final sequence of the film showing his "liberation," the narrative of *Mambrú se fue a la guerra* is the opposite, dealing with the life of the "mole" after he is at long last able to appear in public. Only the initial sequence of the film deals with his long concealment. Fernán Gómez artfully expresses the passage of time during the mole's concealment in the opening sequence: in a beautiful example of visual metonymy, we see a sequence of cross-cut shots of Emiliano's feet pacing back and forth in close-up, and girls playing and singing the popular children's song which constitutes the title of the film as they grow older and wear fashions from different decades. The main narrative then begins with the news of the death of Franco (November 20, 1975). Florentina announces to the other members of the family that Emiliano is alive, a fact celebrated with Manolín's shout of "Long Live the Republic." Emiliano emerges from his subterranean hiding place through the entrance concealed by a watering trough, and sings the "Hymn to Riego" (the national anthem of the second Republic). With the statement, "Con tanta luz no veo" (I can't see with so much light), he confirms the validity of the nickname given to men like him ("mole"). His grandchildren want to know about him and his concealed past, and when Manolín asks if he were a decent person, he responds, "Yo era honrado" (I was an honorable man). This, of course, makes Emiliano an even greater victim, since the only crime that he committed was to be on the losing side in the war. Emiliano begins to explore the world that he has not known by observing the street activities from his apartment window with a pair of binoculars. By using a telephoto lens, Ungría underscores further the empathy between the viewer and the protagonist since he uses a subjective, or point of view, shot so that we see as if we were seeing with Emilio's eyes. When he spies his former political rival in town, Paco, who is now the mayor, Emiliano ironically exclaims, "¡Uy, uy, qué viejo está!" (Oh my, he looks so old!), and he quickly adds, "Claro, los remordimientos" (No wonder, it's on account of his remorse), a humorous statement that is politically charged.

Events take a drastic twist when Hilario discovers that Florentina would now be eligible for payment from the government, but only as a widow whose husband was killed in the war. The son-in-law's plan is to hide the old man--until after elections!--so that the family can escape from penury. Thus, a conflict in which moraland ideological idealism versus materialism takes shape. As

Emiliano retreats to his basement abode, heated discussions occur between family members about the accumulation of objects and debts under their new life style. With a new television set, vacuum cleaner, etc., they symbolically blow the fuses in the house. The antagonism between Emiliano and Hilario is manifested in the visual image of the son-in-law begrudgingly carrying Emiliano on his back after the latter has twisted his ankle. Metaphorically, Hilario feels that he has carried Emiliano for many years, and his resentment culminates in his statement to Florentina, "No me ponga usted los dientes largos, que por matar a un muerto no le pasa a uno nada" (Don't test me, because nothing ever happens to anybody for killing a dead man). Emiliano, who hears the discussion, becomes afraid and decides to flee, upon the advice of his alter-ego, Manolo, a "companion" who speaks to the "mole" through ventriloquism: "Ellos tienen razón. Tú los estorbas" (They're right. You're just in the way).

Emiliano is not the only one who feels the necessity to escape difficult circumstances. His granddaughter Juanita, and Rafa, Paco's grandson, are in love, but since their families fought on opposite sides of the war, they have a star-crossed relationship. The confrontation between Rafa and his grandfather manifests how the Civil War continues to have repercussions on later generations of Spaniards. When Paco accuses the boy of going to the movies with the granddaughter of a "red," Rafa retorts, "Yo no tengo nada que ver con tu guerra, abuelo" (I don't have anything to do with your war, grandpa). The next shot of the youths sitting in front of a *noria*, or wheel for drawing water, and planning to go to France is a visual expression of the circularity of history, of how events (in this case old animosities) repeat themselves. Rafa's comments to Juanita further underscore the disassociation, but at the same time, victimization, of Spanish youth from the conflict of their forebears: "Vaya mierda de guerra. ¿Qué tenemos nosotros que ver con sus peleas?" (Fucking war. What do we have to do with their fights?). The youths steal Hilario's ambulance in order to flee to the neighboring country to the north, where they hope to find Rafa's father, an oblique reference to the divisiveness of the fratricidal combat, since father and grandfather must have been on opposite sides. When they rob the vehicle, Hilario, who hears the motor start, erroneously thinks that the culprit is Emiliano, and he exclaims, "El viejo de mierda. Mejor estaba muerto" (Fucking old man. He was better off dead), a further indication of his

The "mole" becomes a burden: Fernán Gómez's <u>Mambrú se fue a la guerra</u>, with Agustín González and Fernando Fernán Gómez. Courtesy Pro-Cines.

animosity toward his father-in-law.

Hilario's son is also in conflict with the "mole," but instead of materialism, Manolín simply represents self-centeredness, or a total lack of ideals. In a conversation between the two, Emiliano maintains that without ideals, "No se puede ser nada" (You can't be anything). Nevertheless, the youth replies, "Yo de política paso" (I don't want to have anything to do with politics). In this conflict, an object which acquires important symbolic connotations is Emiliano's drum. He tells Manolín that he was a drum-sergeant during the war, and that when the drum sounds, it is history. He explains that he served at the front "a servicio de la libertad" (serving freedom) and he cannot comprehend why Manolín wants to learn how to play if he has no ideals. His grandson's answer: for the discotheque, not for war. As Emiliano plays for the youth with "love and sweetness," the zoom-in to a close-up of the instrument confirms the ideals that Emiliano still holds.

After Emiliano leaves his home, he seems to suffer a series of existential crises when his sister Ramona rejects him as an imposter (since she regularly "communicates" with Emiliano's spirit in seances), and he mistakes a youth named Andrés for the boy's grandfather. The drum becomes his means of existential affirmation, as he roams the town beating the instrument and shouting "Soy Emiliano, soy Emiliano" (I am Emiliano, I am Emiliano), "Decid quién soy, decid quién soy" (Say who I am, say who I am), as well as the names of objects ("Rose water") from his pre-war occupation of pharmacist's helper. As he awakens the neighbors, they think that he must be crazy or drunk, and they want to call the police. Hilario and the other family members locate him first however, on a hilltop where, amidst coughs, he cries, "Libertad, libertad, libertad" (Freedom, freedom, freedom), as a long shot shows the others climbing the hill like enemy soldiers. Hilario throws Emiliano to the ground, and throws his drum down the hill. As the son-in-law puts a bandage on the old man, the camera pans the hillside to discover the broken drum, a visual image which reflects its owner's soul. Since Hilario wants to continue the cover-up of Emiliano's existence, they take him home to treat him, and the final close-up of the "mole's" face, with the bandage and blood, shows the blank look of a beaten man. The final shot of the water in the trough which has served as the coverture to his hiding place indicates that he must return, defeated, to his subterranean imprisonment. J. R. Pérez Ornia calls *Mambrú se fue a la guerra* "a bitter film about the death of the pre-war ideals and hopes, and about the deception of the left today," and actor and director Fernando Fernán Gómez points out that "the society that you see in the film is not observed or judged from a political point of view, but from a moral one" (Pérez Ornia, "*Mambrú*" 30). Although the film suffers from problems in the script, especially in the second half, its merits outweigh its defects, and it makes a poignant statement which goes well beyond the theme of the "mole" to touch on the complex question of the abandonment of ideals.

Chapter 7

Returning to the Past

Of those contemporary Spanish films which manifest the theme of *cainismo*, many deal with the attempt to come to terms with the fratricidal conflict by means of evoking one's memories of that important period, or in the case of political exiles, by returning to their homeland. As censorship in Spain began to slowly loosen its grip and the Franco regime finally came to an end, there was an ever greater opportunity for Republicans to return both in body and mind. Jean Tena, in his study, "Carlos Saura et la Mémoire du Temps Escamoté," points out two important attitudes of many Spanish intellectuals regarding the problem of their past under an oppressive dictatorship: in Carlos Sampayo's *Los que no volvieron* (Those Who Didn't Return, 1975), we read, "The worst thing wasn't that they won the war on us, but rather, that they won History on us"; the obsession of a character in the 1983 novel by Juan Marsé, *Señoras y señores* (Ladies and Gentlemen), is "to recover the lost memory of the country, the memory that was manipulated, camouflaged, and adulterated" (qtd. in Tena 11 and 16).

In *España otra vez* (Spain Again), an American member of the Abraham Lincoln Brigade returns to Spain; in *El amor del capitán Brando* (Captain Brando's Love) and *Volver a empezar* (To Begin Again), Republican exiles come back to their native land; in *Los paraísos perdidos* (Lost Paradises), it is the daughter of an exile who returns. In one of the most important films about the memories of these events, *La prima Angélica* (Cousin Angelica), a man whose parents were Republicans returns to the house of his Nationalist aunt with whom he had lived during the conflict. At times, the protagonists or their families pertained to the Nationalist side, such as in *El jardín de las delicias* (The Garden of Delights) and *La muchacha de las bragas de oro* (The Girl of the Golden Panties), and in these films there is a scathing attack on society during the Franco regime. In each case, the memories of the protagonists manifest the contrasts between the present and the past, or the subjective past and the objective past in order to provide valuable insights into both the individuals and Spanish society.

España otra vez (Spain Again) is a 1968 film directed by Jaime Camino with a script written by the director and Román Gubern. The opening shots--documentary images of soldiers during the civil war which contain a black diagonal streak that divides the frame in two--visually underscore the *cainismo* theme. The film narrates the return to Barcelona by an American doctor, David Foster (Mark Stevens) for an international congress. Gubern points out that the life of the Canadian physician Norman Bethune, who worked in Madrid during the war with the Lincoln Brigade and whose courageous effort appears in the 1937 documentary film *Heart of Spain*, served as an inspiration for the film, as did the personal experiences of Alvah Bessie, another Lincoln Brigade member and script-writer for Warner Brothers who not only contributed to the script of this film, but also played the part of Dr. Thompson, a colleague who accompanies Dr. Foster to the symposium (*1936* 162-63). During Foster's return to Spain, he encounters both places and people from the civil war years which result in a contrast between past and present. For the former, Camino utilizes a flash-back technique based on the inclusion of documentary footage from the 1930's: in these flashbacks, which appear in black and white, the Hotel Ritz appears as "Hotel Gastronomic No. 1" adorned with UCT and CNT banners, a street with children in Barcelona also appears with a CNT banner, and the countryside is filled with soldiers and gunfire. Of primary importance is the still black and white image of María, a nurse who worked with Dr. Foster during the war. When Manolo, the son of a war-time friend, brings his American guest a box of old photographs, the image of David in a beret embracing María foreshadows the melodramatic trajectory of the rest of the film. David asks his old friends--Manuel and a priest--about María, and he discovers that she married a man from Sevilla and now has a daughter who is a flamenco dancer in Barcelona. Gubern admits that the movie was commissioned to promote the flamenco dancing of Manuela Vargas (*1936* 161-62), and the length of the flamenco scenes, together with certain clichéd dialogues, such as the one in which Foster defends bullfighting, give the impression that the producer hoped to reach an American audience with this movie; however, they take away from the over-all quality of the film.

Camino uses brown tinted shots to create "documentary" film of David and María, and the physician sees the María of the 1930's in the daughter. During the trip that they take to an insane asylum, images of Roman ruins trigger David's interior monologue of self-deprecating remarks that show a remorse at not having stayed with the nurse that he loved: "The Romans survived no matter what happened. Why didn't I pay more attention to them?" Shots of the bombed-out buildings of Corbera del Ebro provide impressive testimony of the harshness of the civil war, and on the personal level, they evoke a sense of loss for Foster ("una parte de mí mismo quedó enterrada en estas ruinas" [part of myself is buried in these ruins]). His inner conflict culminates after his wife joins him in Barcelona; after throwing an ashtray to the floor in a gesture of frustration, he blurts out, "I should never have come back. . . . You can't go back to it [the past]," thus overtly stating the main theme of all of the films that deal with an attempted return to the past. As was to be expected, David's attempt to see María one last time in the train station ends futilely: shots of the physician running alongside her train form a parallel with the earlier shot of the elder María running alongside of David's train in the 1930's.

Foster's conversations with his old friends (sometimes accompanied by the music of the civil war tune, "Si me quieres escribir" [If you want to write to me]) provide the vehicle for a criticism of war while at the same time justifying the physician's labor during the conflict. The aging Manuel refers to the war, saying, "Qué locura. Aquello sí que era una locura" (What madness. That really was madness), and his priest friend refers to the conflict in the same terms, saying, "Esos tiempos tan locos no volverán. No volverán ya. No pueden volver." (Those crazy times won't return. They won't return any more. They can't return). David's justification of his own role, that of healing, also provides a subtle endorsement for the Republican cause: "Ayudamos a gente que sufría . . . buena gente" (We helped people who suffered . . . good people). Later in the film, the montage sequence in which Dr. Foster's visit to an insane asylum is intercut with flashbacks to a combat scene, together with the subsequent visit to the ruins from the battle of the Ebro can only bring to mind the themes of insanity and war developed in *King of Hearts*. *España otra vez* received great difficulties from censors, since as Gubern points out, it is the first Spanish film that had "someone from the vanquished side

The inability to re-live the past: Camino's <u>España otra vez</u>, with Mark Stevens and Manuela Vargas. Courtesy Filmoteca Nacional.

of the civil war as the protagonist which didn't conclude with the veneration of or submission to the victors" (*1936* 163). Not only David, but his Spanish Republican friends as well, appear as good people: Manuel, who even utters a few expressions in Catalan; his son Manolo; Father Jacinto; and most of all, the two Marías, since, as David says to the young flamenco dancer, "eres muy buena, como tu madre" (you are a very good person, just like your mother). Although the film has its defects in its script, it represents an important new direction in the development of the *cainismo* theme in Spanish cinema.

El jardín de las delicias (The Garden of Delights) is a film from 1970 directed by Carlos Saura. The narration centers around Antonio Cano (José Luis López Vázquez), a rich Spanish industrialist who has lost his memory due to an automobile accident and whose family desperately attempts to jar his memory loose so as to get at the family fortune that Antonio has stashed in Swiss bank accounts. The real-life accident of Juan March, the Spanish industrialist who helped bankroll the 1936 uprising that initiated the civil war, inspired the creative impulse of Saura on this film. There is also a good deal of autobiographic element in both this film and in *La prima Angélica*, since both films center on the theme of memory, and in particular, memories of the civil war. In an interview in 1976 with Vicen Camos, he stated, "the Spanish civil war has been and is still weighing down on us; it belongs to an immediate past that can hardly be separated from our present," and he added that although he was only four years of age when the war broke out, "I experienced it dramatically at times, and in some ways I have suffered, like many Spaniards, its consequences" (34).

The title of the film corresponds to that of the famous triptych by Hieronymous Bosch which hangs in the Prado Museum in Madrid. The director has commented on his selection of this title for the film, saying, "First of all, because I really love the painting. And also because Spain is a little bit like a garden of delights filled with little monsters" (Cohn 164). In addition, he has commented that he wished the film to be a "grotesque reredos," thus achieving an aesthetic parallel with the Bosch painting (Brasó, *Carlos Saura*, 288).

Elements that Jean Tena points out as keys to Saura's works -- disguises, the theme of the double, and theatrical representation, (18) are manifest from the opening shots of *El jardín de las delicias*: a woman applies makeup to her face, trying to copy the image of an old photograph. When family members bring in a pig into a room where Antonio, in a wheelchair, observes the couple that is acting as his parents of yesteryear tell him--as if he were a five-year-old--that he is bad and that the pig is going to eat his hands, it is evident that the narration will consist of a Cervantine layering of reality and imagination. The latter appears in the theatrical representations made by family members, memories that Antonio has of his past, and sheer projections of his imagination. The father's comment that "Los símbolos son todo" is important both within the narrative, as characters attempt to recreate Antonio's past, and as a self-reflexive comment about the nature of this cinematographic text. D'Lugo also comments that these words "transcend the context in which they are uttered" since the elder Cano's actions are "synonymous with the process of ideological coercion of the Spaniard by state cultural apparatuses" (*Films* 99).

Saura discovers in this film a technique that he will later utilize in *La prima Angélica*: José Luis López Vázquez plays both the adult Antonio and the young Antonio, such as in the scene in which his aunt gives the eleven-year-old Antonio medicine, an idea that Claude Clouzot regards as an ingenious innovation in film syntax (Gubern

Carlos Saura 28). López Vázquez's brilliant performance won him the
Hugo Award for Best Actor at the Chicago Film Festival. This casting
allows for a much more subtle interplay between past and present, since
the actions of the past do not appear in and of themselves, as they
would in a normal flashback, but as an adult remembers them, with all
of the imperfections and deformations that such a process implies.
Kinder (63) notes Saura's explanation of the conceptual genesis for *La
prima Angélica*: "One day I looked in the mirror and said, 'My
goodness, what did I look like as a child?' I can't remember myself
as a child in the mirror. I have photographs, but when I look at them,
I feel as if it's someone I don't know."

The most important syntactic element of the film is the combination
of different levels of reality--the present, the past in flashback,
memories of the past, representation of the past--and this requires a
very attentive viewing of the movie (or multiple viewings).[40]   The
result of this procedure is the distanciation of the film text from the
spectator so that he can better ponder the ideological message of the
movie, and all levels of the narrative reinforce the same message.

The film portrays the despicable aspects of Antonio Cano's
character in each level. His greed even as a young man is manifest in
the flashback to his father's factory when Antonio has just graduated
from college: he complains that the factory is antiquated and that they
have to produce more. His avarice and egoism--illegally depositing the
family fortune in Swiss bank accounts--ironically twists against
everyone in the family when he loses his memory and they are left with
no funds.   His perverse sexual appetite and infidelity appear in the
present--even paralyzed in the wheelchair, he requires his nurse to bear
her breast before he will eat--and in represented reality: the family uses
his lover Nicole as an "actress" to help jar his memory. His family
members view his defects as attributes, however;   when he has
recuperated enough so that he can walk and talk a bit, he prepares to
attend a board meeting and becomes angry at a maid over the selection
of neckties, saying that he wants to fire her. His father becomes elated

---

[40]Enrique Brasó notes the confusing relationship between the different narrative
planes: the real, the imagined, the remembered, the represented, the deformed, and the
oneiric   (Carlos Saura 266-67). Kovacs divides the film narrative into five different
planes: the recreated past, the present-day frame, the evoked past, the oneiric world, and
a future plane ("Loss" 45-54).

at his son's reaction, saying, "Tiene carácter" (He has character). The culmination of his negative characterization occurs at the end of the film when he wants to commit a homicide, although the narrative only connotes this through intertextual referentiality. Antonio and his wife Luchy visit Aranjuez, where they go for an outing in a rowboat. Antonio remembers and even identifies the spot, but his memories do not appear visually. Instead, the reality of the present combines with Antonio's memories, imagination, and desires, which express themselves through his verbal reference to *An American Tragedy* and the visual sign of his desire to kill his wife: he rocks the boat and pushes at her with an oar.

The other family members, with perhaps the exception of his wife, Luchy, are equally reviling in their relationship with Antonio, and their attempts to obtain the family fortune. The dramatic scenes that they represent to him in order to jar his subconscious are often cruel and degrading--threatening a five-year-old that a pig will eat his hands, having a prostitute visit him, showing him the death of his mother. Luchy is the only member of the family who protests the cruelty and perversion of these representations. The death of his mother is one of two key memories that the family attempts to recreate from the civil war. The first is the day of his first communion, April 14, 1931, the day in which Spaniards proclaim the Second Republic. As the priest speaks to "Antoñito," Republicans enter the church, shouting, and begin to fight with parishioners. In a touch of irony, Saura has López Vázquez look at their flag, and ask, "¿Los santos, tía?" (Is it the saints, auntie?) The sirens, bombs, and gunfire heard "off" connote the civil conflict, as Antonio quickly recognizes: "No, la guerra, los rojos, el '36" (No, the war, the reds, '36). Thus, the memories of the civil war are viewed as so deeply entrenched in the subconscious that they, among all of his memories, will provide the key to reawakening his mental faculties. For that reason, the family provides a second civil war representation that corresponds to when he was twelve years old. They show a documentary film of the war with the reading "off" of Rubén Darío's famous poem, "La marcha triunfal" (The Triumphal March): "Ya viene el cortejo / Ya se oyen los claros clarines" (Now the cortege is coming / Now you can hear the clear clarions). Suddenly Antonio's father, dressed as a soldier, jumps through the screen. By this time, however, Antonio has regained enough consciousness to distinguish between reality and representation; indeed,

Reenacting the Republic to jar the memory: Saura's <u>El jardín de las delicias</u>, starring José Luis López Vázquez and Francisco Pierrá. Courtesy Elías Querejeta, P.C.

in an earlier hunting scene, he was able to discern that his friends had rigged his own performance by tying the foot of his prey with a string. His words, "No, la película" (No, the film), is complemented by his next comment when they show him a woman meant to be his dead mother lying in a fountain: "No, no es mamá" (No, it's not Mom). The theme of *cainismo* and a symbolic reference to the civil war also appear in the imaginary plane in which two rows of boys who wield red shields and orange shields throw balls at each other. The shields, in turn, recall two earlier scenes. In the first, which must be taken in syntagmatic relationship with the latter two, Antonio "hears" the whinny of a horse and turns to "see" two knights in armor with lances riding at him. In a later interior scene, we observe that a painting of the knights covers the wall safe where Antonio kept the Swiss account numbers. The combative knights can represent his family that has turned against him and pursue him to claim his wealth, or perhaps on a more abstract plane, Antonio's greed, avarice, and egotism which, in an ironic twist of fate, have also turned against him. Another scene that may evoke the civil war occurs after a confrontation between Antonio and his son when the latter hits his father and throws him out of his bedroom. Antonio falls against the wall, but it is the wall of his

factory that lies in ruins before him. Is this the fantasy of an
egotistical man who sees his son as lazy and incompetent and who
cannot carry on the family "empire," or is it the memory of a loss
suffered at the hands of the "reds"?

The progress in Antonio's recuperation is never enough to achieve
a return to normalcy, and after a flashback to his automobile accident,
the final shot of the film is a gripping one indeed: the entire family is
now in wheelchairs, and in an open field, they perform a grotesque
metaphorical dance "like a macabre social carrousel" (Martialay, "*El
jardín*" 23). Oms interprets this final shot as the metaphorical paralysis
of the family as an institution, and indeed, of the entire Spanish society
(*Carlos Saura* 49). Indeed, the aggressive attack on Spanish society
did not go unnoticed by authorities, and key political elements--the
possible allegorical relationship between the protagonist and the
physically debilitated General Franco, the image of Republican flags
entering the church, and the text of the poem, "La marcha triunfal" by
Rubén Darío--caused problems with the censors. However, the success
of *El jardín de las delicias* at the New York Film Festival insured the
success of what is one of Saura's best films.

Saura's *La prima Angélica* (Cousin Angelica), a film from 1973
and winner of the Jury Prize at the Cannes Film Festival of that year,
would elaborate on many of the themes and narrative techniques seen
in *El jardín de las delicias*. Unlike the earlier film, however, *La prima
Angélica* contains the first Spanish cinematographic narration about the
civil war as seen from the perspective of Spanish Republicans.
(Although Jaime Camino's 1968 *España otra vez* manifests the
perspective of a character who worked for the losing cause, the
protagonist was a foreigner). In this film, Luis, brilliantly portrayed
by José Luis López Vázquez, is an editor from Barcelona who journeys
to Segovia to bury his mother's remains. As a child, his parents had
taken him to Segovia to spend his summer vacation at the home of his
Aunt Pilar, but the war broke out, and he was to remain there as
somewhat of an outcast, since his parents supported the Republicans,
and his aunt, the Nationalists. Upon his return, Luis sees both places
and people--his aunt's house, his school, and above all, his Cousin
Angélica--that flood his mind with memories from the past. Saura
follows the same narrative technique that he used in *El jardín de las
delicias* to portray Luis's memories: José Luis López Vázquez again
plays both the adult and the child, using gestures, facial expressions,

and vocal intonations to admirably capture the soul of the youngster.

Luis is a man of literature--he even "borrowed" a poem from Antonio Machado to woo his cousin as a youngster--and he is conscious of his own mental processes and their relation to literature.   While looking at old photographs, he cites Proust's madeleines to explain the phenomenon, and in the next scene, the hot chocolate that his aunt offers him serves as a stimulus for a flashback.   Indeed, different sensorial stimuli trigger Luis's jumps to memories of his youth in a total of eighteen structural segments in the narrative.   Here, while the adult Luis savors the chocolate, his Aunt Pilar looks at him, and a zoom-in converts the protagonist into the young Luis who is drinking chocolate at his aunt's house in 1936 and complains to his mother that he does not want to stay there.   Luis's memories begin with the opening shot of the film, which provides what Marsha Kinder calls a "powerful germinal image": "As we hear choir boys singing, we see white mist drifting through a church schoolroom, which is illuminated by strange overexposed lighting; the camera slowly glides through wreckage, observing signs of violence from some unknown disaster. We do not yet know what happened, nor do we recognize the mode of reality--present event, nightmare, or memory.   Yet the image immediately engages our attention and opens the door to Luis's consciousness" ("Carlos Saura" 20).   We only fully understand this image when we take it in syntagmatic relationship with a later segment in the film: after a priest at school gives an emotional sermon about death and eternity, stressing that even they as young boys can be victims of "the red fury," we see the schoolboys in the cafeteria and hear the sound of airplanes and of bombs falling and exploding. There is then a repetition of the initial scene, a scene that forms an indelible memory from the civil war--the bombing of the schoolhouse.

Luis's journey to the past begins even before he reaches his aunt's house.   Luis makes the journey in his Seat automobile, and a long shot of the town provides the visual image that triggers a jump to the past: as Luis turns around, the car is now a 1930's model, and his parents attribute his car-sickness to travelling in the back seat.   Once at his aunt's house, the camera shows us the building through Luis's eyes-- closeups of the front door to the building, the door knocker, and the railing all provide the potential for triggering memories of the past. The visit to his schoolhouse provides a sequence that is both memory and imagination: "The Eyes of London" was a film that the priests used to show.   A music rehearsal and the image of a religious painting of Saint Sebastian provide both auditory and visual stimuli to transport Luis back to the time when he participated in a religious festivity; the zoom into "the boy Luis" dressed as a Roman soldier with a fake beard marks the visual transition. The priest's instructions to the boy, "Inmovilidad absoluta" (Absolute immobility), must be taken in both a literal (physical) and a figurative (spiritual) sense regarding the attitude of the church. A second religious painting, that of the mortified nun (with the motto, "Pereció el mundo y su concupiscencia" [The world and its concupiscence perished]), which hung in the bedroom in Aunt Pilar's house, also provides the visual stimulus for presenting a combination of memory and dream. With Luis in bed, the nun, with symbolic images that criticize the role of the church--a lock on her lips, and a worm coming out of her heart--appears at the foot of his bed. At Luis's shouts of "No, no, me lleva, no" (No, no, she's taking me away, no), a young Aunt Pilar awakens the boy from his nightmare. The image of the nun later merges with that of a nun with bandaged hands who offers her mortification for the good of the Nationalist cause, and in particular, so that Luis's Republican father would see the light. Another memory regarding the doubt and fear that religion instilled in him as a youth is that of a priest accusing the twelve-year old of erotic relations with his cousin.

Luis's relationship with Angélica in both temporal planes is the crux of the narrative. Their games in the countryside and exploration of the house attic both in the present and in 1936 provide a feeling of counterpoint in the film. In the past, their game of hide and seek while raspberry picking, and the sexy promenade by the young Angélica (that even includes her showing her bra to Luis while a train whistle "off" imbues the scene with Freudian undertones) exude an erotic tension of desire between the two young cousins. As adults, Luis accompanies Angélica and her family to a plot of land where they intend to build a home, and they play with a frisbee. Here, in contrast, the two cousins admit their failure and unhappiness to each other: Luis, a bachelor, is free, but alone; Angélica is married, but to a man who has simply grown weary of her. When the two adults later examine several old articles in Aunt Pilar's attic, they sit together on the roof of the house, and their kiss--accompanied by the 1930's music of Imperio Argentina, which evokes the days of their youth--is interrupted by the call, "Luisito, Luisito." Indeed, we have again returned to 1936, for it is Angélica's father, with a prominent Nationalist uniform and fascist belt-buckle, who is calling, and the young Angélica in pony-tails emerges

Absolute immobility: Saura's <u>La prima Angélica</u>, starring José Luis López Vázquez. Courtesy Elías Querejeta, P. C.

from the attic window. In the development of the story, this interruption foreshadows the more definitive break in their relationship that Angelica's father also causes. In the present, Luis realizes that he cannot recapture the past: in spite of Angélica's advances--she initiates the romantic encounter on the roof, gives Luis a rubbing of their names that were engraved on a stone cross before the war, hugs him and exclaims that she is lonely--Luis believes that there is nothing else for him to do in the town and that he should leave. Kinder feels that the final separation between Luis and his cousin "repeats what has already happened in the previous generation between Luis's father and his Aunt Pilar. When the lonely lady bids farewell to her nephew, she says, 'Tell your father that . . . no, nothing.' For the same reasons, Luis already has nothing to say to his cousin Angelica" ("Carlos Saura" 22). However, the division between the brother and sister of the older generation was based on conscious ideological and political decisions on their part; Luis and Angela were victims of these decisions--their relationship was destroyed by *cainismo*, and not of their own accord.

One of the most gripping sequences of the film consists of a key memory from the war. As his aunt gives Luis a letter from his parents dated July 5th, 1936 that ironically informs him that they will come to

Erotic tension: Saura's <u>La prima Angélica</u>, starring José Luis López Vázquez and María Clara Fernández. Courtesy Elías Querejeta, P. C.

get him at the end of the month, we hear gunfire in the street--a symbol of all of the conflict that is to come. The family awaits anxiously, praying and listening to the radio for news. The announcement that the city has joined the "Movement of Salvation" of Franco's troops brings shouts of joy to the family members ("Son los nuestros" [They're on our side]) and cognac to accompany the fascist hymn, "Cara al sol" (Facing the Sun), on the piano. The image of Luis apart from the group--the camera zooms into him next to the door--symbolizes that he is now the "black sheep" of the family.

Nevertheless, this germinal memory leads to a questioning of the very process of remembering. When Luis tells Anselmo that although thirty years have passed, "te estoy viendo cerrando ventanas el 18 de julio de 1936" (I can see you closing the windows on July 18th, 1936), his cousin's husband insists that he is mistaken, because he (Anselmo) was in Burgos that day. Angélica later confronts Luis with his confusion of her husband and her father, and she shows him an old photograph of the latter to prove that they look nothing alike. Nevertheless, Fernando Lara points that the equivocation between the father and the husband, who, in the film are portrayed by the same actor (Fernando Delgado) corresponds to historical memory's accuracy in seeing different people who display the same type of authoritarian personality as indeed one and the same ("Estructura" 158). We do not only see Luis's distorted memories however, but also his imagination in the past which was equally distorting. During Luis's memory of his outing with his cousin in 1936 to pick raspberries, Angélica tells him that Nationalists will execute his father when they enter Madrid. The camera zooms into a surprised and worried Luis who answers with the rhetorical, "¿A mi padre?" (My father?). Luis then "sees" his father being executed, an event that never really occurred. Thus, as Fernando Lara points out, there is a complicated presentation of reality in the film, one that appears on various levels: the imaginative (Luis "sees" his father executed); the oneiric (the "Eyes of London" sequence, and the dream about the nun); and the irrational (with relationships between objects that are apparently unconnected such as a ship that leaves Barcelona and a painting in the dining room) ("Estructura" 155).

As the adult Luis leaves his cousin's home, he encounters her daughter (played by María Clara Fernández de Loayza, who also plays the Angélica of 1936) and has one final jump into the past. The final trigger here is the girl's bicycle, which the adult Luis asks to borrow. The young girl sits on the handlebars, and they take off. A close-up of the spinning pedals separates the present from the past, as does important color symbolism that Saura uses in this moment: the bicycle of the present is blue, but the one from the past is red. In 1936, their attempt to escape to Madrid terminates in failure when Nationalist soldiers stop them and return them to Angélica's home. In the final gripping scene, the girl's angry father quotes a Spanish proverb, "Cría cuervos y te sacarán los ojos" (Raise ravens and they will pluck out your eyes), and proceeds to punish Luis: he whips the boy, who is on his knees, with his belt while Angélica's mother combs the crying girl's hair in the next room. (This final image of the film and the first two words from the proverb provide Saura with the opening image and the title of a later film.) Kinder comments that "this moment imprints on them forever, splitting them not only from each other, but also from their own passionate feelings, transforming them into detached spectators of both the present and the past" ("Children" 64). Thus, the beating that Luis receives transcends the physical, broaching the spiritual level between the two characters. In even broader terms, Fernando Lara sees the final sequence as the "perfect image-symbol of

Punishment of the black sheep: Saura's <u>La prima Angélica</u>, starring José Luis López Vázquez and Fernando Delgado. Courtesy Elías Querejeta, P. C.

the relation between victors and vanquished" ("Estructura" 158).[41]

The other politically charged image of the film is Luis's memory of Angélica's father with his arm in a cast from a wound that he received during the war: his arm is straight and pointing at an angle upward in what appears to be a frozen fascist salute. Although reactionary elements in Spain took great offense to this image, Carlos Saura defended it, saying that it was "a very coherent sequence . . . that worked marvelously" ("Entrevista" 15). The comment that Anselmo makes to Luis, "Han pasado más de treinta años y todavía hay quien se acuerda de la guerra civil" (More than thirty wars have gone by, and some people still remember the civil war), contains a good bit of irony. For Luis, the war is much more than a distant memory; rather, it is a weight that he carries everywhere and that shapes his life every day. Indeed, Saura has declared, "Luis ends up devoured by his past. The force of those ghosts, of those characters from the past, of

---

[41]Oms offers a similar opinion, stating that this final scene symbolizes the "reality not only of the war, but above all, of a post-war period where the total physical, intellectual, moral, and spiritual elimination of the adversary was the order of the day" (<u>Carlos Saura</u> 58).

those life experiences, of those images, and above all, of those
memories, is such that they end up devouring the character" (Galán:
Venturas 53).

The emotional reaction to the film was unprecedented. In addition
to denunciatory letters to the editors that appeared in *Pueblo* and *El
Alcázar*, a scathing article that appeared in the falangist newspaper
Arriba, and phone calls of protest to the Minister of Information and
Tourism, rightist elements took action against the film.[42] On July 11,
1974, the debut of the film in Barcelona was cut short because of a fire
bombing of the Balmes cinema. In Madrid, at the Amaya cinema,
rightist elements not only threw stinkbombs, but also broke into the
projection box and stole several meters of the film, an act that the
right-wing newspaper *Fuerza Nueva* defended on June 1st, 1974, as an
act "in the face of a tolerance that should never exist . . . which was
carried out by those who have the obligation of being the guardians of
heroic symbols like that one" ("No son ladrones" 17).

Perhaps the most important aspect of these two films by Carlos
Saura is that both *El jardín de las delicias* and *La prima Angélica*
provided Spaniards who did not support the Nationalist cause with an
opportunity for catharsis, since they could finally empathize with an
artistic expression of their reality. Critic Jean Tena notes that like
many novelists of his generation, Saura constructs a new vision of
Spanish history, of Spanish reality based on a polysemic text that
constitutes a rebellion against the monosemic ideology and culture
imposed by the Franco regime (Tena 18, 23). *La prima Angélica*, after
being banned following the incidents in Barcelona and Madrid, returned
to Spanish movie-theaters and proved to be one of the top grossing
Spanish films during a period of more than two years.

In 1974, Jaime de Armiñán directed *El amor del Capitán Brando*,
starring Ana Belén, Fernando Fernán Gómez, Jaime Gamboa and
Amparo Soler Leal. This film is the first to favorably treat a returning
exile. The film enjoyed great commercial success, and was second
only to Borau's *Furtivos* in box office returns for Spanish films during
1975. With beautiful photography by Luis Cuadrado, there are many
picture-postcard shots of the valley, the mountains, and the small
village of Trescabañas, which is actually the very picturesque Pedraza

---

[42]An English translation of the main segments of the letter from <u>Arriba</u> appears in
Besas: 125-26.

de la Sierra in the province of Segovia. An aging Fernando returns to the village of his youth to find that many things have changed. He asks for a "porrón" (a type of wine bottle with a long spout) in the bar, only to find that no one drinks wine in that fashion any more. This scene represents the constant dialectic between the fossilized past that the exile carries within and the new society that he encounters. After noting a change in the bar's decor, Fernando's admission that he has not returned since 1939 connotes the political reason for his absence, and the exact cause of Fernando's exile surfaces during a conversation with a young teacher named Aurora as the exile examines old books and a photograph of his father. Fernando not only uses the normal euphemism to describe his father's assassination at the hands of right-wing extremists, but adds a gruesome note to further reflect the fascists' violence: "Le dieron el paseo, pero antes lo arrastraban atado a la cola de un caballo" (They took him on a "stroll," but first they dragged him around tied to the tail of a horse). This represents the first reference in Spanish cinema to the brutality of those related to the Nationalist cause.

Fernando's affection toward Aurora grows, but the narrative contains a love triangle, the third member of which is Juan, a thirteen-year-old student in Aurora's school. (Drawings of scenes from the old west during the initial credits foreshadow the fact that Juan enjoys play-acting in westerns, and his imitation of Marlon Brando gives the film its title.) The possibility of a sexual relationship between the teacher and her charge culminates during a class field-trip to Segovia when she and Juan miss the bus to return home, and share a hotel room together. With a gratuitous *destape* scene--Aurora removes her blouse in front of the bathroom mirror--director Armiñán momentarily panders to the Spanish audiences who suffered through decades of screen censorship. This is not *The Summer of '42*, however, and Aurora takes on a rather maternal role at this point, telling Juan, "Eres un niño. ¿Qué te has creído?" (You are a little boy. Who do you think you are?). Armiñán intertwines the political and sexual themes when the local authorities relieve Aurora of her position on the charges that she corrupted a minor. The students respond with a strike in which placards with slogans such as "Justicia" reflect the desire for freedoms in Spanish society in both an intratextual an extratextual sense. Indeed, the political satire of the scene in which the mayor addresses the crowd in a speech which could have been given by the Caudillo himself caused

The problems of returning home: Armiñán's <u>El amor del Capitán Brando</u>, starring Fernando Fernán Gómez and Ana Belén. Courtesy Filmoteca Nacional.

problems for Armiñán: censors must have thought that the political resemblance between the mayor and Franco was too close, since the director had difficulty obtaining approval of the film script, and censors especially required cuts and modifications of this scene with the mayor.

Aurora follows Fernando to Madrid, where his crisis about being old and an outsider continues to grow.   After a self-deprecating conversation with Aurora in which he proclaims, "No sirvo para nada" (I'm not good for anything) and "Este país parece otro" (This seems like another country), he approaches a kiosk and asks for newspapers of yesteryear--*El Sol, Ahora*, etc. This inquiry can only be an example of more self-deprecation, as if he wanted to prove to himself the sad fact that he is out of touch and out of place. Fernando has been living in Amsterdam, and the linguistic element constitutes a further barrier to reintegration. To further manifest his role of outcast, he mentions that his two children do not speak a word of Spanish, and that sometimes he feels that he does not either. Nevertheless, the physical contact with places associated with his past trigger memories in Fernando, and he comments, "De este barrio, no quedó ni un ladrillo" (Not a brick was left standing in this neighborhood). Aurora's ingenuous response, "¿Cuándo?" (When?), brings this retort: "En la guerra. No sabes de qué guerra te estoy hablando" (In the war. You don't even know what war I'm talking to you about). Fernando, however, is not the only one who mentions the war. Other characters in the film make references to it, showing that it marked everyone of his generation and younger Spaniards as well. The old woman who accompanies the cows at the beginning of the film remarks, "Murió demasiada gente en la guerra" (Too many people died in the war). When the mayor charges that Aurora is corrupting the boys that will be the men of tomorrow, his maid states, with a gesture of great contempt, "Y bastante nos ha pasado en la guerra" (We already had enough happen to us in the war). Even young Juan shows that he has been marked by the stereotypes imposed upon him by his elders when he inquires of Fernando, "¿Eres rojo?" (Are you a red?). In order to defuse this emotionally charged term, Armiñán has the aging character respond with the rhetorical, "¿Qué entiendes tú por rojo?" (What does red mean to you?). Indeed, the characterization of this returning exile in the film is most favorable and designed to elicit our sympathy for him. If anything, perhaps Armiñán went too far in stripping Fernando of any political or ideological attributes.

Aside from the political caricature with the mayor, the only negative character is a truck driver. A long shot of Aurora embracing Juan during their play-acting constitutes the perspective of the truck driver who is observing them, and because of the distance between observer and observed, he draws a false conclusion about Aurora's sexual conduct. The truck driver later visits the teacher at her home, and after being rejected, he makes another visit to brutally murder her pet German shepherd, and he finally attempts to rape her. Apart from the sensationalist element, this scene can only serve to exemplify violent uncontrollables in society, and thus, in part, confirm the hypothesis made by both Fernando and Aurora that, in spite of all the years, people have not changed after all. Although Aurora successfully defends herself from the attack, this is only one of two gratuitous mentions of rape in the film, the other being when Fernando says that he cannot remember (!) if he ever raped any women when he was a soldier. Indeed, the film is replete with sexual innuendo, beginning with the voyeuristic opening scene in which young peeping Toms try to get a glimpse of Aurora dressing in her bedroom at night. Of course, *El amor del Capitán Brando* is a product of its time, the waning years of the Franco regime. Indeed, director Armiñán has stated that in *El amor del Capitán Brando*, he attempted to tell a parable of Spain under the Franco regime (Besas 144-45), and this is particularly evident in the sequences involving the student strike. Although it has defects, its treatment of political and sexual themes opened the doors for many films to come.

In 1975, Armiñán filmed *Jo, papá* (Gosh, Dad), starring Ana Belén, Antonio Ferrandis, Amparo Soler Leal, and Fernando Fernán Gómez, a movie that was not allowed to be released until after the death of Franco. The film narrates the trip of a Spanish family from Vigo, in north-western Spain, to the Mediterranean coast. The trip is not an ordinary vacation, however; the father of the family, Enrique, attempts to retrace his participation as a Nationalist soldier in the Civil War, and thus relive the events not only for himself, but as a history lesson for his wife, Alicia, and his two daughters, Pilar and Carmen: "Quiero que me lo recordéis conmigo, paso a paso" (I want you to remember it with me, step by step). Enrique's glorification of his role in the war is evident in the memorabilia in his office: a close-up shows a photograph of soldiers, and there is a Spanish flag on his desk, his old rifle and a map of Spain on the wall. At each stop along the route, Enrique shows that he is still living in the past. At a cafe in Asturias, he elicits bewilderment from a young employee when he asks, "¿Vive aún doña Concha?" (Is doña Concha still alive?) and his wife has to repeatedly call his name to break him out of his day-dream. While camping in the countryside, Enrique's day-dream while gazing at a valley is intensified by the sound "off" of the bagpipes and gunshots of his Galician regiment, and he tells his daughter that this was the first place where he entered battle. Armiñán later repeats this technique of adding the bagpipe music "off" at the end of the film when Enrique wades into the Mediterranean.

He meets two persons from his past on his journey, and they both serve as contrasts to the character of Enrique, underscoring the idea that he is living in the past. At a bar in Oviedo, Enrique orders "sidra" (an alcoholic beverage made from apples), which he says tastes just like it did many years ago. When he wanders out the back door of the bar, he sees an old woman in a chair and says, "Fuiste tú, ¿verdad? De mí no te acuerdas, claro, pero yo no he podido olvidarte" (It was you, wasn't it? Of course you don't remember me, but I haven't been able to forget you). When the woman gets up without responding to him, he attempts to manifest an air of superiority that comes from being on the victorious side: "A pesar de todo, ganamos nosotros" (In spite of everything, we were the ones who won). The woman's response connotes years of hardship forced upon the vanquished, but at the same time a desire not to open up old wounds: "¿Crees que no me he enterado en todo este tiempo? No es de buena ley recordar todo aquello. . . . Vete, estamos en paz" (Do you think I haven't found out in all this time? It's just not right to remember all that. . . . Go, we are at peace). She underscores her sentiments of reconciliation by offering him an olive branch in the form of country ham. Later in the trip, Enrique wants to visit a priest who served with him during the war, Father Comesaña. His friend's greeting in the form of billingsgate, "Me cago en la mar" (Holy Shit), indicates that things are not as they were. Indeed, Comesaña has left the priesthood, become a teacher, is married and has a family. Enrique, clinging to the past, accuses his friend, "Tú lo que eres es chaquetero" (You're a turncoat, that's what you are). Comesaña defends himself, however, saying, "No seas más papista que el papa" (Don't be holier than thou). The ex-priest certainly does not live in the past, and he reacts with incredulity to Enrique's journey with his family, warning him that it is time to forget the days gone by. In particular, he advises him not to go to visit Teruel, because there are too many dead there. This advice helps advance the subplot, an amorous relationship between the twenty-three year old daughter, Pilar, and a young disk-jockey whom she meets along the way named Carlos. Armiñán intertwines this with the main narration by means of the generation gap theme. Enrique, living in the past, still calls his daughter "Pili," much to her dislike, and remembers times when they used to bathe together. He chides Carlos, "Ustedes los jóvenes no respetan nada" (You young people don't have any respect for anything), and when Carlos admits that he did not fight in the war, Enrique assumes a defensive posture of one who knows, at least subconsciously, that his victory, after so many years, is empty: "Pero yo sí, y la gané. No nos lo perdonan, ¿verdad?" (But I did, and I won it. You'll never forgive us, will you?). Because of Comesaña's advice, Pilar must travel alone to Teruel, where she had promised to meet Carlos. There, in a scene which includes some "obligatory" *destape*, Pilar and Carlos finally decide to sleep together, perhaps so that Carlos will not have the same opinion of her that he has of her father: "Que se le ha parado el reloj" (His watch has stopped on him). A second amorous intrigue that is not fully developed is that between

A veteran's attempt to retrace history with his family: Armiñán's <u>Jo, papá</u>, starring Antonio Ferrandis and Ana Belén. Courtesy Sogepaq, S.A.

Alicia, Enrique's wife, and Julio, an old flame whom she happens to meet at an opera performance at the beginning of the film. This intrigue serves as an analogy to her husband's trip, and shows the impossibility of recovering the past.

Isabel Muñoz notes that *Jo, papá* has a basic theme analogous to that of *El amor del Capitán Brando* with protagonists who live in the past and resist change; here he is a Nationalist, in the former film, he was a Republican (33). According to Peter Besas, however, "The script for *Jo, papá* had a much harder time than Armiñán's earlier films because the two Spains were clearly represented, that of the "reds" and that of the Nationalists. Since the script was prohibited, Armiñán shot three different versions. When the completed film was submitted to the censors, Armiñán was told that "while Franco was still alive the film could not be released, to a great extent because it poked fun at the veteran father who, like Franco, was a total anachronism" (Besas 145). Perhaps some of the problems with the censors are the cause of the rather mediocre value of the film, whose main problem lies in the script, both in terms of over-all conception of the narration, and in the dialogue, which is often as inane as the title.

Jaime de Armiñán's *Al servicio de la mujer española* (In Service to the Spanish Woman, 1978) centers on a radio program in which the female protagonist (Marilina Ross) gives advice to forlorn women. The film uses the gaze into a mirror to trigger its first return to the past. The male protagonist, Julio Hernández (Adolfo Marsillach), is seemingly a homosexual, and as he sits before a mirror in his bedroom, he applies make-up to his face. When his Aunt Celsa enters, he explains that he is going to a costume party, and when she comments how much he looks like his mother, a dissolve transforms the mirror to the "movie screen" of Julio's memory, as we see him sitting in front of the mirror, watching a scene from his childhood. The memory then fills the entire frame, as a priest calls school boys in the yard as a siren sounds. Young Julio runs into a bathroom stall and locks the door. Although the boy has gone there to defecate, the priest accuses him of doing "porquerías" (indecent acts) and puts a hose under the door and sprays him with water. A cut to the classroom reveals an equally oppressive atmosphere. The initial long shot reveals a priest sitting below a crucifix that is flanked by portraits of Franco and José Antonio. The history lesson, about Hannibal and other "caudillos" (leaders) of the ancient world, leads into a glorification of the current "caudillo." Since young Hernández does not make the analogy, the priest insults and belittles him, and it is left to another boy to literally sing the praises of "Francisco Franco, born in Ferrol . . . " who led the fight against the Marxist hordes. As the class ends, the priest and the students raise their right hands in the fascist salute as they sing "Viva España" (Long Live Spain). The close-up of the priest, with his extended right hand almost touching the camera lens, and the deep focus showing the crucifix on the wall behind his head, is an especially compelling image. A dinner conversation with Irene triggers a second flashback to Julio's school days, and is also related obliquely to his mother. When Irene defends certain moral principles and laws regarding the family, Julio responds "Me parece que he oído esto en alguna parte" (It seems to me that I have heard that somewhere before), and a dissolve takes us back to the corridor of his school. A priest calls out the names of the other boys and tells them each a time. Since Julio's mother has not come, however, he receives a slap in the face from the priest, an image that portends a later comment by the adult Julio that a priest once slapped him so hard that a tooth fell out. Although Irene says that you cannot judge a system by the actions of an individual, Julio's retort is an accusation against the repressiveness of the Franco regime, which consisted of "cuarenta años de mal gusto, mentiras y aburrimiento, sobre todo de aburrimiento" (forty years of bad taste, lies and boredom, above all, boredom). Julio condemns Irene for her role in maintaining the repressiveness of the regime: "Bien nos habéis jodido. La familia, el orden, la decencia, el honor, la autoridad. Esos valores eternos que no sirven para nada y que tú defiendes todos los días" (You all have really screwed us. The family, order, decency, honor, authority. Those eternal values that are not worth anything and that you defend every day).

However, Irene's adhesion to traditional values slowly disintegrates throughout the narrative. Her sister Mari, who lives with Irene, tries to keep the radio show hostess in line: Mari tells her that she should defend transcendental values, and asks, "¿O también has cambiado de chaqueta?" (Or have you become a turncoat, too?), an expression that reflects the political divisions contributing to the *cainismo* in Spain. When Irene tries out some of the freedom to which Julio has alluded, not arriving home until three-thirty in the morning, Mari's attempts to control her sister range from verbal attack (comparing Irene's private and public lives), the threat of physical violence (she raises her hand to slap Irene), and psychological blackmail (her tachycardia suddenly acts up). Nevertheless, Irene continues to exercise her newfound freedom, and performs a strip-tease in front of her bedroom mirror. When the spying Mari discovers Irene, her reaction exemplifies the values of the regime: she returns to her room to pray, "mea culpa."

The duplicity of Julio's character also develops throughout the film. He claims to be a homosexual, and refers to himself as Soledad. Nevertheless, even in an early stroll with Irene near the beach, his actions seem to negate his words. When she inquires whether or not he had ever tried sex with women, he responds that he doesn't like women. While saying this, however, he gently caresses Irene's face and lips with his hand. Julio takes photographs of Irene at the beach, and when he invites her to his home, he tells her that he wants to photograph her in the nude. She declines, so he later cuts one of her photographs and pastes the head onto the photograph of a nude woman, which he then projects onto a screen. His gaze of desire in this heterosexual context seems to belie his homosexuality. He claims that he owes his affluence to his grandfather, who became rich through the black market, and yet he shows no remorse for this ill-gotten gain. His Aunt Celsa later confronts Julio in the garden, and tells him to stop lying to Irene about his grandfather's role in the civil war. Finally, after Irene gets advice from her friend and co-worker Manolo (Emilio Gutiérrez Caba), Armiñán cuts to a scene with Julio and Irene in bed in which he admits that he is not homosexual and has been lying to her all this time. His final words to her, "Ni siquiera sabes hacer el amor. Márchate" (You don't even know how to make love. Just leave), only confirm his earlier opinion of himself: "Soy la persona más desgraciada que conozco" (I'm the most wretched person that I know). Irene's final anagnorisis comes during her radio show, when she is unable to come up with a response to one of her listeners: she admits, "Creo que lo que estaba diciendo todos estos años no vale" (I believe that everything that I was saying all these years is no good), and after the camera pans down from her face to her hands in close-up, she crumples the listener's letter.

In *Al servicio de la mujer española,* Armiñán seems unable to fully address the theme of homosexuality, or sexuality and its relationship to the oppressiveness of the Franco regime. Problems with the script make some aspects of the plot seem especially weak: the scene of the sisters in bed saying dirty words as a symbol of their new liberation, or the scene at the factory when the working women all laugh at Irene's radio show both seem ill-contrived. The same can be said of the film's ending: Irene catches a ride on a school bus in which the teacher loses control over her rowdy--read "independent"--students while attempting to deliver a lecture about medieval monarchs. When Irene asks a young student (who seems to be a boy) of about nine what his name is, he replies, "Soledad"--the same pseudonym used by Julio. Is this to imply that the next generation is truly liberated? The dedication of the film appears as an epilogue: "A todos los que empiezan a vivir alegremente" (To all those who are beginning to live happily). Although Armiñán surely conceived the film as a paean to liberation and freedom, it falls short.

According to Román Gubern, a statement by Ramón del Valle-Inclán inspired Saura to explore the complex mechanism of memory and the relationship between the present and the past in *La prima Angélica*: "Las cosas no son tal como las vemos, sino como las recordamos" (*1936* 158). This same statement becomes of even greater importance in the 1979 film directed by Vicente Aranda, *La muchacha de las bragas de oro* (The Girl With the Golden Panties), which is based on the novel by Juan Marsé. The aging falangist Luys Forest (Lautaro Murúa) decides to write an autobiography in order to understand himself: in his own words, "Me voy enterando de mi vida en la medida en que la escribo" (I'm finding out about my life as I write about it). The film begins with the voice-over of this character as he walks along the beach: "Los trágicos sucesos de aquellos años que me convirtieron en nómada. Era un extraño en mi propio pueblo. Habían de trastornar para siempre el curso de mi vida, convirtiéndome en ese buscador furtivo de una segunda identidad, abandonada en algún recodo del pasado, quizás basada en el cenagoso entusiasmo de aquellos años arrogantes obligatoriamente calificados como victoriosos" (The tragic events of those years made a nomad out of me. I was a stranger in my own town. Those events were to change the course of my life forever, making me a furtive seeker of a second identity that was abandoned in some corner of the past, and perhaps based on the muddy enthusiasm of those arrogant years that were obligatorily certified as victorious). This opening statement reveals some important characteristics of the protagonist as well as major themes of the film. Luys is Catalan but was a Falangist, unlike the majority of his regional compatriots who supported the Republic, and he was therefore an outcast among his own people. This division is particularly acute among his own family. Luys's voice "off" corresponds to the act of writing his memoirs, and we see an early flashback to October of 1942 when his father's burial took place. Luys's comment, "Consigo las miradas acusadoras de los pocos amigos que han acudido al entierro" (I get accusing looks from the few friends who have attended the funeral), manifests the aforementioned division, which is even further underscored by a woman's shout in Catalan of "Visca la República" (Long Live the Republic). In contrast, Luys is on the side of the victorious Nationalists; indeed, he was the "cronista oficial de la victoria" (official chronicler of the victory). Nevertheless, Luys would have us believe that he slowly began to doubt his ideological stance; hence the search for his real self. Luys writes, "No era posible para mí tras la celebración de la eufórica victoria ignorar más tiempo una serie de pequeños acontecimientos que golpeaban mi conciencia" (After the celebration of the euphoric victory, it was no longer possible for me to ignore a series of little incidents that knocked at my conscience). A flashback takes us to a key scene in the development of a new political consciousness: as we see workers who speak Catalan being detained as they leave a factory, the camera recedes back to behind a bar window where Luys and a friend view the scene and complain that, in the words in Luys's memoirs, "Se están pisoteando una lengua y una cultura" (A language and a culture are being trampled on). In the next scene, the young mustachioed Luys paces up and down in his blue Falangist uniform while a friend reads Luys's resignation from the party.

These flashbacks constitute Luys's memories, and he overtly tells his niece Mariana (Victoria Abril), "Nada es como es, sino como se recuerda, dijo Valle-Inclán" (Nothing is as it is, but rather, as it is remembered, Valle-Inclán said). After a disagreement over the identity of a woman in an old painting--Luys thinks that it is Mariana's mother, and Mariana believes that it is her Aunt Sole, Luys's estranged wife--he begins the same line of thought, saying, "Las cosas no son como son . . ." (Things aren't as they are). His niece quickly corrects him, however, saying, "Pues tampoco son como se recuerdan" (They are not as they are remembered, either). Thus, as the plot progresses, we see the constant negation of Luys's false memories. Although an early scene shows a close-up of the young Luys shaving his "bigotito cursi y simbólico" (pretentious and symbolic little mustache), a physical attribute that linked him to the fascist ideology, Mariana later calls this memory into question, saying "Sin embargo, yo de niña te acuerdo con bigote, y no hace tanto tiempo" (Nevertheless, as a little girl I remember you as having a mustache, and that wasn't long ago). All of the subsequent flashbacks show the young Luys with the mustache, belying his claims. Indeed, Luys admits, "No lo hice, pero lo pensé infinidad de veces" (I didn't do it, but I thought about it an infinite number of times). Although at the beginning of his memoirs, he states that he was able to gain his father's freedom from a fascist prison, Luys later admits that his father died in jail. His resignation from the Falange is likewise false, as Luys admits to his niece, "Esa carta no la escribí nunca, pero me la sabía de memoria" (I never wrote that letter, but I knew it by heart). Luys also confuses and falsifies his relationship with his wife, Sole, her sister Mariana, and the latter's husband, José María Tey. While writing his memories, he says, "Habrá que reinventar fielmente aquel piso" (That flat will have to be faithfully reinvented), but the dissolves linking the image of the elder Mariana in a gray shawl and Sole in a pink shawl and then both in the same image while playing the piano, indicate an inability to faithfully reconstruct the past, or perhaps even a conscious effort to falsify it. A flashback to a love-making scene at the piano is the justification for Luys's marriage to Sole, since he says that he later realized that it was she, and not Mariana who had been playing in the darkened room.

Nevertheless, later flashbacks show that subsequent encounters between Mariana and Luys were charged with eroticism: in a close-up of Mariana in a smoky bar, she says to Luys, "¿Quieres que te la chupe?" (Do you want me to give you a blow-job?) and in long shot of a naked Mariana swinging on a swing on Luys's lawn we hear her shouting, "Quiero chupársela al camarada Forest" (I want to give comrade Forest a blow-job). Luys negates any wrongdoing, however, telling his niece, "Estuvimos a punto de cometer un serio disparate. No pasó nada, pero José María Tey pensaba que sí" (We were at the point of committing a serious mistake. Nothing happened, but José María Tey thought so).

Time and time again, Luys Forest attempts to manipulate the past to his advantage, but in each case, the naked truth finally emerges to discredit him. In Luys's statement, "Me voy enterando de mi vida en la medida en que la escribo" (I'm finding out about my life as I write about it), the verb "to write" here does not connote "to faithfully preserve" but "to invent," "to embellish" and "to falsify." Ramón Freixas notes that the film acquires a "magnificent dimension regarding the political tergiversation sustained by the Franco regime" (62).

The fact that his niece, Mariana, has the same name as her mother immediately causes an identification between the two. The younger girl is a hippie, in a characterization that seems almost overdrawn at times. She visits her uncle with her female, yet androgynous lover, Elmyr, who paints the golden panties of the title onto Mariana's anatomy. The latter uses cocaine, has burn marks on her breasts, does not mind Elmyr's infidelity, and, half naked, alternately repels and seduces her uncle (she warns him, "Había pensado poner un gillete en el coño el día que te decides a penetrar" [I had thought about putting a razor blade in my cunt for the day that you make up your mind to get in] but later invites him, "¿Quieres ver cómo me corro, tío?" [You want to see how I jerk off, uncle?]). The consummation of the sexual act between them occurs at the end of the film, just before the elder Mariana, in a visit to Luys, thanks him for his discretion for the young Mariana's sake during all these years. Thus, Forest "learns" of his incest, and he goes to his bedroom to get his pistol. While we see an exterior shot of his window, we hear a shot, and can only guess that he has committed suicide. However, Forest has merely shot himself in the hand, a bit of poetic justice for his repugnant act in the 1930's of shooting a young man in the hand who was urinating while leaning against an exterior wall of his house where the yoke and arrows (symbol of the Falangist party) were displayed. In the final scene of the film, Forest tells

Mariana that she is his daughter. Her flippant response, "Bueno, ¿y qué?" (Well, so what?), represents the final manifestation of her rejection of his moral and ideological code. Critic Ramón Freixas points out that the role of the young Mariana in the film represents the dichotomy of provocation and destruction by the female, but that in this narration, the dichotomy transcends a merely sexual context and acquires a political meaning as a "settling of accounts" (62).

While the nudity and sexual scenes caused some Spanish critics to object to the film as being pornographic, novelist Juan Marsé has defended his narrative, stating, "This is the convulsive story of two characters that strip in public with very different moral spirit. One does it on the outside, the other on the inside . . . the truth is that the nakedness of Forest-Lautaro Murúa . . . is the only exhaustive, immodest, and immoral nudity that the movie offers. Contrary to what is normally believed, the interior 'nudity' can be more scandalous--and in this case it certainly is--than the exterior. As the character himself would say, 'Things aren't as they seem" ("Vicente Aranda" 23).

Carlos Saura's 1982 film, *Dulces horas* (Sweet Hours) repeats many of the thematic and narrative elements of his earlier films about the civil war. At question are history and memory: how traumatic experiences of the past influence the present, and how an individual's memory, while recreating the past, also falsifies it. Saura manifests the primordial importance of memory beginning with the opening scene in which Juan Sahagún (Iñaki Aierra) is sitting on a sofa looking at old photographs in an album, and the sound track underscores the theme with the music of Imperio Argentina singing "Recordar" (To remember). Juan disagrees with his sister Marta (May García) about the true nature of their mother, and whether or not she committed suicide. A zoom into Juan triggers the first flashback to a scene when young Juanico (young Juan, played by Pablo Hernández) enters his mother's bedroom with a packet from the pharmacy. His mother had been reading a letter and is very upset. After she tells him that she loves him more than anyone else, she tells him to leave, and he does. The scene ends with a close up of the packet in her hand and a shot of a glass of water. This same scene is repeated later in the film, but with different camera angles: the visual point of view is now from the foot of the bed, instead of the side of the bed in the first version. More importantly, instead of leaving the bedroom, Juan stays to see his mother empty the contents of the packet in the glass and drink it. He confesses, "Fui testigo de su muerte. Que maldad la suya" (I was a witness to her death. How wicked she was). This transformation of the past--a manipulation of Juan's memory--occurs after Juan has discovered new information about his mother that has caused him to change his opinion about her. The information came in letters given to him by his sister Marta. Juan now admits, "bajo aquella capa de dulzura y sensibilidad se escondió una mujer voluntariosa y dominante . . ." (underneath that façade of sweetness and sensitivity, a headstrong and domineering woman was hidden). He also comprehends and justifies the abandonment of his mother by his father: "Ahora veo claro que la única opción que tenía para escapar a la sumisión total" (Now I clearly see that it was the only option he had to escape total submission).

After Juan leaves an old elevator and enters an elegant old flat in downtown Madrid, he fondles a maid; only when he pays her with an old peseta, and she calls him Juanico do we realize that we have left the contemporary frame of the narrative and have made a temporal jump to the past. Juan enters a living room in which his mother, uncle, sister, aunt, and grandmother--all dressed in clothing from decades ago--are chatting. A close-up of a newspaper that his uncle is reading shows news about the German invasion of Russia. His uncle and grandmother chide Juan for coming home late, and he explains that he lost track of time while at the movies, watching the film *Gilda*. His grandmother's comment that *Gilda* had its debut in Madrid in 1947 is incompatible with the temporal framework that was indicated by the close-up of the newspaper, and again manifests the falsification of the past by Juan's memory. As the family eats dinner in the dining room, they listen to a radio broadcast with news of the invasion of Stalingrad. After a further flashback to a brothel, the dinner scene is interrupted when Juan's uncle suddenly scratches his nose, and announces "Bueno, por hoy es suficiente" (Well, that's enough for today) as he takes off his sweater. We suddenly realize that this has been a representation, a dramatic recreation of the past, and that these characters are merely actors who are playing out the parts written by Juan Sahagún for his work, *Dulces horas*. What seemed to be a reworking of the principal narrative device in *La prima Angélica*--the adult actor also playing the part of the child--acquires a slightly different twist, since the flashbacks are played by a child actor, and Juan is merely representing himself in his youth. Nevertheless, past and present converge as Juanico walks down a path in a park toward the camera and the adult Juan passes by him; Juanico also interrupts the embrace of Juan and his lover Berta at the same picnic spot where the young boy interrupted the embrace of his mother, Teresa, and father. Berta represents Teresa in Juan's play, and in Juan's mind, they are the same woman. When Juan takes Berta to the picnic spot visited by his parents and himself years ago, his lover asks who was there besides his mother; Juan responds, "Estabas tú y yo" (You and I were), thus confirming his mental identification of the two women. As in *La prima Angélica*, the same actress (Assumpta Serra) plays both roles, and again a photo serves as objective proof of the subjective falsification of memory, since Berta sees a picture of Teresa and comments that they don't really look that much alike.

Aside from acting, Berta also dubs films. As Juan watches her dubbing rehearsal, a scene is repeated several times with slightly different nuances. Of course, dubbing is an act of manipulating, transforming, and this is accentuated here by the repetition of different versions of the same scene, which echoes the repetition of key scenes within the film narrative (the possible suicide, and the young boy's separation of the embracing man and woman). The film projected on a screen during the dubbing rehearsal cuts to a documentary film of the Nationalist bombing of Madrid during the civil war. Sirens sound and bombs explode as civilians run for subway entrances to head to bomb shelters. A piano substitutes for the bellicose sound effects, and using the same yellowish tint of the documentary film, Teresa and Juanico also run for shelter. By combining fiction within the documentary footage, Saura intertwines fiction and reality, memory and history, and thus manifests the irony of the statement made by the actor who portrays Sahagún's Uncle Pepe (Alvaro de Luna): "No se puede confundir la vida con la ficción" (You can't confuse life with fiction). This confusion also occurs when the actor who plays Uncle Antoñito becomes so involved in his role as a fascist hero from the Blue Division who fought at the Russian front that he departs from the script and begins to rant Nationalist slogans: "Este país. España. Hay que volver a las cruzadas" (This country. Spain. We have to return to the crusades).

Uncle Antoñito's narration of his deeds at the Russian front tells of his early morning sentinel duty: "Había una luz incierta . . ." (There was an uncertain light . . .). As he utters this phrase, a voice "off" is heard to utter, "Luz. Esta luz. Apague esta luz" (Light. This light.

Turn off this light). This voice in the background is unconnected to Uncle Antoñito's narrative, and its meaning only becomes clear later in the film when it is repeated during a flashback when Juanico has a light turned on at his bedside. Spot lights outside the window, and the sound of planes and bombs exploding repeat the traumatic civil war experience.

Just as the second version of Teresa's supposed suicide is different from the first, Juanico's interruption of the lovers' embrace is significantly transformed during a second version of this scene. Initially, Juanico pushes his father aside, and substitutes for him in receiving the affection of his mother. In the second version, Juanico likewise separates the adults, but after kissing Berta, he also kisses Juan, all to the strains of Imperio Argentina's "Recordar". This "repetition" of the past cannot be an exact repetition, and its transformation is fundamentally due to Juan's new understanding of and reconciliation with his past, and in particular, with the true character of his mother. The final sequence with Berta echoes the repetitive nature of the other narrative elements: she is pregnant, just as Teresa was pregnant with Juan, his sister Marta was pregnant, and her young daughters played at being pregnant--a foreshadowing of their participation in this cyclical event.

Spanish critics bashed *Dulces horas*: could Saura only repeat the same old themes? Did he not have anything new to say filmically? Hooper (158) goes so far to consider the film a self-parody of Saura's earlier movies. It is significant to note that Saura did indeed abandon the civil war and its repercussions during his films from the 1980's--the dance trilogy of *Bodas de sangre, Carmen*, and *El amor brujo*; *El dorado*; and *La noche oscura*. However, the accusation that Marta's husband makes to her and to Juan in *Dulces horas*, "Siempre con el pasado a cuestas" (The past always haunts you), could also be made to director Saura. He will return to the civil war, but when he finally does so, in *¡Ay Carmela!* (1990), it will be in a very different tone and narrative style.

In 1983, Spain won its first Oscar for a feature length film with José Luis Garci's *Volver a empezar* (To Begin Again), Academy Award winner for Best Foreign Film for that year,   starring Antonio Ferrandis, Encarna Pasó, José Bódalo, and Agustín González. The film narrates the return to his native Gijón of Antonio Miguel Albajara, an exiled Republican who is a professor of Spanish literature at the

University of California, and has been awarded the Nobel prize for literature, and who is on his way to Stockholm to garner the award. The scene containing a surprise phone call of felicitation from King Juan Carlos to the author often elicited standing ovations among Spanish movie audiences. Garci takes a melodramatic approach to the return theme, since the reason for Antonio's visit to Gijón is that he has discovered that he is terminally ill, and he wants to visit the places and friends of his youth one last time before dying. The narrative is imbued with a good deal of melancholy, with comic relief that is occasionally exaggerated from Geuvasio Losada (Agustín González), the hotel desk clerk. Antonio's journey to the past is mainly sentimental; Besas calls the scene in which Antonio confesses to his old friend, "Roxu," that he has only a few more months to live "one of the most touching scenes in Spanish cinema" (239). The real search for the past of this film is personal and amorous, as Antonio seeks out his old girlfriend, Elena. Their affair (Elena says, "Vamos a pasar la noche como amantes lujuriosos" [Let's spend the night together like lustful lovers]) constitutes an attempt to recuperate the lost love of their lives, as well as an homage to mature lovers, as Antonio says, "Los hombres y mujeres son capaces de amar hasta el último momento de la vida. En realidad, sólo se envejece cuando no se ama" (Men and women are capable of loving until the last moment of their lives. In truth, you only grow old when you don't love).

Touristic long shots of Asturias (the beach at Gijón, the chapel to the Virgin of Covadonga), and of the city of the Golden Gate upon Antonio's return to the United States, together with the ever-popular "Begin the Beguine," which provides the sub-title of the movie as well as important moments of the soundtrack, all contributed to the success of the film. Garci concluded the film with an epilogue in which he gave thanks to the generation of Spaniards whose lives were interrupted. But Garci glosses over the reason for the interruption, with scant references to Antonio's stay in a concentration camp in France. The political dimension in this film is even less than in *El amor del Capitán Brando*. One can only speculate as to what extent that this lack of historical specificity contributed to the film's recognition outside of Spain, but the lack of political involvement certainly irked many Spanish critics who had to begrudgingly concede his international success (Besas 240-41).[43] Indeed, its recognition by the Academy caused *Volver a empezar* to have an important role in raising the overall international status of the Spanish film industry.

In *Los paraísos perdidos* (The Lost Paradises, 1985), Basilio Martín Patino narrates the return to Spain of Concha (Charo López), the daughter of a Republican intellectual who went into exile, and her encounter with the physical surroundings and the friends of her youth. Martín Patino uses the voice-over as a fundamental technique in the narrative to enter into the inner thoughts of the protagonist. Near the beginning of the film, as Concha passes a romanesque church and opens the large door of an old house, we hear her voice "off" proclaim "vuelvo a las regiones abandonadas de mi vida" (I return to the abandoned regions of my life). The image of the disordered patio that she enters, with boxes, bricks, and ceiling tiles lying about, underscores the sense of this abandoned past. Now living in Germany with her husband Walter and daughter, she returns to Salamanca because her mother is dying. As she puts some order into her old home, she works on a translation of Hölderin's *Hyperion*, "whose quotes so subtly guide and mark the moral states and fantasies of the central character" (Molina Foix, "*Los paraísos*" 151). Quotes such as "¿No habrá un lugar donde yo pueda vivir?" (Isn't there any place where I can live?) and "Me encierro en mí mismo como una larva" (I close into myself like a larva) manifest the inner anguish of an exile. In addition to the *Hyperion*, another important aspect of the narrative's lyrical dimension comes from the lyrics of Amancio Prada's song, "Libre te quiero" (I love you free).

The political element of the film surfaces when Concha is interviewed on the local radio program dedicated to "Current Protagonists." Concha's friend Benito (Alfredo Landa) refers to the radio interviewer as "that fascist" and insists during the interview that Concha mention the foundation that she intends to create in her father's memory. Concha declares to the radio host, "De protagonista, no me veo, ni de triunfadora mucho menos" (I don't see myself as a protagonist, much less as a victor), and when questioned "¿Qué se siente al volver?" (What do you feel upon returning?) her response is "Se trata de empezar una nueva etapa en mi vida" (It's a matter of

---

[43] Not all Spanish critics panned the film; Norberto Alcover, for example, cites the excellent qualities of Antonio Ferrandis's performance ("José Luis Garci" 226).

Beginning a new stage in life: Martín Patino's <u>Los paraísos perdidos</u>, starring Alfredo Landa and Charo López. Courtesy La Linterna Mágica, S.A.

beginning a new stage in my life). Both of these comments manifest a subtle political and personal theme of this and the other films that deal with the return from exile: the impossibility to return to the past. However, the film script somewhat minimizes the historical and political events that shaped Concha's existential circumstances: she states that "El mío ha sido un silencio normal de cualquier otra mujer" (Mine has been a normal silence of any woman) and the disruption in the painting career of her mother was like that of so many other women, who for different reasons, found it impossible to fully live their lives. By minimizing the importance of her return, Martín Patino eschews the triumphalism that characterized the victory of the Nationalists, and he also implies a certain disillusionment with the present political situation in Spain. He later expands on this theme when Concha visits the town hall to visit the mayor. The idea of a foundation in her father's memory is reduced to a mere marble plaque; Benito inquires, "¿Sólo eso?" (Is that all?), a question that disinflates the hypocrisy of the intellectual/political ruling class. The inability to return to the past also is manifest in Concha's affair with Miguel. As with the sexual consummation in other exile films, the fleeting attempt to travel down a path that has already been discarded leaves a sense of sadness and unfulfillment.

Los paraísos perdidos also constitutes an homage to Salamanca by
Martín Patino. The camera lingers on the architectural beauty of the
city--the cathedral, the Plaza Mayor, the University, etc. The director
also captures the atmosphere of this Castilian community in the carnival
festivities, its music (*pasodobles* such as "El gato montero" [The
Mountain Lion]) and in the outdoor cafés of the Plaza, in which prize-
winning novelist and Salamanca resident Gonzalo Torrente Ballester has
a cameo role. In the end, however, it is the *Hyperion* that sets the final
tone. The last voice-over is the quote, "¿Qué son, pues, la muerte y
todo el sufrimiento de los hombres?" (What are death and all the
suffering of mankind?).

Fernando Fernán Gómez's *El viaje a ninguna parte* (The Trip to
Nowhere, 1986) was winner of several prestigious awards, including
Goyas for Best Picture, Best Director, and Best Script. The film
portrays a company of itinerant actors during the 1940's and '50's, and
stars Fernán Gómez, José Sacristán, and Gabino Diego as three
generations of comedians: Don Arturo, Carlos, and Carlitos Galván.
The structure of the film consists of a series of twelve flashbacks
following the opening close-up of an elderly Carlos saying, "Hay que
recordar" (One must remember). The shadowing space of this
preliminary shot turns out to be an old-folks home in 1973 where
Carlos undergoes sessions with a psychiatrist about his memories--or
about his memory, since the very act of remembering is called into
question. After Carlos rediscovers his long-lost seventeen-year-old son
and incorporates him into the troupe (a process that contains some of
the most humorous sequences of the film), the actors travel from town
to town, fighting for their survival. Their enemies include other
troupes of actors as well as rival entertainment such as soccer ("our
worst enemy"--even Carlitos momentarily abandons the troupe), and
cinema, which evokes anger on the part of the clan elder. Don
Arturo's outbursts, with typical Spanish billingsgate, humorously
counterbalances the tragedy of their situation: he threatens the movie
entrepreneur, Solís, saying, "Me cago en el jodido peliculero. Le
mato. Voy a estrangularlo con sus jodidas películas" (Fuck the fucking
movie-man. I'll kill him. I'm going to strangle him with his fucking
movies). Nevertheless, Juanita (Laura del Sol), Carlos's lover and
member of the troupe, succinctly captures their misery with the lament,
"Tengo hambre, Carlos" (I'm hungry, Carlos). She later complains,
"Esto no es un oficio, Carlos. Somos vagabundos" (This is not an

occupation, Carlos. We're bums), and says that people prefer the movies, and she does, too. Ironically, she abandons Carlos "with somebody from the movies" in order to work at a bar in Rota (where there are American sailors with money), and this is the first in a series of death-blows to both the troupe and Carlos. Eventually even Carlos capitulates, and he decides to go to Madrid to work as an extra in the movies, to which his die-hard father-actor exclaims, "Me cago en el padre de los hermanos Lumière" (Fuck the father of the Lumière brothers). The inherent humor in this billingsgate helps mitigate the pathetic situation of the actors. Don Arturo himself had attempted to work in the movies, but much to the consternation of the film director, the old man was unable to accommodate his dramatic declamation to the cinema. The director's exacerbation grows until he shouts, "Corte o me corto yo los huevos" (Cut, or I'll cut my balls off), and Don Arturo must retire from the scene crying, a defeated man.

The socio-political element of the film appears very subtly. One of the initial reasons for the economic hardships that the actors face is a satirical comment about the social life of the Caudillo, and how his personal mores were imposed on the nation: the theaters had to close early--"cosas de Franco, como no salía" (it was one of Franco's things, since he never went out at night). The moral climate is intertwined with political ramifications when Don Arturo expresses his surprise and chagrin at seeing a rival theatrical troupe in town. The setting is during mass, and his use of more curse words ("¡Coño, son los Calleja Ruiz!" [Shit, it's the Calleja Ruiz family]) offends a local matron, Doña Florentina. Although Don Arturo, with hat in hand, contritely apologizes in the plaza after mass, Doña Florentina will have none of it: "Hay que apedrarlos. Son rojos, rojos, rojos" (We should stone them. They are reds, reds, reds). The repetition of the term underscores the political divisions that culminated in the fratricidal conflict of almost twenty years before.

Another competing theatrical company was a student group sponsored by the government, as Don Arturo angrily informs us ("they are from the Falange"). Nevertheless, the relationship between these itinerant dramatists and the government or the *falange* also brings them favor; this is due to the fact that one actor, Juan Maldonado (Juan Diego) fought in the "Blue Division" in Russia and therefore had "inside influence." Indeed, it is through Juan's contacts that Carlos, as an old man, is able to obtain a place in the old folks' home.

Maldonado's fascist past, however, leads to what is the weakest segment of the film, a drunk scene in which the script, especially Carlitos's dialogue, is marred by ill attempts at humor. The drunk Maldonado brags of his "privileges": "tengo pistola y carnet" (I have a pistol and party i.d. card). This "privilege" allows him to terrorize and humiliate a young couple that he finds kissing in the shadows; Carlitos's "humor" does not mitigate the degradation of the scene. Maldonado's privileged place as "ex-combatiente" (veteran) helps to get him housing at a *pensión* in Madrid, and Galván also subtly refers to it when his psychiatrist questions what would have been normally unacceptable behavior during the Franco regime. The interrogative refers to the episode when Solís offers the troupe work as actors in a film. The local men who want the work threaten the itinerant actors, "Ningún forastero nos quita el pan" (No outsider is going to take our bread and butter away), and after the shot that culminates the threatening posture--an extreme close-up of the local mayor--Carlos responds with an eloquent verbal rebuff in which he extols the locals' hard work, justifies his mission in life ("la gente necesita reírse y nosotros les llevamos la risa" [people need to laugh, and we bring laughter to them]) and appeals to their sense of solidarity: "somos vuestros hermanos en el trabajo, o la falta de trabajo y la falta de pan" (we are your brothers in labor, or lack of labor and lack of bread). A cut to the present shows an incredulous psychiatrist: "¿Y usted, Galván, dijo todo esto en un pueblo de España en los años 50?" (And you, Galván, said all this in a town in Spain in the 1950's?). The retired actor's response is two-fold: that is the way that he remembers it, and that Juan Maldonado also spoke. The second half of the response indicates Maldonado's privileged place as a veteran; he would be allowed to speak words that would have been prohibited of others; the first half reflects the problem of the mechanism of remembering.

Indeed, the scenes in the present with the psychiatrist often refute Carlos's memory. When the actor remembers Kennedy's visit to Spain (the visual image of the plaza festively decorated and Spaniards waving American flags as the cars pass by is an homage to García Berlanga's 1952 *Bienvenido, Mr. Marshall*), a cut to the psychiatrist not only rectifies Carlos's faulty memory, but also subtly criticizes the Franco regime: "Kennedy nunca visitó España. Ni el Caudillo quitó la censura" (Kennedy never visited Spain. Nor did the Leader remove censorship). Carlos's flawed memories of his successful screen-acting career (festivals in Venice, Cannes; his photograph on the cover of *Primer plano* film magazine) are ironically counterbalanced by the arrival at the old folks' home of the famous actor Daniel Otero, who has a trunk full of newspaper clippings that attest to his brilliant career. Why does Carlos confuse reality? As the elderly Maldonado (now a bookseller) observes to his friend, "Tu oficio es mentir" (Your occupation is lying).

In films such as *La prima Angélica* or *La muchacha de las bragas de oro*, the function of memory has more of a political and historical dimension; here it is more personal and addresses the question of the fine line between fiction (drama) and fact, memory and imagination. The multiple fade-outs at the end of the film formally underscore the fusion of these opposites: the images of a young Carlos dancing with Marilyn Monroe, the troupe walking through the Spanish countryside, the cars from the Kennedy entourage stopping to pick them up, and the final long shot of the bus on the country road constitute the dreams and reality of an itinerant actor in the Spain of the 1950's. The final shot of the bus on the empty road graphically captures the title of the film; reality, in the end, outweighs fantasy.

El mar y el tiempo is a film directed by Fernando Fernán Gómez which had its debut in October of 1989. The film stars José Soriano as a Republican who returns to Madrid in 1968 from Buenos Aires after twenty-nine years of exile, Fernán Gómez as his brother Eusebio, and Rafaela Aparicio as their aging mother--a role which immediately brings to mind an intertextual relationship between this film and her role as mother-figure in Saura's *Ana y los lobos* and *Mamá cumple cien años*. The first dialogue between the reunited brothers addresses the political question, and delineates a marked difference between the two: Jesús inquires what Eusebio thinks of the work of the exiles, and the latter's cynical response is, "¿Qué labor?" (What work?). Generally, however, the political dimension in the film is displaced from the exile question to that of the younger generation of Eusebio's daughters and their friends. The latter live in an apartment adorned with a poster of Ché Guevara, sing "Al vent" (To the Wind, the protest song by the Valencian singer-songwriter Raimon that was popular at the time), name their daughter "Libertad," and participate in student demonstrations in both Madrid and Paris. The only intersection of the two political components occurs when the young Mariano meets Jesús and expresses his political solidarity with the older generation:

"Estamos con todos los que se fueron como usted" (We are with everyone that left like you did). The action is set in 1968, and the official news from Spanish radio and television differentiate the socio-political situation in Spain from that of the rest of the world: the assassination of Martin Luther King, the war in Vietnam, and student rebellions in Paris manifest a turbulent world that contrasts with the news that manifests thirty years of "peace": the Franco regime's "Birth Prize" for a family with nineteen children.

Jesús experiences the normal reactions of the exile: he is unable to relate to his changed homeland. He expresses his lack of reintegration throughout the film narrative with statements such as "No reconozco nada" (I don't recognize anything), "Yo lo recuerdo de otra manera" (I remember it in another way), "No es lo que yo dejé" (It's not the same as I left it). Eusebio takes his brother to see a statue that he remembers from his youth as one in which they could see its sexual organ protruding from the side. A low-angle circular tracking shot reflects the brothers' vain attempt to confirm the boyhood memory; the close-up of the statue shows no protruding organ, and the sudden appearance of green leaves in front of the camera causes Jesús to remark, "Lo taparon con el arbolito" (They covered it up with the little tree). More than a veiled barb at censorship during the Franco regime, this statement functions as a safety-valve so that Jesús can avoid admitting his faulty memory.

Unlike in *El amor del Capitán Brando*, where the linguistic element is a cause of alienation (as Fernando complains that he does not even seem to speak Spanish), in this film, the linguistic element manifests the reintegration theme. During a card game in the restaurant, the players insult each other with expressions of typical Spanish billingsgate ("Tonto del culo" [Asshole], "Vete a hacer puñetas" [Fuck off], etc.), and this strikes a real chord in Jesús, who exclaims, "Sentí por primera vez que había vuelto" (For the first time, I felt that I had returned).

Jesús's inability to achieve reintegration into Spanish society is manifest in allusions to visits to old friends in Vallecas. Since this community forms part of the "red belt" around Madrid, the narrative connotes an attempt to reformulate the friendship with old leftist companions from the pre-war days. This attempt is unsuccessful, however, as Jesús notes on two occasions that he found them "different" and that "No me entendí con ellos" (I didn't get along with them). The greatest breach, however, is between the brothers

Brothers reunited: Fernán Gómez's <u>El mar y el tiempo</u>, starring Fernando Fernán Gómez and Pepe Soriano. Courtesy Ión Producciones, S.A.

themselves.   Both reminisce about the hard times that they went through during the post-war. Jesús became a pimp in Buenos Aires; Eusebio was a black-marketeer in Madrid, and only later was able to find work in the restaurant where he is currently employed.   His admission that a member of the Opus Dei backed him in the restaurant draws a protest from his brother and provides a glimpse into how Eusebio betrayed his prior intellectual and political point of view. The change in Eusebio is confirmed during the most poignant scene in the film, when Jesús visits his brother's ex-wife, Marcela.   As in many Saura films, music functions here as a Proustian device to trigger memories of the past: with songs such as "La canastera" (The Basket Maker) and "En el barranco del lobo" (In the Wolf's Ravine) from the 1930's, Jesús comments to Marcela that he can see her skipping rope. But times have changed: Marcela is now an alcoholic, and her tragedy stems from the war, since her husband was a different man before the war, one with ideals who wanted to change the world, not the "desecho que es ahora" (wreck that he is now). Indeed, the relationship between Eusebio and Lupe, his young "compañera," confirms Marcela's opinion of him: steeped in cynicism, Eusebio seems happy to have as his female companion a woman who deals in a world of drugs, bribery, and influence peddling.

Ontological questions: <u>El mar y el tiempo</u>, with R. Aparicio, Fernán Gómez, A. Sánchez-Gijón, I. Miramón, C. Marsillach. Courtesy Ión Producciones.

Doña Eusebia cannot accept the fact that her son has returned. She has a fossilized image of her son, that shown in the close-up of the young Jesús in a soldier's uniform that Eusebia wears in a locket. After a close-up of a tin box of "dulce de membrillo" (quince-meat) that she has prepared for him, she complains that although he loved it as a boy, he did not even look at it during their reunion, proof for her that this man is not Jesús.   For Eusebia, this man is an impostor; her son drowned in the sea trying to escape after the war. When Jesús decides to return to Argentina, he expresses to his mother yet another statement reflecting his lack of integration: "Esta España no es la que yo conocía" (This Spain is not the one that I knew); her response, "Ni usted es usted" (And you are not you), represents the ontological underpinning of the dilemma faced by all exiles. The relationship between exiles and the motherland is one of fossilization: while both the individual and the society change, the act of separation freezes the dynamics of the inter- relationship between the two and makes the possibility of successful repatriation ever more difficult with the passage of time. The final shot of the film, the superimposed image of the sea and phonograph speakers, manifests a circularity in the narrative, since the opening shot was of the sea and a radio; it thus underscores both in visual imagery as well as the accompanying sound track of the tango, "Mi Buenos Aires querido" (My Dear Buenos Aires), the inevitable failure of repatriation, and ineluctable departure from Spain of the exiled Republican to return to his adopted land.

Vicente Aranda's *Si te dicen que caí* (If They Tell You That I Fell, 1989) interweaves different layers of fiction in several different temporal planes. At the beginning of the film, a caption indicates that the action begins in 1970. An ambulance delivers a dead body to a hospital, and as Ñito prepares the cadaver, he sees a large ring on its left hand and recognizes the drowning victim. He asks Sor Paulina "¿Se acuerda usted de Java, verdad?" (You remember Java, don't you?). Ñito then evokes events of the past: a second caption identifies the temporal plane as 1940 as the shabbily dressed Ñito (or Sarnita) as a boy tells "aventis" or tales that constitute a "handy and cheap way of dreaming" to the other boys in his gang of friends. A close-up of Sarnita saying "I'm going to tell you..." cuts to the rag man Java (Jorge Sanz) on the way to his first sexual encounter with Ramona. The line between history and fiction blurs and becomes murkier as the film progresses.

One of the principal causes for confusion is the prostitute character(s). There are three whores: Ramona, with whom Java has sex in front of the voyeuristic eye of Conrado, and with whom he later falls in love; Aurora Nin, the "red" whore who had worked as a housekeeper for Conrado, and whom Conrado and the other fascists are looking for as responsible for the death of Conrado's father; and Menchu, the platinum blonde lover of the rich blackmarketeer. The narrative itself creates a confusion among these three characters as others give information that links them together: that Aurora probably changed her name and dyed her hair (is she now Menchu?), that Menchu's name could not be mentioned at a girls home because of something terrible that she had done (did she, and not Aurora, cause the death of Conrado's father?), or that when Java finds Ramona in a bar he calls her Aurora. Director Aranda underscores the confusion in the narrative by casting Victoria Abril in the roles of all three prostitutes. The most distinguishing physical characteristic of the whore(s) is a scarred breast. Java's brother Marcos (Antonio Banderas) tells him that the fascist Conrado caused the scar with a champagne bottle, but Java replies that it was a wound from a bomb. Jumping back in time to the beginning of the war, Marcos confronts Conrado's mother about the incident, saying that her son caused it with a corkscrew, but Aurora says that it was an accident. Sarnita tells the other boys that the "red" whore has a microfilmed document implanted in her breast. These multiple and contradictory versions of the cause of the scar create an atmosphere of total ambiguity in the narrative.

The blurring of reality and fiction also occurs in dramatic representations. The children rehearse for a religious play directed by the former fascist lieutenant, Conrado. Java has the part of Lucifer, and Saint Michael is played by a girl.   As Java's representation switches from confrontation to seduction, Conrado voyeuristically observes them as if they were the paid prostitutes in his bedroom. The children also practice another drama, a surprise for Conrado, during which Java interrogates Fueguiña. The costumes of the other children, (especially the use of skulls, which underscore the sex/violence/death motif) manifest the playacting qualities of the scene. When Java interrogates Fueguiña about the prostitute, he assigns her the role of Aurora,   and the girl's declamatory style emphasizes the dramatic, unreal quality of the narrative in this scene.

Sarnita often has the role as unreliable narrator in the film. As an adult in the morgue, he even admits to his dead friend that his sordid tale is better than what occurred in reality: "Deberías darme las gracias, Java, por lo bien que quedas en mis aventis" (You should thank me, Java, for how well you come out in my tales). When the boys see Java sitting on a park bench with Justiano, the one-eyed fascist, Sarnita says that he can read lips even at that distance, and he tells what they are saying. His narrative, however, is transformed into the dialogue of a western: "Yo buscarte, Flecha Negra. Yo fumar contigo la pipa de la paz. Yo decirte toda la verdad" (I look for you, Black Arrow. I smoke peace pipe with you. I tell you whole truth). This scene cuts to a scene in which Java, arriving at Conrado's house, learns that he will earn triple for today's performance, only to enter the bedroom and discover a young man waiting for him in bed. We then return to Java and Justiano on the bench, and the young rag man tells the fascist, "Oiga, camarada, tengo que abrirme camino como sea. Quiero quitarme el mugre y los piojos de la trapería. El quiere volver a la sarna y el odio, a la sangre y a las barricadas. Quiere quemar las iglesias otra vez y saquear a los ricos. Ese no es mi hermano, no. Nunca pensé que pudiera ser mi hermano ese sucio guiñapo. Les quitarán el miedo. Podrán descansar al fin." (Listen, comrade, I have to get out no matter what. I want to be rid of the crud and the lice of the old clothes shop. He wants to go back to rage and the hate, the

blood and the barricades. He wants to burn churches again and sack
the rich. That's not my brother. I never thought that dirty bum could
be my brother. They'll take their fear away from them. They will be
able to rest at last). Juxtaposed with the scene in which the level of
Java's prostitution reaches its greatest degradation (as indicated by the
face that Java makes when he discovers his new assignment), the
dialogue manifest Java's willingness to climb the social ladder at any
cost. The switch to an unidentified third person singular (he) in Java's
dialogue causes momentary confusion, but we realize that the mention
of his brother means that Java has sunk down so low as to betray him.
(A later scene in which the one-eyed Justiano arrives at the old clothes
shop with a carload of armed fascists confirms the betrayal.) Java's
further shift to third person plural (they) adds another layer of
confusion. Is Sarnita not reading Java's lips correctly? Does "they"
refer to Marcos and Aurora? The couple escapes just before the
armed fascists arrive, but the blast from a bomb or buried mine in the
empty lot that they were crossing causes the irate Justiano to shout,
"Ya nos han jodido otra vez estos cabrones" (Those bastards have
screwed us again). Has their escape frustrated the fascists again, or
is it their death that has done so? The camera pans vertically through
the dust and smoke, and we see a low-angle long shot of the couple
running in slow motion. Are they now amidst the clouds of a celestial
sphere for lovers? Sarnita and the boys comment on the victim that lies
in the empty lot. Was she the whore who gave hand jobs in the
movies? Only the lover of a blackmarketeer could afford the coat that
she was wearing. Did the *maquis* dump Menchu's body in the lot so
as to appear to be the victim of the mine, or was her appearance there
a mere coincidence? The epilogue adds to the confusion. In the present
(1989) when the elderly Luis asks Palau what ever became of that
blonde, the former *maquis* dismisses him, but from the back seat of a
taxi, he sees the old whore and an elderly man begging at an outdoor
cafe. Dressed in shabby clothes with a hat that has what looks like
small pieces of paper on it--bringing to mind Marcos's origami birds--
the brief glimpse of the couple underscores the fact that all of the
characters in the film are losers.

Aranda's use of the soundtrack adds to the ambiguity of the film
with regard to the multiple temporal planes of the narrative. As we
jump from 1970 to 1940, or to 1936 (at the beginning of the war, in
the army headquarters) or to the single episode before the war when

Conrado can walk and begins his voyeuristic activities as he spies Marcos and Aurora having sex in his bedroom, Aranda often marks the transition from one moment to another with sound, such as music, or the moaning love-making. Since these sounds occur on both sides of the cut from one scene to another (on two temporal planes) the result is a fusion--or confusion--of time.

Si te dicen que caí is a harsh, brutal, negative, ambiguous film that reflects a reality of equal qualities. Critic Ramón Freixas ("*Si te dicen*" 42) calls it "one of the key films of recent Spanish cinema" and the critics from the Spanish film journal *Dirigido* voted it one of the best Spanish films of the decade. Yet the controversial brutality of the film, together with its decidedly confusing narrative, detract from the film's positive qualities.

Chapter 8

Divisions Run Deep

The divisions caused by the civil war persisted for decades after the end of the fratricidal conflict. In the final years of the Franco regime, and even into the transitional period in which Spanish democracy once again began to stand on its own two feet, the war was a touchstone in society. The legacy of the conflict--the division of Spanish society into victors and vanquished, the alliance between the military and the church in order to impose a single ideology, state control of the media and labor unions--all make these years of the regime very difficult ones for many Spaniards. Film makers capture these years in a variety of films that include: Carlos Saura's *La caza* (The Hunt, 1965), *Cría cuervos* (Cria! [The Spirit of Ana], 1972), *Ana y los lobos* (Ana and the Wolves, 1972), and *Mamá cumple 100 años* (Mama Turns 100, 1979); Basilio Martín Patino's *Nueve cartas a Berta* (Nine Letters to Berta, 1965); José Luis Garci's *Asignatura pendiente* (Course Incomplete, 1975); José Luis Borau's *Furtivos* (Poachers, 1975) and *Tata mía* (My Nanny, 1986); Francisco Rodríguez's *La casa grande* (The Big House, 1975), Jaime Camino's *El desencanto* (The Disenchantment, 1976), Manuel Gutiérrez Aragón's *Camada negra* (Black Litter, 1977), *Guerra de papá* (Daddy's War, 1977) by Antonio Mercero, Jordi Feliú's *Alicia en la España de las maravillas* (Alice in Spanish Wonderland, 1977), Gutiérrez Aragón's *Sonámbulos* (Somnambulists, 1978), Luis García Berlanga's *La escopeta nacional* (The National Shotgun, 1978), *Patrimonio nacional* (National Patrimony, 1981), and *Nacional III* (National III, 1982), José María Gutiérrez Santos's *Arriba Hazaña* (Up With Hazaña, 1978), Juan Antonio Bardem's *Siete días de enero* (Seven Days in January, 1979), Antonio Hernández's *F.E.N.* (F.E.N., 1980), Jaime de Armiñán's *El nido* (The Nest, 1980), *Kargus* (Kargus), directed by Miguel Angel Trujillo and Juan Miñón (1981), Víctor Erice's *El sur* (The South, 1983), Mario Camus's *Los santos inocentes* (The Holy Innocents, 1984), Antonio Giménez Rico's *El disputado voto del señor Cayo* (The Disputed Vote of Mr. Cayo, 1986), Vicente Aranda's *Tiempo de silencio* (Time of Silence, 1986), and *La sombra del ciprés es alargada* (The Shadow of the Cypress Is Elongated, 1990), directed by Luis Alcoriza.

The year 1965 marks an important transformation in the treatment of the civil war and its aftermath on the Spanish screen. Carlos Saura's *La caza* (The Hunt) and Basilio Martín Patino's *Nueve cartas a Berta* (Nine Letters to Berta) each constitute a new vision of the *cainismo* theme in which the directors present a very critical look at Spanish society. Caparrós Lera notes that Saura's film, with its profound ideological element, broke away from the amorphous Spanish cinema of the 1960's (*El cine* 118). Saura has defined *La caza* as "a documentary about a crisis situation" (qtd. in Gubern *Carlos Saura* 16) and has stated, "there is an attempt to reflect some Spanish problems and even to recreate a certain atmosphere of the civil war" (qtd. in Brasó 128). This black and white film portrays a group of four men-- José (Ismael Merlo), Luis (José María Prada), Paco (Alfredo Mayo), and Enrique (Emilio Gutiérrez Caba)--who go out to the countryside on a hunting expedition. The first three are middle aged and have been friends for many years; Enrique is of a younger generation. García Fernández points out the intertextual importance of the casting of the older characters in this film: Saura "was able to take advantage of earlier performances--Alfredo Mayo in *Raza* (Race), *A mí la Legión* (The Legion is for Me), and *Un paso al frente* (A Step to the Front); Ismael Merlo in *La fiel infantería* (The Faithful Infantry)--benefitting the characters that they embodied in *La caza*, which conferred that past that the film did not furnish" (254).

The hunting site is a dry deserted area with depressions in the ground. A snare drum "off" provides a military connotation to the inquiry by Enrique, "¿Eso es de la guerra?" (Is that from the war?), and Luis's response "Aquí murió mucha gente--a montones murieron aquí--y ahora sólo quedan los agujeros. Buen lugar para matar" (A lot of people died here--loads died here--and now only the holes are left. It's a good place for killing). Enrique functions in the film as the ingenue who, through the process of defamiliarization, questions--and therefore subverts--the established order. D'Lugo notes that "Enrique's "continual use of field glasses and cameras makes him more a witness-observer than a participant in the action during much of the early part of the film" (61) but his vision of the members of the war-generation becomes an act of subversion, since his views through his telephoto

A violent metaphor for the civil war: Saura's <u>La caza</u>, with Emilio Gutiérrez Cabo, Alfredo Mayo, Ismael Merlo. Courtesy Elías Querejeta, P.C.

lens result in a magnification that "expresses the vain, egotistical, and inflated self-image each man has of himself" and "reaffirms Enrique's private view of his fellow hunters as aging, weak men" (*Films* 65).

Luis's response is the first of a series of references to (and foreshadowings of) violence that builds in a steady crescendo throughout the film. When José gazes across the landscape and comments, "Aquella vez estuvimos más abajo" (That time we were further down below), it is evident that he, Paco, and Luis are indeed veterans of the conflict. Their elevated socio-economic position indicates that they are veterans of the victorious Nationalist cause. Indeed, José is the owner of the land, and his exploitation of Juan, the impoverished caretaker, is, according to García Fernández (254), one of the key elements in a political reading of the film. In addition, Luis sings and speaks in German in the film, and this linguistic element allies him (and by extension, the others) with the fascist ideology.

Although the men have gathered to hunt rabbits, Luis's early comment, "la mejor caza es la caza del hombre" (the best hunt is the hunt for man) underscores the gripping visual images foreshadowing a fratricidal conflict (which is also underscored in an auditory sense by Luis's whistling of the "Battle Hymn of the Republic"). Saura intercuts close-ups of Paco aiming his shotgun to the right of the screen with close-ups of José aiming his to the left, and the Kuleshov effect gives the impression that they are about to shoot each other. From the traps that Juan warns about, to the skeleton that José shows to Paco, death impregnates the landscape. However, the most important aspect of the atmosphere is the oppressive heat which acquires the same existential weight as in Camus's *L'Étranger* (The Stranger). The constant images of wiping the sweat from their brows, their shirts stained with perspiration, and the comments by José ("Este maldito sol me está poniendo nervioso" [This damned sun is making me nervous] and later "Nos estamos asando vivos" [We are roasting alive]) and Paco ("Este calor insoportable" [This unbearable heat] and later "Nos vamos a atizar como siga pegando el sol como está ahora" [If this sun keeps beating down like it is now, we are going to get stirred up]) indicate the importance of this element of nature in the crescendo of antagonism.[44] The climate of violence and death appears in other forms as well: Luis's reading of a science fiction novel with an apocalyptic ending, the slaughter of the lamb in the village, Luis's purchase of a mannequin in order to carry out target practice, and the carnage of the rabbit hunt. The characters' dialogue increasingly points to the violent end as well: the image of Juan limping causes Paco to quip, "Prefiero morirme antes de quedarme cojo o manco" (I would rather die than be lame or one-armed); he later warns Enrique, "A ver si nos pegas un tiro" (Watch out that you don't shoot us). Luis comments--after symbolically turning off the motor to the jeep--"No me importaría quedarme aquí lo que me queda de la vida" (I wouldn't mind spending whatever life I have left here). The tension rises as Luis and Paco have a dispute over money, and José hits a drunken Luis after the latter has been shooting his weapon. The last straw occurs when Paco viciously kills the ferret that Juan had brought to help in the hunt. After Paco kills a rabbit that Enrique had missed, José shoots Paco in the face; Luis, half-crazed in the jeep, shouts, "Mátame, dispara a mí también" (Kill me, shoot me, too). José does indeed shoot Luis, but the latter also kills José before he, too, drops dead. Enrique, the outsider of the group, the ingenue, can only run and escape this madness. The film ends with a freeze-frame of Enrique,

---

[44]This is especially true due to the meanings of the verb <u>atizar</u>, which can refer to stirring up a fire or inflaming passionate feelings.

the only survivor. D'Lugo comments that "by inserting a freeze-frame image as coda to the film which shows the photographer within the frame of the picture attempting to flee from the scene of carnage, Saura's camera is able to crystalize for the spectator the falseness of the individual's contrived distance from the past and his futile effort to avoid the real terms of his relation to history. Our own spectatorial gaze at this image inevitably replicates that same constructed perceptual distance and brings to the surface of narration the underlying project of *The Hunt*: the prodding of an involuntary recognition in the audience of the bogus images that have blocked them from acknowledging their true relation to the war" ("Politics" 50).

A metaphorical reading of *La caza* that relies on the concept of *cainismo* as its intellectual framework makes it an example of film *engagé*; indeed, César Santos Fontenla calls *La caza* "one of the best, most *engagé*, and most effective works of Carlos Saura" (195). In the opinion of Larraz, *La caza* is a veritable political parable that lays bare the latent violence in Spanish society, and in which the moral is that the triumph of Francoism is illusory (180). Other critics, such as Oms (*Carlos Saura* 27) and Brasó (108), concur on the importance of a metaphorical reading of this film text. The film garnered the Silver Bear in the Berlin Film Festival of 1966, and in presenting the award, Pier Paolo Pasolini stated that it represented Carlos Saura's "courage and indignation to present human situations characteristic of his time and society" (qtd. in D'Lugo "Politics" 46). In spite of its limited commercial success, *La caza* represents Carlos Saura's first step in manifesting the theme of *cainismo* on the screen, a theme to which he would later return in many of his films.

Nueve cartas a Berta (Nine Letters to Berta), directed by Basilio Martín Patino and winner of the Silver Shell in the San Sebastián Film Festival, is another film from 1965 that offers a new and critical vision of Spain. Larraz even refers to it as a "fresco" of post-war Spain (175). Lorenzo, a young student at the University of Salamanca, has travelled to England where he has met Berta, the daughter of a exiled Spanish intellectual. Martín Patino presents his nine letters to her in a non-cinematographic style: each represents a chapter that is introduced by a medieval engraving and a title. The choice of visual image for these chapter headings is not fortuitous; his adventure abroad causes Lorenzo to suffer from emotional difficulties, and Spain seems a backward, almost medieval country. Indeed, he admits, "todo aquí

no tiene sentido" (everything here doesn't make sense).   Perhaps the
most important chapter title is "Tiempo de silencio" (Time of Silence),
also the title of Luis Martín Santos's seminal novel of 1961.   Miguel
Bilbatua points out that this title refers not only to the ideological
content of the film (Lorenzo confesses, "uno tiene que vivir callado"
[you have to live in silence]) but also to one of its main stylistic
elements: ellipsis (6).   Nevertheless, Martín Patino uses techniques
such as slow motion (of Lorenzo's mother ironing or of an exterior
shot of the Plaza Mayor) which show the dichotomies between the old
Spain and the new or between Spain and the outside.   Lorenzo's father
is a war veteran whose study of medicine was interrupted by the
conflict; Lorenzo's comment "off" that his father still preserves his
soldier's hat, and "lo quería de joven" (he loved him when he was
young) indicate that he fought on the winning side, and that there is
now an emotional break between father and son.   Lorenzo is tired of
his routine life, the old ways, and feels the necessity to leave.   Leaving
Spain is not necessarily a viable alternative, however: a visiting
professor speaks of emigrants as "desconectados de esta tierra"
(disconnected from this land).

    After Lorenzo accompanies his local girlfriend, Mari Trini, on an
excursion in which we see the traditional Spain--folk dancing, the *tuna*
(a traditional student singing group), and a family passing by on a
donkey--he travels to Madrid, where the personal crisis that Lorenzo
is undergoing takes on a religious hue: while physical symptoms--a
stomach ache and dizziness--manifest his crisis, priests (traditional
Spain) preach about the emptiness of science, and the importance of
faith.   The geographical shift from province to capital evokes the civil
war, as Lorenzo, in his strolls about the city, wonders what it was like
in Madrid during the war.   When Lorenzo invites the foreign friends
that he makes there to visit his home, the contrast between the old
Spain and the new again arises.   As Lorenzo brings his friends into his
home, his mother, sewing, reacts, "Ay, Dios mío, lo que faltaba" (Oh,
God, just what we needed).   The final letter or chapter constitutes a
form of capitulation on the part of Lorenzo and a resolution of his inner
conflict, as he admits in a voice-over, "¿Por qué tengo yo que arreglar
el mundo?" (Why should I have to fix up the world?).   Shots of
Lorenzo participating in the Holy Week procession, his visit to his
uncle's country home in which a long shot of the countryside is
accompanied by the latter's comment, "Mira qué paz" (Look at what

peace we have here), the advice of Lorenzo's father that he dedicate himself to his studies and that as the years go by he will see the world "with tranquility" and the final shot of Lorenzo embracing Mari Trini with his voice-over, "Ahora estoy mucho mejor" (Now I'm much better), all represent this process in the protagonist. The ending must be seen as ironic, however. Indeed, when the film came out, critic José Monleón not only called it one of Spanish cinema's most important films, but also "one of our greatest ironic films" (61). The irony lies in the fact that Lorenzo, in spite of his experiences, becomes part of the Spain that has been laid bare in the film. However, the social criticism remains. Jesús Martínez León indicates that before *Nueve cartas a Berta*, "the fatigue and disillusion of a generation whose mental resources have collapsed had never appeared so clearly in Spanish cinema (344). The war and its aftermath are never brought to the foreground in the film, but they are constantly glimpsing through as the background for the social criticism that Martín Patino carries out in the film.

In 1972, Carlos Saura directed *Ana y los lobos* (Ana and the Wolves), a movie in which Saura attacks, on a very symbolic level, the bastions of the Franco regime and the pillars of Spanish society. He accomplishes this by the introduction of the outsider, the ingenue, in the person of Ana (Geraldine Chaplin), who comes to Spain to work as a house-keeper. The family with whom she stays consists of the aging mother (Rafaela Aparicio), and three sons, Fernando (Fernando Fernán Gómez), José (José María Prada), and Juan (José Vivó), as well as José's wife and children. The house is a large, somewhat decaying building, which, together with the grounds of the house, symbolize Spain. Descriptions of the house made by the mother almost always occur with the civil war as a reference point. When Ana arrives, the mother declares that the house is filthy, "no como antes de la guerra" (not like before the war). The grounds, which are covered with undergrowth that hides dangerous traps like those in the forest in *Furtivos*, were also different before the war. In a voice-over, the mother says, "¿Dónde están las plantas? Antes de la guerra, esto era un jardín espléndido. ¿Dónde están los árboles?" (Where are the plants? Before the war, this was a splendid garden. Where are the trees?). Later, sitting in her chair, she states, "Ya no hay fresones. Antes de la guerra había en todas partes" (There aren't any strawberries any more. Before the war, they were everywhere). The plants, trees, and fruit symbolize the life and vitality that the war truncated.

Each of the three brothers symbolizes one aspect of Spanish society, and this is apparent in their early interactions with Ana. José, who has a fetish with military uniforms and guns, declares that he is responsible for the order in the household. Juan, upon introducing himself to Ana in her room, stares longingly at her empty bed and at the new woman in the house; we later discover that he is the mysterious sender of pornographic letters to Ana, and his brother José declares that he has "la cabeza llena de semen" (his head full of semen). Fernando often retires to his grotto to pray and practice levitation. Guy Braucourt identifies the wolves of the title as "the Religion-wolf, the Army-wolf, and the Moral Order-wolf" (qtd. in Oms, *Carlos Saura* 50) represented, respectively by Fernando, with his mystic tendencies, José, with his collection of military uniforms and arms, and Juan, with his sexual pathology.

A reference to the wolves in the film serves as a foreshadowing of the denouement: when the little girls show Ana a doll that has been tortured, she inquires who could have done such a thing, and they reply, "Han sido los lobos" (It was the wolves). Later, however, Juan accuses Fernando of having tortured the doll, thus indicating a rivalry between the two. Indeed, the *cainismo* grows as the brothers compete for the attention--and affection--of Ana. When José complains to his mother that Ana may choose to stay with Fernando in his cave, and that he cannot live without her, his mother counsels, "Lucha, tú también tienes derecho" (Fight, you've got rights, too). Although José protests ("¿Luchar con mi hermano?" [Fight with my brother?]), fight he does, and when the house-keeper visits Fernando in his grotto, the battle occurs on a symbolic plane in an auditory duel. When we hear martial music (representing José) "off," Fernando grabs a religious text and begins to read in an extremely loud voice, trying to drown out the music. Although Ana leans toward Fernando, denouncing the material world by placing objects such as her hair dryer in the fire, she soon realizes his base intentions and leaves his cave (with martial music in the background, signifying a shift toward José, who awaits her in military uniform on the balcony). The invocation of the mother, "Hijos míos, no peleéis, ella no vale la pena" (My sons, don't fight, she's not worth it), finally causes the brothers to transcend their rivalry and unite: in the last scene, as Ana leaves the house with her suitcase, they

attack her. Juan rapes Ana, Fernando cuts her hair, and José, pistol in
hand, kills her.

Juan Fabián Delgado calls *Ana y los lobos* "an intellectualized and
distanced *esperpento*" (Casado 135), and Hopewell notes that the
esperpento deformations can sometimes be literal, "as in the
grotesquely large scissors Fernando uses to cut Ana's hair" (146) at the
end of the film. Saura admits that he was influenced by Gracián
(Fernando even quotes a text by this seventeenth-century author in the
film), Goya, and Quevedo (Brasó 320). Another aesthetic perspective
of the film would be to view it as a morality play; indeed, director
Saura refers to the film as "a Calderonian reredo in which characters
are representations" (qtd. in Gubern *Carlos Saura* 298). There is no
doubt that the film is allegorical, a characteristic that Hopewell sees as
double-sided: "Francoism as the orchestrated alliance of competing
interests, Spain as a country warped by its frustrations" (146). The
allegorical nature of the text has political implications even on the level
of the discourse, since it has both an ethic and aesthetic quality; as
Tena points out, this ambiguous, polysemic text constitutes a rebellion
against the monosemic discourse of Francoism.

With a screenplay by José Luis Borau and Manuel Gutiérrez
Aragón, *Furtivos* (Poachers) broke onto the scene in 1975 and became
the top grossing Spanish film of the year. It also won the Golden Shell
at the 1975 San Sebastián Film Festival, and the Silver Bear in Berlin.
The film's success must be attributed to Borau's perseverance against
Spanish censors, who initially demanded sixty cuts. Roger Mortimore
notes that the film contains "'the tragedy of Spain,' the brutality, the
incest, the fratricidal strife of a country which has suffered four civil
wars in under two centuries" (15). Unfortunately, the English
translation of the title, "Poachers," does not capture the full meaning
of the original. Director Borau explains that "the Spanish title *Furtivos*
has two meanings--illegal hunters or poachers, and also those who live
their lives in a secretive way. Both meanings apply here--I wanted to
show that under Franco, Spain was living a secret life. Virtually
everyone in this film is a *furtivo*" (qtd. in Kinder 71). The symbolism
of the film appears in the setting, a forest in northern Spain. When the
Governor, played by Borau himself, appears with his friends to
participate in a hunting expedition, he exclaims, "Qué bien huele. Y
qué paz" (It smells so good. And what peace). Franco himself
compared Spain to a peaceful forest, but in the film, we see that it is

a forest that is tranquil on the surface, but teeming with discontentment and violence underneath. The Governor visits the home of Martina, his mother (Lola Gaos), and Angel, his half-brother (Ovidi Montllor). The privileged social status of the Governor and his friends is manifest in the fact that they are hunting after five years of restrictions. Poachers have killed deer, however, and early in the film we discover who one such poacher is. In the opening scene, after Angel helps Milagros (the lover of a thief nicknamed "El Cuqui") successfully escape from a reform school by purchasing her a dress, he offers her venison. The dress has secretive qualities, since it functions as a disguise; the sharing of illegal meat not only implicates Angel, but also represents a communion or intertwining of their furtive destinies. Soon afterwards, when the Governor looks into the attic of his mother's home, he spies deer skins that Antonio has poached. Thus, from the very beginning, there is an antagonistic relationship between the half-brothers. This relationship tends beyond the two individuals, however; Méndez Leite points out that *Furtivos* is a film about the "oppression of the weak by the strong, not only in a social sense, but also in a political or religious sense" ("El cine español en la transición" 13). The characters in the film fall into two antagonistic groups: oppressors--the governor, his friends, the forest rangers, Police, Civil Guards, and priest--and oppressed--Angel, Martina, Milagros, and El Cuqui, as well as secondary characters who live in town. (Martina, as mother figure, constitutes an oppressor in her relationship with Angel, however.) There is a ubiquitous presence of the Civil Guard in the film, and it is somewhat ironic that only two of these Civil Guards were actors--the rest being real guards who, as Besas notes, were not well informed of the contents of the film (141). It is significant that among the townsfolk, Angel is not called a poacher, but an *alimañero*, a gamekeeper who kills animals that destroy game, and even El Cuqui asks for him by that name ("Angel, el alimañero"). He fills this positive social role when he kills a wolf and takes the skin to town, but there is also a tacit understanding that his activities extend beyond the limits imposed by the law, an understanding that is manifested in the laughter after the suggestion that he should be content with the money given him for the wolf skin or he would be denounced as a poacher. Indeed, his prowess at deer slaying appears twice in the film, and on both occasions it manifests the antagonism with his half-brother. During the hunting expedition, the Governor shoots at a deer with no

Fraternal strife in the forest: Borau's <u>Furtivos</u>, with Ovidi Montllor and José Luis Borau. Courtesy José Luis Borau.

success, and as the animal is about to get away, Angel, in another part of the forest, kills the animal and drags it out of sight. Later, Angel kills the prize deer that had been "reserved" for the Governor. The latter is a metaphorical shooting of the Governor himself, and the latter, irate, refers to his half-brother as "ese desgraciado" (that wretch). He tries to save face, however, and Roger Mortimore states that the Governor "emasculates his half-brother Angel, removing his *raison d'être* as a poacher when he makes him a forest warden" (15).

The sexual element of the film is intertwined with the political. The strip-tease performed around a tree by Milagros manifests the new eroticism on the Spanish screen (Angel's voyeuristic gaze matches that of the audience) combined with the socio-political discourse of this film: the forest is the site of furtive, prohibited actions. The tree around which Milagros performs her strip-tease functions both as phallic symbol and concealer, as Milagros's bare bottom flashes out on either side as she swings it back and forth. When Angel brings Milagros to his home, there is a displacement of his mother, an action that is not only metaphorical, but literal, when Angel throws Martina out of her double bed in order to share with his lover. Milagros still loves El Cuqui, however, and even carries mementos such as a

The forest as metaphor for the regime: Borau's Furtivos, with José Luis Borau as the Governor. Courtesy Filmoteca Nacional.

newspaper article about his past crimes. When El Cuqui finds the house in the forest, Milagros furtively packs her things to go with him, but when the Civil Guards begin to pursue her old lover, she promises to stay with Angel in return for his help in letting El Cuqui escape. The Governor, on the other hand, wants Angel to use his knowledge of the forest in order to capture the criminal. Angel does locate him, but in an act of symbolic rebellion against his half-brother, allows the thief to escape. After threatening Angel, El Cuqui steps into a steel trap, symbol of the hidden violence in the forest. When Angel returns to his house empty-handed, the Governor, leaving in disgust, says, "Me has puesto en ridículo otra vez" (You've made me look ridiculous once more). When Angel returns home, Martina informs her son that Milagros has left them, and has even stolen some of their household items. As she helps him take off his wet clothes in the bedroom, she says, "Si estamos mejor así. Los dos solos. Como siempre" (We're better off this way. The two of us alone. Just like always), and as she dries his thigh, her comment "Uy, uy, uy, si se te ve el pajarito" (Oh, your dick is showing), connotes the former sexual relationship between the two, as well as a symbolic one: Martina represents "Spain itself, who wants her children only for herself, who loves, crushes, and devours them" (Hopewell 100). However, the arrival of Milagros

A tale of matricide: Borau's <u>Furtivos</u>, with Lola Gaos. Courtesy José Luis Borau.

radically changed that relationship, and Angel now rejects his mother.
A later chance encounter in town with El Cuqui, who demands to know
where Milagros is, provides a twist in the narrative, and when Angel
returns home, he confirms his mother's lie when he discovers the
wooden box of mementos on top of Milagros's closet; since Milagros
would surely have taken these with her, we know that Martina must
have killed her. Angel takes his mother to confession and mass, and
in the final gripping scene, he shoots her in the back on the way home.
Borau uses a constrained narrative style that brings to mind narrative
techniques used in ancient Spanish ballads.   His use of ellipsis
eliminates some of the key violent acts from the screen, thus resulting
in an excellent fusion of content and form based on "furtiveness."
Vargas Llosa points out that Borau uses transposition to connote the
most violent deaths: "Martina's ax strokes which kill a she-wolf
substitute for (and make us "see" metaphorically) those with which she
strikes her daughter-in-law;   Angel's shooting of a graceful deer
replaces the scene in which he kills his mother" (81). This symbolic
matricide constitutes the radical liberation of Angel. Sánchez Vidal
(111) notes that in order to shoot the final sequence, they had to move
from the province of Segovia to the Pyrenees due to an unusual lack of
snow at the initial filming site, and comments on the "almost polished

snow, purifying like a shroud" (Sánchez Vidal 127) of the final scene, which provides the perfect visual framework for the ritual sacrifice of the matricide.

Furtivos weaves elements of political allegory, myth, and even elements of fairy tale (Kinder 73) into a brilliant symbolic piece on violence and power (Monterde 13). Director José Luis Borau has commented, "Underneath its realist and rural appearances, *Furtivos* is both a tragedy and a children's story--there are even characters that characterize themselves as such: in a given moment they call Lola Gaos a 'witch,' they are the lost children in the forest who return home hand in hand; the mother calls the governor 'my king' . . . like in the stories of kings, princesses and forests" (qtd. in Sánchez Vidal 123-24). Borau also states, "more than reflect reality, what I want to do is *refer* to reality" (qtd. in Escudero 36). This reference to Spanish reality remains as vibrant today as it was when the film had its debut in 1975.

Carlos Saura's 1975 hit, *Cría cuervos* (Cria, [The Spirit of Ana]), takes its title from the ominous Spanish proverb that the fascist father cites at the end of *La prima Angélica*, "Cría cuervos y te sacarán los ojos" (Raise ravens and they will pluck out your eyes). The ravens in this case are three little girls, Irene, Maite, and Ana, the protagonist, played by child actress Ana Torrent, who had earlier starred in Víctor Erice's *El espíritu de la colmena*. The parents are María (Geraldine Chaplin), a sickly woman who fights with her husband, and Anselmo (Héctor Alterio), a military officer who pursues other women. In the opening scene, Anselmo dies while making love to Amelia, and after the latter leaves the house, young Ana enters the bedroom, caresses her dead father's hair, and washes a glass. Ana believes that she has poisoned her lecherous father, and Ana's preoccupation with death constitutes a fusion of the personal and the political planes in the film. Carlos Saura has stated, "for me, *Cría cuervos* is a film about a little girl immersed in a hostile world, and obsessed with death" (qtd. in *Cría cuervos* 125). In its socio-historical context--the Spain of 1975-- the most important death is that of General Franco, and as D'Lugo notes, the scene of the wake for her father, a military officer, "inevitably leads Spanish audiences to read the film's subsequent action as an exploration of a Spain beyond the shadows of the Caudillo" (*Films* 127).

Ana's hostile world is determined by her family and by her society, and after the beginning *in medias res*, Saura weaves a complex temporal narrative that shows Ana's past and even her future. (Ana as an adult twenty years later is also played by Geraldine Chaplin, thus connoting a fusion between mother and daughter; one could argue, then, that the "present" of the narrative is also the past, a flash-back from the confessions of 1995.) One device that Saura uses to trigger shifts in time is music, particularly Imperio Argentina's old melody "Ay, Mari Cruz," which the maid Rosa sings while she cleans a glass door. Ana "sees" her father appear and press his hand against the buxom breast of the maid through the glass. The music also accompanies the camera pan of old photographs pinned to the wall that Ana's mute grandmother views. The melody is thus "a Proustian device, a verbal madeleine that conjures up a visible past" (Insdorf 50).

The adult Ana admits that she does not understand why she wanted to kill her father, but as she says "Lo único que sí recuerdo perfectamente es que entonces me parecía el culpable de toda la tristeza que había embargado a mi madre los últimos años de su vida" (The only thing that I do remember perfectly is that back then he seemed responsible for all the sadness that had seized my mother in the last years of her life), there is a cut from the older Ana to the photograph album in which her father--whether alone or with other soldiers--is always shown in his military uniform. In a later scene, Rosa speaks of Anselmo to Ana, saying, "Se fue de voluntario muy joven y que después estuvo en el frente de Rusia, en la División Azul. . . . Allí fue donde le hirieron en la pierna" (When he was very young he went as a volunteer, and later he was at the Russian front, in the Blue Division. . . . That was where he was wounded in the leg). When Ana asks her when the Civil War ended, she responds, "Yo creo que en 1939" (I think it was in 1939). Rosa's reply concerning the end of the war does not necessarily imply ignorance on her part, but the fact that indeed the fratricidal divisions in Spain continued well beyond the official end of the war. Thus, the Civil War and the fascist background of the father are fundamental underlying elements in the negative portrait that Saura paints of this character. Anselmo is not merely an odious individual, however, but symbolically represents the regime, since, as Annette Insdorf points out, Ana's desire to kill her father is "symbolic of destroying fascism or the political father--Franco" (51).

Visual imagery is particularly important in the film with regards to characters' eyes and photographs. The latter are important from the opening moments of the film when the camera pans the family album: one photograph that shows Ana and her mother is labelled "Mi madre

Victims of post-war oppression: Saura's <u>Cría cuervos</u>, with Ana Torrent and Geraldine Chaplin. Courtesy Elías Querejeta, P.C.

y yo" (My mother and I) in a polished cursive script, showing from the very beginning of the film that the protagonist (Ana) is already an adult. The importance of eyes in the film is understood from the unarticulated second half of the proverb from which Saura takes the title. D'Lugo points out the importance of Ana's eyes in particular: "we are brought to identify with her glance as the principal internal narrative authority of the film. Gradually, her point of view is brought into question as we recognize the shifts in her consciousness as she weaves personal memories with childish fantasies and the curious perception of herself from a future vantage" ("Constructive" 37). The importance of Ana's vision (point of view), her unreliability as narrator, and obsession with death all combine in the scene following the wake for her father: Ana, playing in her garden, "sees" herself standing on the roof of the building across the street. After the low-angle shot zooms in, there is a series of reverse-angle shots in which Ana--in the garden--closes her eyes, and the Ana on the roof jumps off and soars through the air, symbolized by a blurry circular camera motion, while the sound-track strikes the discordant notes of horns honking and sirens blaring. These sounds and the disquieting camera motion capture young Ana's inner malaise. Ana then leaves the garden, and after finding a small jar, she puts some of its contents in her mouth but immediately spits it out. Ana's voice "off" explains that she believed the contents to be poison, which means that the scene that we have just witnessed was a suicide attempt. The camera pans to the adult Ana asking herself why she wanted to kill her father, thus completing the circle of obsession with death.

Another key scene in which we confirm Ana's unreliability as narrator is when her mute grandmother in a wheelchair views photographs pinned to the wall. Both the wheelchair and the photographs connote immobility, paralyzation, not only for the individual, but also for the generation that the grandmother represents. As Ana uses flights of her imagination to describe the photographs, the grandmother's frowns indicate that Ana is an unreliable narrator; when the child offers her grandmother a chance to die, a close-up of the "poison" that Ana holds shows it to be merely bicarbonate of soda, thus further confirming Ana's unreliability and widening the gulf between imagination and reality.

The second half of the proverb of the title almost attains fruition after the death of Ana's mother. Aunt Paulina comes to take care of the three girls, and there is a growing attraction between her and Nicolás, another military officer and friend of Anselmo. Nicolás is also the husband of Amelia, with whom Anselmo was making love when he died, and the affair that Nicolás is attempting to have with Paulina completes the picture of immorality of an entire social class. Ana, who finds her father's military pistol, surprises them while they are kissing on the sofa. The camera seeks them out in a low angle shot, representing the vision of Ana. Nicolás convinces the girl to give him the pistol, and he assures Paulina that the gun is surely not loaded. However, when he removes the live ammunition that could have killed them, we realize that Ana/raven has nearly fulfilled the proverb; Paulina, in a fit of rage, slaps her niece. After this episode, Ana tries to poison her Aunt Paulina, and there is a parallelism in her actions with regard to the opening scene: she comes into Paulina's bedroom, caresses her aunt's hair, and washes the glass. However, we now know that the "poison" was only bicarbonate of soda and that the initial parricide was merely a death-wish fulfilled by coincidence; consequently, Ana's attempt to metonymically carry out the second half of the proverb does not succeed.

At the end of the summer, the girls must return to class, and the final long shot of them in the street as they approach their school also has symbolic meaning. As critics Helène Marinot and Michel Sineux point out, the last shot acquires symbolic value, since it takes us back to the beginning of the film: "The school uniforms correspond to the military and religious emblems of the beginning. Individual history moves to collective history. We know that the girl will become the mother, a closed loop at the end of an evolution/involution that is not linear, but circular, and that Saura without doubt invites us to compare with that of Spain, frozen in its obsessions" (qtd. in Gubern, *Carlos Saura* 38). Gabriel Blanco comments that a detail of the final shot underscores the social symbolism: "the external negation of freedom is seen in the effaced graffiti on the wall" (32). Ana, young and innocent, is, then, a victim of circumstances on a personal or psychological level as well as on the social level. As Hopewell comments, "Saura's political thesis in *Cría cuervos* is that Francoism as a political force could pass away, as Ana's parents literally pass away, but its psychological legacies would remain" (138). *Cría cuervos* is an excellent film that portrays the legacy of the civil war and the Franco regime on the next generation of Spaniards.

Another film from 1975 that proved to be immensely popular was José Luis Garci's *Asignatura pendiente* (Course Incomplete), a film that deals with the situation in Spain during the transition to democracy. The way in which Garci combines politics and sex in the film is manifested very succinctly in the still that shows the protagonists, José (José Sacristán) and Elena (Fiorella Faltoyano) in bed together with a poster of Lenin looming over them (see photograph). José is a leftist lawyer, "de la 6,8 de la izquierda española" (a 6.8 on the Spanish scale of the left) by his own definition, who has suffered imprisonment on various occasions for being a "red." Elena was his childhood sweetheart, but each went their separate way, and their respective married lives, portrayed in the opening cross-cut scenes, seem to offer only boredom, especially in contrast with the musing voice-overs in which the two characters remember each other. In a chiaroscuro shot worthy of *Birth of a Nation* (Garci's fascination with and influence by American film is well known), Elena interrupts her reading with a cry, indicating her basic unhappiness. This changes, however, when José encounters her on a busy street in downtown Madrid. When they take a drive to a small town outside of the capital, José justifies their impending and inevitable affair: "Acostarnos sería como recuperar algo nuestro. . . . Nos han robado tantas cosas . . . las veces que tú y yo debimos hacer el amor y no lo hicimos, los libros que debimos leer, las cosas que debimos pensar" (Going to bed together would be like recuperating something of ours. . . . They have stolen so many things from us . . . the times that you and I should have made love and didn't, the books that we should have read, the things that we should have thought). Thus, the political and social (sexual) oppression of the Franco regime is the basic theme of the film. In his speech to Elena, José also uses a simile that illuminates the title of the movie: "Queda algo colgado, como aquellas asignaturas pendientes de un curso para otro" (Something is left hanging, like those incomplete courses from one year to the next).

Their affair is set against a background of contemporary political events, and it is even interwoven with them. References abound to contemporary politicians--calls to Ruiz Jiménez, appointments with Pujol--as well as to the most important event of the year in Spain: the death of Franco. A montage of calendar shots from the upcoming year--"el año de la apertura" (the year in which things would open up) --manifests the optimism and ebullience of the transition. The love affair soon begins to take second place to José's political commitment, however, as he tries to defend Rafa, an imprisoned member of the communist labor union, *Comisiones Obreras*. Elena complains that the apartment that they have rented to consummate their affair has become more like José's office when he constantly calls his fellow lawyer, nicknamed "Trotsky." Their initial ardor gives way to a relationship that begins to parallel the emptiness of their married lives; when Elena complains that she seldom sees him, and when she does, he is always on the phone, José retorts "Lo mismo que dice mi mujer" (That's just what my wife says). Garci leads us up to the inevitable end to their romance with two narrative devices: José revisits the town where he took Elena on their initial reencounter, but this time he is alone; and a drunk José loses the expensive cigarette lighter that Elena gave him as a Christmas gift. From an early simile in which José likens dictatorships to bicycles that fall when they stop, their "bicycle" also falls as they learn the lesson that you can never recapture the past. Elena, the more mature of the two characters, realizes that José was not searching for her, but for his adolescence, "la época de las grandes sinceridades cuando no había mentiras" (the age of great sincerity when there were no lies), and she realizes that it was an impossible quest. Although Hopewell (111) states that "in a contradiction typical of transition films, a 'progressive' act of political commitment is cast in

Sexual and political liberation: Garci's <u>Asignatura pendiente</u>, with José Sacristán and Fiorella Faltoyano. Courtesy Filmoteca Nacional.

the most conservative of 'classic' film traditions. Like John Wayne leaving his girl behind as he rides out to war, José rides off to rejoin the democratic advance guard," Elena's statement that "La mujer siempre sale peor en este país" (Women always get the worst in this country) and José's response that one must fight for a better future implicitly recognizes the hope for social change that will affect all of society. The script writers, Garci and José María González Sinde, indicate that "If there is a clear political idea in the film, it is that of national reconciliation . . . we want our generation to look to the past, to take it upon themselves, and to enter into the future without anger, without rancor" (González Sinde 7). Though somewhat dated today, *Asignatura pendiente* is a film that not only captured the nation's sensibility at the moment it was released, but also achieved commercial success and fame for José Luis Garci, the only Spanish director to this date who would go on to win an Oscar for Best Foreign Film.

Francisco Rodríguez's 1975 film, *La casa grande* (The Big House), stars Antonio Ferrandis, Juan Diego, and Fernando Sánchez-Polack, and Maribel Martín. The film deals with unpaid crimes and the climate of repression following the war. Andrea (Maribel Martín), a young woman around twenty years of age, lives with her uncle Raúl (Antonio

Ferrandis) and her father Gerardo (Sánchez-Polack) in a small town. Raúl is the mayor, and from the opening shots in which he listens to the radio broadcast about German advances, and consults his map to check the progress of the war, he is associated with fascism. In his office with the priest and a civil servant, they speak of how to become rich in the black market, and photographs of Franco and José Antonio on the wall provide an association between corruption and the political regime. Gerardo, however, belongs to the vanquished, and now, three years after the end of the war, he lives secluded and seems to have lost his mental faculties: he believes that it is time for him to die, and he accuses his brother-in-law of being responsible for the death of his wife while he was away at war. Raúl's violent reaction and threat to put Gerardo in an insane asylum, followed by Andrea's defense of her father--that he is not insane--constitute a purposely ambiguous narrative, and leave the viewer wondering about the truth of the situation.

The relationship between Raúl and Andrea is not the normal uncle/niece relationship, however. After supper, Raúl leaves the house only to go to a vantage point in the barn from where he can see Andrea undress, and the cross-cutting of a close-up of his eye spying her and Andrea in her bedroom underscore the voyeuristic nature of the uncle. He also whets his sexual appetite with Sara, the maid, a situation that manifests how Raúl abuses his power. The sexual, political, and religious themes combine after Diego, Andrea's secret boy-friend, visits Raúl to ask for work. The mayor, speaking of himself in the third person, ironically comments to his niece, "Tu tío sabe cuál es su deber. Lleva muchos años dando trabajo y limosnas en este pueblo. Algún día recibiré la recompensa si es la voluntad de Dios" (Your uncle knows what his duty is. He has been handing out work and alms for many years in this town. Some day I will receive my compensation if it is God's will). His recompense comes indeed, when Raúl is about to have Gerardo committed, and Andrea decides to sacrifice herself for her father's sake. Director Rodríguez treats the grotesque sexual encounter with ellipsis, however, as a close-up of her grimacing face as her uncle kisses her and a fade out is followed by a long shot of the house as a symbolic rooster crows.

Gerardo's ranting about the war combines the sexual and the political themes: he laments the death of his wife during the war, saying that she was found so badly beaten, she was hardly recognizable. Diego captures the repressive atmosphere in town when he says, "No se atreven a abrir la boca. Están atemorizados" (They don't dare open their mouths. They are terrified), but he is determined to inquire at the "big house" to see if he can find out more information about the crime. Raúl angrily blames both Andrea's mother and Gerardo for her death: "Era una zorra que se cavó su tumba . . . y él tuvo la culpa. Tenía la cabeza llena de pájaros, siempre metido en politiquerías de mierda" (She was a bitch that dug her own grave . . . and he was at fault. He was a flake, always mixed up in fucking politics). Aside from revealing Gerardo's past leftist activities, this statement serves to deflect guilt from an ever more suspicious Raúl. Diego presses on in his investigation, and extracts a confession from Raúl's foreman before killing him. Although Diego successfully hides from the Civil Guard in Andrea's barn, Raúl eventually discovers him, and Diego is only saved when Gerardo stabs his brother-in-law from behind. The final sequence does not reveal a happy ending for Andrea, however; with Gerardo being led away by the Civil Guard and Diego escaping through the fields, she has lost the two men that she has loved. The final low-angle shot of her on a balcony shutting her window is one that connotes a cutting-off of life, freedom, and love.

The film has some technical deficiencies--the red tinting that marks a flashback in Gerardo's mind is unnecessary, although Andrea's dream sequence--a double image of Diego being hanged--is much more fortuitous. Nevertheless, the main theme of the film, the need to bring the silenced crimes of the victors to justice, is unique in Spanish films that deal with *cainismo*.

Jaime Chávarri's *El desencanto* (The Disenchantment, 1976) is a non-fiction film about the family of Spanish poet Leopoldo Panero. The frontier between documentary film and fiction is at times rather difficult to discern, and the classification of this film as non-fiction goes against that of several Spanish critics. Juan Hernández Les believes that "*El desencanto* stops being a documentary in order to become a fiction film" (32). Miguel Marías states that the Paneros "thought that they were characters--they live in an almost constant *representation* of roles . . . [and] they are interesting as *fictional characters*" (52). P. Gimferrer is of the opinion that the structure of the film is that of fiction, and it is the Paneros "themselves who make the film slide from a documentary to a narrative film" (133). For Jenaro Talens, the difference between a documentary and a narrative film lies not in the "referent (with autonomous existence, outside of the discourse), but in the referential effect (that is produced)" ("Documentalidad" 11). The director himself, when asked about this dichotomy, responded, "As far as I'm concerned, all film is fiction" (Hernández Les, *El cine* 133). It is perhaps fitting that one of the Panero sons draws attention to a book by Argentine author Jorge Luis Borges in his library: fiction and reality are indeed intertwined in both life and art. Unlike the documentary films analyzed in the Chapter 9 of this study, however, Chávarri does not use archival footage in the exploration of his subject. Instead, surviving members of the deceased poet's family--his wife and sons--all speak to the camera. The poet's widow, Francisca Blanc, noted in an interview that at times the camera would "disappear" during the course of the conversations: "And Leopoldo María would intervene and say a series of things that were quite cruel, and imagine, the camera is there, but I don't see it any more; my eyelids quiver, the discussion was raw, and I am trying to defend myself . . ." (Sánchez, "*El desencanto*" 21). The portrait that emerges of the Panero family-- and by extension, of Spanish society--is a devastating one, or in the words of one of his sons, "la sordidez más puñetera que he visto en mi vida" (the most fucking sordidness that I have seen in my life).

Chávarri shot almost eight hours of material during 1974 and 1975; he finally edited his material into a movie of about an hour and a half. Hernández Les notes that the fact that the film is in black and white has an important aesthetic consideration, since it "corresponds exactly to our most recent history" ("*El desencanto*" 33). The film begins with the unveiling of a statue of the poet in Astorga twelve years after his death in 1962. Many consider Panero as the official poet of the Franco regime, and Caperrós Lera states, "it is obvious that this demythification of the Paneros coincides with the "disenchantment" that the Spanish regime which it surreptitiously evokes is suffering today" (*El cine* 86). Indeed, son Leopoldo María notes that the history of his family consists of two distinct histories: the "epic legend" and the true history; he clearly states his intention in this regard: "pretendo desmantelar la leyenda épica" (I intend to dismantle the epic legend). Indeed, all of the members of the family seem to achieve this goal as we hear stories of the father's drinking and exploits in bordellos, the drug problems, suicide attempts, incarceration of the sons, the oppression of the mother, and the total lack of communication, understanding, or any sense of love among family members. Although his widow, Francisca Blanc, deeply mourned Leopoldo's passing, his death also represented a liberation: she confesses to her son that she never had any female friends--"tu padre me barrió todas mis amistades femeninas" (your father took away all my female friendships)--and she says that she was "sojuzgada por la parte Panero de la familia" (subjugated by the Panero part of the family), calling 1962, the year of her husband's death, "un descubrimiento en mi vida" (a discovery in my life). Mother-son relations are based on a total lack of mutual understanding, and one of the most gripping conversations of the film is between Francisca and Leopoldo María concerning his drug problems. The son later refers to a vicious circle in their relationship, saying that they were the cause of each other's "disaster." Father-son relationships were "terrible", and son José Luis's membership in the communist party represented an act of rebellion on his part that elicited a reprimand from the father. José Luis blames his father's opposition to his literary career to his lack of success, and it is somewhat ironic that the son still uses a Parker pen that his father gave him. Leopoldo María claims, "Cada uno quiso ocupar el lugar del padre menos yo" (Each one except me tried to take the place of the father), and indeed, in the final sequence of the film, Juan Luis expresses his worries about not having any descendants to carry on the family name, fearing this might mean an end to the "race." This term is used three times in the film, and clearly relates to Francoism and the film by this title for which the *caudillo* wrote the script.

The title for this film comes up in conversation as Michi proclaims, "Para estar desencantado hace falta antes haber estado encantado. Yo, desde luego, no recuerdo nada más que cuatro o cinco momentos muy frágiles, muy huidizos de haber estado en mi vida encantado. Yo diría mejor, ilusionado. Desencanto, aburrimiento, desilusión me ha venido impuesto por muchos y variados elementos" (In order to be disenchanted, first you had to be enchanted. I certainly don't remember more than four or five very fragile, very fleeting moments in my life when I was enchanted. Or, to put it better, when I had illusions. Disenchantment, boredom, disillusionment have all been imposed on me by many varied elements). School, which they call a "penal institution" is also a source of discontent, but of course the main source is the family. The sons feel the weight of the family name: José Luis cites Hemingway's statement that "Quien no es hijo de nadie es hijo de puta" (He who is nobody's son is a son of a bitch)--and Michi speaks of their money and "la incapacidad de los Panero por el trabajo" (the Panero's incapacity for work), a statement that brings to mind generations of aristocratic families that have been satirized in Spanish literature since the sixteenth century. The family's need to sell even their art work and books adds to the sense that the end of the "race" is indeed near.

Hopewell points out that "the family under Franco became the minimum political unit, a fact recognized explicitly in 1967 when heads of families were allowed to elect deputies directly to the Cortes [Spanish Parliament]" and that "Cháverri's point in *El desencanto* is gradually to leave Panero senior to focus on the family as an oppressive institution that endows members with an identity rather than with any individuality" (130, 132). The relationship between art (film) and society in this case seems to be one of facing mirrors that capture and multiply each other's images, since Hernández Les argues that *El desencanto* "reproduces with great exactitude the *disenchantment* and the awakening of Spanish society" ("*El desencanto*" 33), and Diego Galán notes that "the term *disenchantment*, coined in the film, extended throughout the country," and that "without a doubt, their story, although personal, connected with lifestyles of other Spaniards" ("Desintegración" 62). Although the film was withdrawn by its producer, Elías Querejeta, from the 1977 San Sebastián Film Festival for political reasons, it went on to have a long run in commercial theaters, and critics from the Spanish film magazine *Dirigido por* even voted it the second most important Spanish film of the 1970's.

Camada negra (Black Litter) is a film from 1977 directed by Manuel Gutiérrez Aragón, co-written and produced by José Luis Borau. Hopewell states that "no other Spanish film underlines so unequivocally the violence of Spanish fascism" (193). Indeed, the socio-political message of the film was so strong that it elicited a vehement reaction from the far right, including protests, threats, and bombings. The film portrays a family of right-wing extremists whose combination of terrorist acts and (hypocritical) religious piety--their chorus often intones bars of "Dies irae" and "Gloria"--brings to mind the "Guerrillas of Christ the King" rightist group that was active both during and after the Franco regime. Indeed, Gutiérrez Aragón was inspired for the film when members of that group beat him after a protest in a church regarding the famous Burgos trial of 1970.

The opening scene, in which masked hoodlums destroy contemporary paintings in an art gallery, recalls the vandalism against

a Picasso exhibit in Madrid. The mafia in the film is run by the
fanatical mother, Blanca, who, with "holy ire," exhorts "unity" among
the group and who sews a huge Spanish flag as a symbol of the group's
"patriotism." Tatín, (José Luis Alonso), the youngest brother, desires
entry into the group, and to gain it, he must meet three conditions, a
narrative element, which as Hopewell points out, provides a fairy-tale
structure such as that studied by Vladimir Propp (194). These
conditions are that he revenge his brothers, keep the group a secret,
and sacrifice, if necessary, a close friend or relative for the cause.
Tatín's attack on a female bookstore employee who had earlier gone to
the police to accuse the gang-members provides him with the first
opportunity to prove his worthiness to join his brothers' group. He
also attempts to disrupt a supper/political meeting of leftists (his request
for oysters has sexual connotations of machismo), and his brothers save
him by machine-gunning the garden-restaurant, killing a waiter. Tatín
then meets Rosa (Angela Molina), an unwed waitress who provides the
youth's sexual initiation, and she offers him a humane alternative to the
violent conduct of his home environment, an alternative that proves to
be ineffective. In the end, Tatín sacrifices this woman that he "loves."
After his older brother exhorts him that the fatherland needs trees (the
metaphor that Spain is a forest reflects that of Borau's *Furtivos*), Tatín
takes Rosa to a tree nursery, and when they are about to make love,
he bludgeons her to death with a stone while chanting, "España,
España, España" (Spain, Spain, Spain). He deposits her body in a hole
dug for a sapling, which has literal and metaphorical significance: it
serves as an excellent place to hide the evidence of his crime, and the
sacrificial blood will provide nourishment for the new Spain,
symbolized by the young forest.

Kinder notes that the "link between fascist repression and sexual
deviance" is quite direct in the film, not only in the character of Tatín,
but also in that of his mother, Blanca, who denies sexual relations to
her current husband while "her bedroom is dominated by a large
photograph of her late husband in his Falangist uniform, which she has
converted into a fetishized icon" (79). The director claims that his film
is about "fascism in all ages, fascism as seen from the inside" (Besas
182). It is interesting to note that Gutiérrez Aragón chooses as the
protagonist of the film the young fascist hoodlum. Although our point
of view in the narrative is closely associated with him, and in spite of
the fact that there is no antagonist to this figure who would represent

Ultra-right violence: Gutiérrez Aragón's <u>Camada negra</u>, with José Luis Alonso. Courtesy José Luis Borau.

the "good guys," there is no empathy between the audience and Tatín. Given the violent reaction of right-wing groups in Spain upon its release, it is without doubt that the fascism that it portrays is very Spanish in nature. With ultra-right violence on the rise again in Spain as in the rest of Europe (in November of 1992 Spanish skin-heads murdered a young immigrant woman from the Dominican Republic), the message of *Camada negra* is as timely today as when the film was made.

Antonio Mercero's 1977 box-office hit, *La guerra de papá* (Daddy's War), is based on the Delibes novel, *El príncipe destronado* (The Dethroned Prince). The narrative presents the portrayal of a family dominated by the values of the father who fought on the victorious side of the war. The emphasis on the bellicose appears even during the opening stills--a child's drawings include those of a tank and a boy with a pistol. Likewise, the opening scene shows Quico, a three-year old played by child actor Lolo García, awakening in his crib with a cannon in his hand "para ir a la guerra de papá" (to go to Daddy's war). The temporal setting is March of 1964, a full quarter of a century after the end of the Civil War, but a moment in which the deep feelings that contributed to the conflict still reign. The father's role in the war appears both in the images of objects in his study--flags, a photograph of himself as a young soldier, and a pistol in his desk drawer--as well as in a dinner conversation wrought with tension due to the fact that the father wants Pablo, his sixteen-year old son, to enter into the armed forces.   The children question the father about the war, and terms such as "buenos" (good guys), "malos" (bad guys), and "cosa santa" (holy thing) clearly divide the ideological question into two clear-cut areas of black and white, with the father ("naturally") on the side of the good, who are, of course, the victors. He now tries to impose his   ideology on his oldest son, saying, "Sus ideas--si las tiene--serán las mías, digo yo" (His ideas--if he has any at all--should be mine, as far as I'm concerned). The lack of response on Pablo's part leads to accusations by the father toward the mother, who does not support her husband. Her opinion about the righteousness of the cause is that "Esas cosas siempre suelen ser lo que nosotros queremos que sean" (Those things are usually just as we want them to be).

The military element in the film is also underscored by a song that Domi, a maid, sings to the children. Entitled, "El puñal de dos filos" (The two-edged knife), it tells of a soldier who returns from Africa to find that his beloved Rosita has betrayed him. The final verses, "Y sacando un puñal de dos filos /   En su pecho se lo atravesó" (And taking out a two-edged knife, he stabbed it in her chest), is accompanied by a shot of Quico urinating in his   pants in order to underscore the negative consequences of violence on the psyche of young children. The appearance of Femio, the boyfriend of a younger maid, Vito, also underscores the military element. He is in uniform because he is shipping out the next day for service in Africa, and he has come to say goodbye. Quico ingenuously asks him if he is going to kill Rosita Encarnada, the victim in the song, as well as a lot of "bad-guys" (just as his father did). Finally, Pablo's decision to follow his father's wishes stems from a conversation that the youth had with Father Llanes of the Veterans' Association in which the priest explains that the only way to forget old animosities is to join together, "unidos los de un lado con los del otro" (those of one side united with those of the other).   Nevertheless, instead of reconciliation, Pablo's decision represents the continuing oppression of the younger generation of Spaniards by the older, victorious generation.   The final scene shows the end of the day, with the mother putting Quico to bed and reassuring him that "Ya no habrá más guerra de papá" (There won't be any more Daddy's war). The rest of the film consists of a series of mischievous acts carried out by Quico and his brother, including the playing with the father's pistol, which serves to further underscore the bellicose element and adds a small note of tension to the film. Aside from the fact that Spaniards generally adore children, and the fact that one could characterize child actor Lolo García as "cute," the incredible box-office success of the film can only be attributed to the empathy that Spaniards felt toward the socio-political theme of the movie.

Jordi Feliu's 1977 film, *Alicia en la España de las maravillas* (Alice in Spanish Wonderland) is an allegorical film inspired by Lewis Carroll's *Alice in Wonderland*. In an almost surreal tone, it deals with the forty years of the Franco regime and the political and social oppression of those four decades. After the initial foray into the realm of allegory with an ironic twist--Alicia chases a black "playboy bunny" into a hole--the film progresses chronologically, beginning with brief documentary footage from the civil war, and scenes of the oppression of the immediate post-war period: guards who torture their prisoners, firing squads followed by symbolic images of blood dripping onto flowers, priests who burn books, and soldiers who march through the streets. The black market theme that is recurrent in so many films' portrayal of the post-war period appears here with the added theme of sexual exploitation: a nude Alicia covers her sexual organs with a plate, and after we see people waiting in line for something to eat contrasted with mountains of stockpiled food, the black-marketeer attempts to rape Alicia. Criticism of religion is also manifest as a nun next chides Alicia that her accusations against the black-marketeer are impossible since "Los hombres malos desaparecieron con la gloriosa victoria" (Bad men disappeared with the glorious victory); this theme later continues with a misogynous priest who calls woman the "gate of hell."

Cultural oppression is another theme of the film. Alicia follows meters of celluloid of film by prohibited directors--Malraux, Buñuel-- like the thread of Ariadne. In a bit of hyperbole, an author protests that censors have only approved the Prologue and the Epilogue of his book. A line of white masks passes by that represents the writers and artists that are prohibited--Hernández, Picasso, Brecht, Sartre, et al. The theme of linguistic oppression appears more than once with the slogan "En España se habla el idioma del imperio" (In Spain you speak the language of the empire), and a shot of a man with earphones and who speaks with a Catalan accent portrays the struggle to learn the "official" language of the regime. History is also only of the "official" variety: when Alicia writes a sentence on a blackboard that represents the Republican point of view--"La guerra civil española fue provocada por un golpe de estado del general Franco" (The Spanish civil war was provoked by a coup d'état by General Franco)--it must be erased and replaced with "La cruzada de liberación . . ." (The crusade for freedom . . .).

Color symbolism is used rather overtly in the film, as workers in blue overalls and caps paint all of the roses blue (the color of the regime). When Alicia inquires why, they respond, "porque la jefatura nacional lo manda, eso es todo . . . que todas las rosas deben ser iguales" (because the national command orders it, that's all . . . all the roses should be the same) thus symbolizing a uniformity of ideology and of language that previous sequences connote. Alicia's trial for subversion combines folklore with *1984*: the accused appears in a bullring, sitting between large loudspeakers that blast forth accusations made by a computer. This sequence is the weakest of the film, because it over-explains the symbolism of earlier sequences by accompanying earlier scenes with each accusation. The death sentence imposed on Alicia brings to mind the famous Burgos trial of 1970, but here, natural forces (that symbolize the "good") win out as a thunder storm cuts off the power of the computer, and the rain washes the blue paint into the gutter. There are actually three Alicia's in the film, played by three different actresses, a technique perhaps inspired by Buñuel's *That Obscure Object of Desire* but used much less effectively here. Although *Alicia en la España de las maravillas* starts from an ingenious concept, it is a film that falls short.

La escopeta nacional (National Shotgun, 1978) by Luis García Berlanga, is the first of the so-called Leguineche trilogy, also made up of *Patrimonio nacional* (National Patrimony, 1981) and *Nacional III* (National III, 1982). An actual event worthy of a grotesque comedy inspired the first of these three films: during a *franquista* hunting expedition, Manuel Fraga, who was Minister of Information and Tourism at the time, accidentally shot Franco's daughter in the behind. A hunting expedition thus serves as the vehicle for social satire in *La escopeta nacional*. José Canivell represents the parody of a Catalan industrialist who attends the hunting party in order to obtain the favors of the regime in selling electronic doormen. The film satirizes centralized power--a main feature of Franco's policy to squash regionalism and old nationalistic tendencies of the periphery, as the

Catalan, in an example of billingsgate typical of the comedy, curses "el puñetero centralismo de los cojones" (the fucking shitty centralism). Parody of this theme also occurs in the person of the reactionary, foul-mouthed cleric, Father Calvo (Agustín González) who berates priests who are communists or separatists. Canivell's hosts are most bizarre, beginning with the sexual perversion of the Marqués (Luis Escobar), who keeps a collection of pubic hairs. After Canivell suffers many humiliations at their hands (he even has to pay for the hunting expedition, although mentioning this fact would tarnish the "honor" of the Marqués and his family), the Catalan businessman believes that he has struck a deal, when a sudden shift in government ruins his entire effort. The priest advises Ricardo, a member of the Opus Dei who has ascended in power, that he should govern with "mano dura, estaca, estaca" (hard hand and a stick) thus following the hard totalitarian line. Ricardo refuses to tip his hunting assistant and leaves, thus foreboding a less-than-generous future government. Canivell's final expletive, "Es una merde" (What shit), accompanies a close-up of a dead partridge that he smells. This final visual image ties in with the epilogue that is an ironic twist on a Spanish proverb about living happily ever after: "Y ni fueron felices . . ." (And they did not live happily . . .).

The film contains two concrete mentions of the Spanish civil war: shortly after Canivell's arrival, he encounters an airplane propeller-statue dedicated to a "red" plane shot down in 1936. This is one of the worst insults of the film ("No faltaba más" [This is the last straw]) since the Catalan industrialist states that his brother was killed in the war. Toward the end of the film, one of the aristocratic guests refers to his wife as "my Brunete nurse." This reference to the battle of July, 1937 that is considered a Nationalist victory further underscores the relationship of the upper classes to the regime. In this society of vanquished and victors, Canivell's business venture was doomed from the start.

Director Berlanga believes that the theme of the film has universal dimensions; when asked if *La escopeta nacional* is a political film, Berlanga replied, "Yes and no . . . I didn't propose to put *franquismo* on trial . . . the film is about the corruption of power" (Hernández Les, *El último*, 133). Nevertheless, the film is indeed a scathing satire of the Franco regime, as the director recognizes on another occasion: "It is not a national shotgun. It is the national shotgun. Belonging to the class that during forty years, determined the destiny, fortune, and

Grotesque comedy: García Berlanga's La escopeta nacional, with Mónica Randall, Antonio Ferrandis, and José Luis López Vázquez. Courtesy Sogepaq.

misfortune of millions of us Spaniards who did not pertain to that class" (qtd. in Galán, *Carta*, 47).

Sonámbulos (Somnambulists) is a film from 1978 in which director Manuel Gutiérrez Aragón combines fairy tale, history, and dreams in a complex narrative that has a profound visual impact on the viewer. One can intuit the meaning of the title of the film from a comment made by the director regarding choosing between death and insanity, which "is the option when you wake up from a nightmare. A nightmare lasting forty years in which we were somnambulists" (qtd. in Caparrós Lera, *Travelling* 51). Gutiérrez Aragón intertwines different levels of narrative beginning with the initial scenes: the opening shot of an old book and a large, ancient key immediately points to the idea of a fairy tale and the need for allegorical interpretation (the key of knowledge, etc.). A shot of the Spanish National Library in Madrid reinforces the initial reference to books and knowledge, as well as setting the spatial location of the narrative. A voice-over that accompanies a shot of protesters in the street sets the historical circumstances: the so-called "Burgos Trial" at the end of 1970 in which six young Basques were tried for killing a police officer and were sentenced to death. The next shot, which is one of the most spectacular and memorable in recent Spanish cinema, provides an oneiric dimension to the film: Ana (Ana Belén) is asleep in a chair in the National Library and in the background there is a large picture window; suddenly, mounted police charge though the window in pursuit of protesters, clubbing everyone in sight while Ana sleeps. The oneiric imagery of the film leads Isabel Escudero to place *Sonámbulos* in the tradition of "oneiric-moral expressionistic experiments" such as that in P. Weine's 1919 classic, *The Cabinet of Doctor Caligari* (18). Comments made by director Gutiérrez Aragón help further elucidate both the title of the film and this scene: "the Franco regime was a very long nightmare, where we did nightmarish things; we did things only because we were sleeping, we don't do them when we are conscious. In this sense, they were somewhat unreal because they corresponded to that nightmare" (qtd. in Antolín 47). The police charge through the library window is a symbol of oppression, particularly against freedom of thought and knowledge. This socio-political plane intersects with that of the fairy tale not only in the person of Ana, but also her uncle, Norman (Norman Brinsky).

Ana is a militant who has become terminally ill, and her Uncle Norman is a physician who has lost his title but who has a medicine that he claims will cure his niece, with the following caveat: "Mis medicinas producen una liberación de tal clase que colocan al paciente más allá del bien y del mal, más allá de la memoria que se va borrando poco a poco, más allá de la historia que se va convirtiendo en un libro, más allá de las ideas habituales que se vuelven originales.   Ana, entrégame tu mente y te salvaré" (My medicine produces a liberation that places the patient beyond good and evil, beyond memory that is erased little by little, beyond history that becomes a book, beyond habitual ideas that become original. Ana, surrender your mind to me, and I will save you). The intersection in planes occurs when Norman, with a large book, reads a story about a deathly sick princess, a sad queen, and a magician who has the book of knowledge. Naturally, the princess is Ana, the queen is her mother María Rosa, and the magician is the physician. Norman reminds Ana that he hid his medicines in the "drawer of surprises" of a mirrored dresser, a piece of furniture that appears in various locations in María Rosa's house, and which acquires the mythological status of a modern Pandora's box. In the fairy tale, the magician tells the princess that in order to have knowledge, one must be free, and in order to be free, she must destroy the queen (her mother). After a brutal police interrogation, Ana divulges that her mother is also a militant and collaborator with ETA, and this confession represents the allegorical destruction of María Rosa. The fact that Ana opens the drawer with the key to the *Libro de todas las cosas* further underscores the Pandora's box metaphor, and the laughter after she sees a communist flag represents Gutiérrez Aragón's disillusionment with the party in which he had participated from 1962 until 1977. Indeed, when communist director Juan Antonio Bardem viewed *Sonámbulos*, he said "We have just received his letter" of resignation from the communist party (qtd. in Torres 88).

The narrative has a further dimension in the intercalated theatrical scenes from Strindberg's *Ghost Sonata*. The inspiration for the movie came from a protest by Spanish actress Julia Peña, who interrupted a production of the Strindberg play during the Burgos trial in order to register a social protest. Gutiérrez Aragón echoes this protest with a voice-over during one of the dramatic sections. The dialogue from the play that the director incorporates into the movie seems to counterpoint each of the narrative moments of the film: thus, the first time this occurs, the line, "But you think that you're going to die" immediately follows Norman's description of his cure; in a dramatic intercalation following Ana's interrogation, a symbolic noose drops into the scene and a young actress chokes an older one, thus showing yet another symbolic destruction of the mother.

Other important symbols in the film include the lentils that the characters have eaten all of their lives, even though they hate them. Gutiérrez Aragón explains, "the lentils represent the period in which you had to eat everything, without any explanations. That cruelty is a symptom of our society" (Aguilar 6). The lentils take on an additional political significance because of the fact that Ana's father loved them, and the nurse who helps administer Ana's treatment is identified as having supplied the lentils. The mother cannot dismiss the nurse, who also works in María Rosa's house, in spite of the fact that she hates the servant, because the latter knows too much. Her dictatorial behavior (she ran off all of the other maids and now does what she wants), her association with the absent father, and employment by the new father figure (Norman) all underscore the physician's negative character, that of the evil magician. Indeed, María Rosa attacks him and calls him "un loco y un criminal" (a madman and a criminal). On the historical, political level, Norman can represent Franco, since his "cure" for Ana represents precisely what the dictator attempted to do with Spanish society: saving it by controlling minds, allowing no moral choices, and erasing memory and reshaping history. The identification of the father figure with Franco appears in other Gutiérrez Aragón films as well, most notably, *Demonios en el jardín.*

In the final scene, Ana, now insane, is institutionalized, and she reads from a book of things that she needs to remember: "Hay que levantarse para orinar. Pertenezco al pueblo y quiero a mi madre . . . mi color favorito es el azul" (You have to get up to urinate. I belong to the people and I love my mother . . . my favorite color is blue). The blue color symbolism and the fact that the statement regarding her mother is the opposite of what was the truth indicate that Ana is now completely controlled, without a will of her own. A librarian presents her with another book--the one that contains all answers to all questions, and she reads, "Guárdate de la reina, la reina es la muerte. Pero guárdate igualmente del mago . . . el mago es la locura. La reina posee el libro pero sólo el mago puede descifrarlo . . . si quieres conocer todas las respuestas a todas las preguntas, te destruyes. Si renuncias a conocer, te salvas" (Stay away from the queen, the queen is death. But also stay away from the magician . . . the magician is madness. The queen possesses the book, but only the magician can decipher it. . . if you want to know all the answers to all the questions, you destroy yourself. If you renounce knowing, you save yourself). The final shot of the film is of two men in white uniforms and water falling endlessly from sprinklers. John Hopewell notes that "the film ends framing a typical paradox: our personality is defined by habits which alienate or violate our true selves but whose absence connotes madness." (196). The final quotes from the book of all things not only closes the cycle of the fairy tale narrative announced in the opening shot, but also underscores themes of knowledge/ignorance and action/passivity. The fairy tale narrative elicits a symbolic reading of the text, and although Gutiérrez Aragón believes that "more than symbolic, it is hyperrealistic," he concedes that "undoubtedly the film has various levels of reading" (qtd. in Martínez 37). The other symbolic aspect of the text is the oneiric quality which derives from the visual imagery. Matías Antolín notes that in *Sonámbulos*, only a visual explosion of suggestive images, full of signifieds, exists" (47), and the director admits that "scenes are done in function of the pure image" (qtd. in Torres 93).

Although Gutiérrez Aragón links *Sonámbulos* together with Ricardo Franco's *Los restos del naufragio* (The Remains of the Shipwreck) and Carlos Saura's *Los ojos vendados* (Blindfolded Eyes) in that the three films have common links, in many regards *Sonámbulos* stands alone as what Hopewell calls "one of the most intelligent reflections made about militancy under Franco" (197). *Sonámbulos* was nominated for an Oscar, and earned Gutiérrez Aragón the Best Director award at the San Sebastián Film Festival.

José M. Gutiérrez Santos's 1978 film, *Arriba Hazaña* (Up With Hazaña), is about the religious education system during the Franco regime, and in a broader sense, about political repression and the transition to democracy. The title is a clear play on words, satirizing the Franco regime's slogan, "Arriba España" (Up With Spain); the satire consists of multiple levels, since *hazaña* means "heroic feat" or "exploit," and is also a homophone of the surname of the president of the Republic in 1936, Manuel Azaña. The priests who represent the oppressors at the school are Brother Ramiro (Fernando Fernán Gómez) and Brother Eluterio (Héctor Alterio). The former represents the hard-line approach and often metes out physical punishment to the students and his bywords are "disciplina y autoridad" (discipline and authority); the latter represents a more subtle, psychological type of repression. Indeed, Méndez Leite notes that in the film there is a "suggestive duel between two forms of oppression" represented by these two characters ("El cine español en la transición" 23). The male teenage students become more and more rebellious as the film progresses. Some of their rebellious acts have a specific motivation against the system; in this case the system is, superficially at least, religion, and the pranks border on blasphemy (putting a dead bird on a crucifix, placing hosts and a chalice with Coca-cola in someone's bed, letting a dove--symbol of the Holy Spirit--loose during chapel and then shooting it). Others are typical teenage pranks--smoke bombs and writing slogans on the blackboards--but barricading themselves into the dormitory quarters takes on specific political connotations as the act is carried out with the anarchist tune "A las barricadas" (To the barricades) repeating itself on the soundtrack, and as the students use terms like "la primera jornada revolucionaria" (the first day of the revolution) and "camarada" (comrade). The resolution of the conflict--expulsion of the ringleaders, and a new director who implements some superficial reforms such as student referenda--points allegorically to the transition to democracy in

Spain after the death of Franco. The final shot of the students singing the same song with which the film began hints that nothing has really changed.[45]

The character of Brother Ramiro manifests the effects of the civil war on this segment of Spanish society. During an early crisis in which a student who has been locked in a closet starts a fire and almost dies of smoke inhalation, Ramiro quips "bastante sufrí en la guerra" (I suffered enough in the war). When he enters a classroom to punish the students, Brother Ramiro clearly carries a book with him entitled *La legión* (The Legion), which refers to soldiers of Franco's Nationalist army. The director tries to assuage Brother Ramiro at one point, saying, "Yo sé que usted ha sufrido mucho en la guerra, pero los tiempos han cambiado" (I know that you suffered a lot in the war, but times have changed)--a point that Ramiro and many like him during the regime found difficult to acknowledge. Indeed, even the terminology used by the priests reflects a war-time mentality: when the students carry out another prank and have someone call the priests' residence inquiring about a massage parlor, a priest reacts, "atacan por todos los frentes" (they are attacking on every front). During a search of students' quarters, two brothers lament that perhaps the overextension of authority is the cause of the rebellion among the students: "La culpa la tiene el Hermano Ramiro que cree que todavía es sargento de la Legión" (Brother Ramiro, who thinks he's still a sergeant in the Legion, is to blame). Thus, the civil war imposes itself on the psyche of its participants and shapes their interaction with others for years to come.

In 1979, Carlos Saura directed *Mamá cumple 100 años* (Mama Turns 100), a film that is a sequel to his 1972 production, *Ana y los lobos*. With the return to the thematics of the earlier film, many Spanish critics felt that Saura's career had played itself out, and that he was only capable of a narcissistic repetition of the same old themes, a fear that was not born out in the last decade, given the variety of Saura's productions, ranging from the so-called dance trilogy (*Bodas de sangre* [Blood Wedding], *Carmen*, and *El amor brujo* [Love the Enchanter]) to his historical films dealing with the sixteenth-century

---

[45]Luis Urbez analyzes the film as a political allegory that shows the old regime (repression), the reaction of the opposition, resolution of the conflict, and a superficial change in the regime (117).

figures, the conquistador Lope de Aguirre (*El dorado*) and the mystic poet San Juan de la Cruz (*La noche oscura* [The Obscure Night]). The cast is essentially the same as in the earlier film, with the exception of the untimely death of José María Prada, who played José in *Ana y los lobos*, the addition of the Argentine actor Norman Brinsky as Ana's husband, and the actresses who play Juan's daughters now as grown-ups. The fact that Saura has brought Ana back to life (she was murdered at the end of *Ana y los lobos*) sets the tone for the rest of the film, and in particular foreshadows the mother's overcoming death at the end of this movie. Ana's initial comments upon her return to the mansion, "Está igual . . . todo igual" (It is the same as before . . . just the same), indicates a sense of continuity from the previous film, and yet naively overlooks the changes that have occurred. There is a certain irony that both actor José María Prada, who played José (symbol of the military in *Ana y los lobos*), and General Franco died between the filming of the two movies. As Luchy says, José was the only one capable of imposing order, and the behavior of Juan's daughter represents that of a new generation of uninhibited Spaniards: she smokes marijuana and seduces Antonio, Ana's husband, into numerous love-making episodes. In spite of his physical absence, José continues to impose himself somewhat, however. When the women and girls search through an old trunk in the attic, the military past seems to dominate the moment: the smell of camphor from moth balls affects Victoria, Carlota dresses up in a military hat, and Luchy, contemplating José's military medals, states, "Es nuestro patrimonio, hija, con esto no se juega" (It's our patrimony, girl, and you don't fool with it). Juan continues to be what his mother calls "a slave of his passions," although the director deflates the Don Juan myth in a scene in which Juan suffers from sexual failure and Luchy shouts, "No hay mujeres frígidas, sólo hombres incompetentes" (There is no such thing as frigid women, only incompetent men). Saura takes Fernando's character in a comic leap from levitation to hang-gliding, as Fernando becomes a modern-day Don Quixote when his acts of faith come crashing--literally--down to reality. Even this generation of Spaniards seems to change with the times, however, as Fernando considers ingesting a hallucinogenic plant in order to "fly." However, Luchy helps bring Fernando down to reality with regard to the plight of the family: they have run out of money. Luchy forges promissory notes and plots with Juan and Fernando to kill Mother by withholding her

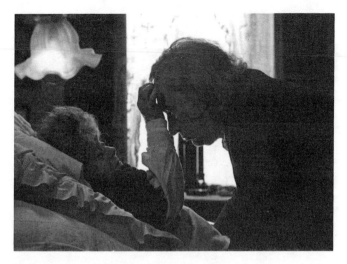

Maternal symbolism: Saura's <u>Mamá cumple 100 años,</u> starring Rafaela Aparicio and Fernando Fernán Gómez. Courtesy Elías Querejeta, P.C.

medicine so that they can sell the land to real-estate developers. Mother, however, is doted with supernatural powers, and not only hears their conversations from her bed, but also communicates with Ana when the latter takes refuge in the grotto after a row with her husband. That the voice reaches Ana in this religious place after she catches her boot in a steel trap continues the themes of religion and violence from *Ana y los lobos*. Mother's message, "Mis hijos me quieren matar y sólo tú puedes salvarme. Para eso has venido" (My children want to kill me and only you can save me. That is what you have come for), conveys a sense of supernatural intervention, but also reinforces the irony that only someone who is "different" and a foreigner can save Mother, and indeed Spain, from her children, a theme that Unamuno also developed in his writings on the need to "Europize" Spain. Another element of the supernatural is the return of José for Mother's birthday celebration, also accomplished through an act of faith: with strong winds that blow out a candle and the sound of a helicopter (representing José's military connection) "off," and the visual image of characters frozen in place (and time), José appears to his Mother. Hopewell points out that Mamá's entrance for her party, lowering into the scene on a giant swing, recalls the Elche miracle play

Quixotic adventures: Saura's <u>Mamá cumple 100 años</u>, starring Fernando Fernán Gómez, Geraldine Chaplin, Norman Brinsky, and Elisa Nandi. Courtesy Elías Querejeta, P.C.

(149), as Saura continues to emphasize the importance of the supernatural. Although Mamá has an attack during the celebration and Carlota declares her dead, a second intervention of the supernatural using the same techniques as before (strong wind and the sound of a helicopter, lights go out, images freeze) brings Mamá back to life, an event that Saura underscores with a symbolic turning on of lights and Mamá's comical retort, "Me ha sentado mal el chocolate" (The chocolate didn't agree with me). Her brush with death allowed her to see her life pass before her eyes as if she were looking out of a train window, and among her visions is one that is central to Spanish society and to Saura's film-making: the civil war. "Cuando empezó la guerra, los bombardeos, las sirenas. Qué horror. Veía pasar mi vida toda por delante de la ventanilla. Cuánta crueldad, cuánta estupidez, cuánta mezquindad, hijos míos. Cuánto sufrimiento inútil, cuánto sacrificio inútil" (When the war began, the bombings, the sirens. What horror. I saw my whole life in front of the window. Such cruelty, such stupidity, such pettiness, my children. So much useless suffering, so much useless sacrifice). The film ends with a rapid tracking shot through the door and out of the mansion, and Hopewell comments that this exemplifies Saura's change in shooting style and handling of inner and outer spaces in this, his first comedy (147-48). The soundtrack also plays an important role in the film; the *sevillanas* and Chueca's "Military March" that create what Saura calls "'a farcical tone which is very Spanish'" (qtd. in Hopewell, 259). Although this film received negative reviews in the Spanish press, it was Saura's most commercially successful movie up to that point, a situation not without irony.

Siete días de enero (Seven Days in January) is a 1979 film by inveterate director Juan Antonio Bardem, whose career in Spanish cinema started in 1952. The movie is a reflection of Bardem's political leanings and of the end of censorship of political themes, as it relates the assassination in January of 1977 of leftist labor leaders at their headquarters on Atocha Street in Madrid by a group of right-wing fanatics. The film begins with a mixture of stills and documentary footage related to the social turmoil during the 23rd to the 29th of January of that year, with the assassination of the lawyers occurring on the 24th. The narration of the film covers a longer time span, however. Beginning with a meeting of the fascist thugs at a firing range on January 22, the narrative moves day by day until the 27th, and then jumps to the 7th, 11th, and 26th of February, the 8th, 11th, 12th, and 23rd of March, and the 23rd and 24th of October, followed by a segment that shows the funeral of the lawyers in a scene that nearly reaches the level of apotheosis, a scene that would correspond to January 26th.

The social and political divisions in Spanish society that remain forty years after the civil war appear very clearly in the film. The rightist fanatics always refer to the leftists in pejorative terms--"rojo," "masón," "cabrones," "rojillos" (reds, mason, bastards, little reds). The rightists' homes and offices are decorated with photographs of Franco and José Antonio, as well as swastikas and other fascist memorabilia. Older rightists, like Sebastián, also view their younger comrades with a certain disdain, making comments like, "Con gente como tú aún no habríamos ganado la guerra" (With people like you we wouldn't have even won the war yet). Indeed, the war shapes the attitude of the victors as much as that of the vanquished: Don Tomás declares, "Nuestra cruzada de liberación no ha terminado todavía" (Our crusade of liberation has not finished yet), and warns against the eternal enemies of Spain. Bardem mainly focuses on the background of Luis María, who abandons his girlfriend Pilar on the night of the 24th with the excuse, "Tengo que hacer cosas . . . cosas de hombres" (I have some things to do . . . men's things). Bardem incorporates television and radio news to document the reaction to the assassination of the lawyers: the demonstrations, general strike, and police man-hunt. A close-up of Luis María shouting at Pilar indicates that things did not turn out as he had hoped and leads to his abandoning Madrid and eventual capture by the police in Murcia.

The event of the assassination, which is the turning point of the film, appears three times. First, it occurs in the normal chronology of the narrative on the 24th. The second occurrence is when one of the survivors of the attack gives an account from his hospital bed on the 26th; this flashback occurs in slow-motion and adds the perspective of survivors of the attack who had fortuitously left the office minutes before the shootings. The third occurrence is during a police line-up of suspects on October 24th, and this final return to that scene incorporates not only slow-motion, but a change in camera angle with an absence of sound followed by a pan of the bloodied bodies piled on the floor. Hopewell comments that the repetition of this gripping scene together with the special effects that Bardem uses contrasts with the documentary style that dominates the rest of the film (108). The final epilogue, recounting the legalization of the communist party in Spain in April of 1977 and the first democratic elections of that year in which ultra-rightist parties did not elect a single delegate or senator, underscores the political message of the film. Director Bardem stated in an interview with Fernando Lara, "With *Siete días de enero*, what I am attempting to basically communicate to the spectator is that he be careful, that the assassins are among us" (11). Although the film was not a huge success either in commercial or critical terms, it is a good example of *cinéma engagé* in recent Spanish film-making.

El nido (The Nest) is a film from 1980 directed by Jaime de Armiñán that was nominated for an Oscar in the Best Foreign Film category. It is a haunting film with beautiful photography by Teo Escamilla, music by Haydn, and excellent performances by Argentine actors Héctor Alterio and Luis Politti as well as by actress Ana Torrent. The love story that comprises the narrative contains both literary and political overtones. The widowed Don Alejandro (Alterio) is a quixotic figure who listens to classical music and rides his white horse in the woods. On one of these outings, he discovers a series of notes that contain clues as to the whereabouts of their composer. This leads him to Goyita (Torrent), a thirteen-year old "Lolita" who is

playing the role of Lady MacBeth in a school play.   A montage
sequence of their various activities together--"directing" Haydn, bicycle
and horseback riding, playing leapfrog, observing a nest that provides
the film title--show a joyful plenitude in their relationship that is like
that of a father and daughter.   However, the foreshadowing in the
scene in which Don Alejandro shoots his shotgun to Goyita's applause,
and the erotic advances that the adolescent makes toward the widower
move the relationship toward its tragic end.   Indeed, the oath that
Goyita recites, "Siempre estaremos juntos por los siglos de los siglos"
(We will always be together, for ever and ever), is an oath in blood
(Goyita cuts her hand and his and joins them together), blood that
serves as another foreshadowing of the blood to be shed.   (The
blood/hands/Lady MacBeth combination also points to the tragic
ending). This ritual also includes an exchange of tokens: Goyita gives
Don Alejandro a handkerchief, and he responds with a chain and
identification tag that he received in a French concentration camp. This
object metonymically represents the political dimension of the film.
Don Alejandro is the Republican outcast, the eccentric who lives apart
from the town, and who will, in the end, pay a high price once more.

In a final scene, an older and more mature Goyita visits Don
Goyita is the daughter of a pusillanimous Civil Guard who is
dominated by his wife and his sergeant, "El Muñeco."   The latter,
standing in the shadows, sees Goyita and Don Alejandro drive off
together, and the Sergeant chides the girl's father.   "El Muñeco" gets
rid of Goyita's pet bird because civil guard regulations prohibit pets in
their living quarters, and he also confiscates the tag and chain given to
her by Don Alejandro. These two acts represent a symbolic loss of
freedom and of life. Seeking revenge, Goyita asks Don Alejandro to
kill the civil guard, something that he confesses himself incapable of
doing. Nevertheless, the close-up of Don Alejandro and the stills from
the earlier montage sequence connote the type of flashbacks that one
experiences before death.   Since the Sergeant rejects Alejandro's
quixotic challenge to a duel, the widower ambushes the civil guard and
is killed. The blanks that Goyita's father discovers near Alejandro's
body are the final testimony of his gentle character and of his love for
Goyita.

In a final scene, an older and more mature Goyita visits Don
Alejandro's grave to ask his pardon and to confess her love for him in
a repetition of the blood ritual (she cuts an "A"--for "Amor" [Love]
in her hand and places it on the marble tomb). The final shot, a long
shot of a white horse running to the accompaniment of Haydn's

"Creation" is a repeat of the opening shot and thus brings the narrative full circle. Pedro Miguel Lamet refers to the horse as a "symbol of freedom" (220), and in the context of this narrative, the horse also functions as a metonymic device, as the eccentric Republican himself fully symbolizes freedom. The principal actors provide excellent performances in this film. This is especially true of Ana Torrent; Ramón G. Redondo notes that Torrent provides a mysterious dimension to the film (115), and Jesús Fernández Santos adds regarding Torrent's portrayal of Goyita, "she acquires a tragic nuance that is infrequent on the Spanish screen" (31). The fine acting contributes to make *El nido* a haunting film that leaves an indelible imprint on its audiences.

In *Patrimonio nacional* (National Patrimony), the 1981 sequel to *La escopeta nacional*, García Berlanga moves the Marquis of Leguineche retinue to the capital as the aristocrats "return" from exile. García Berlanga filmed this movie at an old palace adjacent to the centrally-located Cibeles Plaza. We meet the eccentric Condesa (Mary Santpere) who never leaves her bed, whom Leguineche describes as "una acérrima franquista" (a very strong supporter of Franco). That she has not paid any taxes in forty years implies that she is part of the social class allied with the regime that received numerous privileges of the "haves," a group that García Berlanga satirizes again in this second part of the trilogy. Indeed, Luis José remarks that instead of a portrait of the king, she has two of Franco. The political divisions in the family based on the same epithets as in the first film of the series appear from the opening sequence, as the Condesa refuses to allow Leguineche and his son into her home: "Se van a enterar este par de rojos de lo que vale un peine" (That pair of reds is going to find out what's what). When they finally gain access to the house, she tries to restrict their movement again referring to this political division: "Como sois unos rojos, esta planta no la pisaréis porque aquí es zona nacional" (Since you're a bunch of reds, you won't set foot on this floor because this is the Nationalist zone). The Marquis and his son attempt to have the Condesa committed so that they can take over her property, a move that becomes unnecessary when she is killed while "cleaning" her shotgun (it ironically misfired as she was about to shoot at the marquis). García Berlanga continues the ironic vein of the film as the government seizes the building and makes it "national patrimony"; the palace becomes a museum, and the marquis and his son try to eke out a living by giving tours to Japanese tourists. The

Social satire: García Berlanga's <u>Patrimonio nacional</u>, with Mary Santpere, Amparo Soler Leal, Luis Ciges, Luis Escobar, and José Luis López Vázquez. Courtesy Sogepaq, S.A.

final quote (in English) "Marquis of Leguineche and son, end of the saga," is the last barb at the social class that has declined to this point.

The film contains many of Berlanga's trademarks, including a "choral" structure with a large cast of zany characters (tax collectors, a gay manservant, cousin Alvaro and his French wife, Father Calvo, who continues to rave about Marxist priests, and the over-sexed Luis José) and the long sequence shot, which as Hopewell notes, becomes "hypertrophied" in this film with a seven-minute shot (62). Although not as good a film as *La escopeta nacional*, it was nevertheless popular enough among Spanish audiences to merit another sequel.

Kargus (Kargus), the 1981 debut of film-makers Juan Miñón and Miguel Angel Trujillo, consists of a series of six sketches that portray Spain from the end of the civil war to the death of Franco in 1975. The common themes throughout the film are sex and politics. The sketches are tied together, albeit loosely, by the tale of Juan, a reporter who hopes to interview the wealthy J. R. H. Kargus when he visits Spain. After the first sketch concerning the theme of the maquis, (see Chapter 3), the second sketch deals with the misery of the postwar period. In the ruins of a large abandoned factory building, a man and a woman chase and kill cats that they then sell, and they successfully resist an attempt to place the young woman in an institution for wayward women. This suggests a preference for freedom, even in misery, over oppression in comfort. The third sketch deals with the sexual awakening of some adolescents who voyeuristically spy the naked breasts of a maid. Although the narrative of this sketch takes place in 1953, the presence of the war hangs heavily, as the boys have a school lesson in logic regarding the civil war uniform placed on a mannequin: since the hole in the uniform shows that the bullet entered from behind, the teacher remarks that they must deduce that the soldier was either a deserter or an enemy who was shot in the back. The fourth sketch is the most humorous of the series, and it brings us up to the sixties, and shows the changes in Spanish society. Julián, the aging and impoverished suitor of the shy Carmencita, borrows a SEAT 600, the tiny automobile that is the symbol of a new prosperity in Spain, in order to take her on a drive as part of his courtship. They go out to the country, and after successfully making advances on the girl, in spite of the cramped space, a park ranger catches them *in flagrante delicto* and puts a real damper on the relationship, thus manifesting once again the freedom/oppression theme. The next sketch features some real stars of the Spanish screen--Héctor Alterio and Francisco Algora as members of a work crew who patrol urban streets at night in order to paint over any graffiti of a political nature--or at least those that are anti-Franco in nature, since the crew clearly decides to pass by the graffito "Gibraltar, español" (Gibraltar, Spanish), which was indeed the only one allowed during the late sixties and early seventies. In one humorous scene, the bewildered boss of the crew consults a little notebook with reference to the graffito, "Viva Lola" (Long Live Lola), and says, "Tiene que significar otra cosa" (It's got to mean something else), in an attempt to decipher the hidden political meaning of such an innocuous message. In the final sketch, a young couple make love in an apartment bedroom; a poster of James Dean and music by Bob Dylan connote the progressive attitude of the young woman. Their sleep is interrupted, however, and the young man has to hide under the bed when her whole family comes into the bedroom to listen to the Requiem on the radio, a signal that the Caudillo has died. Political divisions among family members are manifested in exclamations such as "¡Qué calamidad! ¡Ya tenéis lo que queríais!" (What a calamity! Now you've got what you wanted!).

Although *Kargus* is somewhat irregular, there are touches of brilliance in the film, and each of its segments shows an example--sometimes tragic, sometimes humorous--of how the civil war and its aftermath shaped Spanish society for almost forty years.

Nacional III (National III) is García Berlanga's 1982 sequel to *Patrimonio nacional* and the final of the so-called Leguineche trilogy. The film derives much of its humor from references to socio-political events that occur during the early years of democracy, such as the unsuccessful coup attempt by Colonel Tejero that took place in February 23, 1981. García Berlanga even includes the famous television footage of the coup attempt in the film. Father Calvo, who thinks he hears tanks in the street, continues with his invectives seen in the previous films: "ahora van a ver esos rojos" (now those reds are going to see). Ironically, the tanks of "liberation" turn out to be only large digging equipment. Indeed, the historical event of what Spaniards refer to as "23 F" is one of the main plot motivators in the film, since Chus's father on his ranch in Extremadura, upon hearing about the coup, put on his civil war army uniform in order to take over the city hall, ("el alcalde, los concejales son todos rojos con la jodida democracia" [the mayor and the alderman are all reds with the fucking democracy]) but he died of a heart attack. His property is inherited by his daughter, and Luis José quickly tries to improve relations with his estranged wife in order to cash in on this bonanza. (After leaving the cemetery, someone comments, "El dinero, el dinero, lo han olido desde Madrid" [Money, money, they smelled it all the way from Madrid]). A ridiculous money-making scheme by Luis José--to patent paella in order to sell it at the world-cup soccer competition to be held in Barcelona--was met by disdain by the Marquis; his response, "En nuestra familia no ha trabajado nunca nadie y hemos vivido divinamente" (In our family, nobody has ever worked, and we have lived divinely), manifests a theme of social criticism that dates back to the gentleman in the sixteenth-century picaresque narrative, *Lazarillo de Tormes*. The sale of the property, however, results in a suitcase full of money and the problem of how to get it out of the country. The sight-gag of Luis José in a body cast from which jewels are falling during his train trip on a "pilgrimage" to Lourdes gives a hint of the overall comic tone of the film. In a final ironic twist, the trilogy comes to an end as these "aristocrats" arrive in France just at the moment in which the socialists, led by François Mitterand, win the election.

The end of a saga: García Berlanga's <u>Nacional III</u>, with José Luis López Vázquez, Luis Escobar, and Amparo Soler Leal. **Courtesy Sogepaq, S.A.**

Víctor Erice's beautiful film from 1983, *El sur* (The South), is based on the novel by Adelaida García Morales.   The voice-over narration of the protagonist, Estrella, is one of the most important technical elements in the film, and it represents the memories of her youth ("No lo recuerdo ahora con exactitud . . . Nunca olvidaré la cara que se puso mi padre" [I don't remember precisely . . . I will never forget the face my father made]), a reading of her childhood diary ("Hoy cuando vuelvo a leer las páginas que dan cuenta de aquellos días . . ." [Today when I re-read the pages that tell about those days]) and a confession to her dead father. The chronology of the narrative covers the youth and adolescence of Estrella.   Just as Erice obtained a masterful performance from child actress Ana Torrent in *El espíritu de la colmena* (1973), he also receives stunning interpretations from Sonsoles Aranguren and Iciar Bollain, the two young actresses who portray Estrella, as well as from Omero Antonutti, who plays her father, Agustín.   Erice artfully jumps from youth to adolescence in a scene in which the young Estrella goes down her country road on a white bicycle accompanied by a puppy in late fall, and following an elliptical dissolve, the older Estrella returns on a red bicycle with a grown dog as newly fallen leaves now cover the road.

The war dramatically shapes the destiny of Estrella's family; there is a brief mention of the fact that her mother was a "maestra represaliada después de la guerra civil" (a teacher who was blacklisted after the civil war) who could not find work and who therefore taught the young girl at home. However, the impact of the war is especially acute in the case of her father, Agustín. Erice emphasizes this theme with the character of Milagros (Rafaela Aparicio), who, during a visit from the south where Agustín lived as a boy, talks to Estrella about her father's past: in a clear reference to the civil war, she talks of "la cantidad de muertos que han [sic] habido; todo por las ideas" (so many dead; all because of ideas). She later explains that Agustín and his father quarreled over political ideas, and that it was never clear if her father left home or if her grandfather kicked him out. To make clear Agustín's political persuasion, Milagros states that before the war, Grandfather was a "bad guy" and Agustín was a "good guy," but when Franco triumphed, Grandfather became a "saint," and Agustín, a "devil" who went to jail. Erice has admitted that Agustín represents "many men who have a split personality--the civil war exemplifies that split--and who cannot find themselves" (Hidalgo, "El espíritu" 2).

The difficulties that Agustín had in finding employment are alluded to less overtly than in the case of the mother. Estrella recalls, "Fui creciendo mientras nos trasladábamos de un lado para otro. El buscaba un trabajo fijo" (I grew up as we moved from place to place. He kept looking for a steady job). Aside from being a physician, Agustín has the almost magical powers of augury, which he teaches Estrella. The emotive relationship between the two is expressed in lyrical terms, such as when Agustín sacrifices his ideas in order to attend the first communion of his daughter, and in the scene of the subsequent party, a beautiful low angle shot shows Estrella and her father dancing together in a celebration of their special relationship and love for one another.

Although the south is only evoked in the film through shots of old postcards of Sevilla and music by Granados, an element of Agustín's mysterious past in the south begins to weigh heavily on him. When a film comes to town, Agustín discovers that his first love, Laura, has become a movie star. The scenes inside a cinema in which Agustín views his long-lost love imbue *El sur* with a self-reflexive quality also indelibly marks the director's earlier work (*El espíritu de la colmena*). Agustín's character has a good deal of pathos: his unrequited love

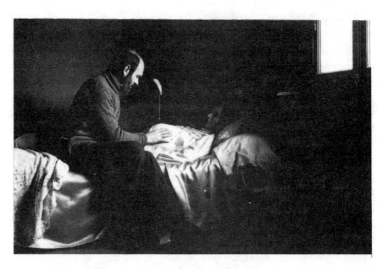

A chiaroscuro vision of the soul: Erice's El sur, with Omero Antonutti and Lola Cardona. Courtesy Elías Querejeta, P.C.

letters to Laura, his increased drinking, quarrels with his wife, and his inability to communicate with his daughter lead to his suicide. Although Estrella is at first despondent, she finally decides that in order to understand her father, she must go to the mysterious place of his origin. The final scene shows her packing her bags as the voice-over proclaims, "Por fin, iba a conocer el sur" (At last, I was going to get to know the south).

Erice's original plans included filming a final segment of the movie in Sevilla; indeed, he considered that a vital aspect of the theme of searching for the past would be the confrontation of "two types of landscape, two worlds" (Cristóbal 7), and the presentation of an "unfinished" film caused considerable controversy. Erice admits to presenting the film even though he was unable to complete his initial concept of the work because of financial reasons: "I'm conscious of the need of the company that has financed the preparation and the filming of the movie to recover its investment" (Rubio 129-30). Nevertheless, I believe that the ending of the film imbues the work with an even greater mysterious and poetic quality and certainly cannot be considered a defect. Indeed, the film won the Golden Hugo at the Chicago Film Festival, as well as a gold medal from the Centro de Investigaciones Cinematográficas for its testimonial character regarding recent Spanish history, and Manuel Fernández calls *El sur* "an authentic allegory about the maturity of thousands of Spaniards who, like the young Estrella, were born after the civil war and tried to know about the past in order to link their lives with the earlier tradition" (40).

Los santos inocentes (The Holy Innocents), director Mario Camus's 1984 cinematographic version of the Delibes novel from 1981 is a masterpiece of Spanish cinema. This film achieved both critical acclaim, with Paco Rabal and Alfredo Landa sharing the best actor award at the Cannes Film Festival, as well as popular acclaim: it was Spanish cinema's biggest box office hit of the year. The film portrays life during the 1960's on a large ranch (*cortijo*) in Extremadura. The characters in the film are divided into two groups: the have's and the have not's, who live in different worlds. The first group consists of the landlords: "el señorito" (master) Iván (Juan Diego), Pedro (Agustín González) and his wife Purita (Agata Lys), as well as the Marquesa who visits the ranch on the occasion of the first communion of her grandson; the have-not's are the servants: Paco (Alfredo Landa) and his family--his wife Régula (Terele Pávez), their children Quirce (Juan Sánchez) and Nieves (Belén Ballesteros). Two special characters of this group are "la niña chica" (the little girl) the youngest child in the family who is infirm and who gives forth occasional heart-wrenching screams, and Azarías (Francisco Rabal), the brother of Régula who is not in possession of all his mental faculties.

Although at the beginning of the story, Paco and his family live in an isolated stone hut, they are called up to serve at the big house. The servile attitude of the members of the lower class appears in their speech--both Paco and Régula repeat "Lo que usted mande, don Pedro" (Whatever you order, don Pedro), and the woman servant underscores the attitude with her phrase, "A mandar, don Pedro, para eso estamos" (Just order, don Pedro, that's what we're here for), as well as in the visual images relating to their demeanor. José Miguel Carión considers that the face of Terele Pávez, who plays Régula, is a "pure symbol of bitterness . . . that the impotence of human submission produces" (93-4). Paco and Régula accept the move to the new house because they do not have any control over their own lives, even knowing that serving there dashes their hopes for a better future for their children. In the stone hut, Paco gives Quirce grammar lessons by candle light, and Régula wants to send her children to school, commenting that "Con una pizca de conocimientos, podrán no ser pobres" (With a pinch of knowledge, they won't have to be poor). The privileged class wants the servants to have some education--but not too much--and they cannot hide their condescending attitude toward the workers. When don Iván shows off the rudimentary writing skills of Paco and Régula to a visiting ambassador, he quips, "Ya no estamos en el '36 . . . hacemos todo lo posible para redimir a esta gente" (We're not in '36 any more . . . we do everything possible to redeem these people). The specific temporal reference here immediately brings the Civil War to mind, and tacitly allies the landlords with the Franco regime. The close-up of the extremely childlike letters that Régula writes constitutes a fitting irony to Iván's contention that there is equality for women in modern Spain; the landlord's command to the couple, "Podéis largaros" (You can leave now) subtly completes the attitude of condescension in this scene. Iván likewise treats Paco in a condescending fashion as he constantly calls him "maricón" (queer). When, during a hunting episode, Paco falls from a tree, Iván's egotism prevails as he snaps, "Serás maricón, por poco me aplastas" (You queer, you almost smashed me). When he discovers that Paco has broken his leg, his only reaction is that it is a "mariconada" (queer-assed thing to do) since it will interfere with his hunting.

The matriarch of the family is the Marquesa, who comes from the city to attend her grandson's first communion. In medieval fashion, she treats the workers like little children, even referring to them as "hijos míos" (my children). As the laborers submissively form a line to receive a monetary present on this happy occasion, the Marquesa speaks to them individually. The combination of inquiring about one's family and one's pigs in the same breath, however, subtly equates these holy innocents with mere animals. Indeed, Paco's skill at retrieving downed prey when assisting Iván at hunting is equated with that of the best bird-dog: in a marvelous tracking shot, Paco, on all fours, sniffs the trail of a wounded bird and leads his master to a lost prize.

Although this equation of the servants with animals is degrading from the point of view of the landlords, it is certainly not so from the point of view of the lower class. Indeed, it represents a harmony with nature that is vital to their happiness and survival. This is best manifested in the personage of Azarías, the mentally-deficient brother of Régula. From the opening sequence of the movie, an evocative tracking shot that shows Azarías racing through the woods at dusk as he runs after the tawny owl, to the accompaniment of the rustic music of tambourine, drums, and rebec which is to become his motif in the film, his love for birds is a central motivating force in this character. When his pet goshawk becomes sick, Azarías's pleas for help at the big house receive only disdainful rejection. The close-ups of Azarías crying when the bird dies are emotionally counter-balanced by the scene in which Camus uses contrasting high- and low-angle shots to show how the faithful servant has trained a new goshawk to fly to his shoulder upon command. The other scene related to this harmony between man and nature which has a double emotional charge occurs at the end of the film when Azarías substitutes for the injured Paco as Iván's hunting assistant. With Azarías now in the tree with a decoy, the rage of the "señorito" over his bad luck leads to the denouement of the film: when Azarías signals the goshawk to come, Iván raises his shotgun and pays no heed to the servant's plea, "No tires, señorito, que es la milana" (Don't shoot, master, it's the goshawk). A circular tracking shot around the crying Azarías who is clutching the dead bird captures the emotions of this, the most innocent of all the characters. Again Camus uses the contrasting low and high-angle shots in the counterbalancing scene: on the next outing, we see Azarías high in the tree with a rope in hand, and shift in angle to show how he hangs the despised Iván is a shot filled with such emotion that it caused audiences in Spain to applaud in approbation.

Camus imbues the film with a high degree of literariness by dividing it into four distinct "chapters" whose titles refer to characters' names: "Quirce," "Nieves," "Paco, el bajo," and "Azarías." The narrative structure of the film consists of a present, marked by Quirce as a soldier and his sister as a factory worker in Zafra, and four flash-backs, each of which is overtly marked by Camus. The first flashback to grammar lessons for Quirce in his stone hut is signalled by three shots (long, medium, and close-up) of the young soldier leaning against a wall in Zafra. This structural unit terminates with the rustic music associated with Azarías and the lyrical refrain with which he greets his pet, "Milana bonita" (Beautiful goshawk). A fade to white signals the transition to the present, where Nieves and Quirce meet and she informs him that their young sister has died. A succession of three stills that represent a zoom-in on Nieves, together with a chapter title with her name, signals the second flashback to the beginning of her service in the big house as a maid. Again Camus uses Azarías and the rustic music to close this narrative segment, and a long shot of Quirce in uniform approaching the stone hut returns us to the present. A medium shot of Paco cleaning a shotgun dissolves into a double image

The haves . . . .   Camus's Los santos inocentes, with Juan Diego, Maribel Martín,
Agata Lys, Mary Carrillo. Courtesy Televisión Española.

(followed by the title, "Paco, el bajo") to signal the commencement of
the next chapter. Following a variant of the   previous pattern, this
flashback terminates with the tambourine music and a fade to white that
brings us again to the present, with Quirce visiting his outcast and
crippled father and aged mother in their isolated hovel. This final
flashback is triggered by an object--a cross that Régula gives to Quirce
so that he can take it to her brother in the mental hospital. A poetic
shot of Azarías holding the cross in the light of his hospital window
precedes the title of the last chapter, which begins with a close-up of
him holding the cross and "la niña chica," (the youngest child who is
mentally deranged and whose animal-like screams add a sense of
helplessness and despair to the household) in his lap. The moment of
his revenge against don Iván--aptly set to the music of the
tambourine--closes this segment with a fade to white before the
epilogue: Azarías, in the mental hospital, repeats his refrain, "Milana
bonita," and Quirce leaves him to contemplate the freedom of animals
so dear to his uncle as a flock of birds passes in the sky.

    Director Camus subtly guides the viewer to the unhappy ending
from the very beginning. After the opening sequence with Azarías,
there appears a still shot of Paco's family in front of their quarters at
the big house which relates to a later moment of the narrative when a

. . . and the have nots: Camus's <u>Los santos inocentes</u>, with Alfredo Landa, Terele Pávez, Belén Ballesteros, Juan Sánchez, Susana Sánchez. Courtesy Televisión Española.

photographer who attends the first communion ceremonies stops to take a family portrait of them. This still shot begins as a negative that is overexposed and gradually grows darker. Instead of this process stopping at the point when the photograph would be perfectly exposed, however, it continues to a point when the photograph is underexposed and barely visible, thus foreshadowing the darkness that eventually overcomes the household. The other technique that Camus utilizes to this end is the visual metaphor contained in the close-ups of excrement. Azarías, the innocent, does not distinguish between acceptable and non-acceptable locations for relieving himself, and he defecates even on the grounds of the big house. The singling out of these remains by the camera lens visually symbolizes a fundamental expression of Spanish billingsgate, "Me cago en . . ." (I shit on . . .). His symbolic curse on those who oppress and exploit turns to reality at the end of the narration as he carries out his vengeance on don Iván.

Although the political element does not receive overt emphasis in *Los santos inocentes*, the prominently displayed photograph of Franco in the big house overtly allies the landlords with the regime. In Iván's opinion, fighting--and winning--the civil war was a fundamental aspect of his family's well-being and indeed of Spanish society: he complains

The most innocent of all: Francisco Rabal as Azarías in Camus's <u>Los santos inocentes</u>.
Courtesy Televisión Española.

about Quirce, "Que los jóvenes de hoy no lucharon una guerra" (The young people of today didn't fight any war). His subsequent remark to the ambassador, "Todos tenemos que aceptar una jerarquía. Unos abajo, otros arriba. Es ley de vida, ¿no?" (We all have to accept a hierarchy. Some below, others on top. It's the law of life, isn't it?), manifests the fundamental social question of the film. *Los santos inocentes* beautifully captures the oppression of the lower classes in Spain during the second half of the Franco regime.

Another portrait of the later postwar years appears in *Tiempo de silencio* (Time of Silence), the 1986 film by Vicente Aranda based on the novel of the same name by Luis Martín Santos and which critics Fanny Rubio and Javier Goñi refer to (together with Cela's *La colmena* and Delibes's *Los santos inocentes*) as novels of the Spanish civil war (153). The narrative portrays Madrid in the late 1940's and early 1950's. Pedro (Imanol Arias), a scientist who studies cancer, has run out of mice in his laboratory, since they do not breed there, and he has no funds to purchase more of these expensive laboratory animals from the United States. Nevertheless, his assistant Amador (Francisco Algora) informs him that he gave some of the mice to his cousin Muecas (Francisco Rabal) who lives in a shanty town outside of

Madrid, and that this poor man has successfully bred them with the help of the "natural heat" of his daughters, Florita and Conchi. The incredulous scientist goes to the shanty town to obtain the mice. After scenes of café life in which intellectuals like Pedro and his friend Matías (Juan Echanove) discuss literature and painting, and those in a bordello in which lights go off due to electric restrictions, Pedro returns to his pensión to make love to Dorita. He is awakened early however, by Amador, who summons him to the shanty town in order to help the dying Florita, whose child was aborted by her incestuous father. The scene of the screaming girl tied to a table next to a bloodied fetus and needle is gripping indeed. Pedro attempts to help her, but to no avail, and Cartucho (splendidly performed by Joaquín Hinojosa), the shanty town thug and beau of Florita, extracts the confession from Amador at knife point that the "doctor" was responsible for Florita's pregnancy. After an autopsy, the police apprehend Pedro, who was hiding out in the bordello, and attempt to extract a false confession from him. Dorita and Matías assist Pedro by setting the case straight, but when Pedro later takes his girlfriend to a fair, Cartucho stabs her to death, extracting his vengeance "hembra por hembra" (woman for woman). The final voice-over of Pedro in his laboratory regarding his sense of futility and oppression both underscores the meaning of the title of the film and lends it an air of literariness of the original narrative. Just as Martín Santos's novel portrays a Spain that is backward and repressed, with its intellectuals trapped in a time of silence, so too does the cinematographic adaptation by Vicente Aranda. Aranda's version of the absurd world in which Pedro lives does not depend on the subtle ironies of the literary text, however; instead, many scenes elicited overt laughter from the audience. Aranda also increases the importance of Dorita, played by Victoria Abril, who seems to be ever-present in his films. Reference to the original narrative is inevitable, and the film cannot and does not capture the important stylistic innovations of Martín Santos's masterpiece. Nevertheless, Aranda's *Tiempo de silencio* is a quality film that deserves much merit in its portrayal of the Spain of the 1950's.

    El disputado voto del señor Cayo (The Disputed Vote of Mr. Cayo, 1986) is director Antonio Giménez Rico's second film adaptation of a Miguel Delibes novel: ten years earlier, Giménez Rico made *Retrato de familia* (Family Portrait) from *Mi idolatrado hijo Sisí* (My Idolized Son Sisí). Delibes indicated in *Un año de mi vida* (A Year in My Life,

34) that *El disputado voto del señor Cayo* would deal with Spanish *cainismo* as well as the problem of rural exodus in Castile. The narrative is placed during the elections of 1977, and centers on the encounter between politicians from the city and a country dweller.

After a night urban aerial shot during the credits that, in retrospect, seems out of place, the film opens in black and white: Rafael (Iñaki Miramón), a parliamentary representative, receives a note in the middle of a debate. A close-up shot reveals the news that Víctor Velasco has died and will be buried tomorrow. After a rainy scene in the cemetery, the first of three flashbacks takes us to the main narrative thread of the film: the elections of 1977, which appears in color. The camera pans the local party headquarters of the PSOE (Partido Socialista Obrero Español), which is adorned with campaign posters of presidential candidate Felipe González and of Víctor Velasco. Indeed, this party propaganda serves as a foreshadowing of a later conflict in the film, as one party member complains that opposing parties cover up his posters with theirs. The sound "off" of breaking glass and shouts, "rojos, maricones de mierda" (reds, fucking queers), further underscores the *cainismo* in the film: political hostilities that are the remnants of the fratricidal conflict of forty years ago. A close-up of a map on the wall in which the camera pans upward in a northerly direction from Burgos indicates the geographical setting where the rest of the narrative is to occur. After exterior shots that include the city's gothic cathedral and evidence along the streets of the "poster war," the three socialist candidates, Rafa, Víctor (Juan Luis Galiardo), and Laly (Lydia Bosch), set forth to campaign in an isolated and poor region of rural Spain. Their vehicle, a red Simca, is not without symbolism, both in terms of its color and model: it seems the appropriate car to connote leftist proletariat ideals. The car does have a cassette player, however, which allows the differences between Víctor, in his forties, and a younger Rafa to become manifest: the former's musical tastes favor the *zarzuela*, while the latter listens to rock music, proclaiming in the modern urban slang that is his "signature," "mola cantidad" (it's really cool). A small ideological rift between Víctor and Laly is also evident: whereas the feminist Laly wants to speak about women's liberation, she cedes to Víctor, who wants to address the campaign theme of emigration. Aerial shots of the car travelling through the Castilian countryside, and a long shot of a beautiful canyon add to the visual quality of the film. This countryside, however, becomes symbolic of the growing division between Víctor and Rafa; the former is in awe of its beauty, whereas the latter condescendingly remarks, "Está bien para ovejas" (It's okay for sheep). The cut to the black and white cemetery scene brings us back to the present. The restaurant dialogue between Rafa and Laly captures the former's disillusionment, as he admits that he has left his revolutionary dreams behind. The images attest to this change: in contrast to the casual look of 1977 elections, Rafael now dresses in a suit, with hair neatly parted and dark-rimmed glasses. (One cannot help but compare this transformation with images of Felipe González in 1977 and in more recent elections.)

The second flashback begins with a 360 degree aerial shot of the candidates at the canyon's edge, and a repetition of the dialogue with which the first flashback ended. In this segment of the narrative, they arrive at a small town and meet Señor Cayo Fernández (Francisco Rabal), a 74 year old who is one of the last inhabitants of the village. Rabal in the role of a rustic and poorly clothed *campesino* cannot help bring to mind his outstanding performance as Azarías, in Mario Camus's 1984 film adaptation of another Delibes novel, *Los santos inocentes*. Although the physical appearance of the two characters is similar, Cayo has full use of his mental faculties, and indeed, shows on many occasions that his "country wisdom" is superior to that of the urban politicians. A close-up of his hand among a swarm of bees shows that Cayo, like Azarías, lives in harmony with nature, and he often shows the visitors his knowledge of the world around him: identifying the elder tree, showing how to catch crayfish, when is the best time for transplanting, or that mallows are used "para aligerar el vientre" (to clear out your innards). The dichotomy between Cayo and the urban visitors also occurs at a linguistic level. When Cayo, puffing smoke on his bees, asks Víctor to hand him "el humeón" (the fumigator), the latter queries, "¿El puchero?" (The smoke-pot?). Later, Rafa mistakenly uses the term "chova" (jay) to identify a "mirlo" (blackbird). The linguistic rift between the *campesino* and the urban politicians symbolizes the greater differences in values and life-styles.

In spite of his knowledge, Cayo has in common with Azarías the trait of the ingenue, the outsider who functions to defamiliarize the narrative, and therefore subtly ridicule the socio-political pretensions of the visitors. When Víctor tells him about the great opportunity of the elections, saying, "Si la desaprovechamos, nos hundiremos sin remedio esta vez para siempre" (If we don't take advantage of it, we'll sink forever this time, with no remedy), the response of the ingenuous *campesino* is "¿Y dónde vamos a hundirnos?" (And where are we going to sink to?). Later, when Laly is aghast that he has no television, Cayo retorts, "¿Para qué?" (What for?). Although he did not learn of Franco's death until four weeks after the fact, he exclaims, "¿Qué prisa me corría?" (Was I in any hurry?).

Ultra-rightists appear in town and use extremist rhetoric that has its root in *cainismo* to scare the *campesino*, warning that if the socialists win, they will take away his lands and set fire to the church. Cayo's ingenuous character continues in this new context: when the rightists assure him that they offer order, his response is, "¿Orden, dice? Es aquí de más" (Order, you say? There's more than enough of that here). Although ultra-rightists earlier attacked the socialists' car, throwing stones at it, the confrontation in the small town before the incredulous eyes of Señor Cayo constitutes the culmination of the *cainismo* in the film. Their provocation of the socialists comes from the "poster war" motif, as they cover over Víctor's propaganda. When Rafa tries to intervene, they stick glue in his mouth, and beat Víctor with a chain.

After meeting with Cayo, a Castilian "noble savage" who seems to have no need for politicians, and after the violence of his encounter with the ultra-rightists, Víctor's disillusionment comes to a head. On the drive home, he tells Laly, "No sé lo que me pasa en los últimos tiempos. Todo por lo que he luchado y en lo que he creído se me va de las manos" (I don't know what's wrong with me lately. Everything that I have fought for and everything that I have believed in is slipping through my fingers). In a later scene in the present, we learn from Rafa that Víctor gave up politics all together.

The *cainismo* of the present is related to that of the past in the film. Cayo takes them to a grotto where he narrates that during the war, the mayors of the town were killed, and everyone had to spend two weeks hiding inside the grotto until a shepherd informed them that the soldiers had left. Possible remnants of *cainismo* persist in the town in the relationship between Cayo and the only remaining neighbor, an unnamed man to whom Cayo disdainfully refers as "ese" (that one). Cayo calls him an animal, saying that he hanged Cayo's cat, an act of spiteful violence that can only reflect a deep-seated hatred between these neighbors.

After Víctor's burial, Rafa returns to the village. The new Opel

The urban/rural dichotomy: Giménez Rico's <u>El disputado voto del señor Cayo</u>, starring Franciso Rabal and Juan Luis Galiardo. Courtesy Penélope, S.A.

with a car telephone, and the *zarzuela* (light opera) music that Rafa now listens to are all symbolic of the profound transformations in Rafa's character: the revolutionary idealist of the first trip has given way to the cynical bourgeois. Nevertheless, two final acts return us to the Rafa of earlier days. The politician finds a sickly and widowed Cayo, and he intervenes to get him proper medical attention (a close-up of the elder-tree flower, with its medicinal qualities that are now insufficient contrasts with the juxtaposed long shot of the ambulance taking the ailing *campesino* away). Rafa then paints on the wall, "Vote for V V"--the political slogan of the 1977 elections, and specifically that of the idealist candidate who later gave up politics "para dedicarse a no sé qué tipo de enloquecidas empresas" (in order to dedicate himself to I don't know what kind of crazy enterprises), according to Rafa. Although his attendance at Víctor's funeral (against the wishes of his superiors) and his subsequent trip to the village may have momentarily rekindled his idealism, the final image of the film, a long shot in the rear-view mirror of the receding town, visually reinforces Rafa's definitive separation from the worlds of both Cayo and Víctor.

Giménez Rico's use of black and white for the narrative in the present constitutes an overly-facile use of color symbolism (the drabness and shallowness of the current life of Rafa and Laly), and it breaks the aesthetic development of the rest of the narrative. Although the narrative in the present causes the viewer to witness the culmination of the theme of *desengaño* that is hinted at in the narrative of the events of 1977, Giménez Rico also seems to use the present narrative and the transitions from present to past (repetitions of dialogue with changes in camera angle that signify a transformation in point of view) as filler: the film is of ninety-eight minutes duration, and would have been excessively short without these scenes.

José Luis Borau's 1986 *Tata mía* (My Nanny), starring Imperio Argentina, Carmen Maura, and Alfredo Landa, is a film that Carlos F. Heredero calls a parable, "an original socio-political reflection about the Spain that comes out of the civil war, about the laborious, conflictive, contradictory, and always difficult conquest of freedom and democracy" ("Un insólito" 42). Clearly set in 1986 (the television news announces current events such as the visit of the King and Queen to England), the film centers on the transformation of Elvira (Carmen Maura), an ex-nun who has recently left the convent. Elvira goes to a ranch to seek the aid and support of her "Tata" (Imperio Argentina), since, as the former confesses, "Tengo muchos problemas" (I've got a lot of problems). As Heredero ("Un insólito" 42) notes, the opening scene of the film in which a train comes out of the darkness of a tunnel into daylight symbolically condenses and synthesizes the trajectory of the two main characters, Elvira and Teo (Alfredo Landa): they evolve from infancy to maturity, from repression to love, and from darkness to light. The metaphor could be taken a step further to refer to the transformation of Spanish society as a whole--emerging from the darkness of a fascist dictatorship to the light of democracy and freedom. A subtle sexual tension in Elvira's character appears in the early sequences in the country. When Germán drives her from the train station to the ranch in a jeep, a close-up shows Elvira, who is wearing a dress, cover her trembling knees. The trembling legs is a sight gag used throughout the film to signify Elvira's weakness for and uncertainty with men. At dinner the first evening, she sits next to the priest, a gesture that symbolizes her as yet close relationship to the church. Cross-cut close-ups of Germán and Elvira, however, indicate that the latter certainly has an interest in the opposite sex.

Elvira and Tata return to Madrid to reside in their old flat. Their old friend Teo, a middle-aged "child" who has a dog, plays with erector sets, and has a fetish for nurses, helps them settle in. Teo is the latest in what Kinder calls the "children of Franco," among whom are "stunted childlike adults who are obsessed with distorted visions of the past, both placed in the social context of a divided family that is fraught with sexual deviations and that functions as a microcosm for the corrupt state" ("Children" 59). They find that Peter, a historian whose mother is English, is in the flat doing research on Elvira's father, General Goicoechea, who had fallen out of grace with the Caudillo. Elvira's brother, however, vehemently objects to Peter's research saying that it is "la piratería inglesa de siempre" (the same old English piracy), that Peter is a "red," and he accuses, "va a cargarse la memoria de papá" (destroy the memory of dad). The brother's association with *franquismo* is also linguistically underscored when Elvira, who refers to the outbreak of the civil war as a "rebelión" (rebellion) is corrected by her brother, who calls it a "lanzamiento" (movement). Alberto represents the repressive and retrograde mentality of certain Spaniards. When his daughter complains that their house is like a dictatorship, he retorts, "¡Ojalá!" (I wish). His supposed domination over his sister is symbolized both physically and verbally, as he slaps her and threatens to return her to the convent. Elvira's retort, "¿Tú en qué mundo vives?" (What world do you live in?), shows how much her brother is out of step with the times. Although Tata does not have the extraordinary powers as the mother in *Mamá cumple cien años*, she does represent the maternal figure who here is able to intervene and smooth over the fratricidal conflict. The metaphorical relationship between Elvira and Alberto is quite clear, and director Borau states that in *Tata mía*, "Evidently, there is a brotherhood, or lack of brotherhood, to the extent that the civil war was also a fratricidal war" (Heredero, "Un insólito" 44).

Although Elvira and Alberto are the most important set of siblings in the film, other fraternal relationships include the elderly Tata and Bordetas, Alberto's young daughters Cristina and Almudena, and the dogs Ollie and Popea. The latter mate in a tent that Teo has set up in his attic. A cut from this scene to Elvira standing before a mirror in a petticoat is indicative of the transformational process in the former nun: the juxtaposition of scenes, together with the connotations of the petticoat and the double image (Elvira and Elvira in the mirror) all indicate that she is moving from her former celibacy toward a sexual relationship. Her comment that she discovered that her father only went to mass when there was a parade represents a further disillusionment with her religious past. The next step in this process of liberation is the scene in which she affirms to a crucifix in her room, "Quiero ser libre y voy a serlo" (I want to be free, and I am going to be). Her bid for freedom must overcome another obstacle, however: two nuns from the convent visit her to try to convince her to return. Elvira initially lacks resolve, and convinces Teo to meet them in her place. Her entrance to face the nuns ("Soy yo quien debería explicarse" [I'm the one who should explain myself]) represents a personal triumph for Elvira. Tata realizes that she is no longer needed, and decides to return to the ranch.

Elvira obtains her father's missing papers from Bordetas, and is finally able to come to an agreement with Peter about publishing them, so that the truth about her father can be known. The sexy pink dress that Elvira wears to the press conference is indicative of her new-found liberation, and when her brother complains, "¿No tenías otra cosa que ponerte?" (Didn't you have anything else to wear?), a close-up of Elvira's high-heel bearing down on Alberto's shoe visually symbolizes her liberation from her domineering brother. Although Peter initially is a rival of Teo for Elvira's affections (after alluding to deer, who let the leaders of rival herds decide the outcome of conflict in singular combat, Teo grabs an artillery shell, and placing it on his forehead like a horn, has a mock fight with Peter that visually underscores their rivalry), it is Teo who wins out in the end. The relationship culminates on a humorous note that characterizes much of the film, as Elvira, who takes off her coat to reveal a nurse's uniform (thus appealing to Teo's fetish), enters Teo's tent and asks, "¿Por qué no hacemos cochinadas?" (Why don't we do some dirty things?). Her meaning is clear because of the syntagmatic relationship between this and previous uses of the term in the film: in the earlier scene of the dogs mating in the tent, they are said to commit "cochinadas," and when Teo, Elvira, and Alberto celebrate the former's birthday in the tent, they remember how they used to play at "cochinadas" when they were young, as Teo protrudes his finger through his open fly. After Elvira's rhetorical question to Teo, a final use of the visual gag of a close-up of Elvira's shaking knees is followed by a kiss between the two: Elvira is "free" at last. Teo, who has finally finished the erector set that he has been working on with "40 años de retraso" (40 years delay)--a number with clear political implications--is free, too. Even Tata's life is now complete, visually symbolized by her acquisition of the second half of

One of Franco's "children": Borau's <u>Tata mía</u>, starring Alfredo Landa. Courtesy José Luis Borau.

a brooch that was given to her by General Goicoechea.

Luis Urbez states that in *Tata mía*, director José Luis Borau insists on "the agreement between brothers, on the difficulties inherited from the past that make living in the present difficult, on the importance of finding truth without losing your roots" ("*Tata mía*" 289). The film accomplishes all this in a tempered humorous vein. It is significant that this film follows García Berlanga's *La vaquilla* by one year. Both of these well-established directors lived through the civil war and its aftermath, and they represent an older generation with regard to the young directors that are emerging today. It is significant that almost fifty years after the war, they both are able to view the fratricidal conflict and its aftermath through a humorous lens and provide an important lesson for Spaniards of today.

La sombra del ciprés es alargada (The Shadow of the Cypress Is Elongated), Luis Alcoriza's 1990 adaptation of the 1948 novel by Miguel Delibes, is a film with two chronological sections. The caption at the beginning of the film, "Avila, 1929" sets the spatial and temporal components of the early part of the film: seven years before the outbreak of the civil war in the Castilian city surrounded by medieval ramparts which is famous as the birthplace of Saint Teresa.

Feminine wisdom and liberation: Borau's <u>Tata mía</u>, starring Imperio Argentina and Carmen Maura. Photo by Teresa Isasi. Courtesy José Luis Borau.

Pedro, an orphan, lives with his teacher, Mateo Lesmes (Emilio Gutiérrez Caba) and his family. Lesmes inculcates Pedro with a certain stoic outlook on life, as he gives the boy texts by Seneca to read, and constantly philosophizes about how the secret of happiness is to resign oneself to having little and accepting destiny. The arrival of another boy, Alfredo, at the boarding house, results in a solid friendship between the two. Although Alfredo is a sickly child, he wants to be a sea captain when he grows up, and he interests Pedro in the life of the sea.   After Alfredo's untimely death, the second part of the film begins: Pedro (Juanjo Guerenabarrena) is now the captain of a merchant vessel, and his ship rescues a group of Americans aboard a stranded yacht.   Pedro shows an interest in Jane (Dany Prius), an American anthropologist who lives in Vera Cruz, Mexico, and when he visits her home, he asks her why she has a Republican flag. Jane responds that her father fought for the Republic in the Abraham Lincoln Brigade, and he is still obsessed with the Spanish Civil War. Pedro, who studied at the Naval Academy in Barcelona, regrets that he was in Galicia when the war broke out, and therefore did not fight for the Republican cause: "Algunas veces pensé en escaparme, quedarme en algún puerto y pasarme al otro lado, pero nos tenían muy vigilados" (Sometimes I thought about escaping, about staying in some port and going over to the other side, but they really kept watch on us). The scene immediately cuts to a dinner party the next day at Jane's house in which Alfonso (Julián Pastor), a Republican exile living in Mexico, irately exclaims, "Eso son leches. Miles del otro bando se pasaron a nuestro lado, y muchos se quedaron en el camino" (That's bullshit. Thousands from the other faction came over to our side, and many of them were left on the road). The excuses offered by Jane's "capitancito de mierda" (fucking little captain) , as Alfonso calls him, are inadmissible. The component of *cainismo* in the film may seem superfluous, since it has nothing to do with the rest of the plot development of the film and does not appear at all in the original novel; it seems that the civil war is not just an obsession for Jane's fictional father, but for director Alcoriza and millions of other Spaniards.

Chapter 9

Images of the Past

The problem of dealing with the past, of reliving and coming to a better understanding of the years of the Spanish Civil War, as well as those of its aftermath, is not exclusively accomplished in contemporary feature films that recreate those crucial years or which show characters of today whose memory takes them back to the 1930's. Spanish film makers also utilize both documentary footage from the Civil War as well as filmed interviews of surviving protagonists of the war in a series of montage films that attempt to shed new light on the important historical events of the period. José Enrique Monterde notes of the trend in documentary films that "the reconstruction of the past by means of fiction films was not sufficient; it was necessary to recover the past in and of itself, through its images, through its protagonists; and you could only accomplish that by means of the documentary montage film" (12). These films include Mariano Ozores's *Morir en España* (To Die in Spain, 1965), Basilio Martín Patino's *Canciones para después de una guerra* (Songs For After a War, 1976) and *Caudillo* (Leader, 1976), Diego Santillán's *¿Por qué perdimos la guerra?* (Why Did We Lose the War, 1977), Jaime Camino's *La vieja memoria* (The Old Memory, 1977), Gonzalo Herralde's *Raza, el espíritu de Franco* (Race, the Spirit of Franco, 1977), and *Dolores* (Dolores, 1980), directed by José Luis García Sánchez and Andrés Linares. It is fitting to end this chapter with a film that inquires into the very essence of documentary film and the very process of capturing the past: Basilio Martín Patino's *Madrid* (1987).

Is it possible to truly recuperate the past in and of itself by means of visual images? Even early theoretical studies on the Kuleshov effect show that the montage of images on screen can easily deceive the viewer. The use of movie footage filmed during the war does not always bring us closer to the objective truth, since as Marcel Oms points out, "it is clear that a montage film is also a fiction film" and that even so-called documentary footage was sometimes staged to maximize its propaganda effects: "thus, for example, the sequences of the Montaña Barracks and the distribution of arms to the popular militia were reconstructed after the fact, since there wasn't enough light to film on the day in question" ("XIV Confrontación" 11). Gubern gives a similar example of "documentary" film that was really staged on request of a war correspondent: the famous shooting of the Christ statue in the Cerro de los Angeles (*1936* 13).

The sometimes vehement reactions to these documentary films, especially on the part of the rightist press, shows that they express a "new" reality, a version of history that is different from the "official" version maintained by the regime during so many years. But this new version is also not a totally objective assessment of the past; indeed, they are often blatantly biased, sometimes only subtly so. Precisely the new focus often made them polemical, and they had problems with censorship until after Franco died.

The date of Mariano Ozores's *Morir en España* (To Die in Spain) is 1965, which indicates that it is different from the other documentary montage films in this category, in that it clearly manifests the regime's point of view. Both the title and the date of release indicate that *Morir en España* is an attempted rebuttal to Fréderick Rossif's anti-Franco documentary, *Mourir à Madrid* (To Die in Madrid), from 1963. Oms states that *Morir en España*, together with the earlier propagandistic films *El camino de la paz* (The Road to Peace, 1959) and *Franco, ese hombre* (Franco, That Man, 1964) constitute a coherent effort to convince Spaniards that they were in the right in their struggle against reds and other outside threats ("XIV Confrontación" 14).

The film constantly attacks the red menace in Spain. The street violence of the Republic is juxtaposed to the newspaper headlines, "Así cumple la República sus promesas" (That is how the Republic keeps its promises). Dolores Ibarruri, "la Pasionaria," threatens Calvo Sotelo, and the next day he is assassinated.[46] As the narrator proclaims, "La independencia de España estaba en juego como se demostró poco después" (The independence of Spain was at stake as was demonstrated shortly afterwards), and a shot of the famous Puerta de Alcalá in Madrid shows the monument decorated with gigantic posters of Stalin, Lenin, and Marx, implying that the Soviet Union would soon make

---

[46]For details surrounding these events, see Ricardo de la Cierva, Los documentos de la primavera trágica and Ian Gibson, La noche en que mataron a Calvo Sotelo.

Spain a puppet state.   The narrator later affirms that during the government of Largo Caballero, "The Soviet Union is governing [Spain]." A close-up of a hand-written document further fans the fear of the reds, since it speaks of "el derecho de expropiar todo lo necesario a la causa y fusilar quien resiste. ¡Viva el comunismo!" (the right to expropriate everything that is necessary for the cause, and to execute by shooting anyone who resists. Long live communism!). Against this menace, the film asserts that the army had no choice but to intervene, and cites Article II of the Army Constitution: "La primera y más importante misión del ejército es sostener la independencia de la patria y defenderla de enemigos externos e internos" (The first and most important mission of the army is to sustain the independence of the fatherland, and to defend it from external and internal enemies). For intellectual support, the film often cites Miguel de Unamuno, a controversial figure who also appears in *Mourir à Madrid* and in *Caudillo* in support of the Republican cause. Although this film quotes the University of Salamanca professor as stating that the Spanish Civil War was not between communism and fascism, but rather, between civilization and anarchy, implying his support of the Nationalist cause as bearers of civilization, the use of this intellectual is not without unwitting irony in the film. When Unamuno proclaims, "Salvadnos, jóvenes" (Young people, save us), the narrator states, "And the young people began to do just that."   The irony is the result of the clash between the sound and visual elements of the filmic discourse, since the accompanying image is not of young Spaniards, but of Moorish mercenaries who fought for Franco, a fact that constitutes one of the greatest ironies of the entire conflict.

The film often defends Franco and the Nationalist cause against criticism at home and abroad on issues such as the bombing of Guernica and the fascist aid to the Nationalist cause. Close-up shots of newspaper headlines from *Ahora* (Now) ("La Aviación leal bombardea aeródromos enemigos y el puerto de Palma, consiguiendo incendiar tres buques" [The Republican air force bombs enemy hangars and the port of Palma, setting three ships on fire]) and *Euskadi* (Basque Country) ("La aviación, adicta al Gobierno, bombardea nuevamente Zaragoza, Mallorca y Melilla" [Air forces that support the government bomb Zaragoza, Mallorca, and Melilla again]) attempt to justify the narrator's contention that Franco was unjustly criticized for being the first military leader to use bombing against civilian populations. Ozores uses old footage of Guernica already used in Joaquín Reig's *España heroica* (Heroic Spain) and repeats the same fallacious argument put forth in that 1937 film, that the destruction of Guernica was due not to bombing by German aviation, but fire-bombs laid by Republicans.[46] Indeed, the film is stridently defensive about international involvement in the Nationalist cause as the narrator repeatedly plays down German and Italian assistance. In the campaign for Madrid, for example, he states, "No hay más que un puñado de aviadores italianos y unos cuantos técnicos alemanes" (There are no more than a handful of Italian aviators and a few German technicians), and he later comments, "se exagera la participación de alemanes e italianos" (the participation of Germans and Italians is exaggerated).[47] On the other hand, the narrator repeatedly mentions the role of the International Brigades, and is adamant about the fact that Soviet help came at the expense of Spanish gold, "que todavía estamos pagando todos los españoles" (that all of us Spaniards are still paying for). This statement, of course, ignores the considerable foreign debt incurred by the Nationalist side

---

[46]Regarding the explanation of "leftist arson" in Guernica, Stanley Payne comments that "this fabrication, once adopted as an official position, was persistently maintained almost to the end of the regime, and is an excellent example of the way in which fundamental facts of the Civil War were obscured by the propaganda inventions of both sides" (141). Payne notes that Guernica was one of two principal routes of retreat toward Bilbao, was district communications center, and contained three military barracks and four arms factories. "The bombing of cities had been made routine practice during the first week of the Civil War by the Republicans, who on several occasions early in the conflict boasted of the damage done to Nationalist-held cities. There is no evidence of any special experiment or massive terror-bombing. Guernica was a routine target of particular importance because of the circumstances of April 26, but it received no special treatment" (140). For further detail, see Herbert R. Southworth, Guernica! Guernica!, Jesús Salas Larrazábal, Guernica: El bombardeo, and Angel Viñas, Guerra, dinero, dictadura.

[47]Thomas states that in the battle of Madrid, which began in November of 1936, the Nationalist contingency of about 20,000 consisted mainly of Moroccans and legionnaires supported by German and Italian tanks and aircraft (322). For more details, see Ramón Salas Larrazábal, Historia del Ejército Popular de la República and his Los datos exactos de la Guerra Civil. For specific information regarding the battle for Madrid, see José Manuel Martínez Bande, La marcha sobre Madrid. For details regarding the air battle during the war, see Salvador Rello, La aviación en la guerra de España, and Jesús Salas Larrazábal, La guerra de España desde el aire.

of the conflict.[48] The film is also defensive about execution of Basque priests who supported the Republic: the narrator states, "unos cuantos curas separatistas vascos cogidos con armas, sancionados de acuerdo el código militar dan origen a una campaña de descreditación contra los nacionales" (a few Basque priests who favor separatism, caught with firearms, and sanctioned according to military code, give rise to a smear campaign against the Nationalists), and counters with statistics regarding the number of priests and bishops killed by the Republicans, and the image of a Christ stature with the anarchist insignia "CNT" on his forehead.

Indeed, the film places particular emphasis on the religious element, justifying Franco's crusade against the atheist reds. Early footage from the period of the Republic shows convents burning and the expulsion of Jesuits. Later, a photograph from an Italian newspaper that depicts priests with pistols held to their heads, and an anarchist is quoted as saying, "Hemos matado a los curas y hemos quemado los templos. El problema religioso está resuelto" (We have killed the priests and burned the temples. The religious problem is resolved). A shot of a newspaper stand shows "El sin Dios" (Godless), which the narrator identifies as the weekly publication of the socialist intellectuals, and to make the point more compelling, the narrator exclaims that on the first Christmas of the war, more than half the children in Spain could not celebrate it, since it had been converted to the non-religious "Popular Night." After all, the narrator states, the pedagogy of the Republic was to teach the children to hate Christ and to love Stalin. Perhaps the most emotional images related to this topic are those of the mummies of nuns displayed in front of the convent of the Salesians in Barcelona. (These gruesome images were originally part of the first film dealing with the Spanish Civil War, the anarchist documentary *Reportaje del movimiento revolucionario en Barcelona* [Report on the Revolutionary Movement in Barcelona], which was directed by Mateo Santos). This film is very anti-clerical, and it

---

[48]Payne (155) notes that Republican expenditures totalled $775 million; Nationalist expenditures consisted of $645 million. The latter figure included $335 million from Italy that was paid back over nearly thirty years; $215 million from Germany, which demanded "hard currency as much as possible and major raw material concessions" although (255) "the obligation was unilaterally canceled by Spain in 1945" and $76 million from other countries. For more details, see Viñas, El oro de Moscú..

affirms that the nuns were victims of their co-religionists. In *Morir en España*, however, these images appear as part of an attack on the anarchists, a phenomenon that Gubern refers to as a propagandistic boomerang (*1936* 14), as the narrator ironically affirms that those who put such a spectacle together must have been aspiring for the Stalin Prize in cinematography. Another aspect of the religious theme in *Morir en España* is that it portrays the Republic as licentious and mired in sin: we not only see a sexual caricature of the time, but also a sign from Barcelona regarding respect for prostitutes: "Compañero: la mujer pública merece todos los respetos. Es una víctima más de la explotación. No la insultes, no la ofendas. Piensa que cumple una función social" (Comrade: the prostitute deserves respect. She is one more victim of exploitation. Don't insult her, don't offend her. She thinks that she is fulfilling a social function), to which the narrator comments, "Y puede ser tu madre o tu hermana" (And she could be your mother or your sister). On the other hand, soldiers who fought and died for the crusade are considered martyrs. The camera lingers on the grave whose epitaph is "Ayer confesé y comulgué si caigo por España ¡No importa!" (Yesterday I confessed and took communion, and if I fall for Spain, it doesn't matter!). The emotional invocation, "Vedlos aquí" (Look at them here) while the camera pans the graves of those who died for the Nationalist cause, elicits the defensive phrase that they are "tan obreros, tan campesinos, tan estudiantes como los de la zona roja, pero sin la bendición de la intelectualidad liberal y de las izquierdas" (just as much laborers, peasants, and students as in the red zone, but without the blessing of liberal and leftist intellectuals). *Morir en España* is such a highly defensive and propagandistic film filled with falsehoods that even film historian Fernández Cuenca (2:548) criticizes it.

An entirely different view of the Franco regime emerges from Basilio Martín Patino's huge box-office hit that had its debut in September of 1976, *Canciones para después de una guerra* (Songs For After a War). Director Martín Patino says that the film is "like an x-ray of that period" (Castro 317), and he has also stated that the concept of basing a film on old songs was the best way to evoke memories, since music, like Proust's madeleine, invariably evokes images from the past (Besas 108). Indeed, the authorities must have concurred with the director's opinion, except that they did not like the memory that Martín Patino was evoking. Although censors exacted

The church and the regime: Martín Patino's <u>Canciones para después de una guerra</u>. Courtesy Filmoteca Nacional.

many cuts on the film, they finally approved it in June of 1971. A virulent attack on the film by the right-wing press, in the voice of Carlos F. de Avellanos writing in *El Alcázar*, accused the director of impartiality and lying (22). Censors not only prohibited the film for over five more years, but even tried to destroy the prints of the film, and it was not allowed to be shown until after Franco's death. At that time, however, the response of the public was overwhelming: audiences applauded at great length at the end of each showing, and the film was a commercial success.

The basic stylistic element of the film is its ironic discourse, which is a result of the deliberate juxtaposition of contrasting images or of the dialectical contrast between the images and the sound track. Although the chronology of the narrative begins with the notice on April 1, 1939 that the war has ended, there is a brief flashback to the bombings of Madrid, and red tinted shots of cadavers lying in the streets. The entrance of triumphant soldiers and the split image of military medals, accompanied by the tune "Yo te daré" (I will give you) constitutes the first ironic composition of image and sound. Martín Patino's use of an old NO-DO documentary regarding the disinterment of cadavers at Torrejón de Ardoz also makes a political statement: the narrator exclaims that they are "víctimas del terror rojo . . . inmolados bárbaramente por pelotones de asesinos y asalariados de Moscú" (victims of the red terror . . . barbarously immolated by the firing squads of assassins and Moscow's henchmen), but the use of the negative of the film serves to subtly negate the narrator's statement.

The film progresses chronologically through the 1940's and '50's, with images from at home and abroad that capture both daily life and the major events in Spain and in the world. Martín Patino often shows women working, either at domestic chores or in factories. Their male counterparts are sometimes absent as a result of the civil war or World War II; a reunion of prisoners and their families takes place at a provincial prison, a headline proclaims the heroism of the "Blue Division," the Spanish troops who fought with the Nazis at the Russian front, and images of the death camp at Malthausen show the Spaniards of the other ideological persuasion who survived the Nazi horrors. There was also entertainment and fun: old movies with Imperio Argentina, bullfights with Dominguín, singing by Antonio Mahín. Patino demythifies this segment of the past as well in a montage sequence in which he juxtaposes scenes from the CIFESA production, *De la España heroica* (Of Heroic Spain)--medieval knights blowing trumpets/soldiers from the 1940's blowing trumpets, etc.--with contemporary images. Segments in yellow and red tints from García Berlanga's 1952 film, *Bienvenido, Mr. Marshall* (Welcome, Mr. Marshall), with the sound track's famous song, "Americanos," deflates the narrator's earlier statement regarding the Hispano-American treaty that "Ahora sí que los tiempos van a cambiar; con el pacto que vamos a hacer con los americanos todo va a ser distinto" (Now certainly times are going to change; with the treaty that we are going to have with the Americans, everything is going to be different). Another satirical use of music is the inclusion of the popular tune, "Se va el caimán" (The Alligator Is Leaving), which, as Besas points out, "referred to hopes that Franco would soon be gone" (107). Entertainment also had an impact on the moral climate of the time. A close-up of a religious message about modern dances shows a devil and the admonition, "Joven . . . diviértete de otra manera" (Young person . . . have fun another way).

The 1940's was a time of economic hardship in Spain, as seen in close-ups of newspaper headlines, "Madrid without gas" and announcements of "Rationing" and "There is no milk" or the long lines at the market. Again Martín Patino ironically underscores the situation with "Tengo una vaca lechera" (I've got a milking cow) on the sound track. Shots from magazines show furniture and refrigerators to the tune of "Encima las montañas tengo un nido" (I've got a nest up in the mountains), and in a moment that is both self-reflexive and ironic, the melody "Rasca-yu, cuando mueras, ¿qué harás tú?" (Rasca-yu, when you die, what will you do?) accompanies the slide commercials that appear during the Intermission at the movies. Martín Patino also shows women modeling hats in a tripartite image with brown, grey, and red tints. Underlying the growing affluence and materialism, however, is the problem of the black market, which is a major theme in films like *Demonios en el jardín* and *Pim, pam, pum, fuego*. This theme appears here in shots of a satirical comic strip and of a demonstration with placards that proclaim it to be a "Student protest against black marketeers." The film ends on an optimistic note, with a still shot of a young Prince Juan Carlos as he enters Spain at the age of twelve. The optimism lies in the future king as a symbol of political change and transition to democracy. [49]

In 1977, Gonzalo Herralde filmed *Raza, el espíritu de Franco* (Race, the Spirit of Franco), a movie that combines clips from the famous film from 1941, *Raza* (Race), together with interviews of Alfredo Mayo, protagonist of the film, and Pilar Franco, sister of the Caudillo. *Raza* was directed by José Luis Sáenz de Heredia but with a script written by none other than General Franco himself under the pseudonym of Jaime de Andrade. Herralde states that his aim in *Raza, el espíritu de Franco* is to "carry out an analysis of Franco through his work" and to point out "the extended doctrine hidden within the film" ("Interview" 264). According to Román Gubern, who worked with Herralde on the interviews, *Raza, el espíritu de Franco* demonstrates that "the fantasy thought up by Franco constituted a compendium of intimate confessions that were filled with autobiographical references" (*1936* 190). Herralde intercuts segments from the film with declarations made about the Caudillo by his sister and by actor Mayo in an attempt to prove this point: when the Churruca family in *Raza*

---

[49]Seen today, the final image of the film further connotes optimism because of the generally high regard with which the king is held in Spain today, especially after his fundamental role in returning the country to democracy, and in thwarting the attempted coup d'état in February of 1981.

is shown with flowers, Pilar Franco states "Teníamos flores siempre" (We always had flowers); when a ship arrives in the 1941 film, she comments that her brother had wanted to be a sailor; the scene showing the firing squad shooting of José Churruca elicits conversation about Franco's stomach wound in Africa, etc. In addition, Mayo declares that "Franco pudo ser un José Churruca" (Franco could have been a José Churruca). However, the juxtaposition of these scenes seems rather superficial at times, giving Herralde limited success in his stated goal. The film provides some valuable insights into the past of Alfredo Mayo and the Franco family, however. Pilar Franco speaks of her father's personality as "hard, demanding," and later declares regarding her brother's lack of political ideology, "No era falangista, nada más que militar" (He wasn't a Falangist, he was nothing more than a military man). Mayo's film credits nearly reach one-hundred movies, and include such classic civil war films as *¡A mí la legión!* (The Legion Is For Me, 1942) and *El santuario no se rinde* (The Sanctuary Doesn't Surrender, 1949). Indeed, García Fernández states, "To say Alfredo Mayo is to say Spanish cinema from the 1940's; perhaps because no one else like him knows how to better offer the image of a heroic and arrogant leading man that the movies of the time demanded" (148). Nevertheless, Mayo denies being an "héroe franquista," stating that he was simply "un actor a servicio de unos héroes que se han hecho después de una guerra" (an actor at the service of heroes that were made after a war) and that "por mi físico, mi constitución, me ha tocado encarnar estos héroes" (because of my physical appearance, my constitution, it was my luck to embody these heroes). In spite of this statement, Mayo noted his disillusionment when the Caudillo screened the film *Raza*, since he thought that Franco might make him a Marquis for his performance. His ingenuousness extends to the political realm, as well: he declares that "en mi casa no entendían de política" (in my house, they didn't understand anything about politics), and war is made between leaders since "a la gente ni les viene ni les va" (common people don't care one way or another about it). Unlike Churruca and Franco, who enlisted as young men, Mayo confesses "No tengo el espíritu militar de sacrificio" (I don't possess the military spirit of sacrifice), and that he served in the armed forces in order to fulfill his duty. Thus, one of the important results of the film is the demythification of Alfredo Mayo.

Pilar Franco's final statement is a defensive one, as if she subconsciously understood that this film and others that attempt a reassessment of Franco's life after his death, such as *Caudillo*, are basically critical of him. "A pesar de las calumnias espantosas que se han dicho sobre mi hermano, no vivió más que para España, y los disgustos, las preocupaciones, y los sinsabores que le dio España lo llevaron al otro mundo. De manera que la gente debería de recordar . . . los cuarenta años de paz que hemos vivido tranquilamente" (In spite of the awful calumnies that have been said about my brother, he only lived for Spain, and the sorrows, worries, and displeasures that Spain gave him took him to his grave. So people should remember . . . the forty years of peace that we have lived through with tranquility). Although the film falls short of its goal, it is not without interesting moments that provide further insight into Francisco Franco and his regime.

In 1977, Jaime Camino filmed the most important movie of this type, *La vieja memoria* (The Old Memory). Although it did not achieve commercial success, it did win critical acclaim, with Spanish critics calling this production "Spanish cinema's best contribution in these years toward the analysis of our civil war" (Monterde 12) and "one of the best documentaries about the Spanish civil war" (Riambau 49). Camino literally went to great lengths (France, Belgium, Russia) in order to interview many of the protagonists of the civil war to elicit their memories of the events from the proclamation of the Republic to the end of the conflict. The subjects interviewed by Camino represent a wide range on the political spectrum: anarchists Federica Montseny and Diego Abad de Santillán; communists Dolores Ibarruri (la Pasionaria) and Enrique Líster; Julián Gorkin and other members of the POUM (Partido Obrero de Unificación Marxista [Workers' Party of Marxist Unification]); falangistas David Jato and Raimundo Fernández Cuesta; Josep Tarradellas, a representative of Esquerra Republicana (Republican Left) and leader of the Catalan government; José María Gil Robles, leader of the Confederación Española de Derechas Autónomas (Spanish Confederation of Autonomous Rightist Parties); José Luis de Villalonga, who served in the Nationalist army as a second lieutenant, and others. Camino was also able to include a segment of film from 1935 in which José Antonio Primo de Rivera, founder of the Falange, briefly expresses his views. In addition, Camino includes stills and other documentary footage from the period.

The discussion of events follows a generally chronological

approach, centering on the declaration of the Republic in 1931, important events during the Republic such as the crushing of the miners' rebellion in Asturias in 1934, the military uprising in July of 1936, the siege of the Alcázar of Toledo, which lasted until September 27 of that year, the conflict in Barcelona between communists and anarchists in May of 1937, and the Nationalist victory in 1939. The interviewees also discuss topics such as the violence of the conflict and the idea of social revolution. Even though *La vieja memoria* is a long film of 160 minutes, it represents only one-tenth of the material that Camino filmed. The producer provided a synopsis of the film that shows his intentions of achieving a new perspective on the fratricidal conflict: "Memory is not objective, be it individual memory or collective memory. Memory is not history, but rather, a subjective remembrance. During forty years, memory was repressed. In order to sustain and defend a totalitarian power, it was necessary to block out memory, and also to tergiversate history."

With regard to each event or each topic, the subjects manifest their diverse, and sometimes contradictory, opinions. Thus, regarding the shortcomings of the Republic and the causes of the rebellion, Líster submits that the leaders did not resolve the problems concerning land reform, church-state relations, and the army; Ibarruri underscores the lack of land reform; Fernández Cuesta calls Republican policy "sectarian of persecution," and José Antonio speaks of a tripartite division of separatism, local parties, and class divisions as being at the root of Spain's problems in 1935. Likewise, regarding the success of the initial resistance of the Republican side in Barcelona, anarchist Ricardo Sanz states, "Si no fuera por la acción del pueblo, los militares hubieran triunfado en unas horas" (If it weren't for the people's action, the military would have triumphed in a few hours), whereas Tarradellas praises the leadership of Catalan President Campanys and Colonel Escobar of the Civil Guard. Camino often included stills or documentary footage to illustrate the statements of his subjects; other times, the sound track plays an equally important role (discordant piano notes for the assassination of Calvo Sotelo; shooting or bombs falling during conflict scenes).

At times, subjective recollections of the protagonists contradict each other or belie the "objective" view of the documentary footage. After a series of scenes in which communists and anarchists disagree over the priority of waging the war or waging a social revolution, Federica

Memories of the war: Camino's <u>La vieja memoria</u>, with Dolores Ibarruri, "La Pasionaria". Courtesy Filmoteca Española.

Montseny characterizes Dolores Ibarruri as "sencilla, simple" (plain, simple), but the latter declares that "Ni siquiera le vi la cara. Nunca" (I never even saw her face. Never), which Camino follows by a photograph of the two women together. Likewise, when Falangist David Jato describes the bombings of Madrid as "extremely light" and proclaims that they have been exaggerated, Camino counters with the photograph of the ruins of bombed-out buildings.

  Some of the most poignant testimony comes from those that were close to the combat. José Luis de Villalonga's account of violence in the Nationalist rear-guard--how Nationalists would go see firing squads at work over lunch after mass; how soldiers would volunteer to be in the firing squads because they received a large cup (*tazón*) of cognac, and how a Lt. Colonel once told his Nationalist troops when they arrived at a small town in Valencia, "Haced lo que queráis durante dos horas" (Do what ever you want to for two hours)--all constitute intimate details of the conflict that provide a deeper dimension to the discussion than that provided by the former political leaders of both sides. After Fernández Cuesta attributes the successful resistance of Madrid to the arrival of the international brigades, and "la Pasionaria" praises their heroism, Camino intercuts footage of Rafael Alberti during the war and in 1976 rendering a poignant reading of his poem, "A la defensa de Madrid" ("To the Defense of Madrid").

Although the film does present a wide variety of viewpoints, it cannot claim total objectivity. Camino, Catalan, certainly stresses events and personalities from his native Barcelona. And in his attempt to rewrite history, the director subtly supports the Republican viewpoint. Gil de Muro notes that in *La vieja memoria*, the "ideological imbalance shows through in the unequal proportion of personages that were interviewed, and in the subtle and differentiating treatment that he gives to some of them" ("Jaime Camino" 326), and Esteve Riambau attributes this bias to technical elements such as the lighting and camera angle that Camino chose for each subject (49). Another example would be the emotive ending of the film, which uses stills and slow-motion film of refugees--women, children, and wounded soldiers--crossing the French border. Nevertheless, the demythification that the film realizes does not only have to do with the right, but with all of the important figures of the past, for as Riambau points out, "Those faces that were hidden by the Franco regime and mythified during so many years of clandestine existence appear 'humanized' in the film" (49).

Martín Patino aptly created a montage of documentary footage for his 1976 film, *Caudillo* (Leader). The film maker went to great trouble and even risk to acquire documentary film that would show a version of historical events that was different from the official version of the regime; he obtained much of the footage for his film in London, Paris, and Lisbon, and had to smuggle the material into Spain in oil barrels. Although some critics ingenuously see the film's portrayal of Franco as ambiguous or eulogistic,[50] a close examination of the film shows that it is, in the words of critic Antonio Castro, "ideologically clear" (61). Indeed, Angel Camiña notes that in the selection and ordering of the documentary materials, there is a clear intention to demythify and condemn the nationalist Crusade, and to denounce the "ascent to power of the man who at the beginning was only Franquito [little Franco], as his military companions called him" (144-45). The demythification begins with the opening shot--a zoom in to a town that lies in ruins,

---

[50]Jesús Fernández Santos calls Caudillo "a eulogy, putting the audience in favor of the protagonist" ("Las segundas intenciones" 27), and Pedro Crespo refers to the film as "a confusing, nebulous film" ("El caudillo" 63).

followed by a shot of a cannon.   The shots of troops and wounded
men and women is accompanied on the soundtrack by the distinctly
Republican war song, "Viva la Quince Brigada" (Long Live the 15th
Brigade).   The voice-over by the narrator, "Hubo una vez un hombre
mandado por Dios para salvar a España" (There once was a man sent
by God to save Spain), can only be taken in the ironic context of the
visual images and the music.   Other popular tunes that had Republican
lyrics and which dominate the soundtrack include "Anda jaleo," "Los
cuatro muleros," and "The Red River Valley" (a Pete Seeger version
in Spanish about the Jarama Valley where fierce fighting occurred).

The film begins with Franco's early career in Morocco, relying on
documentary footage, photographs, and close-ups of comics that were
later used to glorify him.   Martín Patino does not follow a strict
chronological order of events, however, jumping at one point from
Sevilla in 1936 back to Morocco in 1920.   He presents a negative view
of the Nationalist victories by showing a newspaper headline that
proclaims "Tropas nacionalistas avanzan" (Nationalist troops advance)
followed by stills of civilian prisoners of war and of cadavers.
Photographs or footage of many intellectuals adds weight to the
political left in the film.   Three consecutive references to the tragic
death of García Lorca emotionally underscore this event: a shot of a
newspaper headline, "Han asesinado a García Lorca" (They have
assassinated García Lorca), a poster of Lorca covered with blood, and
the voice-over of a narrator that states, "Que fue en Granada el crimen
. . . en su Granada" (The crime was in Granada . . . his Granada).
Rafael Alberti reads his "A Madrid, corazón de España" (To Madrid,
the heart of Spain), and there is a reading of Neruda's "España 1936"
(Spain 1936) to the accompaniment of a rapid montage of bombs
falling, civilians fleeing, women crying, and cadavers of young and
old.   These images follow the hair-raising statement made by Franco,
"Si es necesario, fusilaré a media España" (If it is necessary, I will
execute half of Spain by firing squad), and therefore underscore the
implacable nature of the Caudillo's character.   Unamuno also appears
in support of the left: "Venceréis porque tenéis la fuerza, pero no
convenceréis" (You will win because you have the might, but you will
not win over).   Dolores Ibarruri, known as "La Pasionaria," defends
calling Republican troops her children, saying that they sacrifice
themselves for peace, liberty, and progress.   Martín Patino also
intercuts scenes of the bombing of Guernica with a still of Picasso and
of his famous painting with the town's name.   Not all of those who

Franco and the Church: Martín Patino's Caudillo. Courtesy Filmoteca Nacional.

support the Republican cause are famous however; in a compelling testimony, a simple foot-soldier exclaims that each Spanish fighter is worth fifteen Italian fascists. In addition to individuals, Martín Patino also presents footage of events involving masses, such as the burial of Durruti in Barcelona, or the presentation of Hitler's and Mussolini's ambassadors to Franco in the Plaza Mayor in Salamanca, footage that Martín Patino found in Portugal and which impressed him the most of all the material that he acquired for the film (Besas 113).

In both the narrator's voice-overs and in images of Franco with clergy, Martín Patino stresses the Caudillo's relationship to the church. Thus, the narrator speaks of his fight against Masonic and Judaic tendencies of the Bolshevik revolution (!), "Hubo una vez una cruzada vigilada por Franco" (Once there was a crusade watched over by Franco) etc. Martín Patino follows these statements and images with images of repression and suffering--dead and imprisoned miners in Asturias, or prisoners of war in Santander. Even Franco's personal life does not escape Martín Patino's critical gaze. Angel Camiña indicates that "the fact that he puts light opera music each time that Franco appears with his family is one of the many details that convince us of his lack of neutrality" (146). Perhaps the scene that makes the Caudillo look the most ridiculous is when in a shot of his family, his young daughter wants to deliver a message to the children of Spain. When she tells her father that she does not know what to say, he shrugs his shoulders and says, "Lo que quieras" (Whatever you want). Nevertheless, Franco visibly mouths the message with her, thus destroying any sense of spontaneity or sincerity on her part.

The undermining irony in the film culminates in the final moments. As Nationalist soldiers distribute bread to hungry civilians in Barcelona, the *pasodoble* "La virgen de la Macarena" with shouts of "olé" can be heard in the background on the sound track as the voice-over of the narrator proclaims with ridiculous hyperbole, "Y al frente de todos, él, César, el Cid, Alejandro. ¿Qué grita esa voz de imperio sino Franco, Franco, Franco? El resucita a los muertos; él endurece a los blandos; el estimula a los flojos; él enaltece a los altos" (In front of everyone, him, Caesar, the Cid, Alexander the Great. What does that voice of the empire shout except Franco, Franco, Franco? He resuscitates the dead; he hardens the soft; he inspires the weak, he exalts the noble). After a speech by Franco in which he praises "la vitalidad de una raza y la espiritualidad de un pueblo" (the vitality of a race and the spirituality of a nation), the film cuts to shots that show crying civilians and wounded soldiers crossing the border into France to the accompaniment of "La sagrada espina" (The Holy Thorn), a famous *sardana* tune. This music, which represents the nationalist sentiments of Catalans, contrasts with the earlier *pasodoble*, and the images certainly belie Franco's pronouncement. Franco then receives a medal to the accompaniment of Galician bagpipe music,[51] and the final shot of the film--a painting of Franco dressed in medieval armor, with the narrator's statement, "Era nada más ni nada menos que Franco, por la gracia de Dios, caudillo de España" (He was nothing more and nothing less than Franco, Leader of Spain by the grace of God)--should perhaps bring to mind the standard joke at the end of the regime, "Vaya sentido de gracia que tiene Dios" (God has some sense of humor).[52]

The rightist press understood the unfavorable portrait of their leader

---

[51] Franco was a native of Galicia, and during his regime, the name of his hometown, El Ferrol, was officially changed to make known that it was his place of origin (El Ferrol del Caudillo).

[52] The joke comes from the play on words with <u>gracia</u>, which can mean both "grace" and "humor."

and condemned *El caudillo*, saying that "demagogic partialities . . . invalidate the historical rigor of the film" and that it is "absolutely inane" ("Martialay, *El caudillo*" 24-5). A true fault of the film is that it only takes us up to the end of the Civil War and does not deal with the almost forty years of Franco's regime. Nevertheless, one must mitigate this criticism knowing that although Martín Patino originally intended to make a series of three films about Franco which would have covered those later years, he confessed to having lost interest and abandoned the project after Franco died (Besas 115).

¿Por qué perdimos la guerra? (Why Did We Lose the War?) is a 1977 film by director Diego Santillán, son of Diego Abad de Santillán (Sinesio García Fernández, an anarchist leader during the civil war). With the exception of Ozores's *Morir en España*, this is the most blatantly biased film of the group, professing the anarchist point of view about the conflict which was censored for so many years. Indeed, shortly before the film's release, Diego Santillán attempted to justify the partiality of the film, saying, "It is an absolutely partial film. Partial, in the first place, because it is from the side of the vanquished, who could never tell their story" (27). He clearly stated his purpose of making the film: "to denounce the passivity of the democracies, and the two-faced game of Stalin, who was more interested in achieving a pact with fascism than in a victory for the Spanish people" (27).

The film begins with stills of the subjects that are interviewed in the film. Many, such as Diego Abad de Santillán (who has the largest number of interventions in the film), Juan Manuel Molina, or Eduardo Val, are associated with anarchist groups such as the FAI (Federación Anarquista Ibérica [Iberian Anarchist Federation]) or the CNT (Confederación Nacional de Trabajo [National Confederation of Labor]); other points of view come from Josep Tarradellas (Esquerra de Catalunya [Catalan Left]), José Prat (Partido Socialista Obrero Español [Spanish Socialist Workers' Party]), Manuel de Irujo (Partido Nacionalista Vasco [Nationalist Basque Party]), Valentín González, et al. According to Gubern, González, the famous commander known as "El campesino" (The Peasant), is the only communist to appear in the film because González "broke with the Communist Party during the 1950's and he was available to chime in on anti-Soviet attacks" (*1936* 177).

The dedication of the film states that the only loser in all of the conflicts in the history of Spain has been the Spanish people. It goes on to follow a general chronological progression of events from the end of the monarchy up until early days of the Franco regime. Thus, the narrator begins with the statement that before the Republic, a Spain existed that did not work or produce anything--a Spain comprised of the church and the army. In contrast to the criticism of these institutions, the film praises social changes made under the Republic, and in particular, it eulogizes the figure of anarchist leader Buenaventura Durruti in various ways: stills of the Durruti column going to Aragon, praise of the man from José García Prados, quotes from popular ballads about him, footage of the masses at his funeral, and an extreme close-up of him *in memoria*.

The film proclaims that anarchism and communism are two irreconcilable tendencies, and places much of the blame for the defeat of the Republic on the communists. The film refers to "Stalin's dirty game," accusing him of not wanting a Republican victory, but rather only time in which he could work out a pact with Hitler; it accuses the government of Largo Caballero as serving the interests of the Kremlin, and cites as proof Jesús Hernández's book *Yo fui ministro de Stalin* (I Was a Minister of Stalin). Likewise, it cites the non-intervention of England, which was afraid of Hitler, and the aid of Germany and Italy to the Nationalists, as negative factors. It also emphasizes the delight of Hitler and Mussolini at the defeat of the Republic: the Italian leader refers to it as the great victory of Fascism, and juxtaposed shots show Franco bidding farewell to the Condor Legion, and Hitler praising its heroism.

Another main point of the film is to praise the anarchist movement and its social changes, which Santillán refers to as "la primera revolución social y popular en la historia moderna" (the first popular social revolution of modern history),   with Valentín González contrasting it to the less profound Russian revolution, and Tarradellas calling the collectivization "una idea tan genial" (such an ingenious idea), all supported by documentary footage of factory workers and farmers laboring.

The sound track of the film is filled with renditions of Republican songs, such as "A las barricadas," and "La Quince Brigada." Although Santillán uses emotive slow-motion shots of refugees at the end of the war, he goes one step further in denouncing the fate of the Spanish people. He states that for many, peace did not come, referring not only to refugees, but also to concentration camps where many died of hunger and cold. The final shot of a cemetery is accompanied by the commentary, "En España reinaba la paz, pero también en los sepulcros reina la paz" (In Spain, peace reigned, but peace also reins in sepulchers).

Miguel Rubio notes that the most important aspect of the film is "material that in many cases is extraordinary; some shots shake you for the closeness of the cameraman to the violence. You get a heroic vision of the fight by the Spanish people, both in the rear guard and in the front" (15). The over-partiality of the film is however, a defect that is insurmountable with regard to including it as part of a historically objective new view of the war.

Dolores (Dolores, 1980) is a biographical film co-directed by José Luis García Sánchez and Andrés Linares about Dolores Ibarruri, "la Pasionaria," the famous communist representative to the Spanish Parliament (the *Cortes*) during the Republic. The film interweaves footage of interviews with the 83-year old woman with recent documentary of her return to Spain from Russia and her appearance in the Spanish Parliament, as well as with footage from the 1920's and '30's. Carlos Boyer notes that *Dolores* is not dogmatic nor a glorification of the Communist party; rather, "It is a conversation in which they try to find the human being. The woman who was protagonist and witness of hecatombs that touch us deeply" (11). Indeed, Dolores Ibarruri recounts many details of personal life which reveal more than just her political dimension: how she met King Alfonso XIII as a young school girl, her church marriage, the death of her son Rubén, and how she maintained a "Spanish house" in Russia. However, her political life is inseparable from her private one: she read Marx's *Capital* as a young girl (she attended school up to fifteen years of age) and later acquired her pseudonym when writing an article for *El minero vizcaíno* (Vizcayan Miner) during Holy Week. Her view of life as a struggle was formed in those early days in the mining community where, she says, "the repression was constant." Both during miners' strikes and when her husband was imprisoned in 1917, she attributed her survival to the solidarity of her friends and neighbors. The emotional memories of moments when, as communist representative to Parliament from Asturias during the Republic, she liberated prisoners from jail, and entered a mine to help striking workers, an event that she cites to show that she entered politics in order to solve problems and help people. Her opinions of personalities and events of the civil war are compelling: she admits "No sé cómo resistimos tanto" (I don't know how we resisted so much), and emotionally speaks of her love for the International Brigades. She accuses Blume of hypocrisy and contends that if England and France would have helped, the Republicans would have won the war. More significantly, she offers dispassionate opinions of the regime that caused her to live in exile for so many years: "el franquismo ha dejado poco" (Francoism has left little impact) and that "las dictaduras pasan pero el pueblo pervive" (dictatorships pass on, but the people remain). Songs such as "Ay Carmela" and her own rendition of "Puente de los franceses" (The Frenchmen's Bridge)--site of a key battle in northwestern Madrid--which she sings to the music of "De los cuatro muleros" (The Four Muleteers), add to the soundtrack. The most interesting aspect of the documentary footage deals with the socio-political climate in the mining communities during the 20's and 30's. Hopefully, more film makers will follow in the footsteps of García Sánchez and Linares and record the impressions of other protagonists of the Civil War before they all pass from the scene.

In the 1987 film, *Madrid*, director Basilio Martín Patino uses historical footage of the civil war, but transcends the documentary film genre to create a thought-provoking movie that straddles fiction and reality. The narrative point of departure is the story of Hans (Rüdiger Vogler), a German movie director, who is in Madrid to film a program concerning the fiftieth anniversary of the Spanish Civil War. While in Madrid, Hans becomes enchanted by the Spanish capital and its inhabitants. Hans studies documentary footage of the war, but he also films the vibrant city of 1986, with anti-NATO demonstrations, the outpouring of sentiment during the burial of the city's mayor, Enrique Tierno Galván, the tumultuous atmosphere of a saint's day festival, or the more intimate scene of *madrileños* showing their religious devotion in the ritual kissing of the feet of Christ. While filming, Hans constantly questions his own art, and the limits between fiction and reality: he is unsure of his methodology ("método de trabajo") and uncertain as to what will result from all his work. Does reality become transformed into fiction as it passes through the camera lens? What about the excessive power of a director, who is able to manipulate scenes? Of course, these questions do not come merely from Hans, but from Martín Patino himself, and they relate not only to documentary film in general, but in a certain ironic sense, to this very film, since in an interview, the director admits that some of the documentary footage that he uses was not filmed in Madrid (Heredero, *Madrid* 23).

As Hans travels throughout the city, he often compares the visual image of a photograph of a building with the same building in 1987. His comments in voice-overs, "Están aquí todavía" (They are still here), "Siguen estando aquí" (They remain here), refer not only to buildings that survived the war, and to the old men that we see playing *bolos* in a park, but to those that he refers to while viewing old footage of the distribution of arms to members of the militia: the "anonymous protagonists" who participated in the heroic defense of their city against the Nationalist troops. For this reason, we also see Goya's famous painting, "The 2nd of May," as well as the monument to the people of Madrid who rebelled against the French invaders on that date in 1808. The comment at the beginning of the film about knowing one's antecedents is what conceptually links the images of Goya's Madrid of 1808, the Republican Madrid of the 1930's, and the images of the masses of people that protest against Spanish membership in NATO or show their last respects to socialist mayor Tierno. The people of Madrid turn out to the streets out of a "loyalty to ideas."

The *pueblo* of Madrid also provides another fundamental aspect of the film: the sound track, which consists of a variety of *zarzuela* (operetta) music (*La verbena de la Paloma*, *La revoltosa*, *La Gran Vía*, *El barberillo de Lavapiés*, etc.). Hans learns that the *zarzuela* is "una fiesta que proviene del pueblo" (a festivity that originates with the people) and "símbolo del genio creador de Madrid" (a symbol of the creative genius of Madrid). Martín Patino considers the *zarzuela* music "completely indispensable" as an expressive element in the film (Heredero, *Madrid* 23), and a comment by critic Miguel Bayón shows the director's success in this regard: "the *zarzuela* music over the images of militia members who are radiant with sincere egalitarian passion make your hair stand on end" ("*Madrid*" 176).

Although none of the historical footage in *Madrid* is previously unedited, many of the images are still compelling: the enthusiasm of the crowds at the declaration of the Republic, the bombing of the capital, the separation of children and parents during the evacuation of the city. Some images, such as the sandbagging of the fountain of Neptune or the evacuation of paintings from the Prado, do not frequently appear in the strictly documentary films that have recently appeared on the war. Martín Patino complements these visual images in the film with voice-over testimony or interviews with survivors of the conflict, and readings of poems by Neruda. Regarding the fiftieth anniversary of the conflict, he also includes scenes of a reunion of the Abraham Lincoln Brigade in Madrid, attended by luminaries such as Rafael Alberti. Nevertheless, Hans's German producer feels that he is filming too much of contemporary Madrid, and she cannot understand its relationship to the program on the war. Hans abandons the project, an act that is a reflection of the German director's earlier voiced sentiment that everything that is perfect is already dead. His Spanish assistant Luci (Verónica Forqué) is of the opinion that "La guerra es como todas esas cosas antiguas: es mejor olvidarla" (The war is like all those old things: it's better to forget it), an opinion that may reflect an attitude on the part of some Spaniards, but not of director Martín Patino.

Carlos F. Heredero sees three distinct films in *Madrid*:   an impressionistic portrait of the city, a reflection on the role of the film maker, and a search for traces of the past (*Madrid* 19-20).   The amorous subplot (a sexual encounter between Hans and a young woman, and the flirting between Hans and Luci) seem to be superfluous, as if Martín Patino were trying to provide more commercial interest for the film. His use of captions as part of the self-reflexivity of the film also seems excessive at times; the rhetorical questions in the voice-over of the German director seemed more effective. Nevertheless, the film represents a thought-provoking work on the art of cinematography, and a true homage to Madrid and its people.

Chapter 10

The Persistence of Cain

There are many manifestations of *cainismo* in contemporary Spanish cinema. In films such as García Serrano's *Los ojos perdidos*, Madrid's *Las memorias del General Escobar*, Camino's *Las largas vacaciones del '36*, Gutiérrez Aragón's *Demonios en el jardín*, Saura's *El jardín de las delicias*, *La prima Angélica*, and *Ana y los lobos*, Borau's *Furtivos*, and Aranda's *La muchacha de las bragas de oro*, actual family members oppose each other, usually on opposite sides of the ideological fence. In films that deal with both the pre-war and the post-war era, such as Fernán Gómez's *Mi hija Hildegart*, Armiñán's *Jo, papá*, Martín Patino's *Nueve cartas a Berta*, Saura's *Cría cuervos* and *Mamá cumple cien años*, Chávarri's *El desencanto*, Mercero's *La guerra de papá*, together with *El jardín de las delicias*, and *La muchacha de las bragas de oro*, the ideological division is underscored by a generational division that augments the rift among family members. Sometimes directors present the *cainismo* conflict in visual or allegorical terms; such is the case in *La caza*, *El jardín de las delicias* or *Valentina*. At other times, directors are quite explicit, as in the scene in *Demonios en el jardín* in which the brothers actually fight and the mother calls them "Caínes."

Films during the late sixties and early seventies by directors who sympathized with or supported the Franco regime tended to manifest sub-themes such as an overly facile reconciliation between brothers of the conflict (*La orilla*, *Los ojos perdidos*) or blaming the civil war on the international brigades, which suffer from a negative portrayal (*Posición avanzada*, *A la legión le gustan las mujeres*). Many of these same films that deal with the conflict itself or with the post-war situation contain a large dose of humor; nevertheless, the early comedies--*A la legión le gustan las mujeres*, *Tengamos la guerra en paz*, *No quiero perder la honra*, do not compare with García Berlanga's *La vaquilla*. Of course, the humor in many films is typically Spanish "black" humor, such as that seen in García Berlanga's "esperpento vision" as manifested in the so-called Leguineche trilogy, or in films such as *Kargus, Mambrú se fue a la guerra*, or *Asignatura pendiente*.

Aside from a depiction of the fratricidal divisions in post-war period, many films that deal with the Spain of the 1940's and 1950's manifest sub-themes of the *cainismo* problem: the impossibility of returning to live a happy life in their homeland or to a past filled with marvelous possibilities (*España otra vez, La prima Angélica, El amor del capitán Brando, Volver a empezar, Asignatura pendiente, Los paraísos perdidos*). The impossible return to the past is also true for protagonists of the Nationalist cause (*Jo, papá, La muchacha de las bragas de oro*). Postwar society manifests divisions based on the victor/vanquished dichotomy (*La escopeta nacional, Jo, papá, La colmena*), and many films show the oppression of the vanquished in both subtle and overt ways (*El espíritu de la colmena, Kargus, Pim, pam, pum, fuego, La Plaza del Diamante, La colmena, El hombre oculto, Sonámbulos, Alicia en la España de las maravillas*). Of particular importance is the legacy of the war and of the regime on later generations. Several films manifest or at least imply how these events affected the younger generation both immediately following the fratricidal conflict (*Las bicicletas son para el verano, Demonios en el jardín, El espíritu de la colmena*), during the middle of the regime (*La guerra de papá*), or even at the end of or following the regime (*Cría cuervos, Camada negra*).

José Manuel Fajardo points out that the Spanish civil war had the elements of tragic myth: "an unequal fight, solitude facing the enemy, the fatality of destiny" ("El último" 78). Although the only film produced since 1965 regarding the actual fighting at the front line that contains any of these elements is *Soldados*, they are certainly prominent in the films that deal with the maquis, and they constitute an extratextual element of almost all films about the civil war.

Manuel Hidalgo postulates several conclusions regarding Spanish films about the civil war: the films do not constitute a war genre as such; recent films manifest a change in perspective, with the Republicans seen in a more positive light; films on the civil war continue to show a Manichaean perspective filled with good guys and bad guys; rather than penetrating the history of the period, the historical element that is portrayed is often merely an ornamental addition; some of these films are marked by opportunism; and the civil war will continue to be the subject of many new Spanish films. (Hidalgo "El cine" 31-32). Films about the period from 1936-39 include those about the fighting itself as well as those concerning life in the rear-guard, and each of the films in these categories manifest a variety of perspectives and subthemes: the conflict is seen from the Nationalist perspective or from the Republican point of view; duty versus personal vendettas or even personal ideology, religious versus amorous inclinations, greed and exploitation are examples of themes in these films. To a great measure, one can trace a chronological shift in perspective in Spanish cinema which corresponds to transformations in external political events. Beginning with the transitional period in the mid-1960's, films such as *La caza* and *Nueve cartas a Berta* began to break new ground, and producer Elías Querejeta, who was honored in 1989 by the Spanish Film Academy for his achievements, was an important force behind many of the films that presented "a vision of reality different from the official version" (qtd. in Hopewell 48).[53] Nevertheless, other movies, such as *Posición avanzada, Cruzada en la mar, Los ojos perdidos*, and *Morir en España*, continued to manifest a Nationalist perspective or adamantly defend the Nationalist cause and the Franco regime. The next major shift in perspective came after the death of Franco and the relaxing of censorship. This allowed films to show the conflict and its repercussions from the perspective of the Republicans or those not associated with the regime for the first time: *Soldados, Los días del pasado, Furtivos, Cría cuervos, Asignatura pendiente, La guerra de papá, La escopeta nacional, Pim, pam, pum, fuego, Sonámbulos, La vieja memoria*, and *¿Por qué perdimos la guerra?* are all movies from the period between 1975-78 that constitute the new political dimension on the Spanish screen. Of course, there may be some justification in accusing this surge in films that show the new perspective as opportunistic; nevertheless, the proliferation of movies that show a perspective other than that allowed by the regime also represents four decades of pent-up feelings. There is opportunism in the *destape* that appears in many of the films that saw their release during this same period, however: *Mi hija Hildegart, Tengamos la guerra en paz*, and *Jo, papá* are notable examples of this tendency. Although the Manichaean perspective mentioned by Hidalgo is undoubtedly true for some films, there are also several movies which attempt to transcend such a simplistic view: although early films such as *La orilla, Los ojos perdidos*, or *Golpe de mano* begin to manifest

---

[53]See Hopewell, 71, for what he describes as the "Querejeta look."

this tendency with their reconciliation sub-themes, later films, including *Soldados*, *Las bicicletas son para el verano*, *La vieja memoria*, and *La vaquilla* more fully develop a more complex and more complete vision of the problem.

Written in September of 1978, Hidalgo's words regarding the future production of films about the civil war proved to be true. Many more films about the fratricidal conflict and post-war Spain appeared during the past decade. Although occasionally the Nationalist perspective reappeared on the screen, such as in *¡Biba la banda!*, the majority of these films--*Dragon rápide*, *La vaquilla*, *La guerra de los locos*, *Las bicicletas son para el verano*, *La colmena*, *Mambrú se fue a la guerra*, *El mar y el tiempo*, *El sur*, and *Madrid*, just to name the most important films of the decade from each of the categories that we have examined, all contribute to the important phenomenon begun in 1965 with *La caza* and *Nueve cartas a Berta*: to create a new cultural discourse that attempts to "deconstruct the mythology of the imaginary Spain invented by the regime both in cinematic and social discourses of the early 1940's" (D'Lugo "Spanish" 57).

Several prominent Spanish directors have expressed an interest in making even more films about the civil war. Although in an interview in May of 1977, Carlos Saura expressed a feeling of liberation with Franco's death, and declared that "talking about the Spanish civil war or a series of relating things doesn't interest me at all now" (Torres, "'La guerra'" 78), almost three years later, the director stated, "I would like to make a trilogy about the Spanish civil war and the post-war era, and some day, if they give me a lot of money, I'll do it" (Guerín 58). Saura repeated his plans for this project in the fall of 1990, following the success of *¡Ay, Carmela!*: "*¡Ay, Carmela!* is the first step toward the great film that I want to make about the civil war. It touches on the theme a little bit, but my next project is much more ambitious: a total history of the civil war of 1936, as told through a couple that is very united at the beginning and finds itself separated by the conflict" (Morandini 88). In the spring of 1986, director Vicente Aranda admitted that he had a script already written about the civil war, but admitted, "It is a project for which I haven't been able to find financing," adding, "But I believe that it is a story that has yet to be told, and it has to be done soon, because later on, the people who experienced that drama won't exist" (Gil, "Aquel" 31-2).

The recent past has shown continued attention to the civil war and its aftermath on the Spanish screen. Not only did García Berlanga's *La vaquilla* (1985) become the biggest box-office hit in the history of Spanish cinema, but the three-year period marking the fiftieth anniversary of the conflict (1986-89) showed a heightened awareness of and interest in the war on the part of the Spanish public. Speaking of his 1986 film, *Tata mía*, director José Luis Borau refers to "brotherhood" as the theme or "idea núcleo" of the film, and he goes on to say, "In this sense, it can be considered my contribution to the fiftieth anniversary of the Civil War" (Heredero, "Un insólito" 44). Nor does the interest wane following the fiftieth anniversary of the end of the war. Recent films that continue many of the themes studied here include Jaime Chávarri's *Las cosas del querer*, José Luis Cuerda's *La viuda del capitán Estrada*, Jaime Camino's *El largo invierno*, and Mario Camus's *Después del sueño*. Nevertheless, as time goes on and as the *cainismo* in Spanish society subsides, the theme may disappear from the Spanish screen. Many contemporary Spanish films do not manifest any signs of *cainismo*, and young film makers are beginning to explore other themes and other aspects of Spanish society. Pedro Almodóvar, director of films such as *¿Qué he hecho yo para merecer esto?* (What Have I Done to Deserve This?), *Matador*, *Mujeres al borde de un ataque de nervios* (Women on the Verge of a Nervous Breakdown), and *Tacones lejanos* (High Heels) is the Spanish filmmaker who has gained the most international notoriety of late, and he has declared, "I deliberately construct a past that belongs to me. In that past, Franco doesn't exist" (Ansen 88). In the not too distant future, this will be the case of all Spanish directors, and Cain will at last fade from the Spanish screen.

Filmography

Alcoriza, Luis. *La sombra del ciprés es alargada*. Madrid: Rosa García, P.C., 1989. Script: Luis Alcoriza, based on the novel by Miguel Delibes. Photography: Hans Burmann. Music: Gregorio García Segura. Starring: Emilio Gutiérrez Caba, Fiorella Faltoyano, Juano Guerenabarrena, Dany Prius, María Roso, Claudia Gravy, Julián Pastor, M. Jesús Hoyos, Gustavo Ganema, M. Luisa San José.

Aranda, Vicente. *La muchacha de las bragas de oro*. Morgana, S. A., Prozesa, Proa Cinematográfica C.A., 1979. Script: Vicente Aranda, based on the novel by Juan Marsé. Photography: José Luis Alcaine. Music: Manuel Camps. Starring: Victoria Abril, Lautaro Murúa, Perla Vonacek, Pep Munné, Consuelo de Nieva.

---. *Si te dicen que caí*. Barcelona: I.P.C. Ideas y Producciones Cinematográficas, S. A., 1989. Script: Vicente Aranda, based on the novel by Juan Marsé. Photography: Juan Amorós. Music: José Nieto. Starring: Victoria Abril, Jorge Sanz, Antonio Banderas, Javier Gurruchaga, Guillermo Montesinos, Ferrán Rañe, Lluis Homar, María Bottó, Juan Diego Bottó, Luis Giralte, and Marc Barahona.

---. *Tiempo de silencio*. Lola Films-Morgana Films, 1986. Script: Vicente Aranda and Antonio Rabinat, based on the novel by L. Martín Santos. Photography: Juan Amorós. Starring: Imanol Arias, Paco Rabal, Victoria Abril, Paco Algora, Joaquín Hinojosa, Juan Echanove, Charo López.

Armiñán, Jaime de. *Al servicio de la mujer española*. Madrid: La Linterna Mágica, 1978. Script: Jaime de Armiñán. Photography: Domingo Solano. Music: Carmen Santonja. Starring: MarilinaRoss, Adolfo Marsillach, Mary Carillo, Emilio Gutiérrez Cabo, José Ruiz Lifano, Maite Tojar, Silvia Aguilar, Luis Gaspar.

---. *El amor del Capitán Brando*. Madrid: Incine-Impala, 1974. Script: Jaime de Armiñán and Juan Tebar. Photography: Luis Cuadrado. Music: José Nieto. Starring: Fernando Fernán Gómez, Ana Belén, Jaime Gamboa, Julieta Serrano, Antonio Ferrandis, Pilar Muñoz, Eduardo Calvo, Chus Lampreave, Amparo Soler Leal.

---. *Jo, papá*. Madrid: In-Cine, S. A., 1977. Script: Juan Tébar and José de Armiñán. Photography: Manuel Berenguer Bernabéu. Music: José Nieto. Starring: Ana Belén, Antonio Ferrandis, Amparo Soler Leal, José Maria Flotats, Fernando Fernán Gómez, Eduardo Calvo, and Carmen Armiñán.

---. *El nido*. Madrid: Ados Films, S.A., 1980. Script: Jaime de Armiñán. Photography: Teo Escamilla. Music: Haydn. Starring: Héctor Alterio, Ana Torrent, Luis Politti, Patricia Adriani, Agustín González, María Luisa Ponte, and Ovidi Montllor.

Bardem, Juan Antonio. *Siete días de enero*. Madrid: Goya Films, 1979. Script: Juan Antonio Bardem and Gregorio Morán. Photography: Leopoldo Villaseñor. Music: Nicolas Peyrac. Starring: Manuel Angel Egea, Fernando Sánchez Polack, Madeleine Robinson, Jacques François, Virginia Mataix, José Manuel Cervino, Manuel de Benito, Alberto Alonso, Joaquín Navarro.

Betancor, Antonio. *Valentina*. Madrid: Ofelia Films-Kaktus P.C.-TVE, 1982. Based on the novel *Crónica del alba* by Ramón Sender. Script: Lautaro Murúa, Antonio J. Betancor, Carlos Escobedo and Javier Moro. Photography: Juan Antonio Ruiz Anchía. Music: Riz Ortolani. Starring: Jorge Sanz, Paloma Gómez, Anthony Quinn, Saturno Cerra, Conchita Leza.

Betriu, Francisco. *La Plaza del Diamante*. Figaró Films, S.A., 1982. Script: Francisco Betriu, Benet Rosell, Gustau Herández, based on the novel by M. Rodoreda. Photography: Raúl Artigot. Music: Ramón Muntaner. Starring: Silvia Munt, Lluís Homar, Joaquim Cardona, Elisenda Ribas, José Minguell, Marta Molins, Paca Gabaldón.

---. *Requiem por un campesino español.*   Nemo Films/Venus Producción SA., 1985 Script: Raúl Artigot, Francisco Betriu and Gustav Hernández, based on the novel by Ramón Sender. Photography: Raúl Artigot. Music: Antón García Abril. Actors: Antonio Ferrandis, Antonio Banderas, Fernando Fernán Gómez, Simón Andréu, Emilio Gutiérrez Caba, María Luisa San José, Terere Pávez, Antonio Iranzo.

Borau, José Luis. *Furtivos.* El Imán Cine, 1975. Script: José Luis Borau and Manuel Gutiérrez Aragón.   Photography: Luis Cuadrado. Music: Vainica Doble. Starring: Lola Gaos, Ovidi Montllor, José Luis Borau, Alicia Sánchez, Ismael Merlo, Felipe Solano, José Luis Jeredia, Erasmo Pascual.

---. *Tata mía.*   Madrid: El Imán, S.A./Isasi Prods./TVE, 1986. Script: José Luis Borau. Photography: Teo Escamilla. Music: Jacobo Durán-Lóriga.   Starring: Imperio Argentina, Carmen Maura, Alfredo Landa, Xabier Elorriaga, Marisa Paredes, Julieta Serrano, Enriqueta Caballeira, Miguel Rellán.

Camino, Jaime. *Dragon Rápide.* Madrid: Tibidabo Films, 1986. Script: Jaime Camino and Román Gubern. Photography: Juan Amorós. Music: Xavier Montsalvatge. Starring: Juan Diego, Victoria Peña, Manuel de Blas, Laura García Lorca, Pedro Díez del Corral, Santiago Ramos, Miguel Molina, José Luis Pellicena.

---. *España otra vez.* Pandora, S.A., 1968. Script: Jaime Camino and Román Gubern. Photography: Luis Cuadrado. Music: Xavier Montsalvatge.   Starring: Mark Stevens, Manuela Vargas, Marianne Koch, Enrique Jiménez "El cojo," Luis Serret, Joaquín Pujol, Luis Ciges, William Root (pseudonym of Alvah Bessie).

---. *Las largas vacaciones del 36.* JF Films, S.A., 1976.   Script: Manuel Gutiérrez Aragón and Jaime Camino.   Photography: Fernando Arribas. Music: Xavier Montsalvatge. Principal Actors: Conchita Velasco, José Sacristán, Francisco Rabal, Angela Molina, Amalia Gade, Ismael Merlo, Vicente Parra, Charo Soriano, José Vivó.

---. *La vieja memoria*. Barcelona: Prozesa, 1977. Arrangement: Jaime
Camino and Román Gubern. Featuring interviews with leading
survivors of the Spanish Civil War.

Camus, Mario. *La colmena*. Madrid: Agata Films, S.A., 1982.
Script: José Luis Dibildos, based on the novel by Camilo José
Cela. Photography: Hans Burmann. Music: Antón García Abril.
Starring: José Sacristán, Francisco Rabal, Francisco Algora,
Agustín González, Imanol Arias, Victoria Abril, Concha Velasco,
Ana Belén, Rafael Alonso, José Bódalo, Mary Carrillo, Queta
Claver, Luis Escobar, Fiorella Faltoyano, Emilio Gutiérrez Caba,
Charo López, José Luis López Vázquez, Mario Pardo, Encarna
Pasó, María Luisa Ponte, Elvira Quintilla, Antonio Resines, José
Sazatornil, Elena María Tejeiro.

---. *Los días del pasado*. Madrid: Impala, S.A., 1977. Script:
Antonio Betancor and Mario Camus. Photography: Hans
Burmann. Music: Antón García Abril. Starring: Marisol, Antonio
Gades, Gustavo Berges, Antonio Iranzo, Fernando Sánchez Polack,
Saturno Cerra, Juan Sala, Manuel Alexandre, Mario Pardo.

---. *Los santos inocentes*. Ganesh S.A., 1984. Script: Antonio
Larreta, Manuel Matji, Mario Camus based on the novel by Miguel
Delibes. Photography: Hans Burmann. Music: Antón García
Abril. Starring: Alfredo Landa, Francisco Rabal, Terele Pávez,
Juan Diego, Maribel Martín, Agustín González, Agata Lys, Mary
Carrillo, Belén Ballesteros, Juan Sánchez, Susana Sánchez.

Chávarri, Jaime. *Las bicicletas son para el verano*. Incine S.A.,
1984. Script: Salvador Maldonado, based on the play by Fernando
Fernán Gómez. Photography: Miguel Angel Trujillo. Music:
Francisco Guerrero. Principal Actors: Agustín Gonález, Amparo
Soler Leal, Victoria Abril, Gabino Diego, Aurora Redondo,
Guillermo Redondo, Guillermo Marín, Marisa Paredes, Patxi
Adriani, Carlos Tristancho, Jorge de Juan, Laura del Sol, Emilio
Gutiérrez Caba, Miguel Angel Rellán.

---. *El desencanto*. Madrid: Elías Querejeta P.C., 1976.
Photography: Teodoro Escamilla. Featuring: Felicidad Blanch,

Juan Luis Panero, José Moisés Panero and Leopoldo María Panero.

de la Loma, José Antonio. *Golpe de mano*. Madrid: Profilm, 1969. Script: J. A. de la Loma. Photography: Mario Pacheco Misica and Gianni Marchetti. Starring: Simón Andréu, Patty Shepard, Daniel Martín, Rafael Hernández, Francisco Braña, Fernando Sancho, José Calvo, Antonio Casas, Antonio Domínguez, Oscar Pellicer, Carlos Vasallo.

Erice, Víctor. *El espíritu de la colmena*. Madrid: Elías Querejeta, P.C., 1973. Script: Víctor Erice and Angel Fernández Santos. Photography: Luis Cuadrado. Music: Luis de Pablo. Starring: Fernando Fernán Gómez, Teresa Gimpera, Ana Torrent, Isabel Tellería.

---. *El sur*. Madrid: Elías Querejeta, P. C., 1983. Script: Víctor Erice based on the novel by Adelaida García Morales. Photography: José Luis Alcaine. Music: Ravel, Schubert, Granados. Starring: Omero Antonutti, Sonsoles Aranguren, Icíar Bollain, Lola Cardona, Rafaela Aparicio.

Feliú, Jordi. *Alicia en el país de las maravillas*. Barcelona: Roda Films, 1977. Script: Jesús Borrás, Antoni Colomer, and Jordi Feliú. Photography: Paúl Pérez Cubero. Starring: Mireia Ros, Silvia Aguilar, Montse Móstoles, Conxa Bardem, Rafael Anglada, Jennifer Bertrac.

Fernán Gómez, Fernando. *Mambrú se fue a la guerra*. Madrid: Procines, S.A., 1986. Script: Pedro Beltrán. Photography: José Luis Alcaine. Music: Carmelo Bernaola. Starring: Fernando Fernán Gómez, María Asquerino, Agustín González, Emma Cohen, Jorge Sanz, Nuria Gallardo.

---. *El mar y el tiempo*. Madrid: Ion, 1989. Script: Fernando Fernán Gómez. Photography: José Luis Alcaíne. Starring: Fernando Fernán Gómez, José Soriano, Rafaela Aparicio, Aitana Sánchez Gijón, Cristina Marsillach, Iñaki Miramón, Ramón Madaula, Eulalia Ramón, Gabino Diego, Fernando Guillén Cuervo, María Asquerino, Emma Cohen, Manuel Alexandre.

---. *Mi hija Hildegart*. Madrid: Cámara P.C.-Jet Films, 1977. Script: Fernando Fernán Gómez and Rafael Azcona based on the novel *Aurora de sangre* by Eduardo de Guzmán. Photography: Cecilio Paniagua. Music: Luis Eduardo Aute. Starring: Amparo Soler Leal, Carmen Roldán, Pedro Díez del Corral, Manuel Galiana, José María Mompin, Guillermo Marín.

---. *El viaje a ninguna parte*. Madrid: Ganesh Producciones, 1986. Script: Fernando Fernán Gómez. Photography: José Luis Alcaine. Music: Pedro Iturralde. Starring: Fernando Fernán-Gómez. José Sacristán, Gabino Diego, Laura del Sol, Juan Diego, María Luisa Ponce, Nuria Gallardo.

Franco, Ricardo. *Pascual Duarte*. Madrid: Elías Querejeta, P.C., 1975. Script: Ricardo Franco, Elías Querejeta, and Emilio Martínez Lázaro, based on the novel by Camilo José Cela. Photography: Luis Cuadrado. Music: Luis de Pablo. Starring: José Luis Gómez, Paca Ojea, Héctor Alterio, Diana Pérez de Guzmán, Eduardo Calvo, José Hinojosa, Maribel Ferrero, Eduardo Bea Boluda, Francisco Casares, Eugenio Navarro.

Garci, José Luis. *Asignatura pendiente*. Madrid: José Luis Tafur P. C., 1977. Script: José Luis Garci and José María González Sinde. Photography: Manuel Rojas. Music: Jesús Gluck. Starring: José Sacristán, Fiorella Faltoyano, Antonio Gamero, Silvia Tortosa, Héctor Alterio, Simón Andreu, Covadonga Cadenas, María Casanova.

---. *Volver a empezar*. Nickel Odeon, S.A., 1982. Script: José Luis Garci and Angel Llorente. Photography: Ricardo Navarrete, Manuel Rojas. Music: Johann Pachelbel, Cole Porter, and Jesús Gluck. Starring: Antonio Ferrandis, Encarna Paso, José Bódalo, Agustín González, Pablo Hoyo and Marta Fernández Muro.

García Berlanga, Luis. *La escopeta nacional*. Madrid: Incine, 1978. Script: Luis García Berlanga and Rafael Azcona. Photography: Carlos Suárez. Starring: Luis Escobar, José Luis López Vázquez, Amparo Soler Leal, Agustín González, José Luis de Villalonga, Chus Lampreave, Julio G. Pencha, Francisco Llinás, Andrés

Mejuto, Mónica Randall, Bárbar Rey, José Sazatornil, Laly Soldevilla.

---. *Nacional III*. Madrid: Incine, Jet Films, 1982. Script: Luis García Berlanga and Rafael Azcona. Photography: Carlos Suárez. Starring: Luis Escobar, José Luis López Vázquez, Amparo Soler Leal, Agustín González, José Luis de Villalonga, Chus Lampreave, Julio G. Pencha, Francisco Llinás.

---. *Patrimonio nacional*. Madrid: Incine, 1981. Script: Luis García Berlanga and Rafael Azcona. Photography: Carlos Suárez. Starring: Luis Escobar, José Luis López Vázquez, Amparo Soler Leal, Agustín González, Luis Ciges, Alfredo Mayo, José Ruiz Lifante, Mary Santpere, Syliane Stella, José Luis de Villalonga.

---. *La vaquilla*. Madrid: Incine Jet Films, S. A., 1985. Script: Luis García Berlanga and Rafael Azcona. Photography: Carlos Suárez. Music: Miguel Asins Arbo. Starring: Alfredo Landa, Guillermo Montesinos, Santiago Ramos, José Sacristán, Carlos Velat, Eduardo Calvo, Violeta Cela, Agustín González, María Luisa Ponte, Juanjo Puig Cobre, Amelia de la Torre.

García Sánchez, José Luis. *La corte del faraón*. Madrid: Lince Films, 1985. Script: José Luis García Sánchez and Rafael Azcona. Photography: José Luis Alcaine. Music: Luis Cobos, and the *zarzuela* by Perrín y Palacios and V. Lleó. Starring: Ana Belén, Fernando Fernán Gómez, Antonio Banderas, Josema Yuste, Agustín González, Quique Camoiras, Mary Carmen Ramírez, Juan Diego, Guillermo Montesinos, José Luis López Vázquez.

García Sánchez, José Luis and Andrés Linares. *Dolores*. 1981. Photography: Luis Cano. Montage: Rosario Sainz de Rosas. Music: Songs by Juanita Reina, Ana Belén and Rosa León.

García Serrano, Rafael. *Los ojos perdidos*. Madrid: Estela Films, S.A., 1966. Script: Rafael García Serrano. Photography: Eloy Mella and Julio Ortas. Music: Antón García Abril. Starring: Jesús Aristu, Kianik Zurakowska, Manuel Zarzo, Manuel Tejada, Barbara Teyde, Angela Rhu.

Gil, Rafael. *A la legión le gustan las mujeres.* Madrid: Coral P. C., 1975. Script: Rafael García Serrano and Rafael J. Salvia. Photography: Francisco Sempere. Music: Gregorio García Segura. Starring: Fernando Sancho, Manolo Codeso, Luis Varela, Francisco Cecilio, Ricardo Palacios, Rafael Hernández, Manuel Gil, Susana Mayo, Juanito Narvarro, María Salerno, Mirta Miller, Venancio Muro.

Giménez Rico, Antonio. *El disputado voto del señor Cayo.* Madrid: Penélope, S.A., 1986. Script: Manuel Matji and Antonio Giménez Rico, based on the novel by Miguel Delibes. Photography: Alejandro Ulloa. Starring: Francisco Rabal, Juan Luis Galiardo, Iñaki Maramón, Lydia Bosch, Eusebio Lázaro, Mari Paz Molinero, Abel Vitón, Gabriel Renom, Paco Casares, Juan Jesús Valverde.

---. *Retrato de familia.* Madrid: Sabre Films, S. A., 1976. Script: José Samano and Antonio Giménez Rico, based on the novel *Mi idolotrado hijo Sisí*, by Miguel Delibes. Photography: José Luis Alcaine. Music: Carmelo Bernaola. Starring: Antonio Ferrandis, Amparo Soler Leal, Mónica Randall, Miguel Bosé, Gabriel Llopart, Encarna Pasó, Alberto Fernández, Mirta Miller, Carmen Lozano, Josefina Díaz.

Gutiérrez Aragón, Manuel. *Camada negra.* Madrid: El Imán, 1977. Script: Manuel Gutiérrez Aragón and José Luis Borau. Photography: Magí Torruela. Music: José Nieto. Starring: Angela Molina, María Luisa Aponte, José Hinojoso, José Luis Alonso.

---. *El corazón del bosque.* Madrid: Arándano, P.C., 1979. Script: Manuel Gutiérrez Aragón and Luis Megino. Photography: Teo Escamilla. Starring: Norman Briski, Angela Molina, Luis Politti, Víctor Valverde, Santiago Ramos.

---. *Demonios en el jardín.* Madrid: Luis Megino Producciones Cinematográficas, S.A., 1982. Script: Manuel Gutiérrez Aragón, Luis Megino. Photography: José Luis Alcaine. Music: Javier Iturralde. Starring: Angela Molina, Ana Belén, Encarna Pasó, Imanol Arias, Eusebio Lázaro, Alvaro Sánchez Prieto.

---. *Sonámbulos*. Madrid: Profilmes, 1978. Script: Manolo Gutiérrez Aragón. Photography: Teo Escamilla. Music: José Nieto. Starring: Ana Belén, Norman Brisky, María Rosa Salgado, Lola Gaos, José Luis Gómez, Eduardo MacGregor, Laly Soldevilla.

Gutiérrez Santos, José María. *Arriba hazaña*. Madrid: CB Films, 1978. Script: José María Gutiérrez Santos and José Samano, based on the novel *El infierno y la brisa* by José María Vaz de Soto. Photography: Magi Torruela. Music: Luis Eduardo Aute. Starring: Fernando Fernán Gómez, Héctor Alterio, José Sacristán, Gabriel Llorpart, Luis Ciges, José Cerro.

Herralde, Gonzalo. *Raza, el espíritu de Franco*. Madrid: 1977. Featuring: Pilar Franco, Alfredo Maya, with footage from José Luis Saenz de Heredia's *Raza*.

Klimovsky, León. *La casa de las chivas*. Madrid: Galaxia Films, 1971. Script: Manuel Villegas López, Jose Luis Garci, Carlos Pumares. Photography: Francisco Fraile. Music: Carlos Laporta. Starring: Charo Soriano, Simón Andréu, María Kosti, Ricardo Merino, Pedro María Sánchez, Rafael Herández, Antonio Casas, José Canalejas, Simón Arriaga.

Lazaga, Pedro. *El otro árbol de Guernica*. Madrid: CB Films, 1969. Script: Pedro Masó and Florentino Soria, based on the novel by Luis de Castresana. Music: Antón García Abril. Photography: Juan Marine. Actors: Juan Manuel Barrio, María Fernanda d'Ocon, Inma de Santi, Luis Miguel Toledano, Ramón Corroto, Marcelo Arroita-Jaúregui, José Montejano, Alicia Altabella.

---. *Posición avanzada*. Madrid: Producción Cooperativa Cinematográfica Destillo Films, 1965. Photography: Cecilio Paniagua. Music: Antón García Abril. Starring: Manuel Zarzo, Antonio Ferrandis, Manuel Manzaneque, Angela Bravo, Tomás Blanco, Enrique Avila, Manuel Tejada, Luis Marín, Jesús Colomer, Marcelo Arroita-Jaúregui, Miguel Angel Aristu, Ricardo Buceta, Francisco Vázquez, Fernando Sánchez Polak.

Lucía, Luis. *La orilla*. Madrid: Picasa, 1971. Script: Florentino

Soria, Rafael Sánchez Compoy and Luis Lucía. Photography: Antonio L. Ballesteros. Music: Alfonso Santisteban. Starring: Julián Mateos, María Dolores Pradera, Dianik Zurakowska, Yelena Samarina, Marufa Isbert, Antonio Pica, Tomás Blanco, Tina Sáinz, Lola Lemos, Pedro Luis Lozano, David Areu.

Madrid de la Viña, José Luis. *Memorias del General Escobar*. Madrid: José Luis Madrid, 1984. Script: Pedro Masip, José Luis Madrid. Photography: Antonio Sáinz. Starring: Antonio Ferrandis, Elisa Ramírez, Luis Prendes, José Antonio Ceinos, Jesús Puente, Fernando Guillén, Antonio Iranzo, Alfonso del Real, José María Cafarell, Africa Pratt.

Martín, Eugenio. *No quiero perder la honra*. Madrid: Picasa, 1975. Script: Eugenio Martín. Photography: Raúl Artigot. Music: Alfonso Santisteban. Starring: José Sacristán, Angela Molina, Florina Chico, Laly Soldevila, Josele Román, Rafaela Aparicio, Juanito Navarro.

---. *Tengamos la guerra en paz*. Madrid: Impala, S.A., 1976. Script: Eugenio Martín. Photography: Manuel Rojas. Music: Antón García Abril. Starring: Francisco Celio, Fedra Lorente, Verónica Miriel, Mary Carrillo, Eduardo Calvo, Queta Claver, José María Caffarel, Aurora Redondo.

Martín Patino, Basilio. *Canciones para después de una guerra*. Madrid: Julio Pérez Tabernero, 1971 (debut: 1976). Documentary films and music from the period.

---. *Caudillo* Madrid: Reta Film. 1977. Documentary footage.

---. *Madrid*. Madrid: La Linterna Mágica y RTV Madrid, 1987. Script: Basilio Martín Patino. Photography: Augusto Fernández Balbuena. Music: various zarzuelas. Starring: Rüdiger Volgler, Verónica Forné, Paco Valladoares, María Luisa Ponte, Luis Ciges, Félix Dafauce.

---. *Nueve cartas a Berta*. Eco Film, Transcontinental Films, 1965. Script: Basilio Martín Patino. Photography: Luis E. Torán. Music:

Carmelo Bernaola. Starring: Emilio García Caba, Mary Carrillo, Elsa Baeza, Antonio Casas.

---. *Los paraísos perdidos*. Madrid: La Linterna Mágica, S. A., 1986. Script: Basilio Martín Patino. Photography: José Luis Alcaine. Music: Carmelo Bernaola. Starring: Charo López, Alfredo Landa, Miguel Narros, Juan Diego, Ana Torrent, Paco Rabal, Amancio Prada, Juan Cueto, Walter Haubrich, Enrique Baquedano, Alejandro Sevillano.

Martínez Ferry, Isidoro. *Cruzada en la mar*. Madrid: Documento Films, 1968. Script: Isidoro Martínez Ferry. Photography: Raúl Artigot. Music: Miguel Asins Arbó. Starring: José Rubio, Patty Shepard, Manuel de Blas, Rodrigo Mafry, José Truchado, Miguel Rubio, Pedro Rodríguez de Quevedo, Juan Quintero, Luis Tejada.

Matji, Manuel. *La guerra de los locos*. Madrid: Xaloc, P.C., 1987. Script: Manolo Matji. Photography: Federico Ribes. Starring: Alvaro de Luna, José Manuel Cervino, Juan Luis Galiardo, Pep Munne, Pedro Díez del Corral, Luis Marín, Emilio Laín, Joan Potau, Patxi Catalá, Cesáreo Esebáñez, Francisco Algora, Alberto Alonso, José Vivó, Antonio Drove, Maite Blasco, Emilio Gutiérrez Cabo, Ana Marzoa, Alicia Sánchez.

Mercero, Antonio. *La guerra de papá*. Madrid: J F Films, 1977. Script: Antonio Mercero and Horacio Valcárcel. Photography: Manuel Rojas. Starring Lolo García, Teresa Gimpera, Héctor Alterio, Verónica Forqué, Queta Claver, Rosario García Ortega, Vicente Parra.

Miñón, Juan and Miguel Angel Trujillo. *Kargus*. Madrid: Tallerde cine, S.A., 1981. Script: Juan Miñón and Miguel Angel Trujillo. Photography: Miguel Angel Trujillo and José Luis Martínez. Music: Pedro Luis Domingo. Starring: Patxi Andriani, Héctor Alterio, Agustín González, Francisco Algora, Laura Cepeda, Modesto Fernández, Kiti Manver, Antonio Gamero, Lourdes A. Laso.

Olea, Pedro. *Pim, pam, pum, fuego*. Madrid: José Frade, P. C.,

1975. Script: Pedro Olea and Rafael Azcona. Photography: Fernando Arribas. Music: Carmelo Bernaola. Starring: Concha Velasco, José María Flotats, Fernando Fernán Gómez, José Orjas, Mara Goyanes, José Calvo, Mimí Muñoz, Goyo Lebrero.

Ozores, Mariano. *Morir en España.* Madrid: Pefsa Films, 1965. Music: Miguel Asins Arbó. Montage: Pedro del Rey. Documentary Footage.

Palacios, Ricardo. *¡Biba la banda!* Madrid: Casablanca Films, 1987. Photography: Domingo Solano. Music: Miguel Asins Arbó. Starring: Alfredo Landa, Oscar Ladoire, Fiorella Faltoyando, Antonio Ferrandis, Florinda Chico, José Sancho, Manuel Alexandre, Miguel Ayones.

Rabal, Benito. *El hermano bastardo de Dios.* Madrid: Almadraba Producciones, S.A., 1986. Script: Agustín Cerezales and Benito Rabal based on the novel by José Luis Coll. Photography: Paco Femenia. Music: Juan Pablo Muñoz Zielinski. Starring: Francisco Rabal, Asunción Balaguer, Agustín González, María Luisa Ponte, Mario Pardo, Terele Pávez, Lucas Martín, José Luis Coll, Miguel Angel Rellán, Manolo Zarzo, Juan Diego.

Rodríguez, Francisco. *La casa grande.* Madrid: Zero Film Productores Cinematográficos and profilms, S. A., 1975. Script: José Manuel Hernández, Francisco Rodríguez. Photography: Francisco Sempere. Music: Emilio de Diego. Starring: Maribel Martín, Antonio Ferrandis, Juan Diego, Fernando Sánchez-Polack.

---. *Gusanos de seda.* Belén Films, 1977. Script: Ramón de Diego. Photography: Manuel Rojas. Music: Emilio de Diegos. Starring: Antonio Ferrandis, Esperanza Roy, Rafaela Aparicio, Florinda Chico, Alfredo Mayo, Agustín González.

Sánchez Valdés, Julio. *Luna de lobos.* Madrid: Brezal, PC, S.A., 1987. Script: J. Sánchez Valdés and Julio Llamazares based on the novel by Julio Llamazares. Photography: Juan Molina. Starring: Santiago Ramos, Antonio Resines, Alvaro de Luna, Kiti Manver.

Santillán, Diego de. *¿Por qué perdimos la guerra?* Madrid, 1978. Script: Diego de Santillán. Photography: Julio Bragado. Music: Mario Litwin and songs from the 1930's. Documentary footage.

Saura, Carlos. *Ana y los lobos*. Elías Querejeta, P. C., 1972. Script: Rafael Azcona and Carlos Saura. Photography: Luis Cuadrado. Music: Luis de Pablo. Starring: Geraldine Chaplin, Fernando Fernán Gómez, José María Prada, José Vivó, Rafaela Aparicio, Charo Soriano.

---. *¡Ay, Carmela!* Madrid: Iberoamericana Films, S.A.,1990. Script: Carlos Saura and Rafael Azcona, based on the work by José Sanchis Sinistera. Photography: José Luis Alcaine. Music: Alejandro Massó. Starring: Carmen Maura, Andrés Pajares, Gabino Diego, Maurizio de Razza, Edward Zentara, José Sancho, Mario de Candia, Miguel Angel Rellán.

---. *La caza*. Elías Querejeta, P.C., 1965. Script: Angelino Fons and Carlos Saura. Photography: Luis Cuadrado. Music: Luis de Pablo. Starring: Ismael Merlo, Alfredo Mayo, José María Prada, Emilio Gutiérrez Caba, Fernando Sánchez Polack, Violeta García.

---. *Cría cuervos*. Madrid: Elías Querejeta Ediciones, 1975. Script: Carlos Saura. Photography: Luis Cuadrado. Starring: Geraldine Chaplin, Ana Torrent, Mónica Randall, Florinda Chico, Conchi Pérez, Maite Sánchez, Héctor Alverio, Josefina Díaz, Germán Cobos, and Mirta Miller.

---. *Dulces horas*. Madrid: CB Films, 1982. Script: Carlos Saura. Photography: Teo Escamilla. Music: Imperio Argentina, Ravel, Domenico Scarlatti, Berlioz. Starring: Assumpta Serra, Iñaki Aierra, Alvaro de Luna, Jacques Lelande, Alicia Hermida, Luisa Rodrigo, Alicia Sánchez.

---. *El jardín de las delicias*. Elías Querejeta, P.C., 1970. Script: Rafael Azcona and Carlos Saura. Photography: Luis Cuadrado. Music: Luis de Pablo with additional music by Richard Witting, Joaquín Rodrigo, and Sergei Prokofiev; Starring: José Luis López Vázquez, Francisco Pierrá, Luchy Soto, Lina Canalejas, Julia

Peña, Alberto Alonso, Mayrata O'Wisiedo, Charo Soriano and Esperanza Roy.

---. *Mamá cumple 100 años*. Madrid: Elías Querejeta, P. C., 1979. Script: Carlos Saura. Photography: Teo Escamilla. Music: F. Schubert, E. Chueca, M. García, M. Garrido. Starring: Geraldine Chaplin, Amparo Muñoz, Fernando Fernán Gómez, Rafaela Aparicio, Norman Brisky, Charo Soriano, José Vivó, Angeles Torres, Elisa Nandi, Rita Maiden, Monique Cirón.

---. *La prima Angélica*. Elías Querejeta, P.C., 1973. Script: Rafael Azcona and Carlos Saura. Photography: Luis Cuadrado. Music: "Rocío," sung by Imperio Argentina; "Rosario de la aurora" and "Música de los romanos" by Huesca, "Dolor" by Father San Sebastián, "El Señor es mi pastor" and "Change it all." Starring: José Luis López Vázquez, Lina Canalejas, María Clara Fernández de Loayza, Fernando Delgado, Julieta Serrano, Lola Cardona, Josefina Díaz.

Trueba, Fernando. *El año de las luces*. Madrid: Andrés Vicente Gómez/Iberoamericana Films, S.A., 1986. Script: Rafael Azcona and Fernando Trueba. Photography: Juan Amorós. Music: Jorge Guerrero. Starring: Jorge Sanz, Maribel Verdú, Manuel Alexandre, Santiago Ramos, Violeta Cela, Verónica Forqué, Chus Lampreave, Saza, Lucas Martín, Rafaela Aparicio, Pedro Reyes.

Ungría, Alfonso. *El hombre oculto*. Madrid: Mota Films, 1970. Script: Alfonso Ungría. Photography: Ramón Suárez. Starring: Carlos Otero, Yelena Samarina, Julieta Serrano, Luis Ciges, Carmen G. Maura, Mario Gas, José María Nunes.

---. *Soldados*. Madrid: Antonio Gregori, P.C., 1978. Script: Alfonso Ungría and Antonio Gregori after the novel *Las buenas intenciones*, by Max Aub. Photography: José Luis Alcaine. Music: F. Schubert. Starring: Marilina Ross, Ovidi Montllor, Francisco Algora, Claudia Gravy, José Calvo, Julieta Serrano, José María Muñoz, Lautaro Murua.

Velasco, Andrés. *Uno de un millón de muertos*. Madrid: José Frade,

P. C., 1977.   Script: Emilio Romero and Andrés Velasco. Photography: Antonio L. Ballesteros.   Music: Angel Arteaga. Starring: Sara Lezana, Antonio Mayans, Florinda Chico, José Nieto, Luis Marín, Marisa Medina, José María Cafarell, Ricardo Palacios, Jorge Rigaud.

Secondary Works Cited

Abad, Mercedes. "Juan Marsé: 'La película *Si te dicen que caí* contiene demasiado sadismo.'" *Cambio 16* 931 (2 Oct 1989): 100-101.

Abbondanza, Jorge, "Cuando España se partió en dos." *El país* (Montevideo) 28 Feb. 1979: 11.

Abella, Rafael. *La vida cotidiana durante la Guerra Civil: La España nacional.* Barcelona: Planeta, 1973.

Aberich, Enrique. "Cine español 1972-1982. Memoria de una época." *Dirigido por* 100 (Jan. 1983): 22-33.

---. "*Demonios en el jardín,*" *Dirigido por* 98 (1982): 56-7.

Aguilar, Flor. "*Sonámbulos* o quizá toda la película sea un sueño." *Ya (Suplemento).* 6 Oct 1978: 6.

Aguirre Prado, Luis. *The Church and the Spanish War.* Madrid: SIE, 1965.

Alcover Ibañez, Norberto. *Cine contemporáneo: ética y sociedad.* Barcelona: Don Bosco, 1983.

---. "José Luis Garci. *Volver a empezar.*" *Cine para leer, 1982.* Bilbao: Mensajero, 1983: 225-28.

Ansen, David. "The Man of La Mancha." *Newsweek* 5 Dec 1988: 88.

Antolín, Matías. "Revolucionarios sin revolución. *El corazón del bosque.*" *Cinema 2002* 48 (Feb. 1979): 38-41.

---. "*Sonámbulos.* Habla Manolo Gutiérrez." *Cinema 2002* 40 (June

1978): 46-8.

Arasa, Daniel. *Años 40: Los maquis y el PCE.* Barcelona: Argos Vergara, 1984.

Avellanos, Carlos F. de. *"Canciones para después de una guerra* o llanto para después de una paz." *El Alcázar* 4 Jun 1971: 22.

Bakhtine, Mikael. *The Dialogic Imagination.* Transl. Caryl Emerson and Michael Holquist. Austin: U Texas P, 1981.

Balagué, Carlos. "Entrevista con Ricardo Franco." *Dirigido por* 37 (Oct. 1976): 12-15.

Barral, Carlos. *Años de penitencia.* 3rd ed. Madrid: Alianza Editorial, 1976.

Bayón, Miguel. "Madrid encandila a un teutón." *Cambio 16* 801 (6 abril 1987): 176.

---. "El Madrid sitiado." *Cambio 16.* 22 Aug. 1983: 93.

Besas, Peter. *Behind the Spanish Lens: Spanish Cinema Under Fascism and Democracy.* Denver, Colorado: Arden, 1985

Bilbatua, Miguel. *"Nueve cartas a Berta." Nuestro cine,* 52 (1966): 6-7.

Blanco, Gabriel. "Cine y psicoanálisis: *Cría cuervos." Cinema 2002* 14 (April 1976): 28-32.

---. "Cine y psicoanálisis. Sobre *Pascual Duarte." Cinema 2002* 19 (Sept. 1976): 37-42.

Boyero, Carlos. *"Las bicicletas son para el verano." Guía del ocio.* 20 Feb. 1984, 17.

---.   *"Dolores." Guía del ocio* 31 Mar 1981: 11.
Brasó, Enrique. *Carlos Saura.* Madrid: Taller de Ediciones

Betancor, 1974.

---. *Siete trabajos de base sobre el cine español.* Valencia: Fernando Torres, 1975.

Bufill, Juan. *"Las bicicletas son para el verano*: crónica agridulce de una derrota." *Noticiero universal* (Barcelona). 15 Feb. 1984, 35.

Cacho Viu, Vicente. "La imagen de las dos Españas." *Revista de occidente* 60 (mayo 1986):49-77.

Camiña, Angel. "Basilio Martín Patino: *El caudillo.*" *Cine para leer, 1977.* Bilbao: Mensajero, 1978: 144-46.

---. "*El espíritu de la colmena* de Víctor Erice." *Cine para leer, 1973.* Bilbao: Mensajero, 1974: 120-23.

Camos, Vicen. "Un individualista al habla: Carlos Saura." *Cinema 2002* 14 (April) 34-7.

Caparrós Lera, José María. *El cine de los años 70.* Pamplona: EUNSA, 1976.

---. *El cine político visto después del franquismo.* Barcelona: Dopesa, 1978.

---. *Travelling por el cine contemporáneo.* Madrid: Rialp, 1981.

Cardona, Rodolfo. *Visión del esperpento: teoría y práctica en los esperpentos de Valle-Inclán.* Madrid: Castalia. 1970.

Carión, José Miguel. "Notas sobre cine y literatura: a propósito del último cine español." *Cine español 1975-84.* Madrid: Ministerio de Cultura, 1985, 91-96.

Casado, Francisco and Juan Fabián Delgado, José I. García Gutiérrez, Rafael Utrera. *Cine de aquí y ahora.* Sevilla: Universidad de Sevilla, 1974.

Castro, Antonio. "*¡Ay, Carmela!* Un film atípico de Carlos Saura."
    Dirigido por 178 (1990): 26-9.

---. *El cine en el banquillo.* Valencia: Fernando Trueba, 1974.

---. "*El   caudillo.*" *Dirigido   por*   49   (1977):   61-62.

"*La   caza.*" *Fotogramas.*   22   Dec.   1966:   11.

Cebollada, Pedro. "El hombre oculto." *Ya* 3 Nov. 1971: 42.

El cine español. (Europalia: España, Bruselas, octubre 1985).
    2 vol. Brussels: Musée du Cinéma, 1986.

Clavería, Carlos. *Temas de Unamuno.* 2nd ed. Madrid: Gredos,
    1970.

Cohn, Bernard. "Entretien avec Carlos Saura." *Positif*, May 1974:
    164.

Cominges, Jorge de. "El hombre y su doble," *Noticiero universal*, 3
    April 1980: 29

Cossías, Tomás. *La lucha contra el "maquis" en España.* Madrid:
    Editora Nacional, 1955.

Crespo, Pedro. "*Canciones para después de una guerra* de Basilio
    Martín Patino." *ABC* 3 Nov 1976: 60.4

---. "*El caudillo* de Basilio Martín Patino." *ABC* 23 Oct 1977: 63.

---. "*La colmena* de Mario Camus." *ABC* 12 Oct 1982: 69.

---. "*Volver a empezar* de José Luis Garci." *ABC* 31 Mar 1982:
    30.

Cristóbal, Ramiro. "El paraíso como fascinación." *TeleRadio* 20-26
    May 1985: 5, 7.

Declós, Tomás. "*El corazón del bosque*," *El país* 27 Nov. 1983: 75.

De la Cierva, Ricardo. *Los documentos de la primavera trágica.* Madrid: Secretaría General Técnica, 1967.

---. *Historia de la Guerra civil española.*   Madrid: Librería San Martín, 1969.

Delibes, Miguel. *Un año de mi vida.* Barcelona: Destino, 1972.

D'Lugo, Marvin "Constructive Imagination in Post-Franco Cinema." *Quarterly Review of Film Studies* (Spring 1983): 35-47.

---. *The Films of Carlos Saura. The Practice of Seeing.* Princeton, NJ: Princeton UP, 1991.

---. "The Politics of Memory: Saura and the Civil War on Screen." Kathleen Vernon, ed. *The Spanish Civil War and the Visual Arts.* Ithaca, NY: Cornell UP, 1990.

---. "*Spanish Film Under Franco.*" *Film Quarterly* (spring 1989), 56-58.

Egido, L. G. "*Las bicicletas son para el verano* de Jaime Chávarri." *Pueblo* (Madrid). 27 Jan. 1984.

Elejabeitia, Carmen de and Ignacio F. de Castro. "Prólogo."   In Ricardo Franco, Emilio M. Lázaro and Elías Querejeta, *Pascual Duarte*. Madrid: Elías Querejeta Ediciones, 1977: 7-16.

Escudero, Isabel and Alfonso Silvan and Guillermo Palma. "Al habla con Borau. *Furtivos*: Cine popular, no populista. Entrevista." *Cinema 2002* 9 Nov 1975, 36-9.

Escudero, Isabel. "*Alicia en el país de las maravillas.*" *Cinema 2002* 48 (1979) 17-18.

---.   "*Sonámbulos.*"   *Cinema 2002*   45 (Nov 1978): 18-19.

Fajardo, José Manuel. "Aurora Rodríguez, la tragedia de la Eva futura." *Cambio 16* 806, 11 May 1987, 130-36.

---. "El último mito trágico." *Cambio 16* 3 Abril 1989, 78-9.

Fernández, Alberto E. *La España de los maquis.* Milan: Avance, 1967.

Fernández, Manuel. "Una película excepcional." *Ya* 26 mayo 1983: 40.

Fernández Cuenca, Carlos. *La guerra de España y el cine.* 2 vol. Madrid: Editora Nacional, 1972.

Fernández Santos, Angel. "El cine en la pequeña pantalla: 1974." *El país.* 7 Sept. 1984: 42.

---. "Dureza blanda: cine/*Requiem por un campesino español*," *El país* 19 Sept. 1985, 34.

Fernández Santos, Jesús. "Los amores difíciles: cine/*El nido.*" *El país* 21 Sept 1980: 31.

---. "Las segundas intenciones: cine/*El caudillo.*" *El país* 18 Oct 1977: 27

Freixas, Ramón. "Manuel Gutiérrez Aragón: Las maravillas del bosque," *Dirigido por* 82 (1981): 52.

---. "*La muchacha de las bragas de oro.*" *Dirigido por* 72 (1980): 61-62.

---. "*Si te dicen que caí.* Retrato de una infancia sin inocencia." *Dirigido por* 172 (Sept 1989): 42-45.

---. "*Volver a empezar.*" *Dirigido por* 92 (April 1982): 58-60.

Frugone, Juan Carlos. *Oficio de gente humilde . . . Mario Camus.* Valladolid: 24 Semana de Cine, 1984.

Galán, Diego. *Carta abierta a Berlanga.* Huelva: Semana de cine iberoamericana, 1978.

---. *"El caudillo."* *Triunfo* 22 Oct 1977: 57.

---. "Desintegración de la familia burguesa: *El desencanto.*" *El país* 16 Mar 1983: 62.

---. "Retrato de una familia en exterior: cine / *Demonios en el jardín.*" *El país* 19 Oct. 1982: 41.

---. "Sensible reflejo de lo sórdido." *El país* 13 Oct. 1982: 41.

---. *Venturas y desventuras de la prima Angélica.* Valencia: Fernando Torres, 1974.

García Escudero, José María. *Historia política de las dos Españas.* 4 vol. Madrid: Nacional, 1975.

García Fernández, Emilio C. *Historia ilustrada del cine español.* Madrid: Planeta, 1985.

García Rayo, Antonio. "La década de los setenta en el cinematógrafo español." *Cinema 2002,* 61-2 (1980), 27 (as quoted in Kovács, p. 5).

Genover, Jaume. "*El espíritu de la colmena* de Víctor Erice." *Dirigido por,* 9 (Jan. 1974): 25.

Gibson, Ian. *La noche en que mataron a Calvo Sotelo.* Barcelona: Argos Vergara, 1982.

Gil, Cristina. "Aquel tiempo de silencio." *Ya* 9 Mar 1986: 31-2.

---. "La guerra civil está presente en el cine español de los últimos cinco años." *Ya.* 10 May 1985, vii.

Gil de Muro, T. "Jaime Camino, *La vieja memoria.*" *Cine para leer, 1979.* Bilbao: Mensajero, 1980: 325-27.

Gimferrer, Pere. *Cine y literatura.* Barcelona: Planeta, 1985.

González, M. A. and Santiago de Benito. "Alejado del costumbrismo: *Pascual Duarte.* Elías Querejeta y Ricardo Franco comentan su obra." *Cinema 2002* 14 (April 1976): 38-40.

González Sinde, José María and José Luis Garci. "*Asignatura pendiente*: cine político y fenómeno sociológico.*" Guía del ocio* 15 July 1977: 7.

Guarner, José Luis. "*La vaquilla*," *La vanguardia* 8 Mar. 1985: 34.

Gubern, Román. *Carlos Saura.*   Huelva: Festival de Cine Iberoamericana, 1979.

---. *1936-1939: La guerra de España en la pantalla.* Madrid: Filmoteca Española, 1986.

Guerin, José Luis. "Entrevista: el cumpleaños de Saura." *Cinema 2002*   59 (Jan 1980): 56-63.

Haro Tecglen, Eduardo. "La huella de la memoria o el tiempo de nadie." Prologue to Saura, Carlos and Rafael Azcona. *La prima Angélica.* Madrid: Elías Querejeta Ediciones, 1976.

---. "Pascual Duarte en su contexto." Emilio M. Lázaro and Elías Querejeta, *Pascual Duarte.* Madrid: Elías Querejeta Ediciones, 1977: 18-29.

Heredero, Carlos F. "*¡Biba la banda!* de Ricardo Palacios." *Dirigido por* 149 (1987): 67.

---. "*Los días del pasado.*" *Cinema 2002* 38 (April, 1978):   19-20.

---. "*La guerra de los locos*: En la frontera de la razón." *Dirigido por* 147 (1987): 42-47.

---.   "*Madrid*, la difícil captura de la realidad." *Dirigido por* 146 (1987): 19-23.

---. "Un insólito ejercicio de estilo. *Tata mía. Dirigido por* 143 (1987): 41-45.

Hernández Esteve, Vicente. "Teoría y técnica del análisis fílmico," in Jenaro Talens, ed. *Elementos para una semiótica del texto artístico.* Madrid: Cátedra, 1978: 201-27.

Hernández Les, Juan. "*El desencanto* (Jaime Chávarri)." *Cinema 2002* 21 (Nov. 1976): 32-33.

---. "*Gusanos de seda* (Francisco Rodríguez)." *Cineama 2002* 35 Jan. 1978. 16-17.

---. "*Pascual Duarte.*" *Cinema 2002* 16 (June 1976): 29-30.

---. "*Soldados.* La pasión del estilo." *Cinema 2002* 47 (Jan. 1979): 25.

Hernández Les, Juan and Miguel Gato. *El cine de autor en España.* Madrid: Castellote, 1978.

Hernández Les, Juan and Manuel Hidalgo. *El último austro-húngaro: conversaciones con Berlanga.* Barcelona: Anagrama, 1981.

Hidalgo, Manuel. "El cine sobre la guerra civil en los últimos años del franquismo." *Cinema 2002* 43 (Sept. 1978), 31-33.

---. "El espíritu de Víctor Erice." *Diario 16* Suplemento Cultural. 10 July 1983: 2.

---.   "*La   vaquilla.*"   *Diario   16*   8   Mar.   1985:   36.

Higginbotham, Virginia.   *Spanish Film Under Franco.*   Austin: University of Texas Press, 1988.

Hopewell, John.   *Out of the Past: Spanish Cinema After Franco.* London: British Film Institute, 1986.

Ilie, Paul. *Literature and Inner Exile: Authoritarian Spain, 1939-1975.*

Baltimore: The Johns Hopkins U, 1980.

Insdorf, Annette. "'Soñar con tus ojos': Carlos Saura's Melodic Cinema." *Quarterly Review of Film Studies* (Spring, 1983): 49-53.

Interino. "*Dolores* de José Luis García Sánchez." *ABC* 31 Mar 1981: 69.

"Interview with Gonzalo Herralde." *El cine español.* Europalia/España: Brussels, 1985. Brussels: Musée du Cinéma, 1985.

Jackson, Gabriel. *The Spanish Republic and the Civil War, 1931-1939.* Princeton: Princeton UP, 1965.

"Jeune Cinéma Espagnol aux journées de Poitiers" *Jeune Cinéma*, (July-Aug. 1982), as quoted in Europalia, p. 281.

Kinder, Marsha. "Carlos Saura: The Political Development of Individual Consciousness." *Film Quarterly* 32 April 1979: 14-25.

---. "The Children of Franco in the New Spanish Cinema." *Quarterly Review of Film Studies.* Spring 1983: 57-76.

Kovacs, Kathleen S. "Loss and Recuperation in *The Garden of Delights. Cine-Tracts* 4.2-3: 45-54.

Lamet, Pedro Miguel. "*El nido.*" *Cine para leer, 1980.* Bilbao: Mensajero, 1981: 217-21.

---. "Bardem habla de *Siete días de enero.*" *La calle.* 6-12 Feb 1979: 11.

Lara, Fernando. "Estructura y estilo en *La prima Angélica.*" In Saura, Carlos and Rafael Azcona. *La prima Angélica.* Madrid: Elías Querejeta Ediciones, 1976.

Larraz, Emmanuel. *Le cinèma espagnol des origines nos jours.* Paris: Editions du Cerf, 1986.

Lenne, Gérard. *Le cinéma fantastique et ses mythologies*. Paris: Editions du Cerf, 1970.

Linz, Juan J. *The Breakdown of Democratic Regimes: Europe.* Baltimore: Johns Hopkins UP, 1978.

López i Llaví, J. M. "La guerra civil, va ser cosa de riure?" *Avui* 9 Mar. 1985: 27.

Machado, Antonio. *Poesías*. 7th ed. Buenos Aires: Losada, 1968.

Maliniak, Thierry. "Rire de la guerre civile," *Le monde*, (n.d.) as quoted in *El cine español* I: 312.

March, María Eugenia. *Forma e idea de los esperpentos de Valle-Inclán*. Madrid: Castalia, 1969.

Marías, Miguel. "El cine desencantado de Jaime Chávarri." *Dirigido por* 49 (1977): 44-56.

Marinero, Francisco. "*La colmena*: un fresco histórico." *Diario 16* 12 Oct 1982: 1, 42.

---. "De safari: *La escopeta nacional* de Luis García Berlanga." *Diario 16* 16 Sept 1978: 19.

---. "*Mi hija Hildegart.*" *Diario 16* 16 Dec. 1983: 47.

---. "*La Plaza del Diamante.*" *Diario 16.* 6 Abril 1982: 34.

Marinero, Manolo. "*Pascual Duarte.*" *Diario 16* 28 Nov. 1982: 47.

Martí, Octavi. "El cineasta más rápido: cine/*Memorias del General Escobar.*" *El país* 9 October 1984: 36.

---. "Un encierro difícil: cine/*La vaquilla*," *El país* 9 Mar. 1985: 27.

Martialay, Félix. "*El caudillo* de Basilio Martín Patino." *El Alcázar* 19 Oct 1977: 24-5.

---. "La colmena de Mario Camus." *El Alcázar* 30 Oct. 1982: 30.

---. *"El jardín de las delicias* de Carlos Saura." *El Alcázar*. 11 Nov 1970: 23.

Martín Gaite, Carmen. *Usos amorosos de la postguerra española*. Barcelona: Anagrama, 1987.

Martin Márquez, Susan. *Bifurcaciones en el camino: cinco directores ante la obra de Miguel Delibes*. Diss. U of Pennsylvania, 1991.

Martínez, Raimundo. *"Sonámbulos*, hiperrealismo fílmico." *Noticiero universal* (Barcelona). 26 Oct 1978: 37.

Martínez Bande, José Manuel. *La marcha sobre Madrid* Madrid: San Martín, 1968.

Martínez Lázaro, Emilio and Elías Querejeta. *Pascual Duarte*. Madrid: Elías Querejeta Ediciones, 1977.

Martínez León, Jesús. "Nueve cartas a Berta." *Film Ideal*, 192 (August, 1965): 343-44.

Martínez Montalbán, J. L. *"Los días del pasado* (Mario Camus)" *Cine para leer 1978*. Bilbao: Mensajero, 1979: 180-83.

Masó, Angeles. *"La colmena*: pantalla abierta." *La vanguardia* 16 Oct 1982: 35.

Méndez Leite, Fernando. "El cine español en la transición." *Cine español 1975-84. Primera semana de cine español, Murcia 1984*. Murcia: Universidad de Murcia, 1985: 19.

Michener, James. *Iberia*. New York: Random House, 1968.

Mitry, Jean. *Estética y psicología del cine*. Trans. René Palacios. 2 vols. Madrid: Siglo XXI de España, 1978.

Molina-Foix, Vicente. "La guerra detrás de la ventana." *Revista de occidente* 53 (1985): 112-118.

---. *New Cinema in Spain.* London: British Film Institute, 1977.

---. "Un libro, una ciudad, una historia." *Cambio 16* 4 Nov 1985, 151.

Monleón, José. "San Sebastián." *Nuestro cine* 53 (1966): 54-66.

Monterde, José Enrique. "Crónicas de la transición. Cine político español 1973-78." *Dirigido por* 58 (1978): 8-14.

---. "La guerra civil: 50 años de cine." *Dirigido por* 138 (1986), 27-43.

Montero Moreno, Antonio. *Historia de la persecución religiosa en España, 1936-1939.* Madrid: Editorial Católica, 1961.

Morandini, Norma. "La moda de la guerra civil." *Cambio 16*, 17 Sept 1990, 88.

Mortimore, Roger. "Poachers." *Sight and Sound*, 45,1 Winter 1975-76: 15.

Muñoz, Isabel. "*Jo, papá* de Jaime de Armiñán." *Dirigido por* 30 (1975): 33-34.

"No son ladrones" *Fuerza Nueva* 1 June 1974.

Oms, Marcel. *Carlos Saura.* Paris: Edilig, 1981.

---. *La Guerre d'Espagne au cinéma: Mythes et réalités.* Paris: Editions du Cerf, 1985.

---. "XIV Confrontación. La guerra civil española vista por el cine." *Dirigido por* 55 (1978): 10-15.

Ordoñez, Marcos. "Un *Requiem* que no logra emocionar." *El correo catalán.* 14 Sept. 1985: 27.

Payan, Miguel Juan and José Luis López. *Manuel Gutiérrez Aragón*. Madrid: Ediciones JC, 1985.

Payne, Stanley. *The Spanish Revolution*. New York: Norton, 1970.

Pérez Gómez, Angel A. *"El año de las luces."* *Cine para leer, 1986*. Bilbao: Mensajero, 1987.

---. "Jaime Chávarri, *El desencanto*." *Cine para leer, 1976*. Bilbao: Mensajero, 1977: 117-20.

---. "Ricardo Franco: *Pascual Duarte*." *Cine para leer 1976*. Bilbao: Mensajero, 1977: 217-220.

Pérez Marinero, Carlos and David. *Cine español: algunos materiales por derribo*. Madrid: Cuadernos para el diálogo, 1973.

Pérez Ornia, José Ramón. "El café de doña Rosa, tienda de antiguedades." *El país*, "Suplemento Artes," 23 Jan. 1982: 4.

---. "Fernán Gómez es Mambrú" *El país* 7 April 1986: 30.

---. "Retorno al mundo de La colmena," *El país*, "Suplemento Artes" 23 Jan. 1982: 1, 4.

"Pero Massip ha posuat guió a la vida del General Escobar." Avui 21 Sept. 1984: 28.

Preston, Paul. *The Coming of the Spanish Civil War, 1931-1936*. London: Macmillan, 1978.

---. *Revolution and War in Spain 1931-1939*. London: Methuen, 1984.

Querejeta, Elías. "Anotaciones." In Saura, Carlos and Rafael Azcona. *La prima Angélica*. Madrid: Elías Querejeta Ediciones, 1976: 135-45.

Quesada, Luis. *La novela española y el cine*. Madrid: JC, 1986.

Redondo, Ramón G. "Lolita o Lady Macbeth: cine/*El nido*" de Jaime de Armiñán." *Cambio 16* 12 Oct 1980: 114-15.

Rello, Salvador. *La aviación en la guerra de España*, 4 vols. Madrid: San Martín, 1969-72.

Rentero, Juan Carlos. "Entrevista con Alfonso Ungría." *Dirigido por* 60 (Jan. 1979): 38-45.

---. "Entrevista con Carlos Saura." *Dirigido por* 31 Mar, 1976: 12-17.

---. "Pascual Duarte." *Dirigido por* 33 (May, 1976): 37-8.

Riambau, Esteve. "*La vieja memoria*." *Dirigido por* 58 (1974): 49.

Rice, Miriam. "El hombre masa en una novela de Miguel Delibes." *The USF Language Quarterly* 14.1-2 (1975): 17-19, 22.

Riley, E. C. "The Story of Ana in *El espíritu de la colmena*. *Bulletin of Hispanic Studies* 61 (1984): 491-97.

Rodero, José Angel. *Aquel "nuevo cine español" de los años 60. Espíritu, estética, obra y generación de un movimiento*. Valladolid: 26 Semana Internacional de cine de Valladolid, 1981.

Rovira, Bru. "Estreno nacional en Zaragoza de *Requiem por un campesino español* de Betriu." *La vanguardia*. 14 Sept. 1985: 26.

Rubio, Fanny and Javier Goñi. "Un millón de títulos: las novelas de la guerra de España," in Ramón Tamames, ed., *La guerra civil española. Una reflexión moral 50 años después*. Barcelona: Planeta, 1986: 153-169.

Rubio, José Luis. "Los males de *El sur*." *Cambio 16* 6 June 1983: 129-30.

Rubio, Miguel. "*El hombre oculto* de Alfonso Ungría." *Nuevo Diario*. 11 Nov. 1971: 23.

---. "*Por qué perdimos la guerra* de Diego de Santillán." *El Immparcial* 8 April 1978: 15.

Rubio, Miguel, José Oliver, Manuel Matji, "Víctor Erice, o la conciencia de una generación," *Nuevo Diario* 14 Oct 1973 Suplemento: 2-4.

Ruiz, Jesús. "*El corazón del bosque*: realidad irreal," *El correo catalán* 10 April 1980: 33.

---. "*La colmena*: De lo escrito a lo vivo," *El correo catalán* 17 Oct. 1982: 43.

Salas, Juan Tomás de. "¿Dónde estará?" *Cambio 16* 26 octubre 1987: 7.

---. "Nunca jamás." *Cambio 16* 19-26 Sept 1983: 3.

Salas Larrazábal, Jesús. *La guerra de España desde el aire*. Barcelona: Ariel, 1969.

---. *Guernica*. Madrid: Rialp, 1987.

Salas Larrazábal, Ramón. *Historia del Ejército Popular de la República*. Madrid: Nacional, 1973.

---. *Los datos exactos de la Guerra Civil*. Madrid: Rioduerol, 1980.

---. *Pérdidas de guerra*. Barcelona: Planeta, 1977.

Salvany, Joan. "*La vaquilla*." *Noticiero universal* 9 Mar. 1985: 43.

Sánchez, Alfonso. "*El desencanto* y la presencia de la cámara." *Hoja del lunes* Sept 1976: 21.

---. "*El hombre oculto*." *Informaciones* 3 Nov. 1971: 25.

Sánchez Vidal, Agustín. *Borau*. Zaragoza: Caja de Ahorros de la Inmaculada, 1990.

Santillán, Diego. *"Por qué perdimos la guerra*: cine/ antecrítica.*"
El país 5 April 1978: 27.

Santoro, Patricia. "Novel into Film: The Case of *La familia de
Pascual Duarte* and *Los santos inocentes.*" Diss. Rutgers, 1989.

Santos Fontenla, César "1962-1967." Augusto M. Torres, ed. *Cine
español 1896-1983.* Madrid: Ministerio de Cultura, 1984.

Savater, Fernando. "Riesgos de la iniciación al espíritu," in Víctor
Erice and Angel Fernández Santos, *El espíritu de la colmena.*
Madrid: Elías Querejeta Ediciones, 1976: 9-26.

Sotelo, Ignacio. "Fascismo y memoria histórica," *El país*, 12 Feb.
1986: 11.

Southworth, Herbert R. *Guernica! Guernica!.* Berkeley: U California
P, 1977.

Staehlin, Carlos. *El arte del cine.* 2 vols. Valladolid: Universidad
de Valladolid, 1982.

Sueiro, Daniel and Bernardo Díaz Nosty. *Historia del franquismo.*
Barcelona: Argos Vergara, 1985.

Talens, Jenaro. "Documentalidad vs. ficcionalidad: el efecto
referencial." *Revista del occidente* 53 (Oct 1985): 7-12.

Tena, Jean. "Carlos Saura et la Mémoire du Temps Escamoté." *Le
cinéma de Carlos Saura. Actes du colloque sur le cinéma de
Carlos Saura des 1er février 1983.* Bordeaux: P. Univ., 1983: 11-
29.

Thomas, Hugh. *The Spanish Civil War.* 3rd. ed. New York: Harper
& Row, 1986.

Tirado, Juan Antonio. "Terminó el rodaje de *La vaquilla*," *Liberación*
25 Oct. 1984: 3.

Torbado, Jesús and Miguel Leguineche. *The Forgotten Men.* [*Los topos*]. Trans. Nancy Festinger. New York: Holt, Reinhart, Winston: 1981.

Torreiro, Mirito. "*El corazón del bosque,*" *Dirigido por* 72 (1980): 55-6.

Torreiro, Mirito and Esteve Riambau. "Entrevista con Manuel Gutiérrez Aragón: A propósito de *Demonios en el jardín.*" *Dirigido por* 98 (Nov. 1982): 46-9.

Torres, Augusto M., ed. *Cine español, 1896-1983.* Madrid: Ministerio de Cultura, 1984.

---. *Conversaciones con Manuel Gutiérrez Aragón.* Madrid: Fundamentos, 1985.

---. "Miguel Delibes y el cine." *El país semanal.* 27 abril 1986: 10.

Torres, Augusto M. and Vicente Molina-Foix. "'La guerra civil ha dejado de interesarme.' Entrevista con Carlos Saura." *Cuadernos para el diálogo* 212 (2nd epoch, 14-20 May 1977): 78-79.

Tuñón de Lara, Miguel. *La guerra civil de España cincuenta años después.* Madrid: Planeta, 1985.

Unamuno y Jugo, Miguel de. *La ciudad de Henoc, comentario, 1933.* México, D. F.: Séneca, 1933.

Urbez, Luis. "*¡Arriba Hazaña!* (J.M. Gutiérrez Santos)." *Cine para leer 1978.* Bilbao: Mensajero, 1979: 116-18.

---. "*Tata mía.*" *Cine para leer, 1986.* Bilbao: Mensajero, 1987: 287-89.

Urrutia, Jorge. *Imago litterae: Cine, literatura.* Sevilla: Alfar, 1983.

Valle-Inclán, Ramón del. *Luces de Bohemia* (1920). Madrid: Espasa-Calpe, 1961.

Vaquero, José Manuel. "Garci recupera el encanto en *Volver a empezar.*" *El país* 14 Mar 1982: 38.

Vargas Llosa, Mario. "*Furtivos.*" *Quarterly Review of Film Studies* (Spring, 1983): 77-83.

"Vicente Aranda: 'No he hecho otra cosa que adaptaciones.'" *El país.* 29 Mar. 1980: 23.

Vidal, Nuria. "Barcelona acoge hoy la presentación de las *Memorias del General Escobar.*" *La vanguardia* 21 Sept. 1984: 33.

Viñas, Angel. *El oro de moscú.* Barcelona: Grijalbo, 1979.

---. *Guerra, dinero, dictadura.* Barcelona: Crítica, 1984.

Vizcaíno Casas, Fernando. *Historia y anécdota del cine español.* Madrid: ADRA, 1976.

---. *La España de la posguerra (1939-1953).* Barcelona: Planeta, 1981.

Whealey, Robert H. "How Franco Financed His War--Reconsidered," *JCH* 12:1 (Jan, 1977): 133-52.

Index

About the Author

THOMAS G. DEVENY (B.A., State University of New York at Albany; M.A., University of Florida; Ph.D., University of North Carolina at Chapel Hill) is professor of Spanish at Western Maryland College in Westminster, Maryland. Professor Deveny is author of numerous articles on Spanish film, Spanish literature, and Brazilian literature. He is also the translator of Adelaida García Morales's *The South / Bene* (University of Nebraska Press, 1999), and he is currently finishing a study of screen adaptations of contemporary Spanish narratives.